D1374649

C015544142

RAILWAY MODELLING

THE REALISTIC WAY

IAIN RICE

Dedication

To the memory of my old friend Frank Watts,
master mariner and master model maker, now
wielding his sextant and scriber in a Better Place.

First published in December 2007
Reprinted in July 2008

A catalogue record for this book is available from
the British Library

ISBN 978 1 84425 359 3

Library of Congress catalog card no. 2007922008

Published by Haynes Publishing,
Sparkford, Yeovil, Somerset BA22 7JJ, UK
Tel: 01963 442030 Fax: 01963 440001
Int.tel: +44 1963 442030 Int.fax: +44 1963 440001
E-mail: sales@haynes.co.uk
Website: www.haynes.co.uk

Haynes North America Inc.,
861 Lawrence Drive, Newbury Park,
California 91320, USA

Designed and typeset by James Robertson
Printed and bound in Britain by
J. H. Haynes & Co. Ltd., Sparkford

CONTENTS

INTRODUCTION

Over the past couple of decades, I've written a fair few books and articles on specific aspects of the craft of railway modelling. However, this is the first time I've ever tackled the hobby in the round, trying to cover as many facets of this most diverse of pastimes as possible. Inevitably, the result is to some extent selective and cannot be a complete guide to so broad a field. This is a hobby, after all, that comes in sizes varying from trains you can sit on to ones you can hardly see, ranging in scope from the collection and restoration of antique tinplate toys to the painstaking construction of carefully researched and minutely detailed scale miniatures.

But at the heart of this wide spectrum lies the smaller-scale ('0' and below) indoor, electrically powered scenic model railway – and that's what this book is all about.

The starting point for the present essay was the seminal work by Norman Simmons which first appeared in 1972 and has gone through eight editions and many printings in the subsequent three-and-a-half decades. However, the model railway hobby has, in recent years, experienced such widespread and fundamental changes that it became increasingly apparent that further revision of Norman's book could no longer serve to cover the current state of the railway modelling art. A new work was needed. This, hopefully, is it.

A book like this is inevitably personal. That is, it reflects the preferences, priorities and preoccupations of the author – which, in my case, stem from a quest for realism,

authenticity and that elusive extra, 'atmosphere'. Such an approach does presuppose a certain familiarity with the real railway that is perhaps rather harder to come by these days, at least in the direct sense of standing at the lineside and absorbing what is going on beyond the fence. I have therefore leavened my various ramblings regarding the practical with a smattering of prototype information that will hopefully make sense of the modelling intent.

The illustrations that adorn these pages are drawn largely from my own work and that of friends. As a general commonality of age, interest and approach binds us, there is inevitably something of a bias towards the traditional steam-era railway. On the other hand, most of what I have to say about the *practice* of railway modelling bears an equal relevance to *all* smaller-scale scenic models – irrespective of style, period or subject. So I hope I may be forgiven the pervasive pictorial hiss of steam and excused the lack of an equivalent throb of compression ignition.

If the best contemporary British model railways are distinguished by one characteristic, it is the convincing representation of the railway *in its setting*, both being reproduced to an equally high standard of realism and authenticity. This, I would suggest, stems largely from the inspiration and influence of one unique and precious example: Pendon. There is quite simply nothing to remotely rival – let alone equal – Pendon Museum anywhere else in the world. For here is the art of

Pendon Museum

Open Saturdays and Sundays from 2-5.30pm
Bank holidays and some Wednesdays 11-5.30pm
See website www.pendonmuseum.com
or ring 01865 407365 for more details

modelling – railway and architectural – raised to a level that transcends the materials and the skills involved to truly create a world in miniature, rich in accurate detail and dripping with atmosphere. If you do nothing else or journey nowhere else in the advancement of your hobby, go and visit Pendon. It will for ever alter your perceptions of the possible.

Iain Rice
Bridestowe, West Devon
Autumn 2007

Acknowledgements

Many people have had a hand in this book, either directly or indirectly, by providing information, ideas, inspiration, practical examples, helpful suggestions and constructive criticism, and by granting me facilities, lending me pictures or allowing me to photograph or borrow their models or artefacts. All errors and omissions are, of course, my own, while if I've trodden on any toes or forgotten anybody – my sincere apologies.

So, in no particular order, my thanks go to: Simon de Souza, Barry Norman, Bob Wills, Mike Sharman, the late Frank Watts, Louis Baycock, Don Leeper, Andrew Duncan, Graham Warburton, Steve Earl, Jim Smith-Wright, Alex Hodson and fellow-members of the Launceston Model Railway Club, Dave and Matthew Doe, Graham Baseden, John Chambers, Laurie Griffin, Dave Cleal, Chris Challis, Howard Love, the late Martin Brent, Len de Vries, Vincent de Bode, Phillipe Moniot, Marty McGuirk, Norman Solomons, the Pendon team (in particular, Malcolm Smith), Bob Barlow, Tim Shackleton, Bill Rankine, Chris Longley, Neil Burgess, John Dale and most especially to my daughter Bryony – who had to put up with me while the whole thing was in protracted gestation.

Chapter 1

AN HISTORICAL
INTRODUCTION

There have been models of railways ever since there have been railways to model. Indeed, you could say that the models came first, as Richard Trevithick was demonstrating his high-pressure steam machines – the ancestors of virtually every steam railway locomotive ever built – using models built in the 1790s, when railways were plateways and motive power was the horse. Other pioneers, such as George Stephenson and Timothy Hackworth, built models to try out ideas or for sales purposes. Hackworth's *Sans Pareil* of 1826 existed as an experimental model before the real engine was built, and Stephenson made a demonstration model of his 'Killingworth' design in 1828.

The oldest surviving railway models form an important historical source for students of engineering history as they were made by the men who were at the cutting-edge business of the day – designing and building the real locomotives, rolling stock, track and structures. Their models thus accurately reflect the design features and construction methods of the time. In many cases, the models have survived while the full-size version has not.

Fashionable or practical?

Early railway models were not entirely confined to the workshops of the engineers and apprentices of the new trade, however. In their infancy, railways were seen as exciting, glamorous, mysterious and just a bit dangerous – not surprisingly, when boiler explosions, derailments, bridge failures and other dramatic mishaps were not infrequent and reported in full and gory detail by the sensational press of the day. Given that railways then occupied the same high-tech niche that space travel does now, it is perhaps not surprising that the leisured classes took a keen interest and that railway books, paintings, prints and, of course, models, were much in demand.

A fanciful model steam locomotive – wrought in polished brass and fine woods, often by an artisan who knew more about artifice than he did about engineering – graced many a mantelpiece of the early Victorian era. Ingenious silversmiths made all manner of things – from snuff boxes to inkstands and from clock-cases to cruets – in the form of railway locomotives or complete trains. Diners at fashionable dinners might find the condiments trundling towards them aboard an elegant 'table railway' – again, often entirely made of solid silver, including the track. In the upright and proper households of prosperous suburbia, the first crude toy steam engines fired (and driven!) with spirit wheezed and dribbled their way around the nursery floor, usually to the great detriment of the carpet …

In grander realms, a gentleman of means with a keen interest in the state of progress might decide that a model railway of a very proper sort would grace his garden or coach-house, or make a novel and entertaining alternative to billiards as an indoor pursuit. So he would employ skilled craftsmen to build

him one, in a suitably expansive scale and often of surprising sophistication. Such models often featured track chaired and keyed exactly as the best permanent way of the day, a fully working steam locomotive modelled after the latest and most glamorous prototype, and a couple of fully furnished carriages that were true pinnacles of the joiner's and upholsterer's art. There were no established scales or gauges, no ready-made components and no gamut of tried-and-tested model-making techniques. These models were very much the real thing in miniature and cost a king's ransom to build. The survivors are greatly prized today and the best of them can stand comparison with the finest productions of modern model makers.

Other early railway models were of more serious intent. The great railway companies, the commercial giants of their day, found themselves with the need to train large numbers of people in the practical intricacies

Above: Many of the earliest railway models were built by the men responsible for the construction of the real thing. This is one such, a very interesting example probably dating from the early 1840s and representing a 2-2-2 of the then-new Buddicombe pattern, with outside cylinders and inside mainframes.

The framing detail and axleboxes are complete and the valve motion on the model is fully working, although the boiler is simply a wooden dummy, which suggests that the purpose of the model might well have been to try out what was then a novel arrangement of the chassis components. This layout became famous as the 'Crewe Type', with many hundreds of examples being built by the LNWR from 1845. Mike Sharman

of railway working. The value of models as an educational aid was very soon established. At the shop-floor level, apprentices might learn and hone their skills on a miniature before moving on to build the full-size machines. Simple representations of valve gears, injectors and pumps were used to instruct enginemen and mechanics, while the safe methods of train working were expounded on elaborate and completely signalled layouts. The railway model soon came to occupy a valuable role in the conduct of the real thing.

On a more commercial note, models formed an effective way of promoting the railways and the skills and wares of railway engineering companies. The 1840s were a time of 'grand exhibitions', culminating with the Great Exhibition of 1851 in Hyde Park, London. Such elaborate exhibitions and 'salons' were held in most European cities of note at regular intervals throughout the 19th century – accompanied by the award of medals for innovation, design or quality of manufacture that were eagerly contested. Railway models of superlative quality were built by the railway companies and firms of railway constructors for showing at such exhibitions, or for more general display, demonstration and advertising purposes.

Below: A manufacturer's catalogue engraving of one of the famous 'Birmingham Piddlers', this being a 'Potteries' version by the British Modelling & Electrical Co. of Leek, Staffordshire. It dates from the mid-1880s, was 8½in long and probably used a track gauge of 2¾in or 3½in – not that many of these engines ever ran on track; straight on the nursery floor was more like it! Author's collection

The tinplate era dawns

In the earliest years of railways, such models as were available on general sale were usually large, steam-powered and handmade in very limited quantities. They were also *very* expensive. The very first series-produced toy trains arrived about 1850, in the form of crude pull-along models in cast iron that made do without track. But it was the development of tinplate lithography and associated press-forming and tab-assembly techniques in the early 1890s that led to the production of the model railway as we now understand it; a complete system with track, individual locos and items of rolling stock, effective couplings, signalling, buildings and accessories.

The great German mechanical toymakers – Bing, Marklin, Planck and Carette – produced some wonderful models in the range of 'standard' sizes and gauges introduced by Bing in 1891. These sizes were based on track gauges – quoted as imperial dimensions, 1890s Germany apparently disdaining metric measurements (too French?) – and started at 'No. 1 Gauge' (1¾in). The other popular sizes were '2 Gauge', at 2in, and '3' at 2¾in. Motive power for the new trains was clockwork or steam, and carriages featured full interiors and opening doors. Beautifully decorated and accoutred with a surprising number of refined details and working features, these were toys of superlative quality. They were still very far from cheap and model railways had yet to become a 'popular pastime'.

Cheaper toy trains did arrive around 1900, usually in the new, smaller size of '0' (track gauge 1¼in). Again, in Britain these were usually of German manufacture, and were modelled – usually somewhat loosely but with great charm – after the equipment of the principal railway companies of the day. Both clockwork and steam were used for motive power. These trains were sold through large department stores, notably Gamages in London, and the newly established British model-making firm of Bassett-Lowke & Co. Although much less costly than the 'premier' German ranges, such models were still somewhat beyond the reach of everyman, being

very much a preserve of the more prosperous end of the middle class. Nevertheless, the advent of the clockwork 0 gauge train saw a burgeoning of the infant model railway hobby, and model trains became a frequent topic for popular hobby and scientific magazines. Some surprisingly elaborate layouts were described, and the models were reliable enough to permit proper railway-like operation. These 0 gauge tinplate models were the foundation on which the huge international edifice that is the modern model railway hobby today stands.

The birth of British tinplate

With the onset of the First World War, the supply of German-made models dried up overnight, and the country was anyway bent on much sterner pursuits than railway modelling. The hobby in Britain didn't really get going again until the early 1920s, but when it did, it entered a golden age, when the model train became a widespread part of the childhood of several generations of boys (and not a few girls!). This was due to the inventive genius and commercial nous of one man, whose name came to epitomise the whole world of model trains: Frank Hornby.

Above: The sorry remnants of a typical Bing pre-First World War spirit-fired steam locomotive, as recently unearthed from a garden shed in Devon. This is one of Bing's smaller engines, made for 0 gauge track, and is surprisingly sophisticated, possessing both a lubricator and a whistle.

Hornby, bolstered by the popularity of his 'Meccano' constructional system, set out to make good-quality British 0-gauge tinplate trains that would be accessible to all. The Hornby railway system introduced in 1920 was a huge success and rapidly proliferated. In addition to clockwork power, Hornby was soon offering electric models using – after a brief dalliance with a near-lethal system working directly off the mains – the low-voltage ac three-rail system pioneered by Marklin. To go with the trains a huge range of accessories of every sort was developed, many of them working. Prices ranged from pocket-money pence to several pounds apiece for the fabled 'No. 2 Specials'. If you wanted anything better than these it had to be Bassett-Lowke, who made 'proper' models in limited numbers at what were very much bespoke prices.

Above and right: This is the artwork that graced the lid of Hornby's boxed sets from the late 1920s on – a far cry from what was inside! In this case, a No. 50 0-4-0T in LMS colours and three matching LMS four-wheel coaches with a circle of track, an instruction leaflet and the all-important key!

Below: Classic Hornby 0 gauge tinplate trains of the 'ordinary' kind – rather different from the glamorous 'No. 2 specials'. These tinplate trains, crude as they are, have a great charm however. These examples are post-Second World War, albeit in LMS livery.

Table-top trains

However, the factor which ultimately proved the most influential on the future development of the British hobby was not cost, but size. At much the same time that Hornby was introducing his 0 gauge 'trains for everyman' there began the development in house-building which saw the rapid expansion of suburbia and the emergence of that ubiquitous British institution, the three-bedroomed 'semi-detached villa'. As dwellings, the 'semis' had many virtues, but space for large model railways was not one of them. What was needed was something more

in keeping with the modest dimensions of these new houses, something that demanded only a table-top rather than the entire front parlour. It was Bassett-Lowke, working with their old Nuremburg partners Bing, who first addressed the market for smaller trains, starting out to market them at much the same time as Hornby was releasing his first gauge 0 models.

Using a track gauge exactly half the width of '0' – ⅝in or 16mm – the Bassett-Lowke/Bing table-top system was effectively the first commercial appearance of 'H0' (Half-0) gauge, the size and scale which was eventually to become dominant in world-wide terms. However, when it came to making models of British trains in this new size, there was an immediate problem. If you simply halved the size of '0' you ended up with a model that was too small to house the somewhat chunky mechanical components needed to make it work.

The Greenly Compromise

Bassett-Lowke were advised by Henry Greenly, an 'independent engineering consultant' specialising in miniature railways of all kinds. Greenly had always taken a strictly practical approach to the design of models, being far more concerned with making them work well than bothering too much about scale appearance. His solution to the table-top conundrum was typically pragmatic: keep the track gauge the same but make the bodywork to a slightly larger scale. Thus was born the perverse distortion of the scale-to-track-gauge ratio that has afflicted British railway modelling ever since.

It is probably worth taking a paragraph or two at this point to examine the logic behind Greenly's thinking, given its far-reaching impact. The root of the problem was that full-sized British equipment, most notably locomotives, was built to a smaller loading gauge (set of dimensions in cross-section) than was the case elsewhere. In particular, they were lower and narrower than trains in Europe or America, even though they shared the same track gauge of 4ft 8½in. Not only

were British locomotives smaller, they were also different in form. Until the latter years of steam, British locomotives had low running plates (often called 'footplates') set around 4ft above track level, with the driving wheels encased in close-fitting splashers above this level. To make matters worse, British railway stations used built-up platforms that came almost to running-plate height, platforms which imposed severe restrictions on the width of locomotives.

Greenly, ever the practical engineer, had determined that toy trains (which is what he was designing) called for wheels of a profile far wider in the tyre and a very great deal more generous in the flange than the true scale equivalent of the full-sized wheel. He also needed to allow space for the coiled spring of the clockwork mechanisms, on the size of which depended the length of run. It simply wasn't possible to get these oversized but necessary components under a body made to scale dimensions. Far better, Greenly reasoned, to keep the body proportions (and hence appearance) somewhere near correct and to make room for the chunky running gear by simply making the superstructure of the model to a slightly larger scale than that dictated by the track gauge. The ratio he chose was to make the cosmetic parts of the model 12.5% oversize, using a scale of 4mm:1ft rather than the correct 3.5mm:1ft. This 'oversize ratio' was subsequently perpetuated not just for 00 gauge, but also for TT gauge in 1957 and British N scale in 1970.

Elsewhere in the world, where trains were wider and higher, platforms were lower and locomotives had running plates high-set above the driving wheels, these restrictions didn't apply. Which meant that the correct ratio between modelling scale and track gauge could be maintained. The result was H0 scale, almost universally adopted outside Britain. The British compromise was termed '00' and has ever since been the bugbear of the serious British hobby, leading eventually to the development of separate 'fine scale' standards and track gauges, of which more anon.

Early 00: Bing and Trix systems

The Bing table-top models were initially clockwork-powered and ran on stamped tinplate track which featured an integral base with printed-on sleepers. The trains were British in outline and style rather than in specifics and the models at first appeared

Above and below: Trix Twin at its most basic. If the cabside number of this mid-1950s example of an 0-4-0 is to be believed, Trix thought that this passed muster as an SR Maunsell 2-6-0 – straining credulity more than somewhat! If these Trix locos were short on realism they certainly weren't short on mechanism, *as the 'under the bonnet' shot reveals!*

in pre-Grouping colours; these were soon superseded by the then-current 'Grouping' liveries. There were but two locomotives – neat but nondescript 2-4-0s in tank or tender form which made do without any coupling or connecting rods, together with matching tin-printed four-wheel carriages and wagons. Electric versions of the Bing models followed in 1924, using a simple 6V dc system with mechanical reversing by a clockwork-style 'track trip' and collecting the power from an insulated central third rail. The usual current source was a 'wireless accumulator', the type of rechargeable cell battery used in contemporary radio sets. These Bing trains had great charm but only very limited operational potential. They were not a commercial success, and may well have contributed to the failure of the Bing company in 1932.

Partly from the ashes of Bing arose a new maker – Trix – which, in 1934, introduced the 'Trix Express' H0 electric system. Mechanically and electrically this was very much more sophisticated than Bing, using 14V ac power with on-board relay reversing and a Bakelite-based three-rail track system on which the gauge was 'eased' to 16.5mm. The locos had insulated wheels which – in conjunction with separate pick-up skates on each side and return via the centre third rail – gave the famous 'twin' feature of individual control of two trains on a single track. Perfect for staging the more spectacular style of train smash! However, with Trix trains at what were then very steep prices, the advisability of so doing would have been questionable!

As with Bing, Trix trains were imported to Britain by Bassett-Lowke who described them as '00 size' and marketed them as the 'Twin Train' system. This was at least partly to play down the German origin of the models, a factor which was thought to have hurt sales of the Bing system. At that period, popular sentiment meant that the mark 'Made in Germany' occasioned disdain more often than admiration. The initial 'Twin' set of 1935 used the German loco and carriages, but from 1936 British-style trains and liveries were offered. The locos were, once again generic and somewhat crude and overscale, although solidly made in die-cast metal. The lithographed tinplate rolling stock was more realistic, with proper bogie coaches and goods wagons of recognisable prototype. The liveries of the 'Big Four' companies were made available, and the system was rapidly expanded to include a range of track and a good selection of accessories. In spite of the high cost, Trix Trains soon gained popularity as they offered a system which needed little space but worked well.

Hornby Dublo arrives

The success of the 'Twin Train' showed that there was a market for smaller models. But while they may have been ahead of Hornby in getting their trains on the market, Trix were soon to be left well behind in development terms by the Liverpool firm. Drawing on considerable mechanical and electrical expertise, the Hornby design team developed a radical specification for their new 00 system that was a huge advance on everything else then being made. For a start, they chose 12V dc traction for electric propulsion, taking advantage of state-of-the-art developments in the manufacture of small permanent-magnet motors. This kept the current draw low and permitted simple, centralised control of speed and direction. Thus was initiated a system of electrification that has formed the basis of virtually all model railways ever since.

Hornby Dublo – as the new 00 system was christened – was also made to a very high quality using the latest metal-casting, tinprinting and stamp-forming techniques, processes in which the Binns Road factory was then a world leader. Most significantly, the models were to be realistic scale replicas rather than mere generic approximations. The scale chosen, however, was Greenly's pragmatic 4mm:1ft rather than the more accurate 3.5mm:1ft 'H0' still then favoured by the handful of serious British model railway enthusiasts working to 16.5mm gauge. Apart

Below: The arrival of Hornby-Dublo, the table-top model railway. The Gresley A4 Pacific was Dublo's opening shot – in 1937, a state-of-the-art model of a state-of-the-art prototype. This is an early post-war example and one of the most charismatic and influential model engines ever made…

Above: The true workhorse of the Dublo range was the N2 class 0-6-2T, turned out in versions for all four 'Group' companies and BR. This is one of the more believable variants, a post-war LNER example in green (you could get it in LNER black too, which was authentic). Over 250,000 examples of this model were produced in all, which may well make it the most popular model railway engine of all time.

Below: A lot of what Trix made may have been rather lack-lustre, but every now and then they came up with something truly gorgeous, such as these splendid tinplate Pullmans from the early 1950s. This one even boasts working interior lighting! A sophisticated model for its day.

from all other considerations, Hornby Dublo locos were to have proper rods and valve gear and needed to ensure adequate room for these refinements within the loading gauge – a need which also led to a relatively refined wheel standard. Hornby's adoption of the 00 compromise was a key decision that effectively cemented 4mm:1ft as the principal British modelling scale.

When the first Dublo trains hit the market in 1938 – at prices little more than a quarter of what Bassett-Lowke were charging for Trix – they were quite simply a revelation, with their reliable clockwork or electric mechanisms, realistic outlines and authentic liveries. By the standards of the time these were sophisticated scale models, being sold as toys at toyshop prices. They thus had a far wider appeal than the traditional tinplate approximations. In effect, Hornby – as with Meccano and Dinky Toys before – had created a whole new market: model railways rather than mere toy trains. Hornby Dublo was another Frank Hornby success story, and as such lays claim to be regarded as the progenitor of the indoor model railway hobby centred on 00 that still thrives today.

No sooner had Hornby launched their trains than Hitler launched his war, which thus put an end to production. It was not until 1947 that Binns Road was able to switch back from war-work to toy manufacture again in any meaningful way, battling against shortages of raw material, a depleted workforce, and a British economy that was sluggish at best. However, once Hornby did get back into full swing in the early 1950s, a second golden age dawned. New products poured forth from the factory in a veritable spate, with one or more introductions each month. Soon, the Hornby Dublo system offered a range of realistic locomotives, together with a wide choice of tinplate carriages and wagons. Track was very similar to that of the Bing 'Table Top' system using a pressed-tin base with printed sleepers. The Dublo track system soon included a wide choice of sections to enable a great variety of layouts to be configured. To go with these basics there evolved a veritable cornucopia of accessories: signals, buildings, bridges, level crossings, signs, wagon-loads, figures and even working features like remote uncouplers, electric signals and mail pick-up apparatus. Power came from the mains via superbly-engineered transformer-controllers, running was smooth with good control and the trains had remotely operated automatic couplings. Truly, the small-scale model railway had come of age.

Farish, Rovex and Tri-ang

The success of Hornby Dublo and 00 gauge did not go unnoticed by other manufacturers in the toy and hobby industry. Trix soldiered on, belatedly introducing a few models with a greater claim to realism, although still at very high prices. The next hat to land in the ring was that of Graham Farish, who entered the fray in 1949 with a limited range of 00 equipment. This used an oddball mix of metal and plastic construction and eventually came to include some surprisingly refined models – their Pullman cars were legendary in their day. The early locos were let down by complex and troublesome electrical and mechanical design and were also very costly, although Farish later produced two conventionally engineered GWR locos that were competitive in price and performance. But that was too little, too late; Farish kept going as a 00 bit-part player until British N scale emerged, when they hopped ship and went on to become the main manufacturer in the new scale.

It was left to the Rovex company to exploit the new technology of plastic injection moulding to produce a real rival to Dublo. They started in 1950 as an independent concern based in Richmond upon Thames, Surrey, but were soon swallowed by Lines Brothers Limited, whose 'Tri-ang' (three lines make a triangle ...) empire was rapidly growing to become Hornby's main rival in the toy business. The Rovex 00 system was, in several important aspects, an advance on Hornby Dublo. It used new technology just as Hornby had in 1937, but Rovex's plastic mouldings offered further advantages over printed tinplate and diecast Mazak – most

Above: **The rivals, or Beauty and the Beast. Hornby-Dublo's 'Duchess' was a paragon in its day; big, powerful, sleek, sophisticated, possessed of fully working valve gear, a simply lovely model, with which the upstart Tri-ang 'Princess' couldn't hope to compare, for all its higher aristocratic standing. And yet…two-rail and moulded plastic were the keys to the future. Tri-ang's engineering was pretty good, too – and it was much cheaper than Dublo.**

notably, easy electrical insulation and greater relief detail. Rovex, from the outset, offered what had by then become the 'Holy Grail' of scale model railway aspiration – two-rail electrification.

They also offered excellent mechanical and electrical design with a reasonable degree of authenticity and detail. In other respects the new models were inferior to Hornby Dublo, particularly in the matter of their wheels and their general fidelity to scale. In particular, Tri-ang's locos lacked the delicate see-through spokes that had always been a feature of Dublo wheels, while the tread and flange profile was much less refined, although nowhere near as coarse as Trix.

But, most critically, Tri-ang trains were offered at truly economical prices. Hornby Dublo might have been less costly than Trix, but was still far from 'cheap' as the average post-war British household understood the term. The initial Rovex *Princess Elizabeth* trainset gave you an express passenger engine with tender, two corridor coaches, an oval of track and a simple controller that worked off ordinary torch batteries for just £2 17s 6d (£2.87½) at Marks & Spencer. That was about the price of a Hornby engine alone, and a third of what an equivalent Dublo set cost. True, a Rovex/Tri-ang 'Lizzie' was sadly lacking when compared with a Dublo 'Duchess'; too short, bereft of valve gear, made of plain black plastic, unpainted and relatively crude in detail. However, to many a small boy (your author included!) it was a very great deal better than no loco at all, and – thanks to excellent mechanical design – 'Lizzie' certainly ran and pulled well enough. The grey-based Rovex 'standard track' that came with it boasted moulded sleepers and ballast and just the two rails, held in proper chairs and thus far more realistic than the Dublo tinplate three-rail track, even if more restricted in geometry and range.

The quality and detail of Tri-ang models improved rapidly after the initial introductions, and the new models – especially the moulded-plastic goods wagons – were generally regarded as being more realistic than tin-printed Hornby. Tri-ang also chose a different route to Hornby when it came to expanding their range. While Dublo set out to offer a choice of express passenger engines and carriages for four different BR regions, Tri-ang stuck with mostly LMS and BR prototypes but

Right: Tri-ang's trump card No. 1 – plastic injection moulding. The refinement and crispness of the detail of the pioneering Trackmaster wagons, which formed the basis of Rovex/Tri-ang's goods stock, caused a sensation when first seen in 1949. This early Tri-ang open, in totally mint condition after 50 years, shows what an advance this was on printed tin from Dublo or Trix.

produced a wider range of locomotive types: the immortal 'Jinty' 0-6-0 general purpose tank engine was joined by a truly useful '3F' 0-6-0 tender engine and a modern 2-6-2 tank loco – all general purpose designs well-suited to a 'jack of all trades' role on small layouts. Tri-ang also offered a hook-and-bar coupling design that, while visually obtrusive, was more forgiving than the Peco design used by Hornby.

Below: Tri-ang's trump card No. 2 – two-rail track. It may look crude by today's standards, but in 1951 this track was a real advance. Note that the points are all-metal with live-frog wiring – something Tri-ang later abandoned, to the detriment of reliable running.

The triumph of two-rail

As had Hornby with his 0 gauge range of 1920, the Tri-ang Railway System once again offered 'trains for everyman'. For a while, Binns Road – confident in the superiority of its traditional, all-metal product – looked down its nose at Margate's plastic efforts and rested on its laurels. At Margate, on the other hand, there was no rest at all; not only were new products planned and produced but the existing models were improved or replaced with new versions. And, of course, every Tri-ang model had the key advantage of being made for two-rail, by now well-established as the electrification system of preference for 'proper' model railways. Too late, as it transpired, Binns Road woke up to the threat from Kent.

Above: Tri-ang's immortal 'Jinty' – second only to the Dublo N2 in the ubiquity stakes, but undoubtedly a far more useful prototype. This is a very early example moulded in the original celluloid plastic which – as here – could warp spectacularly! Mechanically, these models were very sophisticated; this specimen still runs sweetly and pulls well, for all that it's more than half a century old!

Below: Hornby-Dublo two-rail made its debut in 1958 with the R1 class 0-6-0T and 'SD6' wagons – high-quality plastic bodies throughout on cast-metal underframes. In their day, these were regarded pretty much as 'scale' models; some of them still are!

Once roused, Hornby went on the offensive by setting out to beat Tri-ang at their own plastic-moulded two-rail game, but played by Binns Road rules. The result was a new system of uncompromised quality. The 'Super Detail' rolling stock that appeared after 1958 was quite magnificent, while the smooth running and brute power of the 1961 'Ring Field' motor was a legend in its own time. Hornby's plastic-sleepered two-rail track used solid nickel-silver rails and was close to scale by the standards of the time, although electrically complex, especially when it came to wiring the live-frog turnouts. But such quality came at a price – particularly in respect of the tooling costs, and as a result, Dublo could not profitably match Tri-ang's prices. Usually, their products cost just that bit more; I know I could never convince my parents that Hornby was worth the extra expense come birthday-present time!

Not only did the new system fail to sell as hoped, but Hornby were also caught with very large stocks of traditional tinplate 0 gauge and old three-rail Dublo that became more-or-less unsaleable once the two-rail system appeared. The result was inevitable, and upstart Tri-ang took over bankrupt Hornby in 1964. The

ranges were rationalised, with most of the two-rail Dublo models being sold on to G. & R. Wrenn, who kept them in limited production for many years, creating what is now a very healthy collectors market. Some Wrenn locos can change hands for sums approaching four figures, so if you've got one look after it! Triang, meanwhile, appropriated the best-known name in the model train business and added it to their own, shifting the hyphen at the same time and 'Triang-Hornby' was for some time the only 00 game in town. More recently, the 'Triang' part has slipped quietly into oblivion, and Hornby is once again one of the world's best-known brand names.

00 gauge expansion

Triang-Hornby was not to remain the only 00 gauge player, however. Trix abandoned their ac range in 1955 and went on to produce some very high quality 12V dc two-rail models in a hybrid scale of 3.8mm:1ft, presumably in the hope of serving two different markets. Their '56XX' GWR 0-6-2 tank, 'Britannia' and BR Class 5 were fully up to the best efforts of Binns Road in terms of quality, with realistic, well-finished and detailed metal bodies and

Above: This close-up of a Dublo 'SD6' van shows what all the fuss was about – superbly refined detail and breathtaking quality of plastic moulding. The cast underframe, with its 'solid' brake rigging, was less admirable – keen modellers spent hours sawing and filing to open this out.

Below: Trix tried to break into the 'scale' market in the late-1950s with models like this GWR 56XX 0-6-2T; the trouble was, they chose the wrong scale – electing to use an oddball ratio of 3.8mm/1ft, presumably as a mid-way compromise between 3.5mm/1ft H0 and 4mm/1ft 00. The body atop the box has been 'scaled up' with finer handrails and a new paint job – a popular ploy in the 1960s.

excellent mechanisms. To go with the new engines, Trix launched scale-length coaches and some nicely finished plastic wagons. Prices were high and availability patchy, while the oddball scale never found favour, being neither 00 fish nor H0 fowl. Trix were never really much of a threat to Triang-Hornby in the mainstream market and finally fizzled out in the 1980s, the remnants passing to Bachmann.

The first real threat to Tri-ang had arrived in the late 1950s when the Mettoy company launched a low-cost British-outline system under the name Playcraft. Although crude and lacking in fidelity, Playcraft was very cheap and was sold aggressively through Woolworth's. It certainly hurt Tri-ang, as although the product was inferior the low prices 'skimmed' the profitable Christmas trainset market. Made by Joueff in France, Playcraft trains were actually to

Below: The next step up was the arrival of second-generation plastic-bodied RTR models that were accurate scale models of their prototypes, avoiding the frequent errors and compromises that marred much of Triang-Hornby's range. These new models, many produced in Hong Kong, offered far more detail, proper wire handrails and sophisticated paint jobs, typified by the Airfix rebuilt 'Royal Scot' of 1980. What these models didn't offer was running to match the looks; this one has a crude tender drive mechanism that does it no favours.

H0 scale, but at the popular end of the market this went unnoticed. Tri-ang and Peco had anyway already muddied the 'scale description' waters by branding their products as '00/H0' – a nonsensical term, as it implied that the models were built simultaneously to two different scales! The common ground was, of course, the 16.5mm track gauge, not the scale. More on the vexed matter of scale and gauge (and the confusion thereof) in a moment.

However, what very nearly finished Triang-Hornby off completely was the entry of two further large toy firms into the 00 train market during the later 1970s: Airfix, of 'two bob kit' fame, and doll-makers Palitoy of Leicester, who set up as Mainline. Both these firms exploited the newly established plastic moulding facility of Hong Kong based toy-maker Kaders, which enabled them to tap into skilled low-cost labour and state-of-the-art tooling. The result was models of high quality at surprisingly low cost. Suddenly, it was Triang-Hornby that looked expensive, dated and crude compared with the newcomers. From the outset, both these new entrants set their sights on the adult 'scale' market and went for greater fidelity to prototype, adopting much finer wheel standards and using newly developed painting and pad-printing techniques to achieve a very high degree of finish.

Where the newcomers fell down somewhat was in the matter of the mechanisms used. Airfix initially opted for an unrefined tender-

drive and Palitoy for an over-complex split-chassis design that rapidly acquired a reputation for unreliability. Worse still, optimistic over-production soon meant that the new trains were being very heavily discounted, which helped no-one; Hornby suffered a grievous loss of sales and the newcomers lost money hand over fist. Worse still, into this fray there now entered further European competition. Joueff, erstwhile producers of Playcraft, ditched their low-cost image and went up-market to produce some nice 4mm scale models, while Italian firm Lima waded in with an odd mix of rather low-end steam trains and some well-detailed model diesel locos, all using the coarse and dated NEM European H0 wheel profile.

The subsequent history of both the Airfix and Mainline ranges is a long and convoluted tale of commercial manoeuvring, confusion, legal confrontation and product duplication that need not trouble us too much here. Names such as Replica Railways, came and went and at times the same models were available under a variety of labels, all of them apparently claiming an exclusive right to the tooling! Eventually, things settled down when American giant Bachmann Industries acquired the former Mainline range and Hornby bought out most of the Airfix line. Subsequently, Joueff has ceased trading, as did Lima, which has now been bought by the resurgent Hornby. Which is where we

basically are today in terms of British 00 gauge RTR, with two strong established brands – Hornby and Bachmann – plus newcomers Heljan of Denmark and ViTrains of Italy. The result? A range of models of unparalleled breadth and quality, mostly now produced in mainland China.

Smaller than 00 – TT and N

Throughout the 1950s, the space shortages that had prompted the move in popularity from 0 to 00 continued to affect the market. Space in newer houses then being built was usually at an even greater premium than in the 1930s 'semi' and once again the need for smaller models became apparent. Like Bing before them, Tri-ang set out to address this need and in 1957 introduced trains in a

Below: Smaller than 4mm. After the brief (1957–1964) heyday of Tri-ang TT, the new serious contender for 'smallest star' in the British railway modelling firmament was N scale. Leaving aside Lone Star's little fling with rubber bands, 'serious' N originated in Germany with Arnold and Trix. Here in Britain, Peco took up the new scale vigorously, introducing Streamline N track and, long before there were any British-prototype RTR N scale locos, making simple whitemetal-cast body kits to fit the German mechanisms. This GWR 1366 class dock tank is one such, designed to fit on to a Minitrix chassis.

new, smaller size – TT – again standing for 'table-top', although the table was now even smaller! Tri-ang adopted the 12mm gauge originally developed in the 1930s, but chose a scale of 3mm:1ft rather than the correct BRMSB-approved 2.5mm:1ft, so once again perpetuating the 'Greenly Compromise' in regard to the scale/gauge ratio.

Tri-ang put a great deal of effort and money into the development of their TT range and produced some very good models, including an excellent 'Britannia' and a three-car diesel multiple unit that was, to all intents and purposes, a true scale model. The initial solid-based track – oddly moulded in a sort of red-oxide shade – was superseded by a more realistic open sleeper design, and a good range of rolling stock and accessories was made available. Although it achieved a measure of popularity, TT failed to have the same impact that 00 had had on 0 20 years previously. Probably, there wasn't a sufficient advantage over 00 either in price or, more importantly, in size. The range was discontinued in 1967 but 3mm has subsequently gone on to thrive as a 'craft' scale.

What later became N scale started out under the more traditional label of 000 and had its origins in pioneering scale models built in the 1920s. It appeared commercially as 'Treble-0', a trademark registered in 1960 by DCMT (Die Casting Machine Tools). The first Treble-0 trains were non-motorised push-alongs, sold under the Lone Star banner, with all the components die-cast in Mazak including sectional track of 5/16in (7.94mm) gauge – that is, half of the original 00 ⅝in. The scale was also halved, at 2mm:1ft with a ratio of 1:152.5, and the models were well-proportioned but basic, with no rods on the locos and a simple single-handed 'hook and eye' coupler. Both British and American subjects were covered in a range which grew rapidly and soon came to have a wide appeal, helped by very low prices and the ability to build a railway on top of a very small table indeed!

Inevitably, Lone Star came under pressure to produce working trains and less than a year after introducing the initial push-along range they released an electric version using 9mm gauge track with nickel-silver rails and moulded plastic sleepering. The locos were powered by tiny 9V dc motors with a rubber-band drive, and initially were of American outline: an F7 diesel and an 0-8-0 steam switcher with the drive in the tender. Existing stock was made available with new plastic wheels and a British diesel was soon added. A miniature version of Tri-ang's tension lock hook-and-bar coupling was used, but the whole system was under-developed and suffered a range of reliability problems that led to its discontinuance in 1964 after a rash of warranty claims. The push-along diecasts continued in production for several more years, however, and are eagerly collected today.

German ingenuity and miniature engineering came to the rescue of the new smallest scale. Arnold GmbH set out at to make commercial micro-models at the same time as Lone Star, in 1960, but from the outset settled on 9mm gauge, electric propulsion and a scale ratio of 1:160 which, curiously, makes the models a little *undersized* in relation to the track gauge. A chunky but very simple and reliable auto-coupling was devised for the new trains, a design still used today. Arnold 'Rapido' trains were of German or American prototype, not quite as crude as Lone Star but still far from being true scale models. However, they worked sensationally well and Arnold mechanisms soon gained a reputation for reliability and high quality – albeit at a price. Arnold were soon joined by Trix, with their 'Minitrix' range, and 'N' – as the new size was now known, from 'neun' (nine), the track gauge – soon established itself in Europe and the USA.

When N arrived in Britain the problems associated with restricted prototype size soon reared their ugly heads and Greenly's Compromise was dusted off yet again. Peco were very early in the field with N gauge flexible track, and to encourage the development of British modelling in the new commercial size, they also introduced a range of cast-whitemetal locomotive body kits to fit Arnold and Trix mechanisms. Again, the German mechanisms were just a tad large

for our wasp-waisted prototypes, so Peco applied Greenly's solution and upped the scale to 1:148, a scale/gauge combination they christened 'British N'. When Graham Farish stepped in to become the home market N scale manufacturer, this was the ratio they adopted – so, yet again, British commercial models were saddled with a fundamental error of proportion. *Plus ça change ...*

Scales, gauges and standards

Thus far in this historical sketch I have been looking at the 'popular' side of British model railways. But alongside the essentially toy-market big manufacturers there has long existed a small but thriving 'specialist trade'. This served the needs of serious, adult enthusiasts who were looking to create model railways that were accurate both in their fidelity to the prototype and in their adherence to true scale dimensions.

A word at this point concerning the key role of correct terminology in understanding all these concepts, for inaccurate use of the terms 'scale' and 'gauge' and a woeful disregard of the importance of 'standards' have long led to confusion among those new to model railways. This is not helped by the fact that terms like

Above: The serious hobby. Following the work of the BRMSB during the Second World War, the hobby started a move to greater fidelity and finer scale standards which had its origins in the fine-scale 0 gauge developments by Norris and Maskelyne in the 1930s, and has continued to the present day. In the now-dominant 4mm scale, the key move was the introduction of a more accurate track gauge – EM. Here is a corner of a pioneering EM layout of the period, 'Rawnook' built by 'Abab', otherwise Alfred Bastaple. Noms de plume *were* de rigueur *in those days!*

'scale' have acquired different meanings according to context, but let's start with the dictionary definitions. So, the *scale* of a model is simply the numerical relationship it bears to the prototype. This can be defined by use of a 'scale ratio', or by quoting dimensional equivalents. A model built at a scale ratio of 1:100 will be one hundredth the size of its subject, and every full-sized dimension can simply be divided by 100 to give the appropriate value for the model. The dimensional equivalent could be quoted as '10mm:1metre' but is probably more familiar as '3mm:1ft'. A model is said to be 'correct to scale' when *all* the dimensions of the real thing are reduced exactly by the scale ratio when sizing the parts of the model. Alas, such a state of affairs is rare in the world of model trains!

The word *gauge*, on the other hand, refers only to the distance between the rails and is defined by a straightforward measurement, usually in millimetres. Both scale and gauge are absolute – that is, they are exactly and numerically defined, often to several places of decimals. So, in that context, one can pronounce with certainty a model is either to a certain scale or is made to run on a given gauge – or it isn't. No room for argument or misunderstanding, surely? If only…

Alas, it is possible to have two models built to the same scale and for the same gauge, yet find they are very different in many respects and quite incompatible in any practical, mechanical sense. This is because they are not built to the same *standard*. A standard is really a measure of the amount by which a model departs from absolute scale accuracy – which most model trains built over the years have done to a greater or lesser extent. In other words, we've come back yet again to Greenly's infamous compromise, where the scale of the model no longer bears a true relationship to the dimensions of its working parts – in many cases, not even in the somewhat basic matter of the track gauge. A standard is thus a combination of a defined scale and gauge with a set of working parameters – normally including such vital practicalities as wheel width and flange size, the distance between the wheel-backs, the clearances for the wheels through pointwork, and the relationship of the wheel profile to the shape of the rails.

Where the confusion has arisen is that these terms have mingled in popular usage, so that people describe things as being to '00 standards' or 'N scale' without really distinguishing what they mean. Taking the most popular size as an example, what actually *is* '00'? A gauge, a scale, or what? To be precise, it is a scale/gauge combination: 4mm:1ft *scale* on a track *gauge* of 16.5mm. This equates to a full-size track gauge of 4ft 1½in, rather than the 4ft 8½in it should be; Greenly's infamous error. However, exactly the same 4mm:1ft

scale is also used by modellers working to EM and P4 gauges and standards – not to mention those modelling Brunel's 'Broad' 7ft 0¼in, Irish 5ft 3in and all manner of narrow-gauge prototypes. The differences come in the track gauges used and associated standards for wheels, rail size and so on – which are, in the case of 'fine' standards like EM or P4, very precisely set out.

You will also note that (just to add to the confusion!) the same gauge is often used by different scales; so, for instance, 16.5mm gauge is common to H0 (3.5mm:1ft), 00 (4mm:1ft) and 0n16.5 (7mm:1ft). In this case, the 16.5mm is used to represent different prototype gauges according to the scale used. Thus, at 3.5mm:1 ft it gives an accurate 4ft 8½in standard gauge, at 4mm:1ft Greenly's erroneous 4ft 1½in and at 7mm:1ft a narrow gauge of 2ft 4½in.

Modelling scales

Before Bing introduced the idea of 'standard' modelling sizes in 1891, individual modellers simply picked some convenient scale (usually very large!) that suited their requirements. Probably the first scale/gauge combination to gain any widespread acceptance as a 'craft' railway modelling scale was 0. This, you'll recall, emerged in the early 1900s using a scale ratio of 1:43.5 (7mm:1ft) on a track gauge of 32mm – which is actually very slightly narrow; the true dead-scale dimension is 32.956mm, usually rounded to 33mm. 0 was – and still is – a very convenient size for modelling in spite of the awkward scale ratio and has long been regarded by many as the ideal size for serious work, especially where the interest lies in the railway models themselves rather than the type of scenic layout that has become popular since the end of the Second World War.

At around the same time that pioneers of railway modelling were setting out to build in 7mm:1ft scale, other British and American enthusiasts were proposing a slightly smaller, all-imperial scale. Technically 7mm:1ft is a 'bastard' scale, in that it mixes two sets of dimensional standards (millimetres and feet) and does not have a nice, simple arithmetic scale ratio in relationship to the prototype (1:43.5). So there was proposed a more logical alternative termed 'S' or 'Half-one' scale. This was half of the No. 1 size of ⅜in:1ft/1:32 proportion and so used a nicely rounded scale ratio of 1:64. As the smallest dimension usually marked on an engineer's rule was ¹⁄₆₄in, this size gave a potential modelling accuracy to the nearest inch without calling for micrometers, special scale rules or a genius for mental arithmetic. However, S scale in Britain has never attracted any significant trade support (although it was taken up commercially in the USA) which means that it has always been the preserve of the dedicated and resourceful modeller who could either make everything he needed for himself or adapt components intended for other scales. And that – give or take a couple of kits and a handful of bits – is how it still is today!

This brings us once again to Greenly and his tinkering with prototype conformity. Where 0 and S offered a scale/gauge ratio that was either exact or very close to correct, Greenly's 00 was fundamentally flawed, making it unappealing to those for whom dimensional accuracy and correct scale proportion were matters of concern. So the next scale to be adopted for 'serious' modelling in the 1920s was not Greenly's 4mm:1ft, but the more accurate 3.5mm:1ft H0. In the context of the time, where few manufactured components were available and most serious railway modellers reckoned to make everything themselves – wheels, motors, track, the lot – then keeping to a 'commercial' scale was nothing like the concern it later became. The pioneering British trade firm of Stewart-Reidpath, one of the first to set out to manufacture parts smaller than 0 scale, adopted H0 and produced some very high-quality wheels, mechanisms and cast parts. But WWII cut short their activities and afterwards they went with the tide and switched to 00.

It was the arrival of Hornby-Dublo that killed off British H0 and established the dominance of 00. The new, realistic models and accessories in 4mm scale soon created a totally new genre – the serious model railway based on mass-produced commercial models. The sheer size and output of Hornby and the quality of their products – especially the mechanisms – swept aside trifling objections as to exact scale fidelity. In the years following the end of the Second World War, 4mm scale and 00 gauge took off in a big way, and before long, firms like Hamblings and Walkers & Holtzapffel were offering a selection of parts: wheels, motors, castings, track components in the new 'popular size' to rival the ranges from the established makers in 0 scale – Bassett-Lowke, Mills Brothers, the Leeds Model Company and Edward Exley. By the early 1950s, the die was cast and 0 gauge – for long the most popular scale – was in headlong retreat, while new firms were jumping on the 00 bandwagon in ever-increasing numbers: Rovex and Graham Farish in the 'ready to run' segment and names like KMR, ERG, Merco, Bilteezi, Kirdon, Gaiety, GEM, Ratio, Anorma, Wills, K's, Jamieson and Rowe in what was now referred to as the 'scale' market – although in this context the term was simply used to distance the products from any taint of the toy train. A lot of them were still very far from true to scale!

Fine scale

The term 'fine scale' is, on the face of it, nonsensical. Given that a scale is a numerical absolute, something is either to scale – or it isn't. So how can a scale be fine? The answer is that some degree of compromise is always necessary in the quest for working models, and the terms 'fine' and 'coarse' scale were devised to describe the degree of compromise accepted – in other words, how far the model departed from true scale in its key dimensions. The 'finer' the model, the smaller the deviation from absolute accuracy.

A few pioneers, usually skilled amateurs or bespoke craftsmen, were building what amounted to 'fine scale' models right from the outset of the hobby, albeit all working to individually determined standards in a variety of scales. The notion of setting out defined 'fine scale' wheel and track standards for

Above: A 'scale' 4mm loco kit of the early 1950s; the KMR LMS Compound, with die-cast body and tender in zinc-lead alloy, brass chassis and Romford wheels to the new BRMSB 'scale 00' wheel profile. The motor and gears on this survivor are also by Romford.

0 gauge – then the popular commercial size – arrived in the mid-1930's, being strongly championed by the inimitable J. N. Maskelyne in the pages of the *Model Railway News*. For several years, debate had raged about how practicable such models were on a working layout and it was an issue over which the hobby divided itself. Maskelyne, in conjunction with his friend W. S. Norris, set out to prove that fine scale 0 was completely practicable, in which endeavour, they were entirely successful. Norris's amazing 'Francisthwaite' layout built in the 1950s simply stunned people with its realism and superlative quality of running. It was, however, very much the indulgence of a rich man who could afford to employ the best professional model makers of the day.

Commercially, Bassett-Lowke, Mills and the Leeds Model Company, the key players in the 'serious' market, persisted with 'Standard 0' using third-rail or stud-contact electrification and oversize rail and wheels. It was well into the 1950s before they eventually capitulated and introduced two-rail models with 'fine scale' wheels. Until then, fine scale two-rail components were produced by very few makers, although Beeson did offer his beautiful wheels and fittings to those with deep enough pockets. In spite of this, the practicality of 'Scale 0' was firmly established and by the mid-1950s virtually all new development concentrated on the 'fine' standard. The death-knell for coarse scale sounded with the demise of Hornby and Bassett-Lowke – and with them, mass-produced 0 gauge trains. The Gauge 0 Guild, founded in 1956, has always embraced both coarse and fine standards in a truly British spirit of compromise, but the fine now predominates.

The BRMSB

In the dark days of the war, when very little practical modelling was really possible, some far-sighted figures in the hobby, notably J. N. Maskelyne and R. J. Raymond, editors – respectively – of the *Model Railway News* and the *Model Railway Constructor* – proposed the setting up of an independent body to evolve a full set of standards for future development in all the popular sizes. Thus was born the British Railway Modelling Standards Bureau (BRMSB) which met periodically throughout the war from early 1940 and in time produced a remarkably full set of proposals for the popular sizes from '1' down to '000'. These standards were very workmanlike and soundly based, but had a fatal flaw: no tolerances (amounts by which components could deviate from the dimensions set out and still conform) were quoted and there was no way of policing conformity; the standards relied entirely on the goodwill of all involved.

Unfortunately, the BRMSB reckoned without two important factors that effectively scuppered these good intentions. The first was the ignorance and laxity of many members of the newly emerged 'trade' in matters of tolerances, with the result that many products that claimed to be 'to BRMSB standards' were absolutely nowhere near them. However, as the bureau lacked any 'teeth', there was no way of bringing these 'sinners' into line. But secondly, and more importantly, they overlooked the rigid competitive ethos that characterised the big commercial makers

Below: The next step up the scale fidelity/ modelling craft ladder was a pre-formed sheet-metal kit like this GWR 57XX pannier from Jamieson, the body parts stamped from nickel-silver sheet with turned and cast fittings. It was pretty basic, but with careful work and some added detail you could make a nice model from one of these kits. Those are Hamblings BRMSB 00 driving wheels – Bakelite centres and brass tyres. This is actually a late (post-decimal) example, although it is a very long time since you could buy a loco kit for £5.49!

Dublo, Trix and Tri-ang. All of these firms subscribed to a commercial doctrine that forsook any notion of conformity to a standard and hence interchangeability of running. The basis for this deliberate incompatibility was that once you had 'hooked' a customer with a Christmas trainset, he could only buy *your* models because no-one else's would work on his layout. Thus, in the mainstream of the hobby, the efforts of the BRMSB came largely to naught.

Below: The new 'realistic' school of railway modelling didn't stop at the boundary fence; in the early 1950s, modellers like P. D. Hancock and John Ahern were creating whole – often slightly whimsical – worlds in miniature, with complete townships and veritable tracts of countryside lovingly modelled. This is Madderport, on John Ahern's 'Madder Valley Railway' (now at Pendon Museum); realistically observed modelling leavened with impish humour – and capturing the very essence of the English country town.

EM and P4

Where the BRMSB did have an impact was in the 'craft' hobby. With 4mm scale so obviously in the ascendant and all these new and tempting goodies flooding on to the market, the enthusiast in search of accuracy could no longer afford to ignore 00, for all its flaws. But how to eliminate Greenly's error? Simple! Keep the 4mm scale – a lot more convenient arithmetically than the truly perverse 3.5mm:1ft – but adopt a more appropriate track gauge. Which is exactly what the Bureau had proposed in its 'scale 00' standard, using a track gauge of 18mm. This equated to a full-size figure of 4ft 6in – still not quite right, but a great deal better than Greenly's effort. To avoid confusion, the standard was re-christened EM (eighteen millimetre) but otherwise adopted the wheel profiles, clearances, flangeway and other dimensions set out by the BRMSB

In the immediate post-war period, many prominent modellers adopted EM, and in some cases – most notably among the group of fine modellers active in the Manchester

club at that time – they set about refining it and moving their models even closer to true scale. The EM Gauge Society was founded in 1954 to promote the new standard, and still flourishes today. In 1979, the society carried out a thorough review of the standard in the light of the components then available and the work of the 'Manchester Boys'. As a result a new, finer 'EM' standard was promulgated, with a new wheel profile (originally coded 'EMf' to distinguish it from BRMSB) and a slightly increased track gauge of 18.2mm. This is the EM standard in use today.

However, this wasn't the end of the development road for fine scale in 4mm scale. The 'Manchester' standard was being further refined with still smaller flanges and a narrower wheel tread as 'EEM'. Then, in the early 1960s, a group of modellers led by Malcolm Cross and Bernard Weller, formed themselves into the Model Railway Study Group (MRSG) to explore the notion of exact-scale modelling in the smaller scales – 7mm:1ft and below. The result was the promulgation, in 1966, of sets of 'exact scale' standards along similar lines to those proposed by the BRMSB a quarter of a century earlier – but this time with the important addition of allowable tolerances.

This 'family' of standards was based closely on full-size practice, the only deviations from strict scale being a pragmatic recognition of the practical limits to which the necessary components could be made and used. Fortunately, the MRSG included people with sound engineering and production backgrounds – including Joe Brook-Smith and, ironically, W. Ward-Platt – at one time the chief draughtsman responsible for much of Hornby Dublo's design. These new 'Proto' standards were set out in a series of seminal

Below: The move toward fully scenic model railways gave birth to the structure kit, often very much along the lines of Ahern's work as described in his book Miniature Building Construction. *These 4mm scale Anorma kits are typical; card based, with printed paper overlays and celluloid windows.*

articles in the *Model Railway Constructor* and covered 7mm, 4mm and 3.5mm scales, the resulting standards being christened respectively Scaleseven (S7), Protofour (P4) and Proto-87 (P87).

Fortunately, these new standards escaped the fate of their BRMSB predecessors, mainly because they were not relevant to the commercial activities of the 'mainstream' model railway trade. In all three scales, the way forward has been 'preach by example', with the protagonists of each scale opting to let their models do the talking. Most of the development took place in 4mm scale, where the need for more accurate standards was most acute. The Protofour Society was formed in 1967, and the EM Gauge Society also embraced the new 4mm fine scale with its 18.83mm track gauge and true-scale wheels. Many found it hard to believe that the miniscule flanges would keep the trains on the rails, but the success of the pioneering P4 layouts soon allayed this fear. A further group, the Scalefour Society, was set up in 1974 to promote the P4 standard, and this eventually absorbed the Protofour Society to share with the EMGS the support and furtherance of 4mm fine scale modelling.

Miniature fine scale

If one overlooks S, the oldest of the fine scale disciplines is that of 2mm scale, which preceded its commercial derivation, N, by some 40 years, using a ratio of 1:152.3 full size and a track gauge of 9.42mm; both 'exact' figures. Early 2mm scale was the preserve of just a few skilled craftsmen, the engineering involved being very much on a par with high-quality watchmaking. It is sobering to consider the audacity of these pioneers in the mid-1920s – when H0 and 00 gauge were often dismissed as 'too small to be practicable' – in producing these miniscule models that not only worked, but were constructed to a far more accurate standard than anything else then being made! Thus 2mm scale has always been a fine standard, albeit one that has never gained the sort of widespread acceptance enjoyed by EM and P4; but it thrives under the aegis of the 2mm Scale Association, founded in 1960. The arrival of better-quality N models that can be adapted to fine-scale standards has given a 2mm fine scale a new impetus – fortunately, the practical and visual differences between 1:148 'British N' and true 1:152.3 are relatively insignificant.

Tri-ang's protégé, 3mm scale TT, also spawned a very flourishing society, founded in 1965 when the RTR product was still current. Like the Gauge 0 Guild, the 3mm Society set out to promote a *scale* rather than a specific wheel or track standard – which meant that eventually it came to embrace no fewer than *four* distinct sets of wheel/track dimensions: coarse for the Tri-ang collectors; 'scale' TT with finer wheels on both 12mm gauge and

Below: True 4mm fine scale arrived with the advent of Protofour in 1966. I suppose I was amongst the first wave of modelling 'Tommies' to go over the top of that particular trench, tackling 'Hesperus' – my first P4 loco – in 1968.

13.5mm gauges, equivalent to 'scale' 00 and EM; and finally a true fine-scale 3mm standard on a correct track gauge of 14.2mm – something that logic suggests should have been called 'Protothree' but somehow never was. Like the 2mm Association, with which it has close links, the 3mm Society is active in providing the wherewithal to model in this attractive size, and today produces or sponsors a wide range of kits and components. In spite of the fact that TT has now been dead as a commercial scale for more than 40 years, 3mm scale modelling continues to thrive.

British railway modelling today

I must now conclude this look back at how we've got to where were are today – not because there's no more to say, but rather so that there's room left in this book to cover the wealth of practical topics that demand attention! As I hope is evident, we have now arrived at a situation where we have three popular indoor modelling 'sizes' in use, with scales of 7mm, 4mm and 2mm:1ft, but using a variety of gauges and standards. Above 0 come the really large sizes 10mm:1ft Gauge 1 and now the re-born 2 and 3 Gauge sizes from the old Bing system, revived for use in garden railways. These are increasingly popular, and also embrace the narrow-gauge sizes of SM32 (16mm:1ft/19:1 scale ratio on 32mm gauge 0 track) and G (for garden) which uses the same scale but on 45mm Gauge 1 track to represent 3ft gauge. (Although be warned – 1:22.5 is also used on the same G track gauge to represent metre gauge prototypes, but only by 'foreigners'!)

The 00/RTR mainstream of the hobby is supported by three large manufacturers: Hornby and Bachmann making the trains with Peco the principal provider of track. Bachmann also control the N gauge market through the revitalised Graham Farish range, and at the opposite end of the range offer an American G system. Alongside the big firms sit some smaller, more specialised RTR ranges, notably the Danish kit-maker Heljan which has recently introduced some excellent models of British diesel locos. All modern 4mm scale RTR is essentially to a common standard; built for 00, but otherwise accurate in all main dimensions and usually readily adaptable to EM and P4 standards. Similarly, the latest N models are far closer to scale and many can be readily converted to 2mm fine scale. H0 scale British-outline clings on as a minority interest, as does S scale and 3mm, but without RTR support; yet...

What the British hobby does have in greater abundance even than that of the USA is a large and incredibly diverse specialist trade, producing a huge range of kits and components in just about all the scales mentioned; even S gets a look in nowadays! Many of the model-making techniques now used world-wide first saw the light of day in Britain, and British fine scale modelling is widely regarded as being the absolute state of the art in world terms. Definitely a third 'Golden Age'!

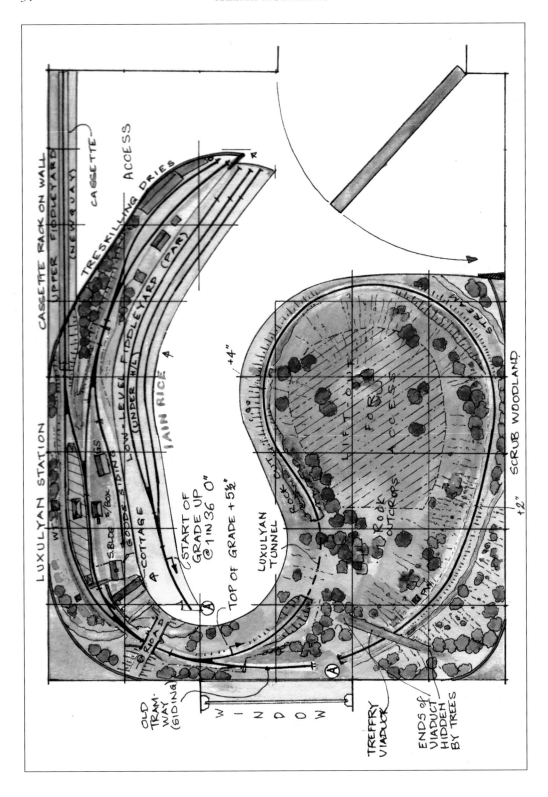

CASSETTE RACK ON WALL

UPPER FIDDLEYARD (NEW&DAY)

CASSETTE

TRESKILLING DRIES

ACCESS

Low-LEVEL FIDDLEYARD (PAR) (UNDER H/L)

IAIN RICE

LUXULYAN STATION

W/BDG

S/BOX

S.BLDG

GOODS SIDING

COTTAGE

ROAD

START OF GRADE UP @ 1 IN 36 0"

TOP OF GRADE + 5½"

LUXULYAN TUNNEL

ROCK CUT

+4"

LIFT-OUT FOR ACCESS

ROCK OUTCROPS

STREAM

+2"

SCRUB WOODLAND

OLD TRAM-WAY (SIDING)

W I N D O W

TREFFRY VIADUCT

ENDS of VIADUCT HIDDEN BY TREES

Chapter 2

PLANNING A MODEL RAILWAY

Layout planning is all about resolving the four 'S' factors: space, subject, scale and scope. These criteria are common to all model railways, from the most modest to the grandest, and from the strictly prototypical to the wildest flight of freelance fancy. Of the four siblings, it is the first which is the most intractable. Without space, it is not possible to create a model railway of any sort, so until a suitable (or usually, more-or-less unsuitable) site has been procured the other factors cannot even be considered.

I touched upon the impact of space – or the lack of it – in my introduction when tracing the evolution of the smaller scales. There are precious few of us who can claim to enjoy an excess of this increasingly scarce commodity – those who do must consider themselves exceedingly fortunate. The trouble is that many of the sites traditionally used to house model railways are effectively disappearing from the modern housing scene. Spare bedrooms get smaller and squarer while the attic area in many a modern house is a dense forest of lightweight gang-nailed roof trusses now that the old-

Opposite: A completed layout design by the author, in this case, an N scale rendition of the Luxulyan Valley section of the Newquay branch set in the early 1980s BR blue-diesel era. The site is a small bedroom, only 8ft x 6ft – typical of the 'third bedroom' in many modern houses. The original drawing was made at a scale of 1in = 1ft; the colouring conveys a good idea of the 'feel' and look of the proposal.

fashioned rafter-and-purlin construction has been superseded. Not only that, but the ever-tighter strictures of building regulations make full-blown loft conversions costly and complex even where they are structurally possible. Gardens, too, get ever-smaller; many more recent lots barely offer enough space for a good-sized shed, and in these days of restricted parking and multiple vehicles per household, the garage is often needed for its intended purpose. What is to do?

Possible sites

Where there's a will there's a way – and with a bit of ingenuity and lateral thinking it's usually possible to find *somewhere* for a model railway in even the most cramped of quarters; I know of at least one layout in the Netherlands tucked into a toilet, while in America I saw a neat H0 logging railroad built into the sleeper-cab of a long-distance truck. Extreme examples, perhaps, but both are workable solutions.

The ultimate site for any model railway is obviously a building erected or adapted specifically to house it. Utopia? For most of us, certainly – except that this is a category in which one could include the ubiquitous garden shed, at least where layout-housing is its prime purpose. (Other raisons d'être may, however, need to be advanced for planning and procurement purposes…) The next best solution must be the exclusive use of a room in the house, preferably of good size and reasonably rectangular proportions, devoid of

Top: Layout sites 1: The garden shed. This standard off-the-peg 12ft x 8ft garden shed served as my own modelling headquarters for more than 15 years. Here, it is housing three layouts (none of them very big, admittedly), as well as my workshop.

The layouts seen in residence are: 1) 'Bodesmeer' (3.7m x 0.75m, HO P87) displayed at high-level top left; 2) 'Cade's Green' (10ft x 1ft 3in, 4mm/P4) under construction on the bench below 'Bodesmeer', and 3) 'Trerice' (7ft x 1ft 9in) stored across the end of the shed.

Middle: Layout Sites 2: Sharing a room. Here is 'Cade's Green' in its current location, occupying one shelf's-worth of space along the wall of my office that otherwise houses my library of railway books and periodicals. This sort of site is ideal for long, narrow layouts; 'Cade's Green' is no wider than 1ft 3in. A backdrop will hide the shelf-tracking holding up both book shelving and the layout.

Bottom: Layout sites 3: The attic. Probably the most traditional of home layout sites, this is the attic of my current abode in the throes of adaptation for railway modelling purposes. I'm lucky that the structure uses traditional rafter-and-purlin construction, as it is easy to adapt to give a clear space. Notice the rigid foil-faced-foam insulation sheets being used to clad the rafters; adequate insulation is essential to render attics usable.

fitted furniture or other such impedimenta, modest in the number and size of its windows and with the door conveniently sited in one corner. If said door opens outwards, so much the better!

Next in the pecking order comes the use of part of a room with a different main use. Studies or home offices are good candidates and can easily accommodate model railways if the latter are carefully designed to integrate with the primary use – a context in which shelf-based layouts can work particularly well. Bedrooms are also tenable if a little prone to dust and fluff, and even the front parlour can serve if other household members are amenable and a good job is done on the presentation and finishing fronts – aspects which I would anyway suggest receive due attention as they are of great benefit to the model as well as its environment. Hallways, passages and lobbies can also provide possibilities where all else fails, while if you've got a spare billiard room you don't need me to tell you what to do with it!

The garage is also a perfectly usable site and there is a long tradition of co-habitation between model railways and motor cars, which can work well if a few simple precautions are taken. Garages are a good shape and are not generally over-endowed with windows (which are bad news in railway modelling terms). It's quite possible to design layouts for garages that don't inhibit the prime use of the structure, although wet motor cars and model railways don't make happy bedfellows. But putting a wet car in an unheated or poorly ventilated garage is bad for the car anyway, let alone any effects it might have on the model. So where there's room, leave the car outside when it's wet. It might as well stay out there when it's dry too – in which case, it's very simple to adapt the garage into a very convivial layout-building environment. Thus adapted, a single or double garage – especially if integral with the house, as many now are – is probably one of the best layout-building sites most of us can hope for.

Dry, spacious, temperate unobstructed basements! The American's have 'em, but by and large we don't. I know of several American homes where the layout was designed first, the shape of the basement configured to contain it, and the house to go on top then designed as an afterthought! A nice order of priorities, although I'm not quite sure how British mortgage lenders, planning law and building regulations would accommodate such an approach... If any such subterranean site is available here, it is most likely to be a basement garage in a modern house or a cellar in an old one. The former falls into the same category as any other garage. Old cellars, on the other hand, often have a regrettable tendency to damp, darkness and poor ventilation. They are also often pokey and sub-divided into several small compartments – usually by load-bearing walls – rather than being a nice open space. It's a fact that what was intended merely to keep the coal dry or the claret cool usually needs quite a bit of adaptation to make it suitable for model railway use.

This brings us at last up into the roof, where this is rendered usable by the nature of its construction. Very much a traditional 'home layout' site in years gone by, the model railway press over the years has featured many loft layouts and accompanying accounts of ad-hoc attic conversions – most of which would make a modern building inspector's hair stand on end! Quite apart from the practicalities, this business of converting attics is nowadays a real minefield in terms of regulation, much of it turning on how the intended adaptation falls in terms of the definition of 'habitable space'.

All of these 'non-habitable' sites will anyway need a spot (or a lot!) of adaptation and improvement to render them suitable to house a model railway. But, by and large, unless you're very unlucky and face extreme structural problems, most of the work that's needed will come down to a bit of fairly straightforward DIY or a couple of days of a jobbing builder's time. More on the practicalities of all this in Chapter 3.

Places to avoid

Before leaving the matter of sites, a word or two on places which experience suggests are definitely *unsuitable* for a layout, at least the sort of small-scale scenic model that forms the subject of this book. Of the things which play merry hell with model railways, wide variations in temperature and humidity head the list, which rules out environments subject to temperature extremes or to excessive dampness. (Excessive aridity is rarely a problem in the British climate!) At the head of this category I firmly place conservatories and greenhouses; what keeps a pot-plant happy is usually the kiss of death to the average model railway. The only exception to this rule might be the 'indoor' portion of a garden railway using robust equipment – such as LGB – designed to withstand outdoor conditions and thus better able to cope with climatic extremes. Uninsulated roof spaces also plumb the depths and scale the heights of the temperature scale, as do structures such as sheds or garages built of sheet metal without properly designed lining and ventilation systems. Such unlined structures are also notoriously subject to condensation, producing an environment damp enough to make things go limp and curly on the days when they aren't cooking. No good at all.

Bathrooms and kitchens are ruled out for obvious reasons; even if the temperature range is more moderate, the humidity levels will quite likely stray into unacceptable areas – not to mention the likely conflicts with the main uses of the rooms! Utility rooms or other confined or poorly ventilated spaces housing boilers, washing machines or – especially – tumble driers not connected to an external extractor vent – can also be bad news, although these are problems that can be addressed if there's nowhere else. Other locations I would always seek to avoid are those with heavy domestic traffic, where not only are you likely to be in constant conflict with people barging through the layout area, but the model itself will usually be vulnerable to accidental damage and hard to keep clean.

Dust rates second only to damp as an invidious destroyer of model railways, so irredeemably dirty environments are definitely ones to avoid. Older roof-spaces are often the devil in this regard, as can be outbuildings of all sorts, and concrete-floored sheds or garages. Considerable site works will be needed to render such environments layout-friendly. Even in the normal domestic environment dust can be an issue, as model railways aren't the easiest of things to keep clean. Dust protection and even simple precautions like keeping the door of the layout room closed as much as possible can help to cut down the menace of the common mite.

Sites directly exposed to large windows – especially south-facing windows – are also problematic, as sunlight is another enemy of the scenic model railway. Not only is it liable to produce unwanted temperature variations, but the high ultra-violet component of direct sunlight will also fade colours badly and degrade many plastics, causing them to warp or become brittle.

To summarise then, the ideal environment for a model railway is temperate, free of damp, as clean and draught-free as possible, shielded from excessive sunlight, out of the way in terms of domestic too-ing and fro-ing, and suitably devoid of cats. (I have absolutely nothing against cats, but I have learned to my cost that they are very bad news for model railways, where they can wreak havoc on a scale to eclipse Godzilla). Almost any domestic site will fulfil these general requirements with little or no alteration; it will also be blessed with power and light and hopefully some form of heating. Sheds, lofts and garages will usually need a little improvement.

Permanent or portable?

Many older traditional model railways were built as very permanent affairs indeed, secured to and integral with the structure of the building in which they were housed. This is fine until the time comes for the layout to be moved, for whatever reason; then, too often, the only course is the complete destruction of the model. If this is of no concern, then all well and good. But most of us, given the investment of time and resources involved in even a modest model railway, would prefer to acknowledge this possibility and design-in a degree of sectionalisation and other aids to dismantling the layout intact for removal to another site if the need arises. This is a type of layout I categorise as 'transportable' rather than portable – you can move it if you *have* to, but probably you wouldn't *want* to!

Opposite: The epitome of the large, traditional permanent layout: the throat of Torreyford Station on Ken Northwood's iconic 'North Devonshire Railway'. Regrettably, layouts like this can rarely be moved and when Ken passed away and the railway room had to be cleared, most of 'North Devonshire' ended up on a bonfire...

Above: A good example of a truly portable compact layout is 'Llenbarff', a Welsh prototype 0n16.5 narrow-gauge model built by Len de Vries, modelling editor of the Dutch Rail magazine. This exquisite model is a scant 2m long without fiddleyard, but thanks to Len's superb backdrop the result appears far from cramped.

The size and weight of section appropriate to a transportable layout is constrained only by the manpower available and the need to get it through doorways, around any corners or up and down any staircases, and finally into a suitable vehicle. The safe rule is smaller and lighter than the theoretical extreme possible; experience suggests anything much bigger than the size of a single bed – say, 6ft x 3ft – is likely to a problem in most domestic environments. Really, it's all about common sense. Moving a transportable layout will almost inevitably involve a certain amount of 'making good' on reassembly and often a degree of adaptation or modification where the new site is at variance with the original.

An alternative to designing the whole layout in the form of movable sections is to divide it into 'key elements' – such as a station or yard, junction, loco depot or some other more-or-less separate feature – which are linked by plain track to form the overall layout. These 'key elements' are built as self-contained (electrically as well as structurally) movable modules, while the plain-track 'linking sections' are regarded as disposable, being easy and quick to replace on rebuilding. This approach, which I have used with particular success in designing 'expandable' layouts for clients in the USA, is very flexible and makes it relatively simple to reconfigure a model to fit a new site.

A true portable layout is a fish from a very different kettle. Here, the objective is not just to make it possible to move and transport the model, but to render the operation as simple and painless as it can be. The features of good portable design include sections which are small and light enough to be wieldy, robust enough to stand frequent handling and which locate together accurately and are quickly and easily assembled into the finished model. In Britain, where model railway exhibitions are thick on the ground and layouts suitable for exhibition ever in demand, portable layout design has become a fine art, and the best of them can be erected or dismantled with a degree of slickness akin to a motor-racing pit stop. Not only that, but they will run faultlessly in the difficult environment of an exhibition hall while exhibiting few signs of the measures needed to render them readily dismembered. A good portable exhibition layout is probably the peak of model railway technology. Even if you have no intention of displaying your handiwork in public however, the truly portable layout has a further virtue, in that it does not demand a permanent site.

No-site layouts

When prospecting for somewhere to create our miniature masterpiece, most of us tend to think in terms of a *permanent* site – a place in which the layout can live whether it is in use or not. Of course, that's the ideal, but it's not the only possible stratagem. It is quite possible to conceive layouts that make use of a non-dedicated space when being operated or worked on, but which are stowed away elsewhere when not in use. This again is an approach with a long tradition – such iconic models as the Rev. Peter Denny's 'Buckingham' (built in a bedsit) or John Charman's 'Charford Branch' (in a caravan) started out thus, and with a little ingenuity it is quite possible to come up with interesting and practical designs based on this 'vanishing trick' precept, using the components and techniques developed for exhibition models.

While you can contrive quite large or complex layouts that come apart like a Chinese puzzle and can be stowed hither and yon about the house – terminus station under the spare bed, fiddleyard in the wardrobe, loco depot in the cupboard under the stairs and so on – my own experience suggests that this is not really such a good idea. The chances are such a set-up will take too long to assemble and will probably be none too reliable into the bargain. If you need to contemplate a 'no site' layout, it's best to think small and box clever, keeping things as self-contained and simple as possible. In which context I have found the 'Cameo' layout concept works particularly well.

Cameo layouts

These are probably the ultimate in 'no-site' railway modelling. Never mind that brooch your granny used to wear, in this context a cameo is a small, self-contained portable layout in diorama form that is complete in itself rather than being an assembly of components. Usually built in lightweight materials like thin ply and foam-core board, a cameo layout uses

Below: The self-contained cameo layout is designed for easy movement and storage – on end, if need be. This is 'Trerice', perched atop the furniture in the spare bedroom in this picture.

a baseboard that is constructed integrally with a backdrop, fascia and side 'wing' pieces to produce a strong, rigid box-like structure which encloses and protects the model as well as displaying it to good advantage. The cameo structure also contains all the necessary electrics and is of a size that is not too big and unwieldy to handle. I have made cameos some two yards long, but something less than 6ft by about 18–20in wide is more typical. My 'Trerice' layout, illustrated here, is just such a cameo, 4ft 9in long by 1ft 9in wide.

To go with the cameo layout there is the 'fiddle case'. Far from being the sort of thing favoured by old-time gangsters toting machine guns, the cameo fiddle case is another ply box that locates on to one end of the actual layout to provide a fiddleyard-cum-stock storage case. The picture shows how this works. Cameo layouts take up very little space as they can be stored on-end – they'll go happily in a normal wardrobe – and the fiddle-case provides a home for the locos and stock when the layout is stowed. If you haven't got room for one of these, you're probably living in a phone box!

Multi-mini layouts

Taking the no-site miniature cameo layout concept one stage further, there's no reason why you need to stop at one. It's inevitable that such small models will be limited in operational scope and modelling potential, so to sustain interest – and given the ease

Below: Here is the inside of a 'fiddle case' for a cameo layout, with a simple two-road sector plate and stock storage shelves.

with which they can be stored, moved and set up – why not have more than one? This is the approach I have used myself for a goodly number of years, living in a small Devon terraced cottage that also had to accommodate a growing family, a large library and an unconscionable collection of junk.

My 'no-site' operating area was a more-or-less vacant shelf in my office, 15in wide, and to fit this space I eventually had a choice of three small layouts, any of which I could also take to exhibitions. The three possibilities were of deliberately disparate subjects, ranging from an H0 Dutch tramway and a 4mm scale East Anglian light railway to an H0 Maine Coast seaport. No lack of variety there! This trio of little models (biggest is 8ft x 15in) kept me busy and happy for the best part of 15 years, and when not in use lived on a series of shelves high up in the utility room or shed, out of the family's (and harm's) way.

There are a number of advantages to this approach. For a start, going the 'multi-mini' route enabled me to dip a toe into a variety of tempting prototype/scale waters rather than needing to plump for just one. I could try out new scales and prototypes, modelling techniques, scenic approaches and technical solutions without ending up with the sort of hotchpotch that arises all-too-easily if you try such experimentation in the context of a single layout. These minnow-size layouts are also readily achievable as they don't call for very much of anything – time, space or cash. They are also readily shared with friends; there's quite a bit to be said for a number of space-starved modellers banding together to produce several such layouts which could then be rotated among the members of the group to keep everyone's interest up.

Prototype choice

Those of us who spent our younger days partaking freely of the greatest free show on earth – watching the trains go by – rarely have much difficulty in the matter of choosing what to model, unless it be the tricky problem of deciding which of a number of equally-tempting possibilities to pursue. Perhaps this

Above: A 'lokaaltrein' calls at Bodesmeer station on my Dutch-prototype H0 layout – one of three alternatives originally built to fit a common display site. The idea was to compensate for the limitations of small size by being able to 'ring the changes' – the layout(s) not in use being stored elsewhere about the house or shed. Simon de Souza

Below: A change is as good as a rest, they say, and here, by contrast, is the second layout of the trio, an H0 P87 effort depicting the Maine Central RR in Northern Maine in the late 1970s.

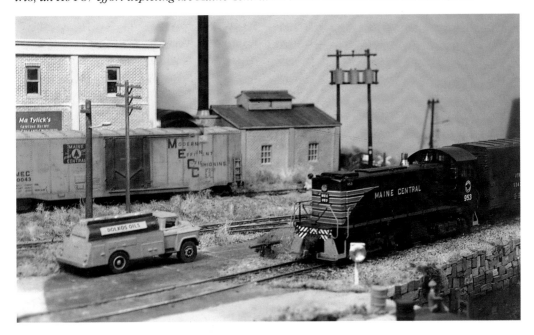

Above: The branch train arrives at the latest in a long line of P4 Suffolk backwaters, Debenham (Cade's Green). The last of my trio of small layouts, and – after a mere nine year's worth of intermittent progress – still a-building.

is still true, although train watching is not what it once was in this age of health-and-safety and security concerns while, I fear, the contemporary scene very often fails to offer the variety and stimulus that made the railways of my youth so fascinating. But apparently, some people are quite happy modelling multiple units of various kinds and block freight trains all pulled by the same type of loco, so perhaps this direct inspiration from the prototype still works its magic…

A quick perusal of the train-makers' catalogues will soon suggest that steam hasn't lost its allure. In fact, there is now a wider choice of model steam locomotives and appropriate-era rolling-stock available in RTR in the popular scales than at any time in the past. For the most part these are sophisticated and historically accurate miniatures carrying a wide choice of liveries, with many models representing prototypes with a working life of half a century or more at different stages

of their existence. This can cause a bit of a problem for many modellers who want to create authentic steam-era model railways but are too young to have been familiar with the real thing when it was still in regular service; what goes with what at which date, and what livery should it be carrying? RTR ranges now include many models carrying the 'Big Four' liveries and – in a few instances, pre-Grouping as well. However, anyone alive today old enough to lay claim to direct acquaintance with the pre-Grouping scene, even from their pram, needs to be in their mid-80s or older!

Even the 'transition' from steam and the earlier years of diesel traction are receding rapidly into history; many of the early diesel classes were very short-lived, and this was a period of rapid and drastic change on the railways. The 'blue diesel' era of the 1970s and 1980s now evokes as strong a nostalgia as steam in the hearts of a generation – now in their mid-40s – that grew up thrilling to the thunder of a 'Deltic' in full cry, the whistle-and-whine of a 'Blue Pullman', the staccato throb of a 'Peak' or the syncopated roar of a pair of 'Fifties' tackling Shap. All these examples of 'heritage diesel' power are now every bit as extinct as the steamers that preceded

them. As some sage once remarked: 'History starts yesterday.'

All of this matters not a hoot if you're not bothered by authenticity. There's a long tradition of 'free and fanciful' model railways on which 'anything goes', when locos and stock of wildly different origins and periods are freely mixed into a colourful mish-mash that, while it may be far from authentic, is at least fun! But, given the sheer quality and prototype fidelity of today's RTR and kit-based models, many people feel behoven to do them justice by selecting items that are appropriate in a historical and geographical

Above: Prototype inspiration comes in many forms, and the 'blue diesel' era depicted here is now every bit as historic, extinct and (to a whole generation of enthusiasts) as nostalgic as the swansong of steam. 'Crompton' No. 33001 trundles the oil empties from Plymouth to Fawley into Newton Abbot in the autumn of 1981. This beautiful photo is by A. O. Wynn.

context as a basis for a layout that has realism and authenticity as core objectives. The challenge now often lies in making the right choices, not just of locos and stock, but of signals, structures, and accessories – not to

Right: A typical selection of source material. Railway history books (the open volume is John Brodribb's Branches and Byways: East Anglia *which, like all the better such tomes, includes maps and track diagrams), periodicals both new and old covering railways, industrial archaeology or topography, maps (the 1930 O.S. 1-inch sheet shown here depicts the Lynton & Barnstaple line), local history books, old postcards and photographs covering both railway and more general subjects. To these could be added personal notes, sketches and snaps from field trips and movie archive material.*

mention the little matter of making the rest of the layout to a good enough standard to do justice to the trains!

The What? and When?

Making informed choices calls, above all, for information. So where should one seek the necessary knowledge? Well, as a general rule – not on preserved railways, many of which often present just as confused and inconsistent a picture as the most fanciful model railway, mixing equipment, liveries and settings in a manner which is quite alien to historical fact. But for the most part they're working railways, not museums, so one should not really expect any different. The exceptions are places like the GW Society complex at Didcot, dedicated to preserving and interpreting a specific railway. The National Railway Museum, in its public collections, covers the whole range and scope of British railway history rather than attempting to cover any one railway or epoch. The true treasure in the museum so far as information goes lies in its archives – not very accessible to most of us, I fear.

Fortunately, the whole business of railway history and the dissemination of information about it has generated an enormous literature. There are literally thousands of books in print covering every aspect of British railway history, often in exhaustive detail. Your local library should be able to find you almost anything you need to research the background to your chosen or prospective modelling subject. Not only are there books, but a every month on the bookstalls you'll find a choice of magazines and journals dedicated to the subject – most notably *Backtrack,* the *British Railway Journal, British Railways Illustrated* and *Bylines.* Some railways even have dedicated titles, like the *Great Western Journal* or *Midland Record.*

Still more specialised, there are the various 'line societies', groups dedicated to the study, promotion and preservation of a particular line or group of lines, who often have large and important documentary and photographic collections as well as publishing yet more specialist literature and staging public meetings, lectures and exhibitions. If you have a particular problem with information, joining such a society will often put you in touch with the one man on the planet who knows the answer! As well as the photographic collections of the museums and line societies, there are also a good number of private collections, either the work of individual photographers or archives of material assembled by enthusiasts or photographic dealers. Prints from these collections are sold at many exhibitions, forming a further valuable source of information and inspiration. Railways must be among the most-photographed of subjects, and the number of images available runs into the millions even for the British scene.

Lastly, often overlooked by 'serious' researchers, there is the enormous amount of railway material captured on movie film (after all, the very first successful movie ever made was of a train!) and now widely available on video or DVD. It is sometimes difficult to pin down particular aspects of your subject on film, but there's nothing like seeing good footage of what it is you're trying to model to inspire you, while moving images convey the 'feel' and atmosphere of a railway scene in a way that often eclipses even the best of photographs. They also provide lots of hard information on things like liveries (and livery combinations), train formations, signalling practice and the minutiae of railway working.

Much of this material can now be tracked down and accessed over the Internet, which bids fair to become the single greatest resource to the railway historian and railway modeller. Just typing your query into a search engine will often produce a surprisingly abundant response, and even if you don't pluck the answer you're looking for straight out of the ether, the chances are you'll come away with enough strong leads to take you in the right direction. When you tire of research, you'll find that the model railway trade is also extremely well represented on the web, as good a place as any to go looking for the models, kits and materials you'll need to turn your knowledge into an authentic and satisfying layout.

Subject and scope

Subject, in this context, refers to sort of prototype installation or installations you're setting out to model: main line or branch, terminus, through station, junction, goods yard, loco depot, industries, docks, mines and quarries and so on. Usually, it will be some combination of several of these elements – the days when layouts reckoned to include The Lot (like the Rev. E. Beal's 'West Midland Railway' of fabled memory) are, I fear, largely past.

Scope is the extent and depth of the project. The greater the number of different aspects of the real railway you're able to replicate, or the higher the standard you're aiming to work to, the greater the scope of the layout – operational in the first instance, modelling in the second. Deciding on scope very much depends on what aspect of the hobby you find most appealing – red-hot operators rarely want to spend any longer than is necessary actually building models and are generally happy with RTR or even vintage tinplate, while on the other hand there are those who spend countless hours and infinite pains producing exquisite models by hand – which they never run other than to test them! Most of us fall somewhere between these extremes …

In an ideal world, choice of subject would be unfettered and scope would be limitless – most of us, I suspect, have some sort of dream model railway of more-or-less-megalomaniac proportions tucked away in the darker

Above: A less usual choice of subject for a model railway – a simple through station in the Scottish Highlands, set in the years immediately preceding the First World War. This is Simon de Souza's 'Corrieshalloch' in P4, a simple L-shaped layout, currently operated with fiddleyards either side of the modelled scene but intended to form part of a larger layout in the future.

Below: Megalomania? It would take an ambitious enthusiast to contemplate this as a subject! In this rare wartime view – an official SR photo taken in May 1942 – 'Merchant Navy' Pacific No. 21C8 Orient Line leaves Waterloo Station (all 21-platform's-worth of it), probably headed for Southampton. A scene like this is practically unmodelable.

corners of our psyches. The trouble is that ruthless reality rules and in all probability we will only have the resources for something far more modest. It's a cruel fact of life that heady visions of a nice 0 gauge Pacific and 15 scale-length coaches streaking along a four-track main line don't square too well with the average British spare bedroom (or the average British spare budget!).

A more realistic approach – in every sense of the word – is to look at the available site with a dispassionate eye in terms of the footprint it presents, with a view to posing the two key questions 'What sort of layout format will fit naturally in this shape of space?' followed by 'What scope does that format offer for the sort subject I want to represent?' For that is the clincher; it's not just a case of the area considered in square units, but rather the way those units are disposed, and how that fits with what you want to do. One of the most intractable problems to be faced in layout design is that one keeps on coming up against things that are set in stone – inconvenient facts about which nothing can be done. A given radius of turnout in a given track gauge, for instance, is a certain length – and no amount of wishful thinking will make it any shorter. The same goes for the length of locomotives or items of rolling stock, horizontal and vertical clearances, maximum permissible gradients and minimum negotiable curves. To ignore these intractables is to invite disaster.

Reconciling format to space and subject is probably the most fundamental (and painful!) part of the whole design process. If you hanker after a main-line continuous run but the only available site is a foot-wide dead-straight shelf along one wall, there just is no way of making the two marry. But you could settle for a station, say, configured as a terminus in scene + fiddleyard format but adaptable at some future point to a 'through' version that could be *incorporated* in a continuous run should a suitable site become available. That gives you something in the short term that is still a useful

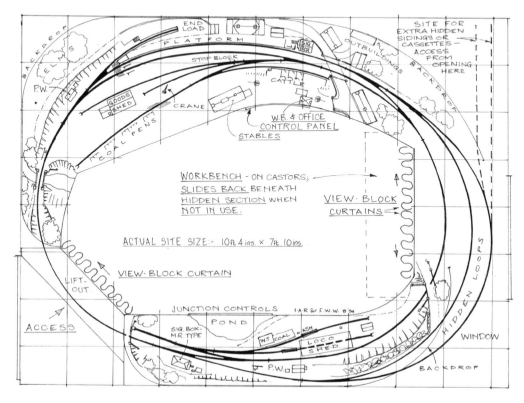

step along the way towards a more fulfilling long-term objective. It's a case of selecting the most appropriate layout format for the space then making your chosen subject fit.

Layout formats

Model railways come in three basic formats: continuous run, end to end or scene + fiddleyard. All, whatever their size or scope, fall into one or the other of these categories, and choosing which one to go for is a fundamental design decision – although, all too often, it's one that's made for you by site constraints and other such unavoidable practicalities. Within each category, however, there are a great number of possible variants, so even though the basic choice may be thrust upon you there's still plenty to exercise the 'leetle grey cells'.

A continuous run is the oldest and most traditional of layout formats, and a circle or oval of track is what you still get in every trainset. It has many virtues but also a lot of drawbacks,

most of them to do with the space needed for the semi-circular end curves involved and hence the necessary width of site and amount of length available for stations, yards and so on. End-to-end layouts (two terminal points linked by a length of running line, usually in an L or U shape) are almost unknown these days for indoor layouts, although still popular in the garden where's there's a lot more room for a decent length of run. It's the last category, the scene + fiddleyard, that is most often used for home layouts nowadays, simply because it is the most flexible and usually offers the greatest potential in a small space.

*Opposite: **A continuous-run layout scheme for a shed; an oval, more-or-less – although in this case, partly concealed by curtaining and incorporating some hidden staging tracks.***

*Below: **Point-to-point layouts are still popular in the USA; this one was designed to use a shelf around the walls of a small bedroom.***

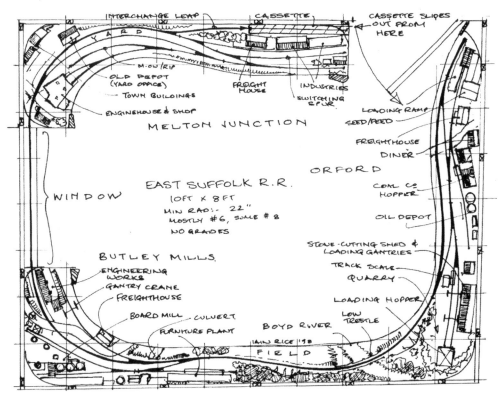

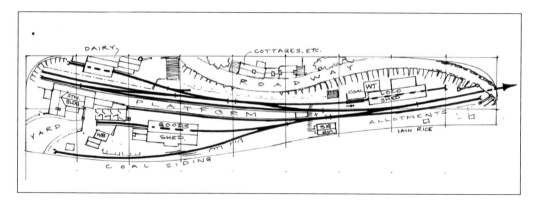

Above: The classic British home layout; a branch line terminus fed from some form of fiddleyard – not specified in this case. The arrowhead at the end of the running line denotes a track leading into a fiddleyard or hidden staging.

The chief virtue of a fiddleyard is that it can represent the 'rest of the rail network' in only a few square feet. The chief drawback is that you usually have to fiddle with it rather a lot, re-marshalling trains, realigning roads or generally doing offstage chores that are not always that much fun. Although scene + fiddleyard layouts usually have good operational potential, that operation consists essentially of shunting and sometimes it's nice to be able to 'let 'er rip'. Looked at another way, however, any form of operation other than the simple 'train passing by' is going to involve shunting of some sort, so in most regards this is the essential basis of model railway working. Scene + fiddleyard layouts are adaptable to almost any site and can take a number of forms, from the common 'terminus-direct-into-fiddleyard' to several scenes linked by fiddleyards or several fiddleyards feeding a single scene.

Presentation

Not the most obvious of design factors, perhaps, but presentation is very much something that needs considering at an early stage. Principally, this comes down to deciding at what height you're going to display the finished model, and how you're

going to light it and 'set it off' in the context of the site. Of these criteria, the height is most fundamental. One of the first steps in moving from the trainset to the model railway has always been seen as 'moving up from the carpet' – getting the model railway to a more suitable height for viewing and operation. Which, traditionally, was 'table top height', or 30–36in from the floor.

Modern thinking on both sides of the Atlantic has seen this traditional mounting height called into question for scenic model railways. In the real world that we're trying to replicate, there's a very inconvenient fact that has implications for those seeking the 'natural' look in a model: the horizon line is always exactly on eye level. This means the display height for our model likewise needs to place the horizon at eye level, which is typically between 4ft 9in and 5ft 6in above the floor for most standing adults. Many American designers are now quoting a 'mean track height' of 54in above the floor as a basic figure for standing operation. This sort of display height also makes it easier to appreciate detail both in the trains – which are much closer to the viewer – and in the scenic modelling, which is seen from a natural viewpoint rather than being seen from a height. Many British layouts – particularly those at exhibitions, which are normally viewed from a standing position – are now being displayed at these levels.

In the context of a home layout, much will depend not only on how you intend to operate (and hence view) the finished thing, but also whether you have to build the model in the final display position. Working on track and scenery 54+in up in the air is not really practicable without standing on some sort of step-up. Everything becomes a lot less daunting where sitting operation is envisaged as this lowers the eye level/horizon line by at least 9in (using a bar stool or similar seat), bringing the suggested rail level down to around 45ins from the floor – a figure now being quite widely adopted. A layout built to this dimension can be quite comfortably worked on in situ, and – being roughly halfway between the floor and ceiling – looks 'balanced' in most domestic spaces. It also allows useful storage/shelving space below baseboard level, while it's high enough to be lit well by ceiling-mounted light fittings. (Light intensity falls off by the square of the distance between the source and the object, so you don't want your lights too far away.)

If you're unsure about what sort of display height will best suit your situation/layout site, then it's well worth spending a little time playing around with simple mock-ups. A flat plank, a locomotive, a few items of stock and a couple of model structures propped up on some boxes stacked on the kitchen table are all you need to gain a good idea of the 'feel' and practicality of different viewing heights. If sitting operation is envisaged, experiment with different seat heights – I have one of those pedestal 'operators chairs' that adjusts over a height range of more than six inches, and I soon found a suitable combination of seat height and baseboard level for my own loft layout, where the slope of the roof mitigates against much in the way of high-level display. For the record, I ended up with a seat height of 17in, which gave me – at 5ft 7in standing on a good day – an eye level of 46in. So I settled on a mean track level of 42in using

*Below: **Modern ideas on layout presentation set great store on displaying the model at a height which provides a natural eye-level view. Here is 'Trerice' set up for exhibition, sitting on trestles atop a normal tabletop which raise the track level to about 52ins above the floor. Note also the use of a neutrally-coloured surround and a drape to 'frame' the model and conceal the supports.***

baseboards with the top edge of the framing 40in from the floor – the best compromise in the circumstances.

Layout theme

What you set out to model is a very personal choice and most people have well-defined preferences. However, some layout themes have become so popular as to attain the status of cliché. Chief amongst these well-worn concepts is the GWR branch-line terminus set in a particularly idyllic bit of the West Country. Visit almost any model railway exhibition and you're sure to encounter several examples of the genre. I'm not going to pass judgement as to whether or not this is a good thing, but given the wide selection of models, kits, detail parts and literature devoted to this theme, its ubiquity is hardly surprising. I would, however, add a few notes of caution. First, amid so many it's hard (but by no means impossible) to produce something fresh and different and truly individual. Secondly, it is very easy to end up building a model of someone else's model rather than starting out from the real

Below: While most of us are happy to model railways familiar at first hand, there are always those who will opt for something a little more exotic. Mike Sharman's interest lies in the railways of the pre-1870 – in this case, Brunel's broad gauge.

thing. Many a chestnut and more than a few howlers have been perpetuated thus!

There are ways of producing a 'classic' steam age branch-line terminus model that is more distinctive. If you're not a committed GWR man, you could look to other, equally attractive prototypes: former SECR branches in Kent, the East Anglian byways of the old GER, the Midland Railway in the Peak District or the North-Eastern in the Dales, almost any Scottish branch line and the doings of the LNWR in North Wales are all equally tempting (and achievable) candidates. While if it must be the GWR, don't overlook the less-modelled parts of Swindon's far-flung empire: West Wales and the Welsh borders, the West and South Midlands, the odd incursions into Hampshire and Dorset. And, of course, there's a long and noble tradition of imaginary GW branches, which could be contrived in any of these locations – with the usual proviso that to be believable, a fiction needs to be rooted in reality as to setting and correct railway practice and not too far-fetched. If you're limited to a typically modest branch line model you can also expand the modelling and operational potential by providing two sets of stock of different periods; my own 'Bodesmeer' was conceived thus, being capable of going back to c1910 or forward to 1949.

If the space you're faced with allows only for a terminus-fiddleyard format, the country branch is far from being the only thematic option. On the prototype, the truly compact stations and yards were more usually found in the inner city – where land is a premium – rather than in some remote rural nook. Urban freight depots can make very satisfying and space-efficient models with a great deal of both operating and modelling potential, as can motive power depots, workshops, industrial or dockside railways, mineral railways, mines and quarries, military railways and agricultural tramways. These are areas I have explored myself over the years, with very rewarding results.

Two fiddleyards either side of a modelled scene give you the possibility of representing a through station without needing to site it on

Above: A popular choice of theme and subject – a GW branch line terminus in Devon. Indeed, perhaps the most popular choice, for this is Ashburton, the prototype for a good number of layouts across all the scales. This – or something like it – is many people's idea of what makes a good model, in spite of limited operational scope and, often, something of a surfeit of Déjà vu…

a continuous run, opening up the possibility of something more main line in character on a narrow linear site. Such an arrangement is not the most efficient use of space in terms of securing the maximum possible area for the modelled scene, but enhanced operational potential and the ability to accommodate a wider choice of locomotives and rolling stock may well outweigh this drawback. Having constructed a couple of examples of this genre, the only other caveat I found was the necessity to do rather a lot of fiddling in the fiddleyards, and careful design of these to make them easy to work will pay dividends.

Layouts of the traditional oval, continuous run form lend themselves to a number of themes, from a simple 'trains passing by' stretch of line in a realistic setting on which to re-create the 'lineside experience' through any number of variations on the through-station from the simple and rural to the large and urban to other settings like junctions or large industrial complexes. These days, oval layouts tend to fall into two formats: the traditional 'home layout', usually around the perimeter of

a loft, garage or good-sized room, where the layout is viewed and operated from within the oval and the whole thing is a scenic model; and the 'exhibition oval', designed to be operated from within but viewed from the front only, or possibly the front and ends. Usually, such layouts represent a busy main line, the rear of the oval being taken up by a large staging/fiddleyard to permit the 'procession of trains' style of working. These are usually club layouts, and many are only ever set up and operated at exhibitions, as they call for a lot of equipment, space and manpower.

Continuous runs can also be adapted to other formats and themes, however. The

Above: Branch line themes don't have to be hackneyed; Neil Burgess's Somerset & Dorset-inspired 00 gauge layout projects a fictional line down the lovely Chew Valley from the Mendip end to Blagdon, in reality served by the GWR coming t'other way. A Johnson 0-4-4T makes a refreshing change from the usual pannier tank. Neil Burgess

traditional flat-sided oval can become an ellipse or even a circle, and I have designed a number of layouts along near-circular lines for typical small shed or spare-bedroom sites. Themes have included simple country stations, junctions, quarries and industries and all manner of urban railways. All-curved layouts like these do pose challenges – often, they will call for custom-built pointwork and careful work in setting out curved platforms and other features. But they are a good way of squeezing a continuous run into a minimal space and can often *look* very attractive – trains rounding curves are

visually more interesting than simply belting along in a straight line, while continuous curvature is a feature of many British railways. But curves can also bring their own problems…

Cursed curves

If the site available to you is a simple straight run down one or two walls – probably the most common scenario these days – then continuous runs are generally out of the question in 00 or larger and probably marginal in N. The critical factor here, of course, is the radius of the return curves involved and the space needed to accommodate them, although RTR models have traditionally been compromised to run around corners that are very far removed from anything approaching scale values. Traditionally, radii as tight as 12in have been used for 00, which contrasts somewhat starkly with the 63in or so that represents the 6-chain minimum normally prescribed for real running lines! Even the usual absolute limiting radius for main line locomotives – 4½ chains – works out at a shade under 4ft. Radii of 4ft and 5ft in 4mm scale have always been regarded as generous rather than minimal!

Fortunately, even scale models can be persuaded to run around too-tight curves and provided things are kept within reasonable bounds we can get away with underscale radii. Reasonable bounds? That mostly comes down to matching the choice of locos and stock to your curves; if you're down at the tight end of things, then 2-10-0s, large Pacifics and 70ft coaches probably aren't the best option. A Mogul or small 4-6-0 with 57ft or even pre-Grouping stock of 50ft or less looks far more at home on tight curves and will run more reliably, with less troublesome offset and overhang. Much depends, of course, on how bothered you are by realism – but for the purposes of this book I'm assuming that a reasonably authentic appearance is part of the design brief.

There is also the matter of horizontal clearances, which can't be ignored. The tighter the curve, the more the ends of vehicles – especially lengthy vehicles like large locomotives or long carriages – will be offset from the centreline of the curve (end throw). Which means, in turn, a greater likelihood of bother; trouble with couplings, buffers, corridor connections and – most critically – clearances with adjacent tracks or fixed features like bridge piers or signals on the outside of curves. Excessive centre overhang (centre throw), meanwhile, will be causing problems on the *inside* of the curve, and it will be necessary to increase the centres (distance apart) of the up and down lines on double track where tight curves are employed. This both looks wrong and takes up more space.

Curve criteria

A *ruling* radius is what you can physically get away with before things start falling over. A *reasonable* one is what looks acceptable. So how does one decide on suitable values for these vital statistics? I could trot out reams of maths and yards of prototype gen on curve criteria, but space is short so I'll simply pass

on some figures I have found workable from my own experience. So, while you *can* persuade a lot of N scale equipment around a 9in radius, I stick with 12in as a ruling figure on hidden sections and aim for 18in or greater on visible trackage. The reason for this apparent liberality has much to do with one of the great virtues of N – that it allows you to model main lines in relatively small spaces. Hence, N gauge layouts often feature large express locomotives and full-length corridor stock – just the sort of equipment that looks worst on over-tight curves, a factor that's as true in N as in any other scale!

Coming up to the most popular scale, 4mm:1ft, we have the extra problem of three track gauges and several sets of standards, that vary in the degree to which they will tolerate underscale curves. So, leaving aside straight RTR trainset trackwork, which is not really relevant to realistic railway modelling, for 'scale' 00 gauge I work to an absolute minimum of 30in radius but aim for 36in or more for anything visible. In EM, I find 36in is the practicable minimum and 42–45in the visual cut-off. P4 takes these figures out another 6in for main line equipment, although smaller locos will live with the same values as EM.

In 7mm:1ft scale, things start to get really expansive. For fine scale standards, main line curves below 6ft in radius are generally held to be undesirable although some biggish locos can be persuaded around 54in or so. The trouble is, they look awful doing it, especially in the context of the realism and degree of detail now normal in 0. Much older coarse-scale equipment was made to squeak around 36in – although that is definitely in the 'trainset' category for appearance! *Desirable* main line curves are in the order of 12ft of more, which perhaps explains why there are precious few indoor main line layouts in 7mm scale!

These figures all assume the need to accommodate main line express passenger locos and coaches. If you're modelling a minor branch line, mineral railway, industrial line or, of course, narrow gauge, then you can bring the minimum radii down a bit – say, 3–6in below main line values – by restricting

Above: Ruling curves on the Launceston Club's 'Lydtor' layout in N gauge; the inner track here is on a 10in radius, the outer a shade over 11in – getting towards the practicable minimum of about 9in. In spite of a modicum of scenic disguise trains look pretty uncomfortable rounding this hairpin, even with the relatively short stock seen in this picture; the corresponding curve at the other end of the layout hides in a tunnel.

the locos and stock used to small, shorter-wheelbase types. However, unless you are modelling a particular prototype that actually used extremely tight curves and equipment designed to operate over them, the acceptable visual limit is not a great deal less. Even some

small loco types (0-4-4Ts come at once to mind), can look diabolical on sharp curves. I'd advise sticking to the main values if at all possible.

Gradients and clearances

Here are a couple of other factors you can't ignore on either practical or visual grounds. On a real railway an incline of 1 in 100 is significant, 1 in 50 is steep and a shade under 1 in 40 the normal limit. Foreigners, mineral, industrial and narrow gauge lines do struggle up steeper hills, but the 1 in 36 of Dainton is the UK main line extreme. As with the curves, we can 'squeeze' these values a bit as many model locomotives will often manage slightly steeper gradients than the real thing – down to about 1 in 30 without gimmicks like rubber traction tyres or magnetically-aided adhesion.

A 1-in-30 grade in any scale looks pretty fearsome and any steeper just looks rather silly, so I regard this as the absolute minimum and 1 in 40 is a lot better. Most gradients on model railways are occasioned by the need for one line to climb up and cross another, and the vertical clearance to achieve this is often a deciding factor in design. In N scale, reckon on around 32mm from rail level to the underside of any bridge, twice that in 4mm scale. Adding on, say, 5–6mm (piece of hardboard or thin ply + underlay) for the thickness of the trackbed supporting the crossing line and you need to achieve a minimum vertical separation of 38mm in N, 70mm or a tad more in 4mm. At 1 in 30, that gives a minimum length of gradient of 44in in N, or a shade under 7ft in 4mm.

Horizontal clearances can also cause bother if adequate allowance isn't made for adjacent tracks, for the clearing point in pointwork and for lateral structural clearances. Even if the trains squeak through the cutting, bridge piers or tunnel, they'll still look wrong if clearances are too tight. The prototype minimum through doorways on sheds was about 12ft with 15ft between girders or piers on single-track bridges. Platforms are another trap for the unwary – be sure that no part of a platform is less than six scale feet wide, and set clearances with your widest outside-cylinder loco and longest bogie coach, especially on curves. Structures, too, need to be set back sufficiently from trackwork, tempting though it is to cram them in close when space is tight. Around six scale feet from the side of the train is a good general guideline. As with so many aspects of railway modelling, studying prototype pictures will help you get these things right

Prototype choice

I'm not going to say much about this as most modellers of my acquaintance have an interest in or allegiance to a particular prototype (not *always* the GWR!) that completely precludes the notion of modelling anything else. This makes life simple, in that it makes one basic choice automatic, but it can also be limiting. For instance, if your *Grande Passion* is the Cambrian or the Highland in Victorian days, pre-World War I French narrow gauge or some obscure 1930s shortline in Nevada, it will inevitably involve you in a lot more research and hands-on modelling than, say, opting for the ubiquity of a GWR 1930s branch line terminus – where you can buy pretty much everything you'll need 'off the peg'. It's important to take this into account when planning and to be realistic about the time, skill levels, facilities and cash that you can call on. Climbing mountains is only fun for mountaineers …

If time and resources are limited and you seek a result sooner rather than later then maybe it would be better to start from the other end of the problem, by finding out what is available and affordable in the way of models that appeal to you or reflect your particular prototype interests, then posing the question: 'What sort of layout can I reasonably build with this lot?' This is not quite the same as the common scenario facing many modellers contemplating a first layout, where a motley and ill-matched collection of equipment has been assembled in haphazard fashion during the 'armchair' phase of the hobby, where a layout is a nebulous dream and models are acquired by chance, on impulse or because they look good on the mantelpiece. Such random collections are rarely the basis for a convincing layout!

However, even if faced with this situation it is usually possible to resolve matters by choosing the most relevant items from the accumulated hoard, then chopping/changing the rest via a Swapmeet, club show bring-and-buy or that great free-for-all of the ether, eBay. It's amazing what you can buy over the Internet and even more amazing what someone else will pay for the things you don't want! But beware – eBaying can become addictive, and you may end up with a larger and even more motley selection than you started out with! As with most aspects of railway modelling, it helps to be clear about what you're trying to achieve and reasonably disciplined as to how you go about things.

As a rule, the availability of models in ready-to-run form is widest in the most popular scale, 4mm, where it is relatively easy to put together a suitable selection for layouts set anywhere between the 'Big Four' pre-Nationalisation era up to the present day. If you're happy to tackle kits, then the 4mm choice today is extremely wide, with a plethora of small cottage-industry makers catering for just about every prototype possibility, even the smaller pre-Grouping companies like the North Staffordshire or the Highland being surprisingly well supported. A similar situation pertains in 7mm and to a lesser extent in 3mm scales, but elsewhere the kit choice is much more limited.

Overseas prototypes

The modeller of US railroads is extremely well-served by the RTR makers, who produce a huge range of very high-quality models, most of them now very sophisticated with inbuilt DCC control and on-board sound. You have to be modelling something pretty obscure if you can't find what you need in one or other of the big ranges, and popular choices like Pennsylvania, Santa Fe, New York Central or Union Pacific are extremely well covered. This is a situation helped by the fact that the majority of US Railroads bought – and still buy – their locomotives and other equipment from large independent makers like Baldwin, Alco, EMD, General Electric, Pullman-Standard, Thrall, Budd, Westinghouse, Union Switch, Signal, and so on. Thus, essentially similar designs could be found in use on most American prototype lines, which makes life easier for everybody. As well as the huge RTR ranges, there are also some very fine kits, particularly for freight cars and structures – but not locos. The British-style loco kit is virtually unknown in the USA.

The same is not true of the European prototype, where there's quite a sharp divide between the German railways and everybody else. Virtually all the main (and quite a few obscure) German designs – which under the Prussian-dominated State system were largely standardised quite early on – are available RTR in both H0 and N and increasingly in Gauge 1, with the most popular types being produced by several makers. But for non-German railways (not forgetting that many European systems, including the French, Dutch, Belgian and Scandinavian railways, bought German equipment or received it as War Reparations), the situation is less rosy. The modeller of French railways, for instance, is surprisingly poorly served – especially in the matter of steam power and older rolling stock. For France and for the smaller networks – the Netherlands, Belgium, Denmark and so on – there is quite a degree of reliance on cast white metal and etched-brass loco and rolling stock kits, often produced by enterprising British makers.

The Swiss prototype is well-served by RTR, much of it of very high quality but far from cheap, but Italy has a limited choice and Spain/Portugal very little; as with Irish railways, the wider-than-standard gauge doesn't help. Eastern Europe is probably better served in H0 RTR – many of the classic Prussian designs were common across the whole of Germany, Poland, Austro-Hungary and the Balkans, if you fancy something a little different by way of the setting, while countries like the Czech Republic and Croatia have native producers making good models of their own equipment. Even Russian and Chinese-prototype RTR is starting to appear now, so the offbeat choice has never been wider!

Scale and standards

Several factors dominate the choice of scale and standards, assuming that prior circumstances haven't already done this for you. Available space, prototype allegiance, availability of suitable models, time, cost and inclination all play their part. Some people are attracted by a certain scale or set of standards in much the same way that they are attracted by a certain prototype. But many of us can see advantages and drawbacks with all the possibilities from Z up to No. 3 gauge. In which case, other factors come into play – most notably the subject/scope criteria already noted. For instance, if the requirement is for high-density operation of a comprehensive main line layout set in a relatively modern era using largely ready-made equipment within a broad overall scenic setting, then N gauge is probably a good choice. But if the attraction is super detailed models of older, offbeat locomotives and vintage rolling stock running on a compact but very fully modelled layout designed for close-up viewing, then 4mm or 7mm finescale – with the availability of high-quality kits and scope for plenty of detail work – is a far better bet. If the challenge of actually *building* the models is the point of the exercise, then an offbeat scale like 3mm or S might have much to offer.

There are some rules of thumb it's worth observing when considering scale choice. Creating a model railway – as a whole, and also in terms of individual items – is subject to the 'eternal triangle' law. To build a model of anything, you need to consider three factors – time, money and satisfaction. These might be regarded as the three sides of a triangle that can have its proportions adjusted; if you're short of time you can compensate by spending more money – paying someone to do the work for you, or buying ready-made models – but at some sacrifice in the loss of the satisfaction that comes from building something yourself. How much that bothers you is a personal judgement, but it's one that is very much part of the planning process – especially in respect of the choice of scale and standard. To build a pre-Grouping layout in P4 will inevitably take much longer – and probably cost more and involve more effort – than modelling a more modern scene in 00 using RTR equipment.

While it is obvious that the choice of scale will dictate what you can realistically attempt in the space available, the standards you opt for will also affect the possibilities. I've already noted the relationship between curve radii and finer wheel and track standards, but choosing to work in fine standards doesn't make much sense unless you're prepared to 'go the extra mile' on all the various aspects of the model. That is, to be uncompromising in matters of fidelity and authenticity and in judging the quality of your own or a manufacturer's work. Just modelling to EM or P4 standards doesn't automatically result in a 'better' layout – I can think of a good few 00 layouts where the builder has taken the trouble to 'get it right' and produced a result that is far superior to many a 'finescale' effort.

Evolving a plan

Having mulled over all the possibilities and taken account of all the pitfalls, it finally behoves the would-be layout builder to distil everything into one great master-stroke – the layout plan. Please note that term; there is a great deal of difference between a full-blown layout plan – which covers all aspects of the proposed model railway, visual and practical – and a simple track plan, which is just what it says – a plan of the track formation. The point being, of course, that there's a great deal more to a realistic model railway than the mere location of the PW. A plan which takes no account of landscape form, structures, viewpoints, visual composition and the host of other, subtle variables that go into a good model railway is not a good starting point. Layouts which have been built only to a track plan are often characterised by unnatural looking scenery – improbable tunnels and bridges, over-steep cutting sides, too-tight clearances and massive retaining walls no real

railway engineer could ever have afforded to contemplate being some of the commoner giveaways. Taking account of all these factors – and the space needed to accommodate them – is a fundamental part of layout planning.

When contemplating a layout design, most people reach for a pencil and paper and start scribbling – but that's not the only option. The modern alternative is to use a specialised layout-designing computer programme, which should produce accurate results and (at least if it's any good) prevent you from designing anything unworkable. However, I'll come clean at this point and confess that I don't like the things; as with all CAD systems, they take away the directness and freedom of hand-drawing, and are often somewhat laborious to use. They also have limitations associated with the way the programme was written in terms of the sort of layout design it was intended to produce.

This is particularly relevant in that in my experience the best ones currently available are American (Third Planit, CadRail). These are highly sophisticated pieces of software and incorporate design tools covering all aspects of the model, scenic and practical. They allow you to perform clever tricks like producing 3-D perspective views from a plan and even to run trains over the prospective layout to check operational aspects. The main drawback is that, being of US origin, they are very much based on the American prototype (very different from British practice) and the type of landscape elements they incorporate are somewhat far removed from the rolling British countryside! They are also costly, complex and demanding in terms of hardware, requiring powerful and sophisticated systems and a high-quality printer to realise their potential.

Coming down from these all-singing design programmes, a lot of the lesser 'layout designing' software is actually simply aimed at track-planning, quite often tied to a specific commercial range of track. These programmes have at best limited capability to plan landscaping or other visual elements, and certainly aren't capable of producing a truly complete layout plan. Often, all they will

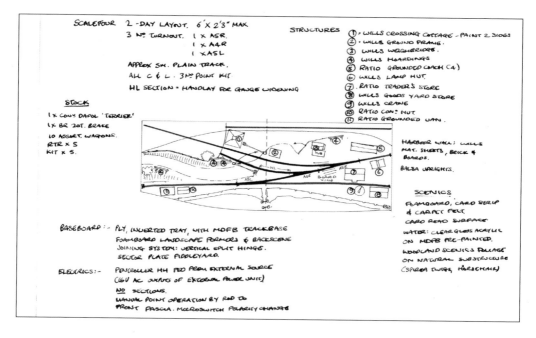

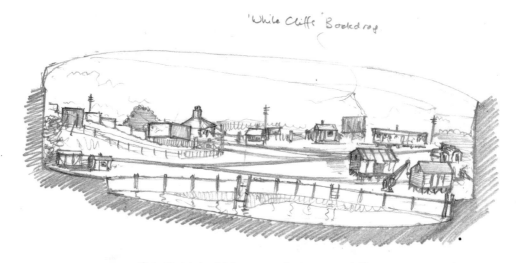

Above and below: The layout design process: a set of design notes, track plan and 3-D pencil sketch for a cameo layout – 'Oldhaven Harbour', inspired by the LBSCR's Newhaven Harbour branch. This was the original scheme for the 1993 'Layout in a Weekend' project at 'Scaleforum', when a team of modellers set out to build a minimum-space cameo during the two days of the show.

 The project was based around RTR equipment that could readily be converted to fine scale – in particular the Dapol (now Hornby) ex-LBSCR 'Terrier' 0-6-0T, which determined the setting. Unfortunately, this loco became unavailable at the critical time and the Dapol ex-L&Y 'Pug' 0-4-0ST was selected as a substitute. A new layout was hurriedly contrived to suit this northern prototype, the result being 'Hepton Wharf'.

tell you is how much track you can physically cram into a given space. I have found them to be of very limited use.

However you produce a layout drawing, it's absolutely essential that this is accurately to scale, otherwise it will be meaningless and probably misleading, You have to take great care to make the lines you put on the paper correspond to the actuality of the model, with the site shape and dimensions accurately portrayed and all the necessary criteria as to curves, clearances, structure placement and so on duly taken account of. A rough freehand scribble on the back of an envelope is not really much use in this context! I've found it helpful always to draw layout designs to the same scale – an inch to the foot, in my case – as by sticking to this one soon becomes familiar with the correct form of things like turnouts, clearances, curve radii and so on.

Above: Mocking up a layout using flexible track, held with Blu-Tack and pins, with landscape and structures roughed up in carton card using a hot glue gun and tape. Trees are crumpled paper on sticks. Once the 3-D design is settled, it can be either marked out at full size or 'surveyed' for a drawing. Snapshots like this are also useful.

Mocking-up a layout design

If relying on scale drawing is not your thing, then in my book the best alternative is the full-size mock-up. I still use this method extensively to check whole plans or aspects of plans at full size, the surest test of whether or not something is workable! The nub of this approach is pretty self-explanatory, and should be evident from the photo above. Note the extensive use of flexible track to establish the formation, overlapping the plain track to give turnouts; I hold it all in place with a mix of pins, weights and the ever-useful Blu-Tack. You can construct a full-size mock up on its final site, or anywhere else that's convenient (on the kitchen table, out in the garden, on the floor, etc.) and big enough to take a full-size plan or site template of the proposed layout. The template can either be of paper (heavy duty wall lining paper is good for this, cheap and easily available) or can be made of the actual baseboard surfacing material, when it can go on to form part of the layout structure.

Buildings, engineering or landscape features, platforms and so on can be mocked-up with scrap card and brown paper, held together with ordinary adhesive tape. The great advantage of the full-size mock-up approach to layout design is that you're working in 3-D – great for visual design – and that it's easy to carry out definitive checks on such vital practicalities as clearances, train lengths, curve radii and so on. If your prize loco won't go around the tightest curve on the mock-up, it won't on the finished layout! I take plenty of photos of the mock-up and use the resulting pictures as guides when building the layout. Using this approach, you don't actually *need* to draw a scale plan at all.

Textbook design

Of necessity, this is only a superficial skit around the whole complex and (to me, anyway!) fascinating topic of layout design. There are many other ideas and techniques that can be employed, and a great deal of 'philosophy' to consider in terms of what you want the layout to do both visually and operationally. There are a good number of books covering the topic in greater detail; if you're seriously intent on building a layout, spending a bit of time and money on this aspect of the whole railway modelling business will be a wise investment.

If, on the other hand, the whole layout design business baffles or bores you, there are plenty of books of 'ready-to-go' layout designs available to suit all manner of sites from the miniscule to the magnificent, while layout suggestions and plans of all sorts form regular fare in the pages of model railway magazines. There are also professional layout designers who will produce a workable and detailed plan to your requirements. So it is possible to shorten, if not skip, the design process and get straight on with construction, starting with preparing the site and building the baseboards – which is where we go next.

Opposite: A completed colour layout plan for a compact home layout in 00, showing not only the track formation, but also all structures, landscape features, view blocks, backdrop positions, fiddleyard details, access points and site features like doors and windows. This 'spare bedroom' plan was required to preserve access to the area by the window – typical of domestic constraints that often impact on layout designs.

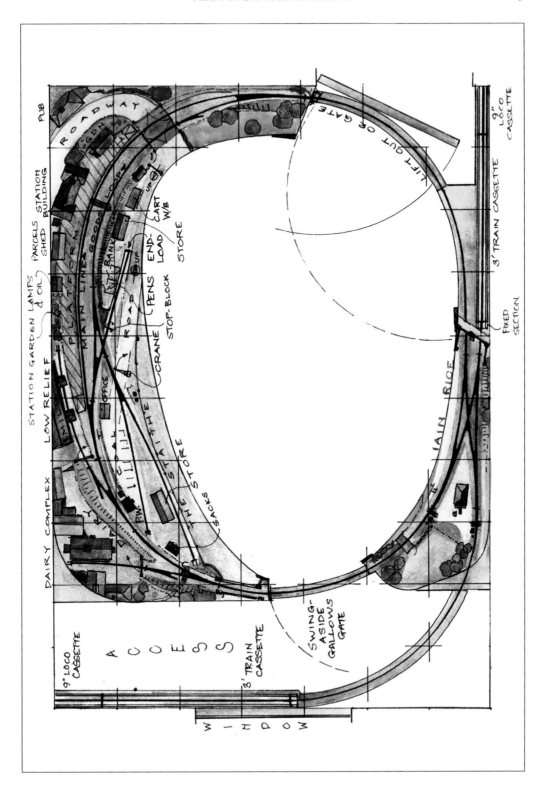

Chapter 3

PRELIMINARIES: TOOLS, SITE PREPARATION AND BASEBOARDS

It's a sad but usual fact of life that before you can get on to the pastries and fancy cakes, you have to chomp your way through the bread and butter. Which, in railway modelling terms, comes down to the need to prepare the site, install power supplies and lighting, build baseboards and generally undertake a range of tasks more associated with normal domestic DIY than 'fun'.

Below: Not a very exciting picture – but then, erecting baseboards isn't generally a very exciting part of the layout-building process. Here is a very simple, lightweight beam-and-bearer 'ladder frame' under construction from good-quality (carefully pick the best bits from your local DIY emporium) 19mm x 38mm softwood, destined to hold up a bit more 4mm scale Suffolk – the extension to 'Cade's Green'.

It is also a fact that you won't get far in any of the many disciplines associated with model railways without the appropriate equipment – which means that some of the hard-won budget that pipe-dreams tend to turn into gleaming models may actually need to be diverted into tools, timber, wiring and paint. Although, that said, most households can assemble at least a basic selection of general carpentry and wiring tools, while should anything be lacking, there's a good chance that it can 'swung' on the general domestic budget rather than making a dent in the modelling piggybank.

General equipment

Almost all the tools needed to undertake the preparatory stages of building a model railway are those familiar from the home improvement field and consequently are readily available from the nearest DIY store. These days, even quite sophisticated power tools are astoundingly cheap from such outlets. In fact, I find that economically priced tools of all sorts are now of a great deal better quality than was the case a few years ago – so there's little point in melting down your credit card in a quest for 'premium' brands.

The first item on my list of general layout-building tools is some sort of fold-up portable workbench of the 'Workmate' variety. A large percentage of DIY accidents involving saws, planes and chisels occur because the work piece is not held properly and slips. Even the most basic versions of these useful contraptions

Above: Still one of the most practical and useful contraptions around, the ubiquitous Workmate is a multi-function friend to layout-builders.

Above: An industrial 'can' vacuum cleaner like this is as great an asset in the cause of domestic harmony as it is in keeping the crud away from your models.

will support, grip and locate wood while you're abusing it with edge tools – as well as providing a flat surface for assembly work, support for things being nailed, glued or screwed together, and somewhere to park your cup of tea. You can also use the sturdier specimens of the breed as a step-up or raised work platform when you need to reach the heights.

Power tools are an absolute boon to the railway modeller, making a lot of the preliminary work quicker and easier and opening up new ways of doing things. A lot of modern tools are cordless, which can be very useful – but are also a curse when the battery gives out while you're in full flow and demands a three-hour recharge. Cordless power can also be expensive and doesn't suit every tool – which means you need somewhere to plug in your mains-power equipment, safely. So I'd put a heavy-duty extension lead of reasonable length (at least 5 metres) with a four-socket termination block and RCD (residual current device) protection on my list. While in the electrical department of the DIY emporium take a look at the portable halogen work lights – preferably on a stand. These are often amazingly cheap and can be a boon at all stages

of the modelling process, from site preparation to photographing the final result. It's a great truism that you won't do good work of *any* sort if you can't see what you're doing.

The next general item is a vacuum cleaner with a hose. An old domestic cylinder cleaner will serve, but if you can swing it, an industrial-style can cleaner like a 'Henry' or a 'Vax' is the thing to have. Mine came from a car boot sale and cost me a tenner; I have it rigged up the whole time I'm working and I find that stopping every few minutes for a spot of 'aspiration' is an effort well repaid in a better job and a cleaner environment for the layout – something which I can't recommend too strongly. Also, there's no doubt that working 'clean' can also avoid conflict with the domestic side of life.

Hand tools

I'll confess that I'm a dyed-in-the-wool tool buff – which means I just love the things, especially of the traditional carpentry variety. A lot of my own gear is thus old and beautiful and cherished, quite a bit of it inherited from my cabinet-maker grandfather. So it pains me to admit that the best, sharpest and truest-cutting handsaw I possess has a plastic handle, a 'hardpoint' blade and cost less than £10 brand new. One such – with a fairly fine cut – is all you'll need in that direction.

I mark out with a traditional carpenter's square and a steel straight-edge, but you can now buy combination squares with a spirit level thrown in that also give you a 45º angle for barely the price of a pint. A plastic builder's spirit level 48in long gives you a useful straight edge, a means of setting accurate verticals as well as horizontals and – if you get a calibrated one – a 4ft ruler. To go with this, a conventional retracting tape measure is needed, but unless you're building something very ambitious, a compact 3m/10ft version is far more wieldy than a big building-site job.

While the advent of the power drill-driver has taken a lot of the tedium out of screw-driving, you can't use them in all situations and conventional hand screwdrivers are still sometimes needed. For layout work of all kinds I find that the modern coarse-thread crosshead 'chipboard screw' is quick and convenient. But beware! Not all crosshead

Below: Power tools to make life quicker and easier. Here are two of the most useful, the cordless drill-driver and the hot glue gun; neither was expensive, being DIY chain 'own brands'. Also shown is a plug-in RCD circuit breaker – always a worthwhile safety measure when using mains-powered tools.

screws are the same – and nothing is worse than trying to work with a screwdriver that doesn't properly fit the screw-head! The right tool is essential – not just in terms of size but with the correct profile tip to match the screw, which comes down to distinguishing what screw system you're using.

Phillips screws have a cross made of two taper-sided V-profile slots at right angles, while in a Pozi-Drive screw the slots forming the cross are much deeper and have near-vertical sides. Such screws are further identified by an 'X' stamped on the screw head 45º out-of-phase with the slots. You will probably 'get away' with using a Phillips driver on a Pozi screw, but a Pozi-driver won't enter the slots on a Phillips screw properly and will simply chew up the screw head. Best is to stick with one type of screw and the appropriate driver. I find Pozi-Drive both easier to use and more widely available.

Nails and pins also have their place in layout-building, so a hammer or two will come in handy. An ordinary claw hammer does most general jobs, but a lighter pin-hammer is also a good idea for more delicate work such as panel-pinning together plywood structures. A useful alternative to pins in many applications – especially building ply baseboards – are construction staples, and a heavy-duty staple gun is a very useful addition to the armoury.

Most model railway carpentry is pretty rough work, so there's not much call for fine edge tools such as planes, chisels and shaves. To simply remove excess wood (or plastic, plaster, filler and half a hundred other things) a wood-rasp of the Surform variety will serve, with a few sheets of coarse glasspaper for such finishing work as might be needed.

Power tools

The power jigsaw and the cordless drill/driver are the two greatest boons to the layout-builder – they not only speed up a lot of routine work, but – especially in the case of the jigsaw – open up a lot of creative possibilities for baseboard construction. Imagine trying to cut scenery profiles, curved trackbed sections or complex bracing and brackets without one!

For model work, you don't need a fancy or expensive jigsaw as you won't be taxing it much, the materials we use being at the 'light' end of the range for which they're usually designed. More important is to find a compact machine, as in the heat of battle its ability to trim errant bits of carpentry in situ and to painlessly pierce vital but forgotten holes is priceless – and the smaller the machine, the tighter the confines within which you can use it. Forget cordless jigsaws – the bulk of a battery is far more of an impediment than a trailing flex, and they're usually gutless.

The cordless drill-driver, on the other hand, is a very versatile tool. As its name suggests, it can perform two basic roles, but to my mind it's the screwdriving function that really makes life a bowl of cherries. If you're not going to waste a lot of effort swapping drill-bits for driver heads and vice-versa, it's best to have separate machines for drilling and driving. A really cheap and basic cordless drill will suffice for the former task, but a good-quality driver with fine speed control, a range of torque settings (use the lowest you can to avoid the likelihood of chewing up screw heads) and decent battery power (12V or 18V) is worth going for.

For heavy drilling – such as into masonry walls for fixing layout supports – then the old-fashioned mains-powered hammer drill is the best bet. Cordless power isn't up to the job unless you've lashed out on a really expensive piece of professional kit, but even the humblest of mains drills will do all we want. The only other job for which power is a real benefit over elbow-grease is sanding, and an orbital sander is a very useful thing to have both for site preparation work and baseboard carpentry.

The modeller's toolkit

Having disposed of the general-purpose kit needed to get us up to the point where we can actually start modelling, what more specialised tools do we then need for the finer work? This is a question that comes into the 'string, but how long?' category. It is one of the great truisms of railway modelling that many of the best models have been built with an absolute minimum of tools and facilities,

Above: **The other true boon power tool for layout builders is undoubtedly the jigsaw. This is a superior specimen by Bosch, with very fine control, variable speed and really accurate blade location – a joy to use.**

while some folk have every imaginable tool, gadget, machine and modelling aid, all housed in an expansive workshop – but never build anything. There is a happy mean, of course, but the question to be posed in the context of a book like this is: 'What tools do you *really* need to go railway modelling?'

The answer is probably 'less than you might think.' After more than forty years at the modelling game, I have a pretty comprehensive collection of tools and gizmos, but when I recently took the trouble to actually note what I used in typical workshop sessions, I found that a relatively few straightforward tools sufficed for well over 90% of what I was doing, whether working on locomotives, rolling stock, track, signals or structures. These frequent-use tools form the basis of this particular tool-list, which I have called the basic list; other, more specific items are discussed in the sections covering the more specialised disciplines of the hobby.

Before I come on to look at individual items of equipment, I must add a few words on modelling tools in general. First and foremost the rule is that it is far better (and cheaper!) to buy a good tool once rather than a shoddy one several times over. Paying a bit more for your workshop basics will not only buy you durability and ease of use, it'll buy you more capability as well. Rule number two is to look after your tools; don't heave them in a heap in a scruffy box, all stained and dirty, or leave them in the damp to go rusty. Rule three follows on from rule two, and warns against misusing tools: pick the right tool for the job, and don't use a precision tool for a purpose for which it was not intended! (This is the Voice of Experience speaking; not so many years ago I wrecked a beautiful and expensive pair of Lundströhm precision needle-nose pliers simply by using them to try and grip an axle tightly. The jaws sheared and the pliers were ruined, all because I'd grabbed the nearest pair off the bench rather than stopping for a moment to open the tool-box and seek out some short-nose ones *intended* for gripping. A lesson hard-learned...)

The basic tool list

All modelling tasks fall into one of six categories, viz: measuring and marking out; cutting and drilling; shaping; gripping and forming; assembly (including soldering), and finishing. So my list is likewise divided into six sections.

Below: Cutting edges. This modest selection will do just about any general cutting job about the layout. The only thing remotely specialised here is the Olfa plastic cutter, but almost all craft shops stock Olfa products and if it's not a stock line they will be able to order one without problem.

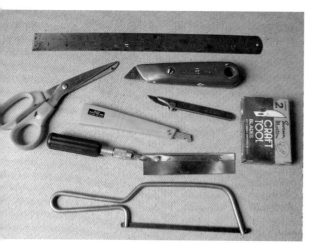

Measuring and marking are tasks which crop up at every stage of railway modelling, from surveying the site to positioning the grab-handles on your prize coach. For model work then, a really good 12in/305mm engineer's steel rule is the thing to have. Clear markings are the key requirement, but it is an unfortunate fact of life that steel rules are very prone to surface corrosion that can obscure the sharpest of engraving, especially likely to happen when they get mixed up with soldering operations and flux. Keep them out of the way during these jobs, or spring the extra from the piggy bank for a rustless chrome-steel rule like the Rabone Chesterman 64R. While you're buying rulers, a 6in/150mm version is also worth having for the more fiddly measuring tasks.

The other key tool in this department is a good engineer's square, the most useful size for general work being about three inches long. To go with this piece of precision kit (remarks re: soldering operations as for steel rules) it is also useful to have a couple of plastic geometry set drawing squares, one with 45° angles and one of 60/30°. To mark on metal or plastic, a scriber is useful and only costs a pound or two; a sharp pencil or a fine ballpoint pen will suffice for wood, plastic and card.

Cutting tools for general modelling work need to be capable of handling the range of materials we're commonly using: card and paper, modelling woods such as balsa or spruce, plastic sheet and sections, and metal in thin sheet, wire and solid-drawn (rail) forms. To take these tasks in order, we're looking at knives, saws, shears and snips.

A good modelling knife and a heavier utility knife are the two key edge-cutting tools. My firm favourites are the brass-handled Swann Morton craft knife and the basic non-retractable Stanley No. 199, both of which have been staple modelling tools since the Ark tied up. The Swann Morton is neat, compact, stiff (essential for all cutting tools where any sort of accuracy is required) and has the ideal 'heft' in the hand; it has three blade profiles available – straight (No. 1), curved (No. 2) and hooked (No. 3). I use the No. 2 blade for almost every delicate cutting task. The Stanley is a design classic, a tool so essentially 'right' that it has never been improved upon but frequently copied. Again, straight, curved and hooked blades may be had; the first is the most useful, and can be set 'in' for a short but very strong blade capable of applying real cutting force, or 'out' for a longer cutting edge for more delicate usage.

To go with these two knives I'd suggest a second steel rule, a cheap-and-cheerful one being quite adequate. Cutting against a fine measuring rule runs the risk of damaging the calibrations and marring the marking edge should a knife slip. The other essential is a self-healing cutting mat, which not only supports and locates the work while you're attacking it, but is kind to your knife-blades and also acts as a great safety-net that'll 'catch' a skidding knife blade – hopefully before it does any damage to you or the work piece. I always opt for a good-size mat, so as to maximise this safety catchment.

A good pair of small craft scissors are the other basic cutting tool. The best ones are those made by Fiskars, which are sharp, very sturdy and will hold their edge and alignment even if horribly abused. They are also rustless chrome steel and have very well-designed handles, but they're not cheap – and many of the less-costly but nameless 'clones' around these days will do the job adequately; err on the sturdy side.

The above trio will cope with paper, card, modelling woods and even – in the case of the scissors – thin sheet metal. However, there's another cutting tool specifically intended for sheet plastics that, while not absolutely essential, is highly desirable if you're going to be doing much with these materials – especially moulded sheet like the Wills Scenic Series. This is the Olfa Plastic Cutter, a 'scrawking' tool designed to take a v-grooved cut from the face of the plastic, which can then be cleanly snapped along the resulting score-line. The same tool is also the very business for scribing planks as it leaves no raised burrs to be smoothed away.

The next class of cutting is sawing, which is usually called for only on chunkier plastic sections, some woods and metal that's too thick to snip. In general modelling, two saws will suffice: a Junior hacksaw and a modeller's stiff-back razor saw. Both are inexpensive and widely available.

Next comes the business of making holes in things. Bigger holes – in model-making terms, anything over an eighth of an inch or so – are the province of the normal domestic electric drill or handbrace; below this, the finer drill diameters call for a pin-vice or two (they

Below: If yer knows a better 'ole… it was probably made like this. Pin vices come in sizes to suit drills from about 1/8th-inch down to the very smallest sizes (0.2mm or so – breathe hard and you'll break it). Pin vices, confusingly, look like conventional drill chucks, while pin chucks look like a miniature vice with a v-groove in one face to take the drill… The little Archimedean drill seen here is ideal for making small holes quickly without too much risk of breaking the drills.

The taper brooch at the bottom of the picture also fits into a pin vice and enables you to open up holes to any required diameter. Twist drills themselves come in differing qualities with price tags to match. The basic economy eight-piece HSS (high speed steel) set at the right is only about a quarter the cost of the 16-piece Titanium-coated set.

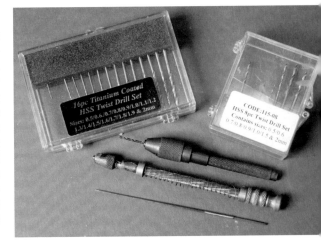

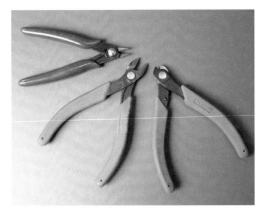

come in a variety of sizes), with perhaps a finger-twiddled 'Archimedean' drill to speed things up. To go with these, a basic set of metric drills in the miniature sizes – generally 0.5 – 2mm – and a taper brooch will allow you to make a hole of any required size.

The last class of cutting tools are snips and shears, which we've already touched on in the matter of scissors. In fact, unless you're going to get involved in a lot of metalwork – in which case metal shears or tin snips might be worthwhile – a pair of craft scissors will do all the sheet-shearing we need. Snipping is a different matter, as here the tool required depends very much on the material you're cutting. The most useful general-purpose snip is a pair of flush-cutting nippers such as those made by Xuron. These are fine for plastic strip and rod, soft wires and strips in metals like

iron, aluminium, copper, brass, phosphor-bronze or nickel silver, plus fine electrical flex. However, they won't look at hard steel wires such as piano wire; if you're going to mix it with this (and it has a good number of uses on the layout) then you need a hardened-jaw snip; Xuron can oblige again. For cutting rail you need to move up a size to Xuron's 'track cutter', which is specifically designed for chopping through rail up to Code 125, while giving a 'square' end to the cut. Even if your trackwork aspirations go no further than trimming Peco Streamline, you need one of these.

Shaping in most model-making applications comes down to filing, so a suitable selection of files must figure in the basic tool list. First, though, a few words on file descriptions, which can be confusing. Files are classified by three criteria: shape, size and 'cut'. File shape refers in the first instance to the cross-section – round, square, rectangular, triangular, half-round and flat (the same as rectangular but thinner!) being the common ones. A file will also be described as parallel or tapered, which is the shape in plan. The size normally refers to the nominal length if described numerically – a 'six inch' file being just that. But there are also 'classes' of file size: Mill files are huge, the real heavyweights, and thus of no concern to modellers. Engineer's files come in large (12in and over) medium (6–12in) and small (6in or less), while jeweller's files (sometimes called needle files) are around 6in or less in length but of miniature cross section – usually only 4–6mm wide. The 'cut' is an indication of the coarseness of a file, numbered from 'first' cut (fierce!) up to sixth cut (virtually smooth). A 'bastard cut' file is one where there are two sets of cutting edges forming a grid; a normal cut has one set of edges set at an angle across the file.

Most modelling tasks can be accomplished with a modest selection of files: an ordinary flat engineer's file about 12in long for the heavy stuff, a nice 6in flat or 8in half-round second-cut file for more delicate smoothing, and a set of needle files containing the standard selection of square, round, triangular, flat, half-round and knife-edge. Such file-sets – made in China and typically sold in a red plastic wallet – are very cheaply available and though a bit coarse (first cut) are fine for basic work. A couple of second-cut jeweller's files for fine finishing work are desirable but not essential; half-round and knife-edge are the shapes to go for. Genuine Swiss files (Vallorbe or Gerber) are nice to have but come at wallet-withering prices and are easily ruined; mid-range files at from £2–£3 apiece are all you really need.

Gripping and Forming – vices and pliers. A good vice is an absolutely key piece of equipment for the railway modeller, the one thing on which you should never compromise. That's not to say you have to take out a second mortgage and buy something exotic

Above: The vice squad? Here, we have two extremes of the model-making vice spectrum. On the right, weighing in at less than a fiver, we have a nameless economy model (Polish, in this case) that nevertheless satisfies the basic requirements. It has 60mm long flat-faced jaws that are amazingly true and square and boasts a nice smooth screw action. Perfectly adequate and very sturdy.

The purpose-designed effort to the left cost five times as much and while it is certainly bigger and more refined – boasting a tilt-and-pan head, 100mm long grooved jaws that close nicely true, removable soft jaw cheeks (seen in place here), and a nicely engineered clamp mounting system – at the basic level it's little more competent. You pays yer money…

from a Hatton Garden toolsmith – it's more about making a careful choice and ensuring that the vice you buy is a good specimen of its type. Certainly, an expensive vice should be straight of jaw and sure of grip – but cheap ones can often be surprisingly good in these fundamentals. Just go through the stock on offer and examine each individual specimen carefully. You're looking for jaws that are true and parallel in all dimensions, and which close accurately over their whole faces – avoid like the plague anything where the jaws have even the tiniest of gaps at one end when t'other end is up tight.

A good way of sorting the wheat from the chaff is to take a piece of thin copy paper or hard tissue paper with you when you go

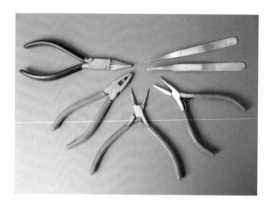

Above: Gripping stuff. Very much a case of 'the right tool for the job in hand'. So, for a firm hand – when force is to be applied – we call on the sturdier members of the pliers family, such as the stout flat-nose affairs at top left, or the square-ended 'combination pliers' below them. Both of these have serrated jaws to prevent slippage.

For more delicate gripping and forming work, the fine-nosed instrument pliers are the required tool; these two – round-nosed at left, smooth-jaw snipe-nose on the right – meet almost every modelling need. For delicate gripping and placing, jeweller's tweezers are the best option – the square-ended 2A below and the pointed medium-fine tip No. 3 above.

vice-buying. Clamp the edge of the paper fully in the jaws of the vice and tear the rest of the sheet off; if you get a nice, crisp tear and a neat outline of the vice-jaw in the torn-off paper, it's a good 'un. A ragged edge or random tearing is the sign of a vice to avoid. While you're at it, test the screw action of the vice spindle for smoothness and try waggling the sliding jaw on the fixed one. Uneven or sticky spindle rotation and sloppy-fitting jaws are also to be avoided. Applying these tests can often reveal surprising results – many a cheap vice of nameless Eastern origin out-performing more expensive 'branded' items. The excellent little vice on my portable bench came from India and cost a whole £1.99 off a market trader's barrow!

The same tissue-paper test holds good for pliers, too – especially the key type at the heart of the modeller's tool-kit, the smooth-jaw 'snipe' or taper-nose precision pliers. This is the one that does all your fine bending and tricky gripping, and if those jaws don't close properly and grip evenly over their whole meeting faces, they're worse than useless. So spend your serious money on your snipes and only use them for this type of delicate work – cheap serrated-jaw combination pliers will do for the rough-and-tumble. A pair of round-nose pliers are also very useful for some bending tasks (handrails come at once to mind) and are the second most useful type. The last basic modelling pliers is the square-ended type with flat, smooth jaws. Otherwise, a small pair of ordinary square-jaw serrated combination pliers are the only other essential, for heavier bending and serious gripping.

Tweezers are the other gripping/handling tool we need, for those tiddly details that add so much to the appearance of our models. Normal chemist's-shop first-aid or eyebrow tweezers are almost useless for model work; what we want are jeweller's stainless-steel forceps in fine (but not too fine – avoid the feeble needle-tipped types coded 'AA') versions. The simple pointed No. 3 and blunt square-ended 2A will do the job. These are delicate tools for delicate tasks and are easily damaged, so protect those vulnerable points by pushing the closed nose of the tweezers into a wine cork before lobbing them into the toolbox. For keeping a hold of anything truly tiny or fiddling their way into awkward places, they're unbeatable, but never use jeweller's tweezers to apply any force – they simply aren't made for it!

Assembly tools: screwdrivers and soldering irons – The larger screwdrivers having been addressed in the general tools list, here, we are only talking miniature items The biggest of these is a small spade-ended electrical screwdriver, essential for those so-useful 'chocolate block' electrical connectors. Also useful is a similarly-sized crosshead screwdriver, for plug and other screws having small Phillips heads. For the really small screws, a selection of jeweller's screwdrivers will suffice – these days, you'll need both flat and

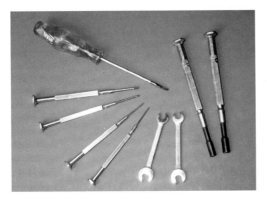

Above: Driving you screwy: there's no doubt that at the smaller sizes met in model making, it pays to have the right screwdriver for the job. A fine electrical 'driver with a good-quality hardened tip is worth the extra over a cheap specimen. A basic set of jeweller's screwdrivers will match miniature screws such as the grub screws in gears; a similar selection with Phillips crossheads is useful for working on RTR models, many of which are held together with small, self-tapping screws. Miniature spanners can be had in BA (left) and metric (right) sizes, but the useful-looking socket-end nut-drivers only seem to come in the metric variant; shame.

crosshead patterns. As with the needle files, you can buy amazingly cheap sets of jeweller's screwdrivers made in the Far East, but they are entirely adequate for our purposes.

You can also buy from the same sources, sets of miniature socket-head drivers. These are usually of metric dimensions, and hence are fine for most of the nuts found on modern RTR locos. However, they won't fit the BA nuts found in loco kits or sold for general use in the British hobby. You can buy BA sockets (but not very easily!), but the pair of square-end flat-nose pliers included in the 'gripping' section above will usually take care of most nut-twiddling needs.

Soldering is, of course, the Black Art of railway modelling – although it's not half as black as some would have you believe! In terms of basic railway modelling, it is the making of good, sound, electrical connections we're concerned with. The technique – such as it is – is described

Above: Tools of the 'black art'. This modest set-up will cover the basics and probably 95% of the clever stuff as well. The key tool is a small instrument iron – this is an Antex 'CS' 18-W version, which is sufficient for most wiring and general tracklaying/kit assembly/detailing work. If more 'oomph' is needed there's a 25W version, the 'XS'. Other makes are available, but Antex have been my choice for the last 25-odd years. This one has a two-pin plug to suit my portable workbench, which uses French electrics.

The stand shown here has a nice heavy cast-iron base (plastic ones are too light), a generous tray for a cleaning sponge and a double coil heatsink/shield. Unfortunately it is anonymous, so it's a case of looking out for something similar. The cleaning pad, incidentally, is just a piece of a domestic 'Spontex' cleaning wipe, kept nice and wet. Cheap and readily available.

The solder is 145°C uncored lead-based wire, which is no longer readily available, but Homebase sells a nice, presumably lead-free, cored solder that makes a very good substitute. The flux here is Fry's 'Powerflow' paste, widely available and a good general-purpose brew. Cleaning up afterwards with a two parts meths/one part water mix applied with a stiff hogshair brush removes any surplus flux and leaves the joints sparkling.

in Chapter 5, but what of the equipment? Well, forget all those fancy electronic temperature-controlled 'soldering stations' – our needs are far simpler. You can also forget instant soldering guns, cordless irons and gas-powered torches;

a small, basic instrument soldering iron costing only a few pounds will do all that is required. I prefer the type with the element actually inside the bit – far more efficient and compact, and easier to use in consequence. The Antex 'XS' 25-watt iron has long been my preferred weapon, being light and wieldy and having a plated bit with an iron tip that is long-lasting and easy to keep clean.

Soldering irons should always be used with a suitable stand – one that will keep the iron safe both from overheating and from painful encounters of the 'Ouch!' variety when you're not using it. You also want a stand with a holder for a damp sponge; keeping the bit clean and shiny (a wipe before and after each use) is a large part of successful soldering. For electrical work, you need a suitable rosin paste flux and some nice, free-flowing cored solder. Your local electronics or DIY store should be able to provide these. The electronics store should also be able to sell you a little round tin of 'tip tinner and cleaner', which will make the business of 'tinning' the bit – getting a nice, clean shiny coating of molten solder over the working faces – a lot easier.

The other main assembly process used in modelling is, of course, gluing. This doesn't call for tools as such, but the modeller's toolkit needs to include a surprising variety of adhesives. The ones you can't be without are five in number: First, a high-strength resin woodworking adhesive for carpentry and for model work in wood and card – for which purposes Evo-Stik Resin W is ideal. Secondly, a low-strength PVA for track ballasting and general scenic work – the sort of white craft glue or kids' glue sold in your local art shop suffices. Thirdly, a general-purpose contact adhesive in tube form – Bostik 1 Clear or UHU are the usual choices. Fourthly, an instant cyano-acrylate 'super glue' such as Loctite 3. Last, plastic cement or – preferably – a liquid plastic solvent, for joining polystyrene and other modelling plastics. Well-known solvent brands include Liquid Poly, Plastic Weld, Mek-Pak and Plastic Magic. Store these carefully and use with caution (yup, read the label…) as they are not particularly nice chemicals.

Finishing in a basic modelling context is basically pre-paint preparation and painting. Again, it's one of those subjects that – to do it justice – calls for a dedicated book, so consider these notes but a skit. However, I can make one useful statement, which is that cleaning and preparation are nine tenths of the finishing game. We need to be able to remove *everything* which will impair the final paint job – excess solder or glue, tool-marks and dirt of all kinds, most especially flux and finger-grease. Some of these tasks can be accomplished with tools already mentioned – files or a craft knife can trim unwanted solder or glue, while tool-marks can also be banished by careful use of a fine file.

However, to really smooth a surface, finer abrasives are needed. Wet-and-dry paper can be bought in grades right down to 1400 grit, but for general modelling work 240, 320 and 400 grit will do most things. Never be afraid to use these papers 'wet', especially on plastics – a drop of washing-up liquid in the water will also help get a really smooth finish. Cut the wet-and-dry into small pieces with scissors (which will also help sharpen the scissors) and make yourself some 'rubbing sticks' and pads by sticking the abrasive to small pieces of wood. The other useful finishing/polishing tool is a glassfibre burnisher. These come either as a 'stick' or in 'propelling pencil' form; I find the former more useful and less prone to produce the little 'whiskers' of glassfibre that, given half a chance, will stick painfully into your fingertips.

Don't confuse smoothing and burnishing with cleaning – these are different processes. Even the shiniest of models can be effectively filthy when it comes to applying paint! Fortunately, no great sophistication is required to remedy this state of affairs; an old toothbrush, a nice stiff hogs-hair paintbrush, a bottle of normal domestic scouring cream, plenty of warm water and some kitchen towel will take care of this necessary task. A hairdryer is also useful for ensuring the model is free of any trapped water. You can't, of course, bathe electric motors and mechanisms generally under the kitchen tap, so here, the judicious use of methylated spirit and the hogshair brush will get rid of encrusted dirt, flux, oil and grease – the main enemies of paint.

The last element in the finishing process is, of course, suitable paint and something with which to apply it. Paint can either be brushed or sprayed, but not all types of paint can be applied by both methods. Generally speaking, enamels (Humbrol, Precision Paints,) are the most universal type of paint, being thick and smooth enough to brush but readily thinned for spraying. Acrylics are a bit more variable – some, like Poly S or Railmatch, are intended for spray work (but will brush as well); others, like Humbrol Acrylic, are essentially brushing paints. Cellulose paints, on the other hand, are really only suited to spray application, as are synthetics like Floquil.

When it comes to spraying, some paints (Railmatch, Precision, Just Like the Real Thing) are available in aerosols, which are often surprisingly effective; or they can be applied through an airbrush of some sort. The latter are very much a topic in their own right and somewhat beyond the 'basic' in terms of modelling equipment – so they don't figure here. Which brings us to brush painting. Here, the quality of the brush is all. Fortunately, the arrival of synthetic bristle materials has resulted in modestly-priced ranges such as Daler's Daylon or Windsor & Newton's Cotman, paintbrushes that are modestly priced but ideal for our purposes. No longer is it necessary to grit the teeth and pay for best-quality artist's watercolour sables. I use both these ranges and find a selection of four brushes does all I want: a quarter-inch flat brush for large surfaces; normal round fine-point brushes in sizes 3 and 1 for general painting and a '00' for fine detail. Look after them – clean them in hot soapy water (washing up liquid) rather than solvents where you can, and always store them 'head in the air' with the bristles twiddled to a fine point and protected by the sleeves that come with the brushes. If you're using enamel paints, use pure artist's turpentine rather than turps substitute (white spirit) for thinning and initial brush cleaning.

The workbench

It's another truism of railway modelling that the average modeller, given a billiard-table to work on, ends up doing everything in a space six inches square in one corner. This suggests that, nice though it is to have an extensive workshop, you don't actually *need* that much space. Being a peripatetic sort of individual, quite a lot of my own modelling is done on a portable workbench that also functions as a toolbox, but even at home my permanent modelling bench is only 48 x 18in. It is also home to two vices and a miniature drill press, so the six-inches-square story isn't far from reality.

I could write a book on the modeller's

Below: Mention has been made of the portable workbench which accompanies me on my travels – or at least those of them which don't involve aeroplanes. Well, here it is, in original form; it's had a refit since the picture was taken. It is surprising just how much can be accomplished in this small space and with the limited selection of tools and materials seen here.

Above: The workbench – well, my workbench. In fact, my new workbench, in the newly adapted attic chez Rice which, as can all-too-readily be seen here, is far from finished at this point. The first working essential is good light, largely assured by the north-facing roof light, augmented by an anglepoise-type fitting with a high-power (18W) 'daylight' low-energy spiral lamp.

The bench is set quite high – 36in from the floor – and I work seated on an old and rather threadbare draughtsman's chair to give a comfortable working height and a decent view out of the window. The work surface is 18in deep and the actual working area is about 48in long – luxury! The contraption with the handle to the right of the bench is my most valued specialised tool – an American PPM precision shear, which makes cutting metal square, straight and accurately to size an absolute doddle.

Hand tools are mostly kept in free-standing racks at the rear of the bench (the most often used), with the rest in the drawers seen. The chest of drawers houses jobs in hand, finished models and – of course – unmade kits. It also supports a selection of vintage hi-fi for suitable music and Radio 4. At the left of the picture can be seen a portable music stand, which I find invaluable for holding any reference books, drawings or photos which I need to consult while modelling.

Left: Good tools are worth looking after. A tool stand like this is simple to make and keeps things safely but conveniently to hand.

workshop, but in the context of the 'basic' approach underlying this chapter, I'd opt for a portable work-board as the most useful way of providing a viable work-space. The workbench photo shows what I mean; a chunk of 15mm MDF or similar (mine is actually 5/8in blockboard), with a strip of wood below the front edge so that it will locate against the edge of any table or other suitable surface and give you a front 'lip' to which things can be clamped. You want a fairly heavy, solid board so that it stays put in use and doesn't wander off around the table-top in the heat of battle – something that can be further prevented by sticking some non-slip material to the underside. Kitchen shops sell a soft anti-slip matting designed to go beneath carving dishes which is ideal; it'll also protect the finish of whatever you've parked the work-board on top of. The modelling vice is screwed or clamped to the front 'lip' of the board, while a 2in high 'fence' around the remaining three sides will contain operations and cut down on lost bits.

The last essential is a work-lamp of some sort. There are all sorts of fancy ones on the market, but at a basic level the sort of small, low-voltage quartz-halogen desk lights widely sold at DIY outlets for around a fiver will do just fine. My preference is for an Anglepoise-type fitting carrying one of the new-generation low-energy, high-output lamps. The one I use is rated at 18W (equivalent to a 100W tungsten bulb) in the colder 'daylight' colour; it provides ample flicker-free light but no unwanted heat.

Site preparation

Model railways can be finicky things to house and – if sited in less-than-ideal environments – have a propensity to malfunction in any number of infuriating ways. Oddly enough, the same is true of their creators; an appropriate level of human creature comforts is equally important to a successful outcome. I've come across many instances of model railways unfinished or abandoned simply because working on or operating them was more of a penance than a pleasure. Railway modelling is a hobby to enjoy, and is more rewarding if

you can stand or sit comfortably, can see what you're doing, aren't being showered with dust and detritus, frozen to death, or boiled alive.

As with any practical problem, in adapting a less-than-ideal site to model railway purposes you can treat the symptoms or cure the causes. In the first category, for instance, the advent of relatively inexpensive dehumidifiers and compact free-standing heating/ventilation/air-conditioning (HVAC) units now makes it much easier to render spaces suffering climatic problems usable at the push of a button and the consumption of a few kilowatts. Realistically, though, this sort of hi-tech approach is only an option for dealing with occasional climatic extremes or for temporary use of a site. If air conditioning is the *only* means of maintaining a suitable environment, the system will need to run continuously and any breakdown or power failure could have a permanently damaging effect on the layout. And in today's ecologically conscientious world it is hardly a very 'green' approach and apt to be costly!

The lower-tech – and ultimately more economic – alternative is to modify the space to eliminate the problems at source. Generally, this comes down to a thorough clean-up and the provision of proper damp-proofing, insulation and ventilation, together with control of sunlight and maybe the provision of low-level background heating. None of which lies beyond the scope of a little DIY and some modest expense.

Fundamentals

Common to many sites is that need for a spring-clean. Sites in old buildings especially will well repay the effort involved in a really comprehensive dust-removal exercise, aided by an industrial style high-power vacuum cleaner. If you can't find an excuse to add one of these to the domestic inventory, they can be hired for a modest sum. Once you've got rid of the dust of ages, any recurrence can be contained by such precautionary measures as the sealing and binding of crumbly wall and floor surfaces and the thorough partitioning of the layout space from its surroundings to keep dirt and draughts (the two usually go together) at bay.

Above: One of the essentials of a usable attic is good access. Here's the 'pedestrian' entry to Rice's attic kingdom; the opening is 36in long by 21in wide; I would have made it wider but there was a beam in the way. I'm fortunate that there is another, even bigger hatch (36in square) through which to get large objects up and down. But, as so often, this is sited on the landing – which meant the ladder got in everybody's way if left rigged. This alternative entrance is in a bedroom, out of harm's way.

Below: Effective insulation is the other layout-space essential – and this is a neat, efficient and not-too-costly way of accomplishing it, using rigid foil-faced polyurethane foam insulation sheet. I used 40mm thick 'Kingspan' in 4ft x 18in panels in my attic (and also in the shed which preceded it). It's very light, easy to cut with a Stanley knife and can be pinned or glued in place. If fitted under a roof, as here, there needs to be a vapour barrier or sarking felt below the slates or tiles and at least a 50mm air-gap between that and the sheet.

Structural alterations to buildings to accommodate layouts are best avoided if possible. Altering or adding non-load-bearing partitions is simple enough, but in these days of convoluted and restrictive building regulation, anything more fundamental is likely to involve professional assistance and hence considerable extra cost. Even simply flooring out an attic is, nowadays, no simple matter if 'acceptable' floor loadings are to achieved. I sometimes wonder what those who pen building regulations think we're going to get up to in our adapted roof space; mass Sumo wrestling, perhaps?

This book is not really the place to dissect the complex ins-and-outs of building alteration. However, one point that is worth making is that you don't need a full-blown attic conversion to house a model railway; an insulated loft-space with a floor strong enough for normal domestic storage should be quite adequate for model railway purposes. Similarly, while permanent staircase access is nice it's not necessary – a good loft-ladder sited in a decent-sized opening will serve. Many loft access hatches are ridiculously small, but are not difficult to enlarge; 3ft x 2ft is a good size to aim for. Add a little insulation and some basic wiring and you're ready to go.

Insulation and dust control

These are the two real essentials in creating a usable layout site in what is otherwise a non-habitable space. Roof spaces, cellars, sheds and garages will all normally need some attention in these areas. Insulation can be addressed in a number of ways, but I have found that by far the simplest approach is to use sheet insulation material of the rigid polyurethane foam variety, widely available from builders' merchants under the Celotex or Kingspan brands.

This versatile material consists of a rigid foam core either faced on one side with heat-reflecting foil and on the other with a white paper-based finished surface, or with foil both sides. The board comes in various thicknesses from 25mm upwards, weighs very little and can be cut with a Stanley knife. It can be fixed using a construction adhesive like No More

Nails or double-sided heavy duty adhesive tape (carpet tape), by nailing with large-head plasterboard nails or, where it is to be fitted between rafters, studs or uprights, by simply cutting tightly to size and jamming in place (sheds and attics, particularly). Celotex is supplied in standard 2,440 x 1,220mm (8ft x 4ft) sheets, but Kingspan comes in smaller 1,220 x 450mm (4ft x 18in) panels that will fit through a normal loft-hatch.

Obviously, the thermal performance and price of sheet insulations are determined by the thickness, but for model railway purposes full domestic performance isn't required; 40mm sheet is usually adequate, especially in a relatively small and easy-to-heat location like a shed or attic where the restricted space keeps the volume down. Don't forget the importance of leaving an airspace behind the insulation (to avoid condensation problems).

Large areas of concrete floor – as in garages or basements – can often be less-than friendly both from the dust-producing and thermal comfort viewpoints. A coat of suitable concrete paint or sealant usually addresses the dust problem, but the propensity of bare concrete to be a cold and uncomfortable surface on which to stand for any time should not be underestimated. Carpeting – preferably on a suitable underlay – is a straightforward solution. The usual timber-floored shed is rather more forgiving on the feet than a concrete-slabbed garage, but floor insulation is still well worthwhile. This is best arranged using rigid styrene floor insulation sheet – which you can get from builders' merchants – slotted tightly between the floor joists under the boards. This is easy to do before the shed is erected, much more difficult once it is, as you'll need to get underneath the floor. It is also beneficial to sit a shed on piers or bearers so that it is at least a few inches clear of the ground, which will keep any damp at bay. I have successfully raised an existing shed on to low concrete-block piers using a small car-type trolley jack, going round it and raising each corner a few inches at a time.

In larger spaces with greater height (particularly tall roof spaces, deep basements and pent-roof garages) it may well be worth considering installing a false ceiling to both exclude dust and to cut down the volume to be heated. Rigid sheet insulation on a lightweight timber framing can provide a simple non-structural insulating ceiling. You won't be able to hang heavy light fittings off such a false ceiling, though. Therefore use modern miniature low-voltage or energy-efficient downlighters or support more substantial fixtures, such as integrated fluorescent fittings, from the main roof structure.

Mad dogs and Englishmen

Avoiding the harmful effects of the mid-day sun is just as wise in the case of model railways as for either canines or coves. As noted in Chapter 2, sites in front of windows – particularly south-facing – are best avoided if possible. If you need to make use of space so afflicted, it will certainly pay to take measures to cut out or control the exposure of the layout to direct sun. Good heavy curtains or, better still, Venetian blinds, are useful, while it is often possible to arrange drapes, covers or removable shutters to protect the model when not in use. Double glazing and UV-filter glass (Pilkington 'K' or similar) in the window will also help. All or any of the above should also ensure the layout doesn't become the cat's favourite sunning spot – something that is always detrimental to any model railway! Although cats rarely seem to agree about this …

Mains power

Hopefully, your model railway site will already be provided with mains power and light – but if it's an attic or a shed it may well be bereft. In these days of ever-tighter building regulation, many of the ad-hoc wiring solutions we used to employ to get mains power into such locations are now somewhat frowned upon. There is very little scope these days for DIY mains wiring, but modest additions to the domestic circuitry can be made under the present (BS 7671/2001) rules. If you feel competent, consult the relevant publications or go online to http://www.iee.org/publish/wireregs/. If you'd rather steer clear of this sort of work (and if you have any doubts, do so …) then there are two alternatives: either employ an electrician to route integrated mains wiring to the site, or use a suitable extension lead to bring power from the nearest extant 13A socket.

Actually, this last approach has quite a lot to recommend it. In terms of the wiring diktats under building regulations, these don't apply once you 'get past the plug', so providing you avoid overloading any cables or creating trip hazards due to carelessly strewn wires, then good quality extension leads (widely available and modestly priced) are a perfectly safe and economical solution. Fortunately, model railways don't require much power, and even if a small (up to 2kW) heater is included in the equation the current involved will lie well within the capacity of a suitably rated domestic extension lead. To ensure plenty of 'headroom' in the power supply, it pays

Below: Power supply by extension lead. Here is the six-outlet switched socket block terminating the main heavy-duty 13A extension lead that feeds my attic, together with one of the four-way 5A 'local' extension leads used in 'daisychain' fashion to provide an adequate number of outlets where they're needed. There are some 20 outlets in all dotted about the whole area, but heavy-duty items like the 2kW room-heater or the 1,600W industrial vacuum cleaner are only powered direct from the main block.

to opt for a heavy-duty lead rated at 13A and preferably used with an RCD trip, which gives an extra layer of protection. The same lead as already recommended in the tool-list could well serve for this higher purpose.

Most ready-made extension leads are terminated in a socket block with at least four outlets. Providing you keep the total load within the capacity of the 'trunk lead' there's no reason why you can't add additional shorter leads with further four-way blocks to provide sockets where you need them and in sufficient quantity to plug in all the 'fixed' devices needed (layout power supplies, lighting, heating and so on), plus any power tools being used. Again, it is important to ensure that the leads are appropriately rated for the job – so a heater, for instance, must always be fed via a heavy-duty lead. In fact, I'd suggest that 'heavy load' appliances like heaters or aircon units are always plugged direct into one of the sockets terminating the main extension lead; putting such a load through too many plug-and-socket joins is not recommended. Note also that the coiled-type extension leads (on a drum or wound into an outer) should not be fully loaded unless they're fully unwound – so choose an uncoiled lead of appropriate length to avoid having unwanted cable snaking all over the place.

One enormous advantage of a layout site powered via an extension lead is that simply unplugging the lead totally isolates the layout and all its ancillaries, reducing any risk from soldering irons inadvertently left on or electrical mishaps occurring while the layout is unattended. My own attic workshop/layout space is powered via a 13-amp extension lead terminating in a six-outlet switched block, fed via an RCD trip from a socket in the room below. The lead has a plug with an inbuilt neon warning light to indicate quite clearly when the attic power is live; it's left in place permanently, being routed up into the attic inside a convenient cupboard, which keeps the cable out of sight and safely out of the way,

If you opt for extension lead power for a shed layout, buy a lead intended for garden or outdoor use as this will withstand the effects of the weather if left exposed. You probably won't want to keep coiling or unwinding such a lead every time you nip out to the railway anyway – but if you do leave it rigged, make sure it's safely out of harm's way and is always unplugged when not in use. Two useful options are to clip it to the garden fence where practicable (that may even dictate the best site for the shed) or, for short distances up to 10ft or so, to suspend it at a good height from the ground on suitable poles. Don't let the lead carry its own weight if you do this – rig a wire or rope support and clip or tape the lead to it. Never, ever, be tempted to bury this type of lead; it's quite unsuited to that purpose and such hidden flex is beset with dangers. A buried supply needs proper armoured cable and has a further flurry of rules to comply with.

Baseboards

Well, here is a topic on which one could write reams, although the result would not, I fear, be a riveting read. Baseboards are as essential as they are unexciting and there are a great number of ways of attaining an adequate result. Rather than conducting a survey of all the manifold possibilities, I'll confine myself to describing the two basic types of board with which I have most experience and that I can, hand on heart, recommend as being both simple to build and satisfactory in service. This handy ploy will permit me to draw a discrete veil over some of the less-successful baseboards I have concocted over the years, when I either got seduced by new-fangled ideas and materials, or just skimped the job in my hurry to get on to the tracklaying and the other interesting bits …

For many years, baseboards were specified without much consideration for what was going on top of them. Countless layouts described in the pages of the best-selling magazine for railway modellers dismissed them in a single unthinking line: 'The baseboards are 4 x 2ft, made of half-inch chipboard sheet on a frame of 2 x 1 softwood, butt-jointed and nailed together.' On being introduced to just such an animal my cousin Jem – a boat builder and joiner of some note – gave it as his opinion that the chipboard top was doing quite a good job of holding the framing up and that 'it was just as well because there's precious little wood around some of those knots.' The moral to be drawn from many a sorry tale of sagging baseboards is that the structural integrity of the framing is the key, no matter what you put on top of it. Good baseboard framing needs to be strong, stable and nice and stiff in the vertical dimension – which rules out a piece of 2 x 1 with an inch-and-a-half knot in it.

A traditional baseboard consisted of a rectangular perimeter frame braced with a grid of cross-members, usually on 12in centres. At its simplest, such a framework supported a flat surface of some suitable sheet material – usually hardboard, chipboard, ply or a 'composition' board such as Sundeala – to give the 'table top' of trainset memory. In terms of realistic railway modelling, such a structure would suit only a layout set in the flatter bits of the Fens – and even then, the dykes and drains would cause a problem. The fact is that even flat land is far from flat, and most terrain goes up and down by a surprising amount – something that the baseboard design needs to take into account, and one reason why it's important to think through the topography of the model at the layout design stage.

Another drawback to the old-fashioned 'grid' type of baseboard frame is that it is based on the presumption of a layout conceived as a series of rectangular or otherwise straight-edged modules – very much at odds with modern thought on layout design, which tends to favour more naturalistic and irregular shapes. The trend is for layout 'footprints' that follow the typical flowing curves found in the British landscape and, very often, in British railway tracks. Both the 'beam and bearer' and glued-ply 'eggbox' baseboard systems I use are far better able to accommodate such considerations than the traditional 'grid'. Both these systems also take account of 'z' – or the vertical dimension. The ability to incorporate different levels into the layout scenery – both above and below the level of the trackwork – is an essential requirement of a supporting system for a realistic model railway.

The other factor that needs to be taken into consideration when pondering baseboards is that of portability – or, at least, transportability. Traditionally, layouts were classified as either 'portable' or 'permanent', this was reflected in the baseboarding. Permanent layouts were often immutably tied to the structure which housed them so that if the need to move or remove them arose, the only answer was total demolition. Almost every model railway will need to be removed from its 'build' location at some stage, so unless you have a great need for kindling or a penchant for starting all over again, planning the baseboards to allow the model to come apart in a manageable manner and to be able to got through the doorway seems only prudent.

I prefer to think of layouts as being either portable or transportable, with baseboards and supporting systems arranged accordingly. If they are to be anything other than a pain in several delicate parts of the anatomy, portable layouts need to be more than simply movable; they need to be light in weight, arranged in chunks small enough to be wieldy, free from sharp extrusions, drooping wires or other things likely to snag. They need to incorporate handles, strong points or other aids to actually getting a grip on the thing. They must

Below: **An all-glued-ply compact baseboard structure.**

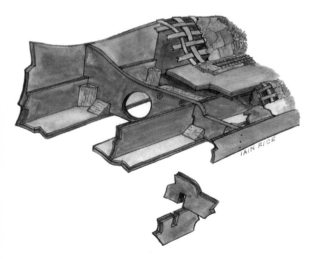

come apart and go together quickly with a minimum of fuss and fiddle, and they have to be well finished to look good wherever they are. For these reasons, I would not now consider building a portable layout that used anything other than a lightweight glued-ply base structure.

Transportable layouts, on the other hand, can ignore many of these requirements. So long as they can be moved in time of need, it doesn't matter too much if that movement requires a little more effort and the help of a few willing pairs of extra hands. In these instances, I've found that heavier timber-framed structures will suffice – in other words, L-girders. Mind you, these don't need to be as substantial as often seen or advocated in the USA. There's no virtue in over-specifying structural timberwork (like the American friend who built his own house then went on to build his model railroad using the same sizes of timber as 'he had some left over'; the result was baseboards strong enough to support a real train!). This merely adds weight and cost without conferring any benefit.

Glued-ply lightweight baseboards

These are essentially a British invention, brought into being by our penchant for exhibitions and the consequent need to build easily-portable layouts to exhibit at them. The key to their development was the introduction to the general DIY market of high-strength resin-based woodworking glues, derived from the adhesives developed during the war to build that wonderful lightweight ply-framed flying machine, the de Havilland Mosquito. In fact, there is quite a close resemblance between a well-built ply baseboard and a Mosquito airframe.

The key structural property of ply as exploited in both applications is that a relatively thin strip of the material is very flexible in one dimension but extremely stiff in the other. Thus, a baseboard member made of ply around a quarter of an inch thick and somewhere between three and six inches wide, used vertically and suitably braced to maintain its longitudinal alignment, gives a principal structural member that weighs very little but is extremely rigid and free from any tendency to sag or flex vertically. Given that ply usually comes in eight-by-four foot sheets, such a member can be readily produced up to the full length of the sheet – quite long enough for our purposes. Normal practice is to maintain the vertical alignment by gluing in cross-bearers at suitable (but reasonably close) intervals, resulting in a sort of 'square honeycomb' structure, often known as an 'eggbox' – presumably after the multiple compartments thus produced.

One of the great advantages of a longitudinal principal ply member like this is that it doesn't have to be straight. So long as it is kept vertical by the cross-bracing, it can be flexed to follow a curved outline, making this a very suitable way of framing irregular-shaped baseboards. Furthermore, there's no need for either the longitudinal member or any of the cross-braces to be constant in their vertical dimensions, so they can be profiled to support different levels of trackbeds, scenery or structures.

The key to the success of this type of structure is the quality of the ply and the strength of the adhesive. Although ultra-cheap Luan ply from the Far East will work, it's worth paying a bit extra for Scandinavian or North American birch ply (second grade is fine). Glue is no problem; Evo-Stik Resin W woodworking adhesive is widely available and amply strong enough. It is also non-toxic and clean to use; wipe away any excess with a damp cloth. To cut the ply into strips, a table saw is the ideal tool; most timber yards or DIY outlets will have one of these and will normally do the job for a small charge. However, at the expense of a little more sweat, it is quite possible to produce suitable strips with a Stanley knife and a straightedge, simply making repeated passes with the knife until the ply parts. For curved profiles and formers, the jigsaw is fine – it's just not so good at cutting dead straight lines, at least when I'm driving it!

For most modestly sized baseboards, I find that structural members around 4in deep are quite sufficient, resulting in a baseboard that is stiff enough but not too bulky. There are a couple of variants on the plain ply member:

Below: Support beams made from ply; L- and T-sections can also be made from solid timber.

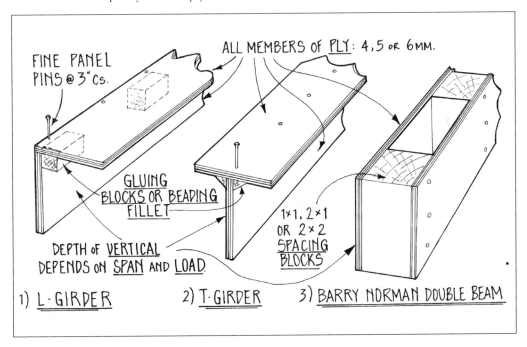

the first – only really applicable to straight members – is to fit ply flanges top, bottom or both – to give either 'L', 'T' or 'H'-section ply beams which are rigid in both directions. The other useful variant is the double-wall 'spaced girder' invented by Barry Norman, where two parallel ply members are kept parallel and vertical by small wooden blocks glued between them. Such a girder is very strong and stiff and can be made straight or curved, and is very useful where conditions don't allow a deep side-member.

For surfacing a ply-framed baseboard, all sorts of materials can be used, according to what that particular area of the baseboard is supporting. You *can* make everything from ply, including the trackbeds – I have, many times – but to cut down resonance I tend to opt for something denser under the track, usually MDF 12mm or 18mm thick, screwed to softwood blocks glued to the cross-formers of the base structure. Apart from all other considerations, making the trackbeds as separate items facilitates my preference for building or laying and ballasting my track on the workbench whenever I can. Away from the track, I use a variety of other, lighter materials as a base for roadways, structures, waterways and other features – thin MDF (the 2mm stuff used as backing board by picture framers is useful), hardboard, thin ply, card, or foam-core board. For plain landscape, I go for my favoured 'glueshell' system (more on that in Chapter 7) which is applied straight to the ply baseboard framing.

The basic constructional technique for building ply baseboards is very simple – the various components are simply edge-glued together, helped by a few fine panel pins or construction staples where you can get at the appropriate face of the join with a hammer or staple gun. The pins don't add much to the strength, but they are useful for holding everything in place while the glue goes off. It's no bad idea to reinforce key joins, such as those where the ends meet the longitudinal members, with 'gluing blocks' of inch-by-inch softwood fitted up the inside of the angle. In fact, I don the belt to aid the braces by adding just such reinforcing fillets to all my joins, using lengths of half-inch quadrant (quarter round) beading, as in the drawing. A further nice refinement is to cut lightening holes a couple of inches or so in diameter through the cross-formers with a hole-saw, which not only takes away unnecessary material, but provides 'ways' for electrical circuits, point control mechanisms and so on. It also looks mighty impressive and high-tech!

Where multiple baseboard sections are needed for a layout, it will be necessary to provide alignment devices and some sort of clamping system to hold the baseboards firmly and accurately together. The established practice is to use pattern-maker's dowels for alignment and 6mm large-headed 'gutter bolts' with wing nuts to clamp things together. When arranging joining faces for ply baseboard structures, it's a good idea to 'beef up' the cross-formers either side of the join, either by cutting them from thicker ply or by using two layers. It is also a good idea to cut and drill the end formers for adjoining baseboards as pairs and to install all the alignment and joining hardware *before* building them into the baseboards.

Beam-and-bearer baseboards

Perhaps more properly, 'benchwork', as the origins of beam-and-bearer – or L-girder – baseboards lie across the water in the USA, birthplace of the large scenic model railway. The principle of the L-girder 'beam' is that each component of the 'L' braces the weak dimension of the other, giving a strong structural member that is very simple to make. The Americans make 'em big, too: often 8in deep by 4in or even 6in wide, but that reflects the size of US layouts (and hence spans needed) – not to mention the weight of the massive plaster mountains they so often seem to stick on top of them! For most British applications a far smaller girder will suffice; one with a 4in vertical web and a 2in top flange is about as big as you'll need, while for spans under 10ft, 3 x 2 or even 2 x 2 L-girders are fine. As shown in the diagrams, I often make these in ply, 6 to 10mm thick. Ply L-girders are light, straight and very strong. For very small or lightweight baseboards, an L-girder beam isn't really needed and straightforward stripwood of good quality can be used.

The beams or girders are used in conjunction with suitable baseboard supports and carry a whole series of simple timber cross-bearers, which are attached by screws driven up through the top flanges. This means said bearers can be fitted, removed or moved from below even when there's a layout sitting on top of them. The cross-bearers support the trackbeds (usually on risers) and the fascia, which can readily be made to follow curved outlines. The girders don't have to be parallel, so can easily be arranged to accommodate odd-shaped 'footprints'. The drawing hereabouts will hopefully make all this clear.

Beam-and-bearer baseboards are a strong, simple and adaptable system ideal for the transportable category of layout, but not really suited to the portable genre. Given their usual application, joining systems between baseboard sections don't need to be of any sophistication as the things won't be taken apart and reassembled on a regular basis. Simple screwed splice plates normally suffice. Trackbed materials, scenic supports and

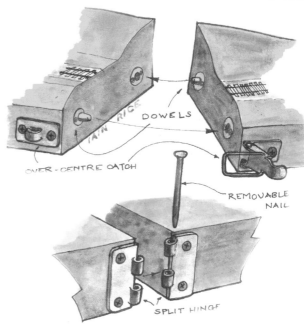

Above: Baseboard joining systems.

Below: Basic baseboard structures using beam-and-bearer principles; Classic L-girder at left, fully profiled with an integrated backdrop at right.

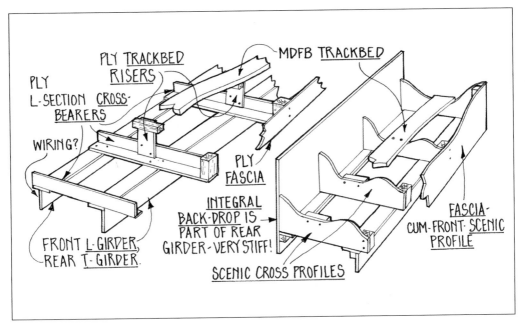

surfacing systems can all be just as described for the ply baseboards. The 'risers' supporting trackbeds are usually made of ply with inch-by-inch locating blocks, on centres of 12in or less, and wide enough to support the trackbed over its full width. The great advantage of the riser system is its adaptability and the ease with which track heights, gradients and alignments can be adjusted while such niceties as superelevation of curves can be introduced.

Baseboard supporting systems

You can support a model railway at the desired height in one of three ways: off the floor, on legs, trestles or pieces of furniture; off the wall, on brackets or battens, or from the ceiling or roof, using hangers. The first is probably the most common approach, but wall-mounting also has much to commend it. The last option is rarely used but can be a good solution for loft layouts, where the rafters form a convenient attachment point. By it's nature, such a solution will need to be devised and tailored to suit particular circumstances, so it's not practicable to discuss it in general terms here.

Portable exhibition layouts will usually need some sort of floor-standing support that can be as readily moved as the layout, in which role the trestle is usually the preferred option. Easy to build, collapsible to the flat for transport, readily adjusted for height, self-bracing, strong and stable, the trestle has much to commend it for home use as well. Recently, rather than cart around full-height floor-standing trestles for exhibition use, I've gone over to using 'mini-trestles' that are designed to sit on top of a standard folding table of the type found in abundance at the majority of exhibition venues. Mini-trestles are typically about 18–24in high, being designed simply to make up the difference between the height of the table and the desired display level of the layout.

Trestles work with all types of baseboard, but the convenient upright web of an L-girder beam makes the bolt-on leg an attractive option. Whether legs or trestles are used, it is important to ensure that the layout sits straight and level without any 'rock'. For permanent or home layouts, this is accomplished by either packing as needed, or by tailoring each leg to its position. For exhibition layouts, screw leg-adjusters are an elegant way of accommodating uneven floors. These can be fitted to legs or trestles.

Not depending on a level floor is one of the many virtues of the wall-mounted layout. The two basic options here are the custom-made 'gallows' bracket or the use of commercial shelf track – of which the latter is by far my preferred method. Speed and ease of erection, adjustability, stability and strength, unobtrusiveness and the ability to integrate seamlessly with domestic environments and other uses of the space are just a few of the benefits. All my portable and exhibition layouts for the past twenty or more years have sat on Spur shelf-track when at home, often integrated with storage or book shelving, and using a further shelf above the layout to carry lighting and provide dust protection.

However you site, support and light your layout, paying due attention to these fundamentals is time, effort and money well spent. Sound underpinnings contribute a huge amount to the success of the model as a whole, while skimping on these preliminaries is something you'll live to regret later. Many a good model has been undermined by trivial defects in the substructure or site preparation that would have taken little cost or effort to put right at the preliminary stages – but which are almost impossible to rectify later.

Chapter 4

TRACK

The trouble with trying to write a book like this is that almost every chapter heading needs a volume to itself! Nowhere is this truer than when it comes to track – the key element in any railway system, real or model. Get this wrong and naught but a vale of tears lies ahead, for without good trackwork a model railway will neither work properly nor look realistic.

Below: What it's all about! A wonderful spread of traditional British bullhead permanent way in all its intricacy and complexity – full of flowing, subtle curves. A Caledonian Railway 'Dunalastair' 4-4-0 leaves Aberdeen early in LMS days. Author's collection

A quick skit around the prototype

The study of prototype trackwork is a topic so broad and so deep that it could occupy a lifetime. Not having too many of those to spare, however, I'll have to content myself with a modest selection of pictures, a spot of analysis as to salient features, and a quick run-down of the whys and wherefores of prototype British PW practice relevant to the modeller. British track evolved over a long period and for most of that time was highly distinctive – only recently has it come to resemble that used in the rest of Europe, while it has always been quite different from anything found in the USA.

Above: Fully chaired 4mm scale model bullhead track on the author's P4 'Trerice' layout. This uses C&L flexible track and hand-laid turnouts using matching C&L chairs. These components are also suited for EM or 'fine' 00, while similar parts are made for 7mm scale. Matt Doe

Below: Vignoles rails in Irish use. Note the lack of any base plates on the 'siding' track at the left. The main line (right) has sole-plates and screw-spikes; Irish economy! Author's collection

The main characteristic of traditional British track was the use of bullhead (dumb-bell section) rail carried in substantial cast-iron chairs and held in place with wooden wedges called 'keys'. This is a very sophisticated form of track construction only encountered in the British Isles (including Ireland) and on a handful of overseas railways originally laid out by British engineers. The various pre-Grouping railway companies developed their own individual patterns of bullhead track, using different chair designs, sleeper sizes and spacings, and lengths and weights of rail. By the early 1920s, however, under the influence of the British Standards Institute, a 'standard' pattern of bullhead PW emerged. This used BS95R rail of 95lb/yard section in 60ft lengths, carried in cast-iron chairs weighing around 56lb each on timber sleepers 10in wide by 5in thick by 8½ft long, spaced on 30in centres except at joints, where the spacing was closed up slightly.

There were still minor variations in exact PW practice between the 'Big Four' companies and, indeed, between the six BR Regions that succeeded them. Most noticeable differences came in chair design, with variations in jaw shape and in the number and type of fastenings used to attach the chairs to the sleepers. The GWR opted to fix each chair with two 'fang

bolts' – substantial steel bolts nutted to 'fang plates' that bit into the underside of each sleeper – while the LNER and the SR used a three-hole chair design held by screw-spikes. The LMS used a four-hole chair with four screw spikes. Modellers refer to these as two, three or four-bolt chairs.

As well as the prevalent bullhead (BH) track, a few minor railways adopted PW of the pattern more common on the Continent. This used Vignoles or flat-bottom (FB) rails, usually of quite small size, spiked or screwed directly to the sleepers without any chairs. This was a cheaper but less durable form of track and in Britain was usually only found on secondary lines with lighter traffic – industrial, mineral and light railways of both standard and narrow gauges, as well as on a good number of Irish lines. Elsewhere in Europe, such FB track was widely adopted and soon developed into a far more substantial form of PW, with heavier rails sitting on cast-iron sole plates using multi-spike, bolted or spring-clipped rail fastenings.

Such heavyweight FB for main line use was trialled in Britain in the late 1930s and adopted as the new BR standard after the end of the Second World War, using rail of 110lb/yard section on cast base plates and held down with laminated spring spikes. At much the same time, cast concrete sleepers started to replace the traditional creosote-impregnated timber variety. All this was in the cause of longer track life and lower maintenance costs. The other main development to this end was the introduction of continuous welded rail (CWR), which did away with the frequent rail-joints and their troublesome fishplates.

However, to resist the resulting expansion forces, welded track has to be much more rigid than traditional bolted BH, which was specifically designed to be flexible. The springs of a steam engine are very stiff and only allow a slight wheel movement, while there are many out-of-balance wheel loadings due to the valve gear and the reciprocating nature of the drive. So flexibility in the track was highly desirable on a steam-powered railway. With the change-over to diesel and

Below: Modern heavyweight flat-bottom track on BR. Here is a newly laid stretch of concrete-sleeper, continuously welded track with 110lb/yd flat-bottom rail. Note the very heavy ballasting, characteristic of welded track which needs to be firmly located. On the adjoining tracks the pointwork being negotiated by the paired Class 37s is on timber sleepering – which is usual as there are very few concrete-sleepered turnouts in use other than on the Channel Tunnel Rail Link (HS1) and associated lines. A. O. Wynn

electric power, where the drive is smooth and softer with long-travel springs and hydraulic damping incorporated, track could be made far more 'solid' without affecting ride or traction. The horse had to change to suit the new course and there seems little doubt that this fundamental change in the nature of the track was a considerable factor in the rapid phasing-out of steam locomotives and traditional short-wheelbase wagons in Britain after about 1960.

Modern British track is a development of this post-war FB PW, although using much more substantial close-spaced concrete sleepers firmly held by heavy ballasting, long, continuously welded rails of around 130lb/yard and sophisticated flexible-composition sole pads between the rail and the sleepers. The rails are held down either by bolted clips or by the highly ingenious spring-steel Pandrol clips invented by Per Pander-Rolfsen of the Norwegian State Railways in 1957. This design of track is now more-or-less universal on main routes throughout Europe, but older PW designs still survive on less-important routes. Here in Britain, it is not hard to find traditional bullhead rail still in situ – lightly used track can have a very long life.

Straight track
Traditional 'standard' British BH track was laid in panels – discrete lengths of track 60ft long (although older, pre-Grouping track came in shorter lengths, 30 or 45 feet) joined by

Below: **A panel of traditional bullhead track showing, at left, the closed-up sleeper spacing and fishplate at the joint. This is GWR track with two-bolt chairs.**

fishplates. This regular joint spacing was the feature that accounted for the regular, rhythmic 'diddly-dum' made by the wheels of British stock when running; overseas railways often used staggered joins and unequal rail lengths, so lacked this characteristic soundtrack. A 60-foot track panel had 24 sleepers spaced on 30in centres, or slightly closer together either side of the joints. The fishplates are straight-shaped steel bars with four holes, bolted either side of the rail to span the joint with the bolt-holes slightly oval to allow movement for expansion. For the same reason, the bolts were not done up too tight and the whole fishplate assembly was kept lubricated.

Full-size BH rail is actually amazingly flexible – which means it will readily take up quite convoluted curves and form all manner of dips and humps if not carefully aligned and packed up to give a true 'top'. Laying a dead-straight, dead-level section of track was actually a difficult and skilled business, and keeping it true required constant careful maintenance.

Curved track
Curves on real railways are very rarely straightforward. In the world of toy trains, track is either straight or curved as part of a circle of fixed radius, but at full size curves are laid out with a continuously varying radius – particularly where they are entered from straight track. These 'transitions' or 'easements' are intended to guide the trains smoothly into the curve, avoiding any abrupt changes of direction by starting on a very wide radius which is gradually reduced until the tightest part of the curve – the 'ruling radius' – is reached. The same progressive

'spiral easing' then gradually unwinds to unite the curve to the next section of straight track. These sinuous curves are a notable feature of British railway track, endowing it with a unique flowing appearance.

Not only are real railway curves of sophisticated form, but they are also, by model railway standards, very gentle. Most 20th century British steam engines were designed to work on a *minimum* radius of six chains (as a chain is 66ft, that is a shade under 400ft). Moreover, such tight radii would only be encountered in works sidings or goods yards, or at confined locations where trains would only be moving very slowly indeed. This may seem reasonable enough – until you do the sums and work out what a six-chain curve scales out at in the popular modelling sizes. In 4mm:1ft scale it is almost 63in. Most 00 modellers would regard a 5ft 3in radius curve as being pretty generous and certainly a very long way from the practical minimum!

Fortunately, both mechanically and visually it is possible to 'get away with' curves on models that are, in strictly scale terms, ridiculously tight. However, as noted back in Chapter 2, the closer to scale you go in terms of wheel and track standards on your models, the less scope there is for 'squeezing' minimum curves. This is, I fear, a fact of life which no amount of wishful thinking will ever overcome! There's no doubt, though, that model track that incorporates easements or transitions both looks and functions a great deal better than track laid as straight-fixed curve-straight, even to the point where it is preferable to accept a *tighter* minimum or ruling radius to make room for easements rather than using a wider curve of fixed radius.

Prototype pointwork

If plain track is convoluted enough in its anatomy and history, pointwork is just plain baffling. British PW made comparatively little use of off-the-peg standard point formations and a high proportion of turnouts were 'one-offs', specifically built to suit a particular location. Many of these were curved, either in opposite directions as a 'Y' point or with both

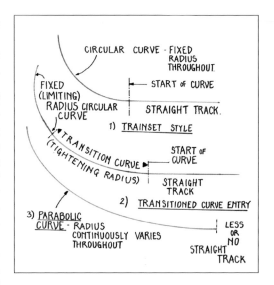

Above: Railway curves.

roads curving to the same hand, while complex formations where several tracks came together at the same location as three-way turnouts or slip crossings were also quite common. The illustrations show a selection of these different point formations. This extensive use of custom-built pointwork was another factor that contributed to the characteristic flowing appearance of British track.

Below: Trackwork of mind-blowing complexity was a characteristic of British railways, as here at the top of Bethnal Green Bank in GER days. Where space was tight, just about anything was possible! Author's collection

Above: Slips – correctly, 'slip diamonds' – were a common space-saver throughout the steam era; some railways had great fondness for them, most notably the Midland and the old GER. Here's a P4 1-in-6 single slip on 'Cade's Green'. Peco do a ready-to-use version of this formation in both 16.5mm and N gauges.

Below: Some specialised pointwork of straightforward PCB-sleepered construction – a short (45°) diamond crossing, a 1-in-6 single slip and a B6left/B8right tandem three-way. All these were constructed using printed templates – by C&L, in this case. This is P4 track, but PCB track can be made for any gauge, standard or rail-type.

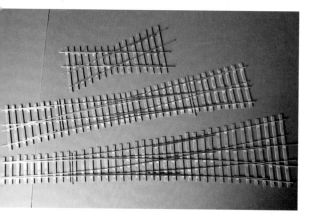

The details of British point and crossing work are even more variable than those for plain track, with the old pre-Grouping companies once again evolving a rich variety of characteristic designs. As well as the differences in rail weight, chairs and sleeper sizes, there were variations in the geometry used, the design of the point blades, the way the timbering was arranged, the construction of the crossings (or 'frogs'), the special chairs used to hold the various rails and the way the parts of the turnout were fastened together. This is an aspect of the historical prototype that repays study by modellers bent on reproducing the pre-Grouping scene, as the nature of the track is just as much a part of the model as the buildings, signals, engineering features and even the trains. But, of course, accurately modelling old-fashioned PW does call for a DIY approach – as do many aspects of historical modelling; all part of the fascination of that branch of the hobby.

Track layouts

Modellers and prototype railway engineers frequently have different ideas on this subject! Many a model railway which 'doesn't look quite right' falls into that category because it incorporates an arrangement of trackwork that just would not be entertained in reality. This is most particularly true in the matter of the facing turnout in a running line, something the Board of Trade's railway inspectors regarded with a great deal of suspicion and to which many railway companies, most notably the Midland, had an almost pathological aversion.

Of course, on single-track railways where trains are running in both directions on the same line of rails, facing turnouts are unavoidable in one direction. They are also inescapable at junctions, at the entry to a loop and in the approaches to terminal stations. Elsewhere, however, they were studiously avoided and things like facing crossovers in normal double-track running lines were very rare indeed. (I write in the past tense; modern train working, signalling and track design varies considerably from the traditional rules, and facing points in running lines – particularly of very wide radius high-speed design – are now far more widely used.)

Modellers are often inclined to sprinkle facing points hither and thither on their layouts in the cause of 'easy' shunting. This is usually in an attempt to avoid reverse or set-back moves – pushing stock backwards through pointwork, an operation that was often fraught with hazard when tried with trainset stock at trainset speeds through trainset curves! In the earlier days of 'scale' modelling such setting-back was also problematic; poorly-matched wheels and track ('universal' pointwork and lax standards) made for a large number of derailments where flanges struck point noses or bumped through unmatched wing rails, while the jerky running of locomotives, excessive slop between wheelsets and track, stiff wheel-bearings, frequent buffer-locking and couplings that did not function well in the 'push' mode also caused many problems. All of which led to such setting-back operations becoming regarded as 'best avoided' – and hence to a rash of layout designs intended to eliminate the need.

The big problem with that approach is the inconvenient fact that the setting back move is the basis of almost all shunting on a real railway, and hence the starting-point for full-size track layout design! So we have had a situation where many models were inauthentic in a very basic sense, in that the

track was arranged in a totally unrealistic manner. This was an early concern of the pioneers of the 'scale' modelling movement and much of the effort directed towards refining wheel and track standards stemmed from a determination to make 'setting back' as easy and reliable in model form as it was on the prototype. Much experimentation and research has resulted in the reduction or elimination of most of the problems, and the more consistent and refined wheel profiles, better pointwork and the superior running qualities of modern model railway equipment all help to facilitate this vital operation. Careful attention to track-laying, taken together with an apt choice of coupling, fine-tuning of locomotives and careful weighting of rolling stock, can all help make this once-hazardous undertaking unremarkable.

Below: Modellers are far fonder of facing points than the prototype ever was. Here are two versions of the same basic layout, with, at top, a typical 'model' arrangement with the facing turnouts starred. Beneath is a rather more prototypical alternative. Note that the latter – with a trailing crossover only – does not facilitate run-round moves. The additional trailing connection to the goods shed – shown dotted – was often put in for handling 'tail traffic' – single goods vehicles attached behind passenger trains to convey urgent consignments.

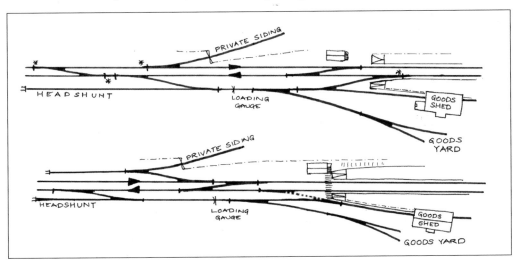

Which in turn means that railway modellers can once again look to the prototype when laying out their trackwork. Rather than attempt to describe what might be termed 'good practice', I've drawn examples of both prototypical and non-prototypical ways of arranging some popular forms of track layout. The proper signalling and operation of these arrangements is discussed later, but for the moment I'm purely looking at the disposition of the pointwork.

Model track

So much for our brief dose of reality. But how do all these prototype niceties relate to the track you're going to be offered at your local model shop? The answer, I fear, is 'not all that much!' At the time of writing, the range and fidelity of mass-produced ready-to-use model railway track – particularly in terms of authentic pointwork – has fallen rather a long way behind the standards of the trains that one can now buy to run on it. There are historical and technical reasons for this, but it is the main area of the hobby in which there is still scope for dramatic improvement.

Model railway trackwork comes in three basic formats: sectional, flexible and hand laid, with mass-production, obviously, confined to the first two categories. Sectional track is what you get with trainsets and hence has usually been produced by the big train-makers like Hornby as part of their branded ranges – although these days firms like Peco in Britain, Tillig in Germany and Atlas in the USA also offer aftermarket sectional systems. In the bad old days of deliberate non-compatibility, every branded train maker offered track of mutually exclusive design, with differing trackbase heights, geometry, rail sections and joining systems. 'Mix and match' was simply not a possibility. To a certain extent, the same is true of some proprietary sectional tracks today (Fleischmann Profi or Bachmann E-Z Track, for instance), which is why the independent track makers like Peco and Atlas can sensibly offer universally applicable alternatives – with the added bonus of compatibility with the same firms' flexible trackage systems.

It was the non-compatibility of different makes and restricted and rigid geometry of traditional sectional tracks that provided the spur for the development of what were described as 'universal' trackage systems. These were intended to accept models from different manufacturers using a whole gamut of unrelated wheel profiles. As the proper and precise matching of wheels to track is the foundation-stone of railway engineering, the very concept of universal track was – in strict functional terms – a complete nonsense. Certainly, to work at all it had to incorporate some pretty startling compromises in the matter of pointwork, which could not use prototype design criteria. The device most widely used – by both individual modellers like John Ahern or manufacturers like GEM or Wrenn – took the form of a moving wing-rail arranged to close against the appropriate side of the crossing vee to eliminate the flangeway gap and hence its relationship with flange thickness and wheel gauging. This worked well enough, but looked awful!

Other track makers tried to use conventional crossing construction with fixed wing rails and check rails, simply increasing clearances to those required by the coarser wheels and hoping against hope that anything more refined would bump its way across somehow without the benefit of any proper guidance. This resulted in running which was at best lumpy and at worst prone to perpetual derailments. Given the huge disparity between something like a Trix 'steam roller' wheel at one extreme and a Romford at the other, this all smacked of hopeless optimism rather than any form of engineering!

Towards a common standard

Fortunately, the situation today is nowhere near as bad as this, as all the main manufacturers of model railway equipment in the popular sizes now use similar wheel profiles. While not of the precisely defined and uniform standard which characterises either the fine-scale disciplines like EM or P4 or agreed national standards like those propounded (as long ago as 1951!) by the

NMRA in America, modern British RTR wheels are now generally close enough in such variables as tyre width and flange size to be able to use common trackwork without engendering poor running. The trend seems increasingly to be to use the NMRA RP25 H0 profile in both H0 and 00, with its N scale equivalent appearing on both new 1:148 'British N' (Bachmann's re-introductions of the old Farish range) and better European and US-outline 1:160 'N'. The old coarse trainset European NEM H0 and N profiles are still around, mostly on products of German origin, but the more progressive European manufacturers now offer a choice between these and RP25.

This gradual move towards uniformity has made life a great deal easier for the track makers, who now only need to accommodate wheels of similar outline. This has resulted in the introduction of finer-scale sectional and flexible tracks and the gradual phasing-out of the chunkier-looking and less precise universal tracks – although even these have become more refined as RTR makers like Hornby have moved away from the really coarse 'steam roller' profiles. For a layout using only current-generation RTR equipment and kits, there is no longer any need to accept the universal compromise; trackage systems using scale-height Code 75 rail will accept the majority of contemporary RTR wheels. Only where it is desired to use older equipment on a layout laid with modern track will a spot of re-wheeling be called for.

Rail codes

You'll have the noticed reference to Code 75 track in the foregoing, so it is perhaps not a bad idea to take a look at model trackwork and the way in which it is classified and described in a little more detail. The term 'code' used in this context refers simply to a single dimension, the height of the rail quoted in thousandths of an inch. There's no-one like a railway modeller for mixing his terminology and measuring units! Thus, Code 75 refers to model rail that is 75 thou. high – although this can be of either the flat-bottom or bullhead profile and is independent of scale. In fact, at 4mm scale 75

thou. high bullhead rail accurately represents British Standard BS95R, the rail size adopted as standard in the early 1920s. At 7mm scale, Code 148 bullhead rail is used, while 3mm scale calls for Code 65 and 2mm for Code 40 – all to represent the same thing!

However, quite a lot of the rail code/profile combinations found in model trackwork don't bear any scale relationship to real rail sizes. Most notably, the Code 100 flat-bottom rail typically used for 00 and H0 sectional track like Hornby, Bachmann or Peco 'Setrack' is really oversize for any scale below 7mm; in 4mm, it works out at something equating to US super-heavy 138lb/yd rail, but about 50% too wide!

Frogs – dead or alive?

Another piece of typically enigmatic model railway jargon concerns the electrical arrangements at point crossings or – as they're often described after the American manner – point frogs. In this context, the point frog consists of the 'vee' and wing rails considered as a discrete unit. Model pointwork is classified electrically as either dead-frog or live-frog, the difference lying in the way that the design

Below: Frogs: Dead or Alive?

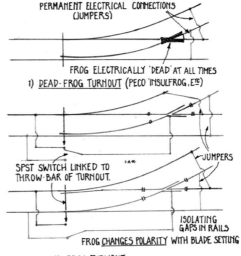

PERMANENT ELECTRICAL CONNECTIONS (JUMPERS)

FROG ELECTRICALLY 'DEAD' AT ALL TIMES
1) DEAD-FROG TURNOUT (PECO 'INSULFROG', E⁗)

SPST SWITCH LINKED TO THROW-BAR OF TURNOUT.

JUMPERS

ISOLATING GAPS IN RAILS
FROG CHANGES POLARITY WITH BLADE SETTING
2) LIVE-FROG TURNOUT

overcomes the basic problem arising from two-rail electrification. This is that at the frog of a model turnout one rail – at one electrical polarity – has to cross over the opposing rail, which will be at the opposite polarity.

To avoid a short circuit, two options are available. The older and simpler option keeps the opposing polarities apart by having the frog as a separate, electrically dead unit – in the case of modern ready-made pointwork, usually in the form of a plastic moulding incorporated as part of the sleeper base. The alternative also keeps the frog as an electrically discrete component, isolated by gaps from all the other rail sections around it – but one that can be fed electrically via a switch to energise it at the appropriate polarity for the route set through the turnout. For obvious reasons, this switching needs to be integrated into the point-changing mechanism so

Below: The median choice: SMP Code 75 bullhead flexible track used in conjunction with PCB-sleepered handmade turnouts, as here on Neil Burgess's 'Blagdon'. A good compromise well suited to 00 fine scale but also used for EM and P4; SMP produce track for all three gauges. **Neil Burgess**

that when the point blades are thrown the frog polarity is changed accordingly. This is usually accomplished by a changeover switch incorporated in the turnout itself or the operating linkages controlling it, or by a set of changeover contacts on a point motor if that is the actuating system used.

The advantage of a dead frog is the simplicity – no switching involved. The drawback is the resulting electrical 'dead patch' in the path of the loco, which can easily give rise to stalling or hesitant running, particularly at slow speeds. Live frog turnouts have long been the preferred choice of the enthusiast, the extra wiring being considered a small price to pay for the improvement in reliability and running quality. Both types of frog are found among ready-to-use turnouts, while most point motors incorporate the necessary changeover contacts for live-frog wiring.

Trackwork choices: 4mm scale

It is a sad fact that the choice of ready-to-use trackwork available to the British modeller in 4mm scale is somewhat restricted. The problem isn't the plain trackage – that's available in a variety of prototype configurations and gauges. No, the difficulty

is ready-to use pointwork. Leaving aside small manufacturers like Marcway, offering a handmade product in limited quantities, the only available comprehensive range is Peco's Streamline system in its many variants. This, of course, is only available for 00 gauge; EM or P4 workers are very much on their own in this regard.

'Twas ever thus, however, so techniques, components, templates and tools to facilitate turnout construction have long formed part of the stock-in-trade of the 'scale' end of the hobby. Building pointwork is not actually as difficult as it first appears, and turnout kits with some or all of the components ready-made are available from sources like SMP, C&L and Exactoscale (The P4 Track Company). The 'scale' societies also put a lot of effort into facilitating track construction, not only in terms of providing the necessary bits and pieces but also in terms of information and guidance, templates, tools and jigs. Many modellers find that once they have taken the plunge, track-building becomes a rewarding aspect of the hobby.

Brewing your own pointwork for use in conjunction with a ready-to-lay flexible track is a well-established middle-of-the-road approach that has a number of practical advantages. Chief amongst these is the ability to tailor your pointwork *exactly* to the needs of the track plan rather than being constrained by the geometry of off-the-peg pointwork. This a valuable asset both in terms of maximising the use of space and also in capturing the characteristic flowing appearance of British track already remarked on – a characteristic at least in part derived from the fact that the real railway custom-built its pointwork! Home-built track is also often more economical than buying ready-made, while fully chaired ranges like C&L or Exactoscale have a truly authentic appearance.

The truly dedicated enthusiast often takes things a stage further, by hand-building all his track – plain or pointwork – using dedicated components from the specialist societies or from 'scale' suppliers like the aforementioned C&L or Exactoscale. There are a number of reasons for taking this approach: consistency of appearance, ultimate authenticity to prototype (particularly where that prototype had oddball or highly characteristic PW), economy of cost and the satisfaction derived from the skilled work involved. However, there's no getting away from the fact that hand-building track requires a great deal of time and trouble – it certainly isn't everybody's cup of tea. That said, with ever-increasing standards of authenticity prevailing throughout the hobby, taking the trouble to build super-realistic track (or paying a specialist to do it for you) is increasingly seen as worthwhile.

But to return to the mainstream: off-the-peg track for modern 00 RTR. What are the choices? Basically, one of two options: using sectional trackage systems – available from Bachmann, Hornby or Peco – or opting for the Peco Streamline flexible trackage system.

Sectional tracks

Any sectional track system is, by its very nature, full of compromises. It is restricted in scope and rigid in geometry, while the need for it to be robust enough to withstand juvenile handling and repeated assembly and dismantling will call for a 'beefy' construction that will be at odds with any pretensions to fine appearance. In terms of a 'proper' model railway with aspirations to authenticity, these are major drawbacks. So, in the context of a book primarily concerned with realistic railway modelling, sectional track systems don't have a great deal of relevance – which is why they only rate a passing reference in these pages.

In the bad old days, every make of sectional track had a mutually exclusive geometry, rail section and sleeper base height – which meant that they couldn't be intermixed. The situation today is somewhat different, in that the three main manufacturers noted above use a common geometry, sleeper base and rail section (Code 100 FB) as well as a set of standard curve radii, denoted as first, second and third radius curves. The three radii chosen – 317mm/12.5in, 438mm/17.25in, 505mm/20.0in – are all extremely tight by any scale-modelling standard, which means the accompanying turnouts are also undesirably tightly curved and hence unrealistically short.

True, the modern sectional track systems are more comprehensive than was traditional with trainset fare; as well as the three radii of curves and a modest selection of different turnouts, all three ranges offer a good selection of standard units of different lengths and a matching 'flex track'. The Code 100 rail is not as gross as some of the massive ironmongery used in the past, while the sleepering, too, is at least 'open' rather than solid, even if it bears little resemblance to the British prototype in matters of size and spacing. But this track is still a long way from being anywhere near as realistic and authentic as modern RTR locomotives and rolling stock, while the turnouts are of a totally unprototypical layout and geometry. They are also all of the dead-frog design – to avoid any additional wiring while retaining the 'plug together' format – and hence don't make for the best slow running.

The role and intent of sectional track is rather different to the requirement posed by the type of built-on-a-baseboard, scenic model railway being considered in these pages. In this context, the limitations imposed by using sectional trackage far outweigh the convenience of its 'plug-and-play' capability, while extreme robustness will not – we hope – be necessary. A flexible track system is far more suited – which, in readily available British 00 terms, comes down to one product range: Peco Streamline.

The Peco Streamline system

Peco has dominated the UK track market with Streamline for very many years and has also carved out a very large slice of the European H0 track market and is a significant player in the USA to boot. That they can achieve all this with the same basic product tells us two things: it's well-proven and of good quality, but it must – given the different scales and prototypes – be less than authentic for at least some of these applications.

In fact, Streamline is – and always has been – strictly speaking an H0 track. The sleeper size and spacing are pure H0, the sleepers being far too small and too close together to accord with British prototype in 4mm scale, while the flat-bottom rail reflects European/American practice. Only the rather chunky rail fixings give a nod towards British-style chaired track, although obtaining a sufficiently robust product probably had more to do with that! Peco, ever adept at marketing, turned the 'too busy' H0 appearance of Streamline in a British context to advantage, branding it the 'fine scale longer look'. Masterly!

This track was certainly state-of-the-art when it first appeared. The flexible plastic sleeper base was a 'first' and was far more malleable and robust than the fibre sleepering typically used at the time. It was also unaffected by climatic conditions – those fibre sleepers could do alarming things if they encountered even a hint of dampness! Streamline also came 'ready to curve', whereas the traditional flexible tracks were only flex-able once the rigid web connecting the sleepers beneath the rails had been suitably cut – a tedious task. The rail chosen for Streamline was Code 100 FB (then the standard NMRA rail size used in the USA) drawn in solid nickel silver – although steel was available as a cheaper option, 'sheridized' to inhibit rust.

To go with the new flex-track came the first ready-to-use Peco Points, which were to a similarly advanced specification. They had a one-piece plastic sleeper-base with the rails moulded in place and used neat pivoted point-blades with an ingenious over-centre spring that held them to whatever position had been selected, obviating the need for a separate point lever. The check rails and the dead frog were incorporated as part of the sleeper base moulding, and all necessary wiring to link the parts of turnout electrically was incorporated in the assembly. The geometry of Peco's turnout range is based around three degrees of curvature, classed – logically – as 'small', 'medium' and 'large'.

These descriptions equate to nominal radii of 24in, 36in and 60in on the curved roads of the turnouts; the radii are 'nominal' because the curves used are not circular, but incorporate transitions and use a prototypical straight path through the crossing. The design is standardised around a 12° diverging angle at the crossing no matter what the nominal radius of the point (that just affects the length of the lead to the crossing and hence the sharpness of the divergence at the point-blades). The various points can thus be intermixed one with another and aligned with diamond crossings incorporating the same 12° angle. Peco's pointwork is thus quite subtle and very cleverly designed. Although the geometry does not exactly follow full-sized practice, it is a great deal more sophisticated than any of the sectional trackwork systems.

The Streamline range has undergone steady development since it first appeared. Not only has the range of pointwork expanded dramatically, but the basic design has been steadily improved. Traditional dead-frog (Insulfrog, in Peco-speak) turnouts have been joined by Peco's own variant on live-frog design (Electrofrog), while finer rail (Code 75 Fine Scale) is now offered as an alternative to the traditional chunky Code 100 (Universal). Even such niceties as catch-points are now included, and there is an accompanying moulded foam track underlay system – of which more anon.

The Peco pointwork range

Peco's plain pointwork includes straight turnouts at all three curvatures, curved turnouts using a 30in inside curvature diverging from the 60in large radius and 'Y'

turnouts of small and large radius, giving diverging angles of 24° and 12° respectively. To match these turnouts there are two diamond crossings, the 12° 'long' version and a short, 24° version that matches the sharper diversion of the 'Y' point. Also on offer is a range of 'compound' pointwork that includes a tandem three-way point (one with tracks diverging to the left and right of a straight centre road) and single and double slips based on the 'long' 12° diamond crossing. The three-way uses the geometry of the medium-radius pointwork but the slips employ the sharper point-blade divergences and nominal radius of the small-radius turnout. All this pointwork is – somewhat confusingly – available in live or dead-frog formats in Code 100 Universal or in live-frog format only in Code 75 Fine Scale – except the diamonds and slips which, to ease potential wiring problems, can be had in either format. To avoid confusion, it's worth

*Below: **About as good as 4mm scale mass-produced, ready-to-use pointwork gets at the moment. This is a Peco Code 75 'Fine Standard' medium radius in all-live (Electrofrog) form. In terms of British steam-era modelling, the rail is a (commendably delicate) FB section, although that is a lot less noticeable to British 4mm eyes than the too-small, too close H0 sleepering. However, the all-rail frog is a vast improvement on the older plastic types.***

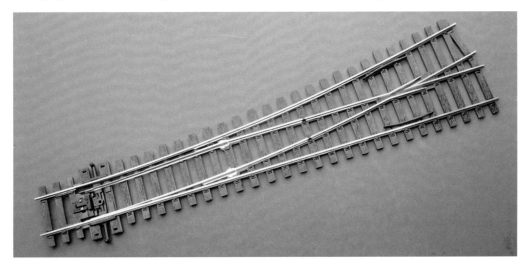

Above: A fully chaired double junction for 00 fine scale built with PCB sleepering and Code 75 bullhead rail, using etched-brass fold-up chairs to match the rail height to C&L flexible track. The underlay is Woodland Scenics expanded-vinyl foam.

pointing out that Peco product numbers prefixed plain 'SL' denote dead-frog Code 100 turnouts, the same numbers with an 'SLE' prefix are live-frog versions of the same thing, while an 'SL-1' or 'SLE-1' prefix denotes Code 75 Fine Scale.

4mm scale bullhead track

Bullhead flexible track in 4mm scale has been available in Britain for quite a long time – originally from SMP of Warwick and more recently from C&L. These tracks use Code 75

bullhead rail with moulded plastic sleepering to typically British sleeper size and spacing and are produced for 00, EM and P4 gauges. They also offer a choice of rail materials – nickel-silver, steel and – in the case of SMP – phosphor bronze. SMP track has the rail sitting level with the tops of the sleepers and a 'generic' chair lacking any keys, whereas the C&L uses a prototypical chair design that lifts the track about a third of a millimetre above the sleeper, in accordance with the inch or so of base thickness found on a prototype chair. A third of a millimetre may not sound much, but it makes a surprising difference to the realistic look of the track, which is further helped by the accurate outline and better detail incorporated in the C&L chairs – a reflection of their more recent origins.

Unfortunately, while it is relatively cheap and straightforward to tool up to produce plain flexible BH track, the opposite is the case for pointwork. SMP has in the past, sold a rather basic normal turnout of 36in radius with a plastic sleeper base in 00, but no comprehensive range of economically priced ready-to-use BH pointwork has been produced by either manufacturer. Reliance has instead been placed on the use of kits of parts for certain point types or the supply of individual components and templates, to enable the enthusiast to build his own pointwork to match these flexible tracks. C&L can supply turnouts ready-built from their own components – but these are effectively hand-built to order and have commensurately high prices. There are a good number of independent specialists who also offer a custom trackwork-building service; try the online UK model shop directory www.ukmodelshops.co.uk for contact details.

Hand-building 4mm track

The how-to of building track and pointwork in 4mm (or any other scale) is a huge subject, far beyond the scope of these pages. All I can do here is give a brief run-down of the basic options and suggest a few sources for help and guidance. So – there are three commonly used approaches to hand-building 4mm scale track. The oldest-established is the ply-and-

rivet system devised by Joe Brook-Smith, a pioneer of fine scale modelling in 4mm scale; the rails are soldered to rivets inserted into ply sleepering – a technique with over half a century of use. The next arrival on the scene was PCB-based trackwork, pioneered by Firmway back in the early 1960s and adopted and refined by SMP, while latterly, we have seen the arrival of several all-plastic trackage systems using components glued together with solvents.

The Brook-Smith ply-and-rivet system is propounded by the two specialist 4mm Societies, EM and P4, reflecting its long association with fine scale modelling. Sleepers are made from 1mm thick ply – pre-stamped to size for plain track, supplied in strip form for pointwork. Holes of 1mm diameter are drilled in the ply at chair locations, and small copper rivets with 2mm diameter heads inserted and spread to secure them. The Code 75 BH rails are then soldered to the rivet heads, which also give the requisite 0.33mm clearance between the rail and the sleepers. Pointwork is built over printed templates, of which a wide selection is available in EM and P4 from the specialist societies. 00 modellers can use the C&L templates sold for use with their plastic components. Nowadays, chair detail is usually added to the bare ply-and-rivet track, using either cosmetic cast, fold-up etched-brass or moulded chairs adapted from

Above: Track construction underway (amid usual untidy clutter) chez Rice. This is the three-way point at the entrance to 'Trerice', being built (sans template) by the methods advocated in my book Finescale Track *(Wild Swan Publications, 1991): a ply and rivet 'skeleton' with C&L plastic chairs used cosmetically, all to match C&L Flex-track. Once again, the underlay is from Woodland Scenics.*

Below: Beattie well tank No. 30586 rumbles out from under the road causeway and enters Trerice yard over the three-way point seen under construction in the preceding picture. The ballast is Woodland Scenics, and the finished track has been carefully painted and weathered with real china-clay dust.

the all-plastic systems. Ply and rivet track is reasonably robust, cheap, adaptable and can be made to look very realistic indeed, but it is laborious to build.

PCB-based track uses sleepering cut from $\frac{1}{16}$-in thick copper-clad Paxolin sheet, or printed circuit board (hence PCB). The rail is usually soldered directly to the copper surface of the sheet, although track built thus lacks the prototypical clearance between sleeper and rail-foot. The SMP flexible track is also made without this clearance so that it matches PCB-based pointwork – SMP having long been the champions of PCB-based systems. They sell point kits that include templates for 00 or EM, nickel-silver rail, all the necessary PCB sleepering and a few sundries such as prepared tiebars. Shaping of components like crossing vees and point blades is left to the modeller, however. The necessary electrical isolation for PCB track is provided by cutting gaps in the copper surface of the sheet – the most tedious part of the track-building process, which is otherwise quick and painless. PCB-based track is easy to adjust, and – due to the continuous solderable surface – readily facilitates the construction of complex pointwork. It is also economical in price and very robust – probably the only hand-built system that will stand lifting and re-laying. Traditionally, fillets of solder were used to represent chairs, but more recently fold-up etched brass chairs have become available. These not only facilitate a more realistic PCB track, but provide the necessary rail-to-sleeper clearance to enable PCB-sleepered pointwork to match the C&L flexible track.

There are currently three all-plastic 4mm track-building systems on the market: C&L, Peco Individulay and Exactoscale/The P4 Track Company. All use moulded plastic sleepers in conjunction with plastic chairs or base plates that are threaded on to the rails before laying. These are then chemically welded to the sleepering using a plastic solvent such as Butanone. The three systems differ in their intent, however. C&L's 'Jack of all Trades' range is by far the widest, covering steam-era BH and more modern FB track, with wooden or concrete sleepers and a good selection of chair types. Their point kits include many pre-finished components such as ready-made crossing vees and fully shaped point blades, and they have a comprehensive selection of templates for 00, EM and P4. Peco's range, by contrast, is very limited and is aimed at modellers of the modern scene, providing only for FB track using Code 83 rail secured with bolt-down or Pandrol clips. Timber and concrete sleepering is offered, and the range includes conductor-rail supports for third-rail electrics. The components are adaptable for 00, EM or P4, but no templates are provided. The Exacto range is, as its subtitle suggests, only made for P4 use. The point kits are self-jigging and are very complete, with all the specialist chairs and pre-finished point blades and crossing assemblies. The track is modelled on the S1 chair design used by the LNER and SR.

All the plastic ranges produce very realistic pointwork. In terms of the work involved, however, they are up there with ply-and-rivet – while it must be said that the result is not as robust as the soldered systems. It's also quite tricky to adjust plastic pointwork, as the solvent welds the chairs very firmly to the sleepers and cutting them free again involves some ticklish work with a sharp knife or razor saw. The plastic systems are also considerably more expensive than either ply or PCB. The latter is probably the most popular choice for handmade pointwork in 00 gauge, with a good compromise between ease of construction, robustness and appearance.

N scale track

The situation with regard to ready-to-use track in N scale is an almost exact duplicate of that in 4mm, with the Peco Streamline flexible system the alternative to a selection of sectional systems that are if anything even more compromised than their 4mm equivalents. The need for robustness makes most sectional N truly 'clunky', with grossly oversize rails and monstrous sleepering, while the point motors or manual throw mechanisms often incorporated with the pointwork are –

of necessity – very large in relation to the size of the point itself. This results in hugely over-wide track centres, while – to take advantage of N scale's potential in tight spaces – curve radii of eye-watering tightness are often used.

As in 4mm, Peco offers a bewildering range, with two parallel N scale Streamline track systems – confusingly labelled 'Universal Standard' and 'Universal Fine', both produced with either timber or concrete sleepering. The Standard system uses a tall-but-narrow rail of Code 80 which was originally designed to accommodate the very deep NEM-profile

flanges of early N scale products, almost all of which originated in Germany. When N spread to the USA, these monster flanges – as well as looking horrible on typical small-diameter American wheelsets – caused all sorts of clearance problems under low-slung American rolling stock. Once the scale became established there as a serious modelling alternative to H0, a far more refined 'Lo-Profile' N scale wheel was not long in appearing and being adopted. I'm glad to report that these finer wheels have now spread to British N, to the great advantage of its appearance.

Top: Peco Code 55 'Universal Fine'(!) N scale track on the Launceston Club's 'Lydtor' layout. Careful painting and ballasting makes for a more realistic PW. The HST is a detailed, weathered and close-coupled Farish model.

Middle: A Peco N Code 55 'Universal Fine' medium radius turnout on 'Lydtor'; the actual point blades are in Code 80 rail, common to the 'Universal Standard' track, but the general appearance does benefit from the lower-section rail.

Bottom: Concrete-sleepered Peco Code 80 'Universal Standard' track on the Croydon Club's 'Acton Main Line'. Again, careful ballasting and painting is the key to realism on this superb modern-prototype exhibition layout. The Class 47 is Farish, but lowered on its bogies; what a difference that makes! Graham Baseden

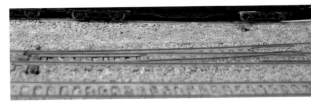

Finer wheels in the USA soon produced finer track, with Code 55 rail becoming the new N scale standard. Peco responded with a Code 55 system of their own that, ingeniously, used a smaller visible rail section but maintained robustness by achieving this with a deeper rail partially 'buried' in the moulded sleeper base. Logically, this new track should have received the same 'Fine Scale' description as the Code 75 version of Streamline in 16.5mm gauge, but here Peco became hoist with their own 'Universal' petard. It soon transpired that the new 'fine' track would, in fact, also accept British and European N scale equipment fitted with deeper flanges. Not wishing to imply that the Code 55 system was only suited to the new finer wheels, Peco fell back on the description 'Universal Fine' – even more of a nonsense than plain 'Universal'. How much simpler life would be if we called a spade a spade and revived the old 'coarse' and 'fine' labels! Not the done thing in marketing-speak, one suspects …Actually, the success of the Code 55 system in N has, in many ways, made the older Universal Standard Code 80 redundant, but it is still around, so there must be a demand. There's no problem joining one system to the other with the standard rail joiners.

The extent of the N scale pointwork range almost equals that in 16.5, the notable absentee being the three-way point. As with all Peco turnouts, the N scale versions incorporate switching and the over-centre spring for blade alignment. The Code 80 points can be had in live or dead-frog variants, the Code 55 in live-frog only. The exceptions to that rule are the Code 55 diamonds and slips which, as in 16.5mm gauge Code 75, are available with dead frogs to ease the wiring. The turnouts are offered in 'medium' (18in) and 'large' (36in) radii, but unlike the 16.5mm range, the diverging angle is not constant. The medium radius gives 14°, the large radius a mean 8°, shared with the long diamonds and slips. There is no 'small radius' turnout or short diamond, although the Code 80 range can use the 9in radius/22½° Setrack turnout and matching diamond in these applications.

Above: This is 2mm fine scale track on Martin Allen's 'Haverhill South' layout. Code 40 rail and PCB-sleepering – components from the 2mm Association. Graham Baseden

Hand-built trackwork in 2mm scale

Hand-built turnouts for N scale are rare but not unknown. The PCB-sleeper system as described for 4mm scale is most commonly used, with Peco rail and purpose-made PCB sleepers from SMP – which match the Peco plastic sleepers in outline and thickness. The Peco Code 80 rail is readily available under code IL4X, but the 'embedded' code 55 rail is quite unsuited for hand-built track and is anyway not supplied separately. For constructing pointwork to go with Peco Code 55 flexible track, the normal option is to use Peco's Code 60 Z gauge rail, which is available separately under Code IL1X. Peco also supply the point blades used in their N scale Code 80 turnouts as a separate item, IL61.

Fine scale 2mm track also uses PCB constructional techniques, but with a much thinner sleeper strip and a code 40 BH rail section. These components are only available from the 2mm Scale Association, but it's unlikely any aspiring 2mm fine-scaler would not be a member. The resulting track is robust but delicate in appearance.

0 gauge track

It'll be no surprise that when it comes to ready-to-lay 0 scale track, Peco is once again the main provider. What is even nicer to report is that Peco's 0 gauge range includes traditional

British BH PW, with nicely moulded plastic chairs on sleepers of correct scale dimensions set at the correct spacing. The rail used is a Code 124 section that, while not a true BH profile, is very close, having a slightly squared-off foot to improve the 'grip' in the moulded chairs. The subterfuge is only apparent on close scrutiny.

As well as the plain flexible track (timber sleepers only) there is a basic range of ready-to-use pointwork incorporating live-frog electrification. Check rails are adjustable to suit different wheel profiles, which does give some validity to the 'Universal Fine' description, while switching and an over-centre spring are included. The ready-to-use turnout range includes catch points, plain left- and right-hand straight turnouts and a 'Y' turnout, a long diamond crossing and a double slip. The nominal radius of the pointwork (described as 'medium', although other curvatures have yet to appear) is 72in, with an 8° diverging angle. Peco also offers an 0 gauge FB track using Code 143 rail on wooden sleepers, with matching plain left-hand and right-hand turnouts with the same geometry as the BH versions.

As might be expected in the 'Senior Scale', hand-built track is also widely used, with several specialist ranges available – some dedicated to modelling the PW of a particular pre-Grouping company. The largest and most accessible component range comes, once again, from C&L, and equates very much to their 4mm product – just twice the size! However, PCB and ply-and-rivet also figure at this scale, as does traditional track using slide-on cast metal chairs nailed to wooden sleepering – good for the garden.

Narrow gauge track

Peco again, has ranges covering everything from 6.5mm Nn3 up to G scale, (1:24 scale on 45mm gauge track). The most relevant to the sort of modelling covered in this book are 009/H0e, 00n3/H0m and 0-16.5. These are, respectively, a 9mm gauge track with Code 80 FB rail for use at 4mm scale to represent a 2ft 3in gauge or at 3.5mm scale to give 2ft

6in/660mm; a 12mm gauge Code 75 FB track to give 3ft gauge at 4mm scale or metre gauge in H0, and a 16.5mm gauge Code 100 FB track with sleepering at 7mm scale to give a 2ft 4½in gauge. The specification of the flexible track and pointwork equates to the standard gauge equivalents. The 00n3 track is also used as a standard gauge track by some modellers building to 3mm scale on 12mm gauge.

Minority scales –
3mm and 2mm finescale, S scale

Unsurprisingly, there is no off-the-peg track available for these scales, so it's down to hand-building. Membership of the relevant societies is essential to acquire the necessary technical information and components, especially rail. Most track in the two smaller scales is PCB-based, although the 3mm Society does have a

Below: Some ingenious and highly realistic 'secondary' PW in fine-scale 0 on 'Arcadia' by Martin Brent. 'Arcadia' was a fictional-but-convincing extension of the Colonel Stephens' light railway empire, and here Martin has caught the look of light railway trackwork to perfection using C&L Code 124 BH rail, spaced off PCB sleepers using tiny pieces of 4mm Code 75 lying on their sides. This raised the rail from the sleepers by just the right distance to allow C&L plastic chairs, cut in half, to be applied cosmetically. The result combined the ease of building, strength and adjustability of PCB-based track with the realism of detailed plastic chairs.

Above: Some utterly convincing light railway track in S scale by Barry Norman on his evocative model of the Bishop's Castle Railway. The basic ingredients are once again from C&L, the 'normal' 4mm scale chairs and Code 75 rail being just right to represent the lightweight rail and older, smaller chairs of the BCR in the slightly larger scale. Sleepers are cut from 1mm ply and the ballast is largely herbaceous!

plastic component system for chaired track. S scale usually uses ply-and-rivet construction embellished with cast cosmetic chairs, with BH rail of Code 95 (the old BRMSB standard BH of half a century since). S scale modellers also adapt a lot of 4mm. scale components for lightweight BH or FB track, using a variety of rail sections. Great stuff if you've got the hair shirt…

Track underlays

Real track is laid on a deep bed of stone ballast that both supports it and holds it in place while allowing it to flex. This raised ballast bed, with its neatly shaped 'shoulders', is a highly visible characteristic of the permanent way. Model track also benefits from a supporting bed that imparts some degree of resilience to the permanent way, a function fulfilled by

a track underlay of some sort. Model track underlay has an additional function over the real thing, in that it absorbs unwanted noise and vibration produced by the mechanisms of model locomotives, which can cause the baseboard to resonate. All manner of materials have been tried over the years to perform this role, but two basic options have consistently proved successful: cork sheet or foam rubber.

Cork is the traditional choice and nowadays is sold either in sheet form to allow for pointwork or multiple tracks, or as shaped strip for a single line of track. The usual thickness is 4–5mm – which gives the right look for plain ballasted track while being thick enough to do an effective job of absorbing sound and imparting resilience. The cork is glued in place on the trackbed, taking care to get it smooth and flat. The track is then laid on top of the cork and finally ballasted and painted. The principle range of cork underlays products is Carr's, sold by C&L for use with their flexible and component tracks. The single-track strip has chamfered-off ballast shoulders and is split down the centreline, the idea being that it can then be easily aligned to a track centreline drawn on the baseboard.

Foam underlays come in two formats: sheet and strip material, very much as described with cork; or as dedicated 'inlay' systems for specific track systems. Peco, in particular, offers a full range of foam 'ballast inlay' strips and bases to match all their track sections. These are moulded with indentations to match the sleepering of the track, which then sits in the foam up to the level of the sleeper-tops. This type of underlay is thus a locating/retaining system as well as a resilient trackbed. The drawback is that the moulded foam inlays don't allow scope for the addition of scale cosmetic ballast; the foam itself represents the ballast, which isn't terribly convincing – although careful painting can help.

Unlike cork, the foam systems come in a range of different densities, from very soft to quite firm and resilient. Generally, the softest foams are those used for the moulded ballast inlays, and there is no doubt that track laid 'floating' (more on that in a moment…) using this type of material is beautifully quiet and accommodating, giving very nice quality of running. Sheet and strip foam such as Woodland Scenics expanded vinyl or Exactoscale's high-density foam is used in the same manner as the equivalent cork underlay, and as the same 4mm or 5mm thicknesses are offered, it is possible to mix the two materials on the same layout. My own personal preference is to use a soft foam such as Woodland Scenics below plain track, but Carr's cork under pointwork, especially where this is being hand-built in situ. It's quite hard to construct trackwork on a soft base, which allows things to move about somewhat when you'd rather they stayed put! The Woodland Scenics strip underlay comes in the same format as Carr's cork – chamfered off shoulders and a centreline split.

To glue either cork or foam underlay to the trackbed, a single-surface, general-purpose contact adhesive like Bostik 1 or UHU is quite adequate; there's no need to become involved with heavy-duty sheet-laminating glues like Evo-Stik or Thixofix. Cork can also be stuck with PVA 'white glue', but this is generally ineffective on foam rubber. Ideally, you want an adhesive that allows an initial period of 'slip', to allow time to get the underlay accurately positioned before the glue 'grabs'. There's no

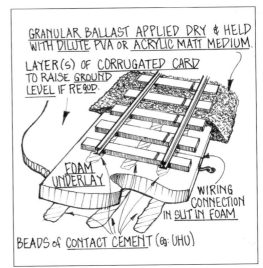

Above: Resilient track on foam underlay.

need, either, to try to get a continuous film of glue over the whole surface of the underlay/trackbed join; beads along each edge and up the centre are all that is needed.

Tracklaying: floating or fixed?

The way that the track is attached to the underlay and trackbed has an enormous influence on the quality of running of the finished layout. The key factor is the degree of resilience allowed, which will determine not just how noisy the layout is, but will also have an effect on the reliability of the electrical pick-up, the haulage power of the engines and the track holding of the rolling stock. Generally speaking, the more unyielding the track, the more problems of noise and vibration interfere with smooth operation. Vibration is the big problem. Not only does it generate that unwelcome soundtrack, it also interferes with the contact between the wheels and the rails on which running quality ultimately depends. With the far higher quality of modern mechanisms, things are nowhere as bad as they once were, but everything that we can do to absorb this unwanted movement will help with the quality of running.

Obviously, we need to ensure that the

track stays where it's supposed to be and doesn't wander hither and thither about the baseboard, but the degree of rigidity imparted by the fixing system is an important factor. At one extreme, you can have 'fully floating' track, which is track that has no direct connection to the baseboard at all; the track is attached to the underlay – usually by occasional dabs of adhesive – and the underlay is in turn glued to the baseboard. The track is thus free to move to a considerable degree in relation to the trackbase, the amount of freedom depending on the firmness or otherwise of the underlay. Peco Streamline sitting in foam ballast inlay strip, held with a dab of Bostik under a sleeper every few inches, produces a very effective fully floating track that provides running of almost uncanny silence. It is ideal for hidden track, ensuring that 'offstage' trains are neither seen nor heard.

However, full-floating track like this is not always practicable. With such a system it's difficult to obtain an exact alignment, as the track can move sideways as well as vertically, while it can also loose its 'top' and bow upwards. So it's usual to add just a few locating pins to maintain vital alignment – an approach described as 'semi-floating'. The important thing here is to make sure that the track has enough freedom of movement on the pins to allow it to flex slightly in the vertical direction; that is, the pins are not driven home firmly, but held to the point where the pinhead is half-a-millimetre or so clear of the sleeper-top when the track is in its 'rest' position. That way, there's less danger of the pins transmitting track noise to the baseboard, while the track will retain that desirable degree of 'give'.

'Fully-fixed' track is much more firmly attached to the trackbase, and is usually associated with the use of cork underlay. It is a system of tracklaying sometimes used in fine scale work in conjunction, particularly, with complex hand-built pointwork built in situ, where precision of alignment and the maintenance of a true 'top' through a formation made up of lots of small track units – crossings, short closure rails, closely fitted point blades and so on – takes precedence

over ultimate resilience. The technique revolves around gluing prepared sleepering to the cork underlay, then soldering the rails in place. Trying to do this in a floating track context would obviously be rather difficult!

For most model railways using pre-made track, the semi-floating system is the best compromise and is simple enough to adopt. Peco's steel track pins are fine for location, and a contact adhesive like Bostik 1 or UHU will do the rest, while the right method of ballasting will finish the job off. But first there are a few other tracklaying techniques to get to grips with.

Cutting, joining and aligning flexible track

Traditional sectional tracks incorporate the joining and aligning system in each discrete track unit. Flexible track, by contrast, comes bare-ended, leaving the business of joining one section to another to the user. There are a number of different ways of doing this job, but the usual approach is to use a push-on rail joiner of some sort, so that's what I'm concentrating on here. A rail joiner does the job that a pair of bolted fishplates do in real trackwork, and for that reason they are sometimes described as such. A typical rail joiner like Peco's effectively combines the side alignment provided by fishplates with vertical location, achieved by use of a base section that makes a tight fit on the foot of the rail.

First essential in using joiners is to make sure that the rail-end is in a fit state to accept the joiner. This means that it is necessary to use the correct techniques to cut track where this is trimmed to length. There are two approaches: sawing or snipping. The trouble with the use of a saw is that it puts a lot of strain on the track – the use of a track-cutting block (a wooden or plastic block with grooves to fit the rails and support them while the saw does its worst) is essential, and a fine-toothed razor saw is preferable to something like the Junior hacksaw sometimes suggested. Opting to snip the rails with a purpose-designed shear such as the Xuron Track Cutter puts far less

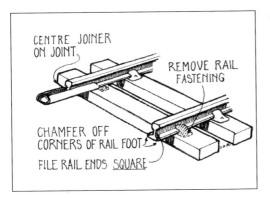

CENTRE JOINER
ON JOINT

REMOVE RAIL
FASTENING

CHAMFER OFF
CORNERS OF RAIL FOOT

FILE RAIL ENDS SQUARE

Above: **The essentials of a joint in flexible track.**

strain on the track, although it won't produce such a square cut. A bit of work with a fine file may be needed to get a nice true end, while taking a whisker of metal off the corners of the rail-foot will ease the fitting of the joiner. Even pre-cut ends on pointwork or complete track lengths will benefit from this treatment.

It will also be necessary to trim back the rail fixings nearest to the joint to make room for the rail joiner. With N scale Streamline Code 55 track, the technique is to remove the last sleeper adjacent to the join entirely and replace it with the special 'joint sleepers' supplied with the N scale rail joiners (Peco SL310). The Peco pointwork has the necessary clearance for rail-joiners built in to the sleeper base. The rail joiners are best pushed on to the prepared rail-ends using a pair of fine-nose pliers to grip the base of the joiner. While there are no rail joiners specifically made for Code 75 BH track such as SMP, the Peco N joiner also serves very well in this role and makes a surprisingly good fit on the BH rail foot.

A well-made rail joint will preserve the line of the track, both in avoiding kinks, dips or bumps, and also in keeping the sleeper spacing correct. Where a join comes on a curve, avoiding kinks is not always easy. For this reason, it is well worth taking the trouble to arrange matters to avoid such things as far as possible – even at the cost of perhaps not making the most economical use of the track lengths. However, a few curved joints are almost inevitable, so the bullet will need to be bitten at some stage. In the USA, where expansive layouts with lots of long curves are common, the technique used to get smooth curved joins involves pre-joining several lengths of flexible track before they are laid. However, owing to the fact that the inner rail on a length of track that has been curved will finish up in advance of the outer rail, this results in staggered joins and the loss of rather too many rail fastenings for comfort, at least with Peco track.

The usual approach is to trim back the inner rail to match the outer and thus preserve a 'square' join. This is made in the usual way, but with great care; once everything is aligned, many modellers solder the rails firmly to the joiners to make sure that the alignment is preserved, come what may. At the very least, a few extra locating pins in the approach to the joint location can help take the lateral strain of the track's natural tendency to try to straighten itself out off of the actual rail joint. Peco track, fortunately, is by nature very flexible (especially with the finer rail sections) and thus presents less of a problem in this regard.

Ballasting

Unlike the real thing, model track will function quite happily without a grain of ballast in site; it just won't look very convincing. Good ballasting of model PW is actually quite a demanding and time-consuming business. Bad ballasting, on the other hand, can wreck both the running quality and appearance of the best-laid track, so it is worth taking the trouble to do the job right.

There's absolutely no point in carefully laying your track to get a nice resilient ride and quiet running if you then lock the whole assembly rigid in a ballast mix that sets off like military-grade concrete. This is exactly what the oft-recommended mixture of 'real stone chippings' and a high-strength woodworking glue like Resin W will do. No; what we need is something that remains flexible when dry and which, hopefully, improves the sound-deadening qualities of the underlay rather than negating them. So long as the glue provides enough of a bond to keep the ballast in place, then all will be well. High-strength bonding is counter-productive, not just on the noise/resilience front, but also should you need to adjust, lift or re-lay track. Resin W and granite chip ballast calls for high explosive when you come to remove it!

The ideal ballast material for model track is light in weight, non-abrasive, relatively soft,

Below: The last stage in the tracklaying process – the final painting and weathering of laid and ballasted track. This is C&L 00 flexible track on Andrew Duncan's 'Maiden Newtown', glued onto Woodland Scenics foam underlay with Bostik Clear then painted overall in a grey-brown 'sleeper colour' using Humbrol acrylic paints brushed over grey acrylic spray car primer. The painted track was then ballasted 'dry' with Woodland Scenics fine light grey ballast held with dilute PVA (school glue). The final job is to pick out the rail sides and chairs in a dark rust colour, finishing by polishing the rail heads with a fine abrasive rubber block.

and easily bonded in place. It will also need to have the correct granular size to look right in the scale being used. Much of what is supplied as 'scale' ballast is actually far too coarse; the typical real ballast stone rarely exceeds 3in on its largest dimension, with most of it quite a bit smaller. Some of the stuff sold for the purpose in model shops is nearer boulders than ballast!

Traditional granulated cork is an excellent ballast material, provided the grains are fine enough and provided that it has been dyed a realistic colour; natural cork shades rarely look convincing! However, these days cork ballast has been largely overtaken by another natural material, ground nut husk. This forms the basis of the excellent Woodland Scenics ballast range, which includes a very good selection of colours and three grades of which the 'fine' is one of the few ballasts that look right in N scale. Nowadays, I rarely use anything other than this material for ballasting any trackwork below 0 scale.

To hold such material in place, all that is needed is a relatively low-strength adhesive

with good flow and penetration qualities and which does not dry 'hard'. These are, fortunately, the precise qualities of ordinary water-based PVA glues when suitably diluted and aided by a wetting agent. In this context, the common white glue sold in art and craft shops for craft use or as Kid's Glue is ideal. For economy, you can buy it in 1-gallon containers from educational suppliers; try your local county council supplies agency or the Educational Supply Association.

Ballasting – wet or dry?

There are two basic ballasting techniques, classified as 'wet' or 'dry'. Wet ballasting involves actually laying the track into a bed of PVA adhesive spread quite thickly over the underlay; once the track is laid and aligned, ballast material is poured on to the wet glue and tamped down; the surplus is removed once the glue has dried. This is a quick and simple method that effectively kills two birds with one stone, as tracklaying and ballasting are effectively combined into one operation. But it is an approach that has several drawbacks. It has to be done very quickly – within the setting time of the glue – and is thus limited to relatively small sections of track. Laying a whole yard of flexible track 'wet' is definitely a two-man operation requiring a considerable degree of slick team-work! Wet ballasting is also a little difficult to control when it comes to the appearance of the resulting PW; much depends on getting the glue bed truly even in thickness. It is also a little imprecise – the need for speed often resulting in a rather a ragged edge to the ballast.

Dry ballasting offers a great deal more control over the placement of the ballast and allows you to be very precise as to its exact depth and extent, particularly when it comes to pointwork. It is, however, laborious and – it must be admitted – a trifle tedious, but I've found it worth the trouble. In dry ballasting, the track is laid and secured in place with pins or contact adhesive, in which state it can be test-run and, if needed, painted and otherwise detailed. Once all is well, the ballast is applied dry using a spoon or similar

(those little plastic ice-cream spoons from the interval Strawberry Vanilla at the Odeon are ideal) and roughly positioned using a small pin-hammer to tap the track and 'settle' the ballast between the sleepers. Finally, a small artist's paintbrush is used to chase any stray grains off the sleeper-tops, chivvy ballast into any bald spots and tidy up the shoulders.

The dry ballast is fixed by first misting it gently with 'wet water' – which is simply normal tap-water to which a few drops of soap solution has been added to lower its surface tension and allow it to percolate the grains more readily. Cheap washing-up liquid (which won't contain Lanolin and other things good for your hands but bad for your ballast) is fine for this de-tensioning. The ballast is then secured by carefully applying diluted and de-tensioned (more soap) PVA adhesive to the wet ballast using a dropper or brush. The resulting mess (which looks horrid at this stage) is then allowed to dry thoroughly.

Painting and weathering track

Real track does not have rails with shiny silver sides, even when new. Neither are real sleepers an intense black or brown – after only a short time in situ they have taken on a pale grey-brown hue that blends into, rather than forming a stark contrast with, the ballast colours. Track is also very greatly affected by the weather and by the traffic passing over it. Even the most basic painting of the rail-sides of normal flexible track with a suitable rust shade will make a huge difference to its appearance, while going to town with a full-house paint job carefully following the colours and shades of real track will transform it. I've found grey Acrylic car primer a good basis to work on, using brushed or sprayed hobby acrylics or enamels to create the subtle colour effects. It is best to paint track before ballasting and often easier to do so before laying. A final mist of weathering sprayed on with an airbrush once the track is ballasted can often unify the finish of the track and ballast and settle everything visually into place. A little experimenting will be well repaid in the realism stakes.

Chapter 5

LAYOUT ELECTRICS

I have quite a large circle of friends and acquaintances in the model railway hobby. I can't, offhand, recall any one of them ever professing to *liking* the job of wiring up a layout. Tolerating the necessary task is about as near to enthusiasm as most modellers get. As with many of the 'non-modelling' aspects of layout construction, wiring can be puzzling, fiddly, frustrating and sometimes just plain tedious. In the context of a working layout

however, good wiring is as vital as accurately gauged track and structurally sound baseboards as a poorly wired layout will never run reliably.

The question open to debate is just what constitutes 'good wiring'. For instance, the electrical side of a local club layout in these parts was undertaken by a member who was a professional electrician (he wired-up aeroplanes for a living!). Was the result the

epitome of neatness and logic? No, it was not; Technicolor spaghetti was more like it. Oh, it worked well enough – so long as the perpetrator was on hand to trouble-shoot any problems, which he would do – with a test-meter and an unerring eye – in about five seconds flat. But if he was absent, nobody else had the ghost of a chance of finding the fault.

There is an opposite school of model railway wiring which I find is also best avoided. This is when someone whose *hobby* is building electrical circuits – a radio buff, computer wizard, electronic guru or similar – offers to wire up the layout. To these people, wiring is an art form, a rich field for intricate self-expression and inventiveness. The result will be colourful, beautifully neat, dotted about with clever gizmos, and about ten times more complicated than it needs to be. As with the spaghetti school, all is doubtless fine so long as those who understand these things are on hand. Take away the expert, however, and Joe Modeller usually hasn't a clue as to what it is all about.

To me – as a non-electrical type – the essence of good model railway wiring can be summed up in two alliterative adjectives: it should be 'comprehensible' and 'consistent'. To wire a layout successfully you need to have a clear understanding of what you're trying to achieve and the simplest means of going about it. You also need to be utterly consistent in the way you undertake the task.

Wiring basics

At the fundamental level, all model railway wiring is basically very simple, although I must make it clear that throughout this discourse I will only be considering contemporary two-rail wiring practice. This is the system used by

Opposite: Wiring – the necessary evil. Here is Don Leeper's cameo layout 'Hepton Wharf' being re-wired after the original circuitry had been in place for 14 years. A spate of corroded joints and other minor ills, together with an upgrade to include signalling and greater track sectionalisation led to a total renewal of the electrics throughout the layout.

the vast majority of model railways of all scales throughout the world, the only exceptions to this 'rule of two' being the various historical systems, which may use any one of a number of three-rail or stud-contact arrangements on either ac or dc over a range of voltages, together with some modern products of Marklin in Germany and Hag in Switzerland which stick to the old Marklin 20V ac stud-contact electrification. These are covered by specialist literature and fall well outside the scope of this tome!

The basic electrification standard current throughout the railway modelling world uses the system and values first introduced to the mass market by Hornby Dublo in 1937 – direct current (dc) at up to 12 volts, and small, permanent-magnet motors typically consuming between 0.25 and 1 amp of current. The control of speed is achieved by regulating the actual voltage supplied to the motor – the fewer the volts, the less the speed. Forward or reverse movement is determined by the direction of the current flow in the circuit – reversing the flow reverses the direction of rotation of the motor. The virtues of this system include simplicity, ease of control, economy, reliability, safety and versatility.

Leaving aside Digital Command Control (DCC) – discussed later – the usual method of powering 12V dc models is to feed the current via a controller, which is interposed between the power supply and the track and determines the voltage supplied and direction of the current flow. The two-rail wiring system uses the two rails of the track and the wheels running on them as the two 'halves' of the necessary electrical circuit; the two halves are strictly insulated from each other throughout the trackwork, locomotive wheelsets and mechanisms, rolling stock wheels, chassis and couplings and layout wiring systems. It is achieving this insulation which lies at the heart of two-rail electrification and which – in the pre-plastic age – was so hard to arrange. Praise be for polystyrene!

The normal type of model railway dc controller will present two output terminals or leads, one identified as '+' (almost invariably coloured red) and one described as '–' (coded black). To complete the circuit which will power our trains, we need to lead the electric current from the + terminal to one rail of the track, described as the 'feed rail', where it will be collected by the wheels of the locomotive on that side and led to one brush of the motor. Having done its stuff in rotating the motor armature, the current then enters the 'return' side of the circuit, being led from the other motor brush via the wheels on that side to the 'return' rail. The wheels on the two sides of the loco being electrically insulated from one another, the current has no option but to pass from one rail to the other via the motor. (It'll try to find other ways, mind – such as anything conductive in accidental contact with both rails – a condition known as a short circuit.)

Feed and return convention

You'll note that throughout my potted explanation of two-rail wiring basics, I used the terms feed and return to describe the two halves of the circuit. This clear and unequivocal division of everything into being either on the feed or return side is, in my experience, the essence of successful model railway wiring. Only when the two sides get muddled does one meet that bane of the railway modeller's life, the 'inexplicable' short circuit. There's no such thing, of course; *any* short circuit is the result of an illicit liaison between feed and return somewhere. Absolute clarity as to what side of the divide every wire, length of rail, wheel or switch is on is the key, both to avoiding short circuits in the first place and in tracking them down when they do occur.

So – how to make this clear distinction? The first essential is to decide which of the two rails is going to be the feed and which is the return. The convention that I have always used to determine this relies on the concept of 'near' and 'far' rails. The first step is to define a 'datum edge' for the layout – that is, to decide which is the *front*. Normally, this is self-evident; it's the side from which you usually view/operate, but there are situations where a layout or part of it can be viewed/operated from either side. If the whole layout

falls into this category, then it is an arbitrary decision as to which is edge is the front; but once the decision has been made it must be – electrically, at least – rigidly adhered to. Where part of a layout is 'either side', but the rest is clearly orientated, then the 'front' is decided by this section.

Why is this so important? Well, once you have a clear datum 'front' edge, you can then define any rail in any track, no matter how many tracks there might be, or how complex a formation they might form, as either a near or a far rail. My convention is that the near side is the feed half of the circuit and the far side therefore forms the return. This is reinforced by the colour-coding of the wiring attached to the two elements, such that the identity of every wire is equally clear. The really essential 'no-no' is *never* to use the same colour of wire on opposing sides of the Great Divide.

Colour-coded wiring

Few modellers would disagree that the use of a clear and logical colour code for circuit identity is the basis of successful and reliable layout wiring. This is where we amateurs differ from the wiring pro, for whom the colour or colour combinations of a wire is simply a means of identifying that particular wire wherever it appears and has no relevance to the function of the circuit of which it is a part. This might be OK for aeroplanes, computers or telephone systems, but as a basis for model railway work it's a recipe for disaster!

Unfortunately, with one or two exceptions such as DCC decoders, there is no standardised code of wiring colours to refer to, more's the pity. The result is that each model railway uses the same wiring colours in different ways. However, so long as those who have to install and maintain the wiring on a given layout know what the code is, then all should be well. So – select a colour code and stick to it, and *write it down* somewhere it can't possibly be mislaid, like the bottom of the baseboard or the underside of the control panel. It is amazing how easy it is to forget what you decided the functions of the various colours would be!

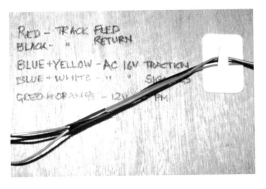

RED – TRACK FEED
BLACK – " RETURN
BLUE + YELLOW – AC 16V TRACTION
BLUE + WHITE " " SIG
GREEN + ORANGE – 12V FM

Above: If you make a note of the basic colour code on the underside of the baseboard, it will be handy when you need it and you won't get lost. Note the use of stick-on cable clips and neatly bundled wiring runs.

The colours normally readily available as 7/40 'layout wire' (see wire types below) are red, black, orange, green, blue, white, brown, purple, grey and yellow. These ten colours should provide enough possibilities to allow a clear wiring colour code for most model railways. For more complex wiring set-ups, it is possible to obtain tracer wires, where the basic wire colour is overlaid with a trace of a second colour, or even several traces. However, this supposes a level of complexity somewhat outside the definition of basic wiring that concerns us here. The key thing at this level is to make the best and clearest use of a simple code – for which ten variables should suffice.

Adopting the red and black colour convention for identifying the two sides of a basic two-rail circuit is a good starting point and I would suggest sticking to this for normal track wiring – red on the near or feed side, black for the return. Where it is desirable to distinguish between various different feed wires – as where the track is divided into section blocks or power districts, or where feeds originate from different controllers – then I use orange and brown as alternatives to red for feed colours. It is rarely necessary to divide the non-feed side of the circuit, which is normally wired as a common return, but some types of electronic controller, however, *do* call for discreet returns,

and green is my usual choice for the 'second return' where this is needed.

Within the more complex elements of two-rail trackwork there are some units of rail that need to be switched from one side of the circuit to the other, depending on the particular route selected. Most particularly, the frogs or crossing rails within pointwork wired 'all live' (that is, without sections of rail made from plastic or otherwise unpowered) will need to be switched in concert with the point blades to keep the electrical sense of the route correct. It is important to clearly identify a connection to any part of the track subject to this change of status from feed to return, for which purpose I reserve the colour grey in my wiring code.

Other circuits that must be clearly identified are the ac power supplies to electronic controllers, or used as controlled ac feeds and returns to accessories such as point or signal solenoids. Here, I use the convention of a blue wire for an ac feed and yellow or white for an ac return. The last group of circuits that need to be clearly identified are those not associated with either track power or accessory control, such as the low-voltage circuits for layout lighting. For these, I reserve the remaining two wire colours of purple and pink.

It goes without saying that no mains wiring should *ever* be mixed up with this low-voltage layout wiring. The best practice is to keep any mains voltages to the 'input' side of layout power supplies and to locate such power supplies away from the layout, only bringing the low-voltage outputs to the layout itself. Unless you're very sure about matters electrical (in which case I doubt you'll be reading these notes!) I'd suggest that by far the safest option lies in buying a dedicated cased power supply from a specialist supplier like Gaugemaster. This will be built to conform to all relevant wiring and safety codes, will be properly insulated and earthed, wired with the correct gauge and type of wire and protected by input fuses and output cut-outs of appropriate value. Long on safety and short on sorrow, in other words.

Wire types

Choosing the correct type of wire to connect up your layout is another important aid to reliable running. The best practice calls for the use of multi-stranded flex of suitable cross-sectional area for the currents involved. 'Layout wire', as widely sold by model shops and specialist suppliers, is normally 7/40-gauge copper/PVC flex; that is, it has seven strands of 40SWG (standard wire gauge) copper wire twisted into a braid inside an insulating casing of PVC. This has a current handling capability of about 1.5 amps, adequate for all normal model railway circuitry. Only for applications where greater currents are encountered, such as on some vintage toy train systems, with older 0 gauge or larger-scale models and in modern DCC power supplies, is a heavier gauge of wire called for.

Unsuitable wire types for layout use include single-core telephone cable (prone to fracture), very fine flexes such as those sold for some electronics uses, mains cables of any sort, fine single-strand wires and wires with cotton or enamel insulation. Stick to the 7/40 layout wire or – in the case of DCC systems, to the gauge and type of wire recommended by the system supplier – and you won't go wrong. Layout wire is either sold in hanks (usually 10 metres or so), off the reel by the metre, or in complete reels of several hundred metres. Buying in bulk on complete reels is the most economical way of obtaining wire – co-operative purchasing by a club or several individual modellers can produce worthwhile savings.

Wiring accessories

For the majority of model railway applications, we're talking about three basic items: switchgear, plugs and connectors. The important things about any wiring accessory used on a layout are the suitability for the purpose and the quality. Virtually none of the fundamental wiring accessories commonly used for model railways are purpose-designed for the job; rather, we adapt components intended for other, more general uses. In this context, it is important to understand what something is intended to do, and how it will function on the layout.

Switchgear

This can be a puzzling area for the electrical tyro. Not only are there many discrete types of switch, but they come in different voltage or current ratings, qualities, configurations and prices. To take these properties in order, the first thing is to establish what the switch descriptions mean and which are appropriate for model railway usage.

Switches are described first by the number of 'poles' they have, which determines how many discrete circuits that they can carry. Thus, single-pole switches carry one circuit, double-pole two, and so on. The second feature is the 'throw' – the number of alternative outputs the switch can connect to its input. A single-throw switch can only connect one, while a double-throw can connect either one of two, and so on. These descriptions are often abbreviated to a set of initials as SPST (single-pole, single-throw – a straightforward off/on switch) for example.

Switches come in different formats, of which the toggle, slide, rotary and push-button are the ones most commonly met in model railway work. For most model railway control purposes the miniature toggle switch is the usual choice, and is widely available

Below: The three most useful varieties of miniature toggle switch, the most commonly used format for model railway control purposes. From left to right, these are DPDT, SPDT and SPST. These neat little switches mount in a 6mm diameter hole in panel material up to about 5mm thick.

and reasonably priced. They usually come in SPST, SPDT and DPDT configurations, either as two-way or centre-off versions. A two-way switch has only two possible positions – 'up' or 'down' – when (except for single-throw switches), one or other set of poles will always be connected to the input. A centre-off switch has a third, mid-way position, when neither set of poles is connected to the input. Such a switch can thus serve two functions – as a selector, to choose which set of poles are energised, and as an 'interrupter' or 'off' switch, when nothing is live to the input. SPDT centre-off switches are widely used for model railway wiring using the 'cab control' system, on which more in a moment.

Slide switches usually come in DPDT format, and their principal use in railway modelling is as a reversing switch on a controller, or for point operation. They can form the basis of a very cheap and reliable point operating system, where the slide switch acts both as a point lever and point lock (to hold the point blades firmly in place) as well as a selector switch to route power to the point frog or crossing. See the point operation section of Chapter 6. This still leaves you a spare set of contacts for niceties

such as signalling or panel lights to indicate point position …

Rotary switches are used where more than two 'throws' are needed – such as in selecting between three or four possible controllers on larger layouts. The one usually met with is the 12-way Yaxley, again widely supplied by model railway retailers. This useful gadget has 12 possible power routes or 'ways' which can be arranged in a number of different configurations by adjusting an ingenious little collar on the switch shaft. Thus, the same basic switch can be set up to give a range of switching possibilities: a single-pole 12-throw, a double-pole six-throw, a three-pole four-throw, or a four-pole three throw. So long as the poles x the throws = 12, you can do it with a Yaxley!

Push-button switches are usually single-pole devices and come in two common variants: 'push to make' and 'latching'. The first is the one most often used for model railway work; and as its title suggests, it is spring-loaded to the 'off' position. When you push the button, you 'make' the circuit, and as soon as you release your pinkie the circuit is broken. The most common applications for this are to give a brief pulse of power to fire a point or signal

Below: The other common type of panel-mount switch is the slider, almost invariably supplied in DPDT format and available in standard and miniature sizes. These switches can be used in a number of ways, either treating them as two SPST switches acting together, or just ignoring any poles/ways you don't need. These switches are very cheap and reliable.

Below: Simple push-to-make push-button switches being used in conjunction with SPST toggle switches for point control; the toggle sets the desired direction and the accompanying push-button provides a brief pulse of power to fire the point motor.

solenoid, and as a protection device for 'dead ends', particularly in fiddleyards or other locations where the track is hidden. Unless the button is held down, the train will stop short of the end-of-track.

Latching push-buttons 'latch' the circuit in the 'make' position, and must be pushed again to release the connection. They're just an alternative form of off/on switch, and their main use in model railway wiring is as a 'panic button'. Wired on the input side of the controller and normally left in the 'latched on' position, they give the ability to shut down the whole layout by just 'hitting the button'. This can be a 'life-saver' when things are rapidly going pear-shaped!

The last point about switches concerns 'lifing'. Modellers are often puzzled to find what are, to the casual eye, identical switches, but selling at widely differing prices. This may smack of sharp practice, but in fact the variation in cost reflects the degree of mechanical and electrical robustness built into the switch, usually expressed as the 'life'. This derives from the number of 'operations' the switch is designed to stand up to before failure is likely, and is expressed as a power of 10. Thus, a cheap switch may only have a life of 10^3 operations (i.e. 10,000 cycles) whereas a seemingly identical but more costly item may be rated at 10^6 (1,000,000 cycles – or ten times the life). This may seem irrelevant – until you tot up the number of times some switches can be thrown in an operating session. Suddenly, 10^3 looks like a short life and a gay one! It's often wiser to pay a bit more in the first instance, especially for a club or exhibition layout where wear is heavy and reliability paramount.

Plugs and sockets

Plugs and sockets used for model railway purposes can have a number of origins. In the old days, my generation of modellers used a lot of Government Surplus components, either ex-military or ex-GPO-telephones. This was wonderful stuff of superlative quality and can still be found in use today as it's virtually everlasting. Alas, it is no longer easy to obtain! This leaves us with connecting

Left: A five-pin DIN audio plug and socket adapted to model railway use. Here, it is being used to connect a signal actuator mounted on the base of the signal to the layout wiring loom. This means the signal can easily be removed from the layout for maintenance or adjustment.

Below: Here, 21-way SCART plugs and sockets are being used to connect the control panel on 'Lydtor' to the layout. The spiral sleeving on the lower cable is a better way of 'bundling' wires than the ties used on the upper connection.

systems basically designed for audio or telephone circuitry, miscellaneous low-voltage connectors such as those meant for car wiring, or – increasingly – multi-way plugs and sockets made for computer/electronics use, many of which are ideally suited to model railway applications.

Useful audio bits include the multi-pin 'DIN' plugs and sockets and the good old GPO quarter-inch in-line jack that originated with manual telephone exchanges and is still used for microphone circuits and on public address audio and amplification systems. It is robust, reliable, easy to use, has substantial current-carrying capability and is cheap – but is limited in the number of circuits available to either two (mono jack) or three (stereo jack). It is useful for applications calling for frequent plugging/unplugging, such as removable sections or connecting power supply inputs to the layout. These days you can buy also 'miniature jacks' of 3.5mm diameter which do the same job in a smaller space, but are less robust and have a lower current rating. They're still adequate for model railway applications, however.

From telephone systems we get the modern five-way (British) or six-way (American) 'telephone jacks'. The former are little used as they have very restricted current-handling and are very fiddly to connect up, calling for use of a special tool. The US phone jack, however, has become the standard for use in DCC systems, but is almost always supplied pre-connected, either as a socket on a device or layout connector, or as a plug on the end of a pre-made cable.

From computer/digital technology we get two really useful forms of multi-way plug and socket: the 'D' series of small-round-pin connectors which come with either 11 or 21 ways, and the heavier, 21-way SCART plugs with angled flat pins. Either of these types make very good inter-baseboard connections, being available in a number of formats and as pre-made connecting leads. The difference between them lies in their current-handling capability. The miniature-pin 'D' plugs are designed for use with computer data circuits

using fine flex and are really only suitable for applications where the current levels in the circuits will not exceed 1 amp. Used with the normal 7/40 wire, they are thus fine for normal dc wiring in the smaller scales – up to 4mm/ft. For larger scales or for any layout using DCC control (where current levels are typically far higher, up to around 5 amps) then the heavier SCART components are the ones to go for. Either type is easily found and reasonably priced.

The main reason for employing a variety of different plug-and-socket types in layout wiring is to reduce or avoid the possibility of errors in connecting up the parts of the system. Thus, I use in-line jack plugs and two-pin DIN speaker plugs for dc and ac power supplies, five-pin DIN audio plugs for connecting hand-held controllers, multi-way computer 'D' or SCART plugs for linking layout sections together, miniature in-line jacks for lift-out sections, cassettes, test-leads and the like, and US telephone jacks for connecting DCC devices to the 'Control BUS'.

Connectors

These are a more permanent means of joining circuits than plugs, but without the inflexibility of a soldered joint. The most common met is the 'chocolate block' type – a strip of 12 brass screw-clamp joints encased in a flexible plastic housing. These are cheap, readily available and have a variety of uses, including connecting up point motors in an 'easy change' mode and making semi-permanent links across baseboard joins in transportable layouts. They can be ganged together or cut down to give any required number of ways and incorporate provision for screw-mounting to the baseboard framing. They are also a lifesaver for making temporary repairs to damaged wiring; a chocolate block has saved my electrical bacon at more than one exhibition!

The other frequently used connectors are those sold for automotive wiring, available in a range of sizes and formats. Most useful are 'crimp on' connectors, which enable circuits to be joined without the need for soldering.

They are particularly useful for afterthought modifications to the wiring, enabling you to add circuits – an additional feed or return, or to power-up some newly laid extra trackwork. Their virtue is that you don't have to disturb the existing wiring to make the additions. Also useful as a semi-permanent connector to things like solenoids or lighting circuits are automotive spade connectors, available in a variety of sizes and with or without plastic sleeving.

Wiring techniques

There have been ponderous text-books written on this subject, but for model railway purposes we can just concentrate on essentials. Wiring really comes down to two factors: routeing and connecting. So these are what we'll concentrate on here.

Routeing wiring in a logical and tidy manner may seem a self-evident pre-requisite – but it is actually something that takes a bit of careful thought and planning to achieve. It also requires a bit of self-discipline when the inclination is just to string the wiring any-old-how in the headlong gallop to get the trains running! Most of the potential problems stem

from the point in the layout construction sequence at which you start to think about getting the wiring in. Some people lay all the track, install all the switchgear, point-motors and so on – then wire the whole lot up as a single operation at the end of the day. Others prefer to install the wiring piecemeal as tracklaying progresses, testing everything in stages as they go along.

I've tried it both ways, but on the whole I find I get on better with the 'wire as you go along' approach. I find it easier to understand and faults show up sooner and – hopefully

*Below: **Wiring wherewithal. The tools needed for layout wiring work are mostly from the 'general' selection, the exceptions being the miniature wire-strippers (from DCC Concepts) and the cheap-and-cheerful multi-meter. This is shown set to the 1 kilo-Ohm range for continuity testing; if the needle swings over all the way, you have a good circuit while a part-way swing is a bad circuit, and no movement is no circuit at all. Powerflow flux is OK for wiring provided you clean joints afterwards with the meths-and-water mix (see Chapter 3).***

– in a more 'find-it friendly' sort of way. The disadvantage of piecemeal wiring is that it's more apt to degenerate into a jungle as more and more wires are added. A bit of trouble and discipline is needed to keep it all neat. It is also important to route wiring so that it is not prone to tangle, to avoid sharp kinks, pinch-points where wires might become trapped or crushed, and slack lengths of wire that will be prone to snag – especially important on portable layouts. However, it is also not a good idea to wire too 'tight' – there should be a little 'extra' in each wiring run to allow a tad of movement. This enables wires to be moved a bit if necessary and means that if a wire *is* snagged there's a bit of give before the load comes on the connections.

Joining wires is a straightforward soldering operation, not needing any great skill with the soldering iron. The usual small instrument iron specified in the basic tool list is the implement needed, used with an electrical paste flux like Fluxite and cored solder. To join plain wires, I always use the 'double hook' system. Trim the wire sleeve back by about 5–6mm and twist the strands tightly together; now smear the bared ends with flux, load the iron with solder and liberally 'tin' them. These tinned ends are then bent through 180° to give 'shepherd's crooks' that can be hooked together then held under light tension while the loaded soldering iron is reapplied, when 'Bingo' – you should have a nice solid joint!

Most devices sold for model railway or electronics use will be fitted with solder terminals, usually a flat 'D' shape with a hole through. Soldering a wire to these is also a case of stripping and tinning the ends, bending them 90° or a bit more and hooking them through the hole. A smear of flux and a touch with the loaded iron should complete the job. A good soldered joint should be bright silver and smooth-surfaced. If you end up with pasty-looking grey joint with a pitted surface, it's 'dry' and will lack both mechanical strength and good electrical conductivity. Dry joints are caused by dirt (is the *solder* clean?), insufficient heat and/or lack of flux – make sure you apply a good smear and hold the iron in place long enough for the solder to become fully molten and flow into a nice silvery blob.

Conventional or DC control

Until recently, this was the only control system on the block, but the growth of DCC (see next main section) in the last few years has now come to provide a complete alternative. DC control consists of three main elements: the Power Supply, the Controller, and the Track Switching or sectionalisation. (I'm leaving out point and signal control here as this need not be electrical and is anyway, described in the next chapter.) We will now look at the basic dc control elements in turn.

DC power supplies

The power supply for model railways nowadays is universally by means of a step-down transformer from the 240V ac house mains. This is obviously a critical piece of equipment and needs to be safely designed and made. I've only ever heard of one railway modeller being fatally electrocuted (and that was a very long time ago), but it is a possibility nonetheless and mains voltages should always be treated with a great deal of respect. Thus, so far as this book is concerned, the construction of mains-fed power units for model railways is not a job for the amateur. Apart from all other considerations, there's no need, as excellent and highly suitable ready-to-use power units are cheaply and widely available from the general electronics trade as well as from specialist model railway suppliers.

As we have already noted, the standard operating voltages for modern model trains fall in the range 0–12V dc, with a current rating of 1 amp or less (usually a lot less in these days of high-efficiency motors). Accessories like point and signal solenoids, however, are non-directional and usually require a bit more 'punch' to ensure reliable operation. These are designed to work off a 15–18V ac supply, as this was the usual output of the mains step-down transformer before it was 'rectified' to dc, which process usually cost around 4–6 volts, hence giving the required 12V dc output.

Traditionally, this output was used to feed a straightforward resistance-mat controller with an inbuilt reversing system, which dropped the 12V progressively to 0 by increasing the resistance between the input and output of the controller. It became usual to combine the power supply and the controller into a single unit, known as a transformer/controller or power pack providing three outputs: 0–12V dc Controlled; straight uncontrolled 12V dc Auxiliary (to power a second resistance controller), and 16V ac Accessory.

Modern power supplies do not need to accommodate this range of outputs, as all modern accessory and electronic control circuits are designed to work from a common supply standard of 16–18V ac. However, electronic controllers (which almost all contemporary designs are and on which more in a moment) usually need a 'discrete' supply, that is, a power source that has nothing else connected to it. 'Shared' power sources can give rise to electrical disturbances that will upset electronic circuitry, so for this reason, many modern dedicated model railway power supplies have two or more separate 16V ac outlets fed by different transformer tappings. You need one such discrete outlet to power each electronic controller and an extra one for the accessories. Nowadays, this need for discrete supply can also be met by using a series of low-cost plug-mounted transformers, dedicating one to each controller and one to accessories. Plug them all into a multi-socket 'power strip' and feed from a single wall socket.

The only other thing we need to know about a power supply for a model railway is the total power output it is capable of producing. This is arrived at by multiplying the operating voltage by the maximum current available, or volts (V) x amps (A), giving an answer normally expressed as 'so many VA'. Somewhere on the power pack will be a printed legend or rating plate giving this power handling figure. Whatever this number is, it represents the *total* power for the whole unit, not the power available at each outlet. So to see how much you have to play with for each controller or accessory circuit, you

need to divide the power handling, VA, by the number of outlets.

A typical dedicated model railway power supply such as the Gaugemaster model M1 is rated at 30VA for two outputs, each of which can thus provide 15VA or 1 amp at 15 volts – just right for a typical electronic controller. A dedicated unit like the M1 also has overload protection to stop these limits being exceeded. It is a good choice for the non-technical. For applications where 15VA is not enough – DCC systems, some types of accessory, high-output controllers for large scales, and garden railways – firms like Gaugemaster offer more potent power supplies. The power required for controllers or other devices is always given with the device – also usually in VA. You will find it stated either on the case of the unit or in the instructions, so it isn't a problem to match it to a suitable power supply.

DC controllers

As a controller, the traditional, simple resistance mat has a lot of limitations. These include inefficiency (a lot of the power gets turned into heat), lack of finesse of control and the chief bugbear of all – the very low voltage supplied to the track at slow speeds, when control and reliable pick-up are at their most critical. Various attempts have been made to address these shortcomings, from 'half wave' or 'pulse power' (only using half the rectifier output to produce power as a series of pulses rather than continuously) to fully mapped electronically generated outputs matched to the motor characteristics, with sophisticated feedback circuits to monitor what the motor is up to.

Apart from speed control, the controller has two other functions: it determines the direction of travel and it keeps the current flowing in the circuit to within safe limits. On traditional single-knob resistance controllers, the 'off' position was usually at 'twelve o'clock' and direction was controlled by turning the knob one way to go forwards, t'other way for aft. Simple, but not very effective, as this only allowed about a 150° sweep to the control knob in either direction, limiting still further

Above: Traditional style dc train control.
Well, antique style, really, as this Hammant
& Morgan 'Minor' is half a century old. Never
mind the patina and the linen-wound flex,
note the centre 'off' control knob, the business-
like cut-out (which operates with a racket
that tells the whole house you've got a short-
circuit), and the manly terminals on the top to
which you connect your track. Sophistication
is not entirely absent, however as there's a
screwdriver-adjustable 'shunt' which enables
you to vary the control resistance. Sockets on
the side panels give you 16V ac to the left and a
rampant 12V dc uncontrolled to the right.
*   The armour-plate case also contains the*
transformer and rectifier, with the whole thing
built like the proverbial battleship. A lot of
this superb H&M equipment is still in use,
although replacing mains flex of this vintage
is advisable; the insulation was rubber, which
can perish.

the possibilities for fine speed control. One
of the first improvements made by the new
breed of transistor controllers that arrived in
the 1970s was to separate these two functions,
with a dedicated switch for reversing and a
control knob with a sweep of 300° or more,
typically giving much more progressive and
accurate speed control.

To limit the current flowing – necessary
to protect the locomotive motor, the

controller itself and the intervening wiring
and switchgear – controllers incorporate an
'overload cut-out', which disconnects the
supply if safe limits are exceeded. This is a
condition caused either by the motor being
stalled (prevented from rotating) or by our old
friend the short circuit. Cut-outs are one of
three types: magnetic, thermal, or solid-state.
You will know right away when you've upset
a magnetic cut-out, as it'll give an annoyed
'click' as everything stops moving. Solid state
cut-outs don't make any noise but usually
switch on or change the colour of a warning
light on the controller panel to tell you that
you have a problem. Thermal cut-outs, by
contrast, are plain sneaky; they just quietly
snip off the power without announcing the
fact. For this reason they're rarely fitted these
days, and you'll usually find either a magnetic
or solid-state device; the specification or
instruction leaflet should tell you which.

It is important to know what sort you have
as ideally, magnetic cut-out should not be left
under the 'overload' condition. In fact, many
older ones had to be manually reset, but
modern ones are automatic; they just don't
like continuous operation. So if it trips, turn
the control knob to 'off' and seek out the
cause before attempting to put power back
on the track. Solid-state electronic devices,
on the other hand, can be left 'overloaded'
until the cows come home, which can be
useful in aiding the tracking-down of the
problem. As soon as you remove the fault, the
light will go out or change back to green and
everything will start running again at the same
settings as before the fault occurred. This can
cause problems of its own if you changed
points, moved engines or stock, or generally
disturbed the status quo while fault hunting.

Electronic controllers

Virtually every model railway controller sold
today uses an electronic circuit of some sort to
generate an output suitable for the powering
of small 12V dc motors. You can always tell an
electronic from a resistance controller, not
only by the label on the box, but also by the
input power required. Electronic controllers

Above: Not quite so antique – although still a couple of decades to the good – is this vintage Gaugemaster electronic controller, a very simple but highly effective design that is still around in updated form as the Model 100. It has a refined speed control with a 300° sweep on the knob and reversing by a separate switch with a centre 'off' position. The LED monitors output, and goes out (accompanied by a sharp 'click' from the auto-resetting magnetic cut-out) if you get a short circuit.

Above: Plain looks conceal the complexity of the Pendon-inspired 'Pentroller', a very sophisticated programmable device designed to cope with the requirements of 'coreless' motors like the legendary RG4 as well as controlling normal 'iron core' types. This is the hand-held version, which connects to the layout via a DIN audio plug. Most electronic controllers are available as hand-held units, which allows for easy substitution or exchange of controllers between layouts.

call for an ac supply of 15–18 volts rather than 12V dc. This is because the rectification of the power from ac to dc takes place within the control circuitry itself.

Electronic controllers address the drawbacks of the old resistance systems by taking the principles of 'pulse power' – power supplied as a series of short bursts rather than continuously – but refining it by controlling the force, duration, 'shape' and frequency of the power burst. By producing a short but powerful burst with an optimised rise and fall time (the 'shape'), delivered at an appropriate interval, the motor can

be kept turning over slowly at low-speed settings without loss of power or stalling, while keeping the actual track voltage at levels where problems with pick-up and motor power output can be mitigated. As speed increases, the nature of the output spikes also changes to give longer but gentler pulses closer together until, at full speed, the output becomes to all intents and purposes continuous and smooth.

As if this wasn't enough cleverness, the boffins then went one stage further. A dc motor and a dc dynamo are electrically identical; if you rotate the armature of a small dc permanent-magnet motor, this creates an electrical output at the brushes, the size of that output depending on how fast the armature is being rotated. On a model driven by the sort of pulsed output just described, the motor is only receiving power for part of the time, although it is (we hope!) rotating continuously. For those parts of the revolution where the motor is 'freewheeling' it acts as a dynamo and generates a small pulse of current that goes in the opposite direction in the circuit, which is known as a 'back-EMF'.

This little nugget of contrary electricity provides a handy means for the controller to check on what the motor armature is up to, which it does by comparing the size of these back-EMF pulses one with another. If they are getting smaller, then the armature is slowing down – or vice-versa. So the control circuit compensates by adjusting the duration, frequency or size of the power pulses until the required armature speed, measured by the back-EMF produced, is reached. This type of controller is known as a feedback device, in that the motor feeds back a signal that enables the control circuit to adjust itself. Clever stuff.

This is a very crude outline of what electronic controllers are basically all about. They have many other virtues and potentials, including artificial 'inertia' with programmable acceleration or deceleration rates, switchable feedback sensitivities to suit different motor types, adjustable speed control ranges, built-in braking systems and all manner of subtle refinements of the basic circuitry. They come with rotary, slider or hold-the-button speed control in panel-mounting or hand-held formats or, increasingly, in a 'split' configuration with the main circuitry in a 'black box' installed on the layout and just the control knob/reversing switch/brake (if any) in a plug-in hand-held unit. The advantage of this is that the bulky, heat-generating power part of the circuit doesn't have to be squeezed into a compact hand-held unit, some of which could get uncomfortably warm in protracted use. Many of the 'split' controllers also have a memory function, so that you can have a variety of plug-in positions around the layout.

The 'memory' enables the controller to carry on running the train 'as commanded' while you unplug the hand unit and move it to another socket; invaluable on larger layouts.

Track switching/sectionalisation

Sectionalisation is the business of dividing the trackwork of a model railway into discrete electrical sections which are energised through a switch and hence can be turned off when required. This division takes place on the feed side of the circuit, by creating breaks in the feed rail to isolate the desired length from the rest of the layout. This separated length of feed rail is then connected to the controller output via a section switch and a separate feed wire. There is no need to do anything on the return side, as an interruption anywhere in the circuit will stop the current flow. The reason for placing the section switch between the feed side of the controller and the track is so that the track is entirely electrically dead when the section is switched off – which would not be the case if the switch was on the return side of the circuit. (If you'll pardon a rather obvious analogy, there wouldn't be a lot of point putting a bath tap on the waste pipe from the plug-hole!)

As soon as you want to accommodate more than one locomotive on a conventionally wired dc layout, sectionalisation becomes essential. However, I'd argue that it is just as essential even if you only have the one engine, in that dividing the track into discrete electrical units makes it far, far easier to track down electrical problems. If you get a short, simply turning off the section switches one by one until the problem goes away will tell you which section has the problem and hence where to start looking. From this it follows that the most logical approach to layout wiring is to divide the whole of the trackwork into sections, rather than the more limited concept of simply creating them as 'parking places' where an engine might need to be isolated for operational reasons. A section can be as big or as small as you like; its essential quality is that the rail on the feed side is electrically separate from all other rails on that side and it is powered through a switch.

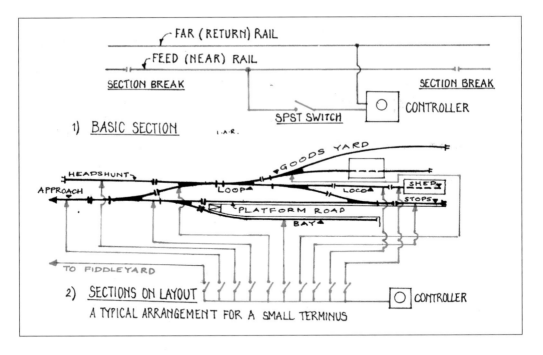

Above: Basic sectional wiring.

Below: Basic cab control for two controllers. Selecting a section feed from more than two controller options would call for a rotary selector switch in place of the SPDT shown.

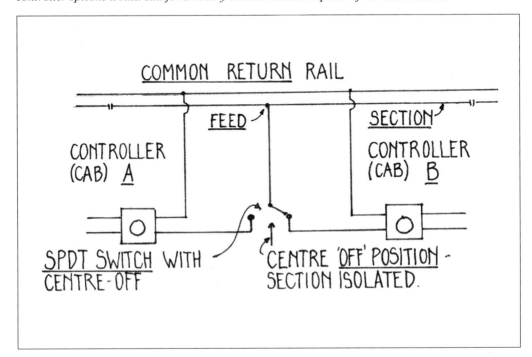

Cab control

Once you have a sectionalised layout, you can move up to the next level of control sophistication, where more than one controller is in use and hence two (or more) trains can be run at the same time. This is achieved by using an extra 'layer' of switching on the feed side of each section to allow it to receive power from any one of two or more controllers, or 'cabs'. (The term cab control is an American one, deriving from the designation of each control position as a 'cab'; multi-cab systems were first developed in the USA, where layouts have always tended to be bigger than here in Blighty.)

The essence of cab control is thus the ability to decide which controller is controlling which sections of track, or put another way, to 'switch' sections between controllers. In the case of the most basic level of cab control, using two controllers, this can be very simply accomplished with our friend the SPDT centre-off switch already mentioned. With the switch in the 'up' position, the section is connected to the output of controller 'A'; throw the switch to the 'down' position, and the section will be powered via controller 'B'. In the centre position, neither controller will be connected and the section will be 'off'.

When it comes to more complex set-ups with three or more controllers, then you need to move to a multi-way rotary switch to route the power to your section from any controller; the 12-way Yaxley type already described would enable you (theoretically, at least!) to consider any one of 11 controller options, leaving the 12th position – not connected to anything on the input side – as the 'off' option. In point of fact, this would be so unwieldy as to be unworkable, and in my experience it is rare for any given section to need the capability of being assigned to so many potential operating positions. Four is the most I've ever had to go to, using the rotary switch in its six-way x two-pole configuration. Positions 1 and 6 were 'dead', so to turn the section off you just rotated the switch to one or other end of its travel. The second set of poles was used to feed coloured indicator lights (red,

green, amber and white) so that it was clear which controller had been selected. To keep things even more logical, the controllers were always described by the colour of the light that came on when they were selected: 'red cab', 'green cab', and so on. All part of the comprehensibility requirement ...

The basic facility of cab control, the ability to link any section to any controller, can easily lead – on larger or more complex layouts – to the need to throw an awful lot of section switches before you can make a particular move. This adds undesirable operational complication and can result in frequent 'pilot error', so is best avoided as much as possible. There are two golden rules to follow in designing a cab control system, both in the cause of simplicity. The first is simply to assess which controllers actually *need* to be able to control a given section, and the other is to restrict the switching capability to meet that need. There's no virtue in having a half-dozen controller options for a section if you only ever use two of them!

The other great way of cutting down on both the number of switches (and hence switch-operations) needed and the complexity of the wiring is to consider your cab control in terms of selecting *groups* of sections rather than trying to extend the selectability to each individual section. This is called 'district' (properly, Power District) control. Any normal model railway is going to divide into logical districts: the main line (or up and down main lines on double track); the goods yard; the loco depot; the sorting sidings; and so on. Each of these districts may include as many sections as you like; the key thing is that there should not be any that will *need* to be under separate control from a neighbouring section. As the majority of layout sections are, essentially 'parking bays' that exist simply to enable a loco to be isolated, it is normal for whole groups of such sections to be able to be combined logically as a single control entity.

The cab control then becomes much simpler and more logical, as only a single rotary selector is needed for each district. The input feeds to the individual section switches within the district are simply grouped together and connected to the output of the rotary switch. Thus, one switch movement of the rotary selector transfers a whole area of the layout from one controller to another. Using this approach, I was once able to simplify the control of a large layout from a situation where some movements were calling for over 20 switches to be thrown to one where only three four-way rotary switches did all that was necessary.

Digital Command Control

What it is, what it does

The arrival of Digital Command Control (DCC) has marked the first fundamental change in the way electric model railways were controlled since they first evolved from their steam or clockwork forebears in the 1930s. Traditionally, the speed and direction of the trains had been governed by the power fed to the track as described above. Such centralised power-regulating control has a number of disadvantages, particularly in the most critical

Below: A DCC master controller. This is the British ZTC 511 which, unlike many equivalent US or European units, eschews the usual computer-keypad format and opts for controls that act in analogue format and attempt – with some success – to impart a 'railway feel' to the control functions. Far more satisfying than prodding push-buttons, although not even ZTC can eliminate them altogether!

areas of electric model railway operation – starting and slow running. If all the trains need to do is to whiz around chasing their own tails at high speed, there are few problems; but real trains don't run like that. As soon as you move away from the train set into the realms of scale model railways and realistic operation, flexibility and consistency of control and excellent starting, stopping and low-speed performance become of overwhelming importance. These are the aspects of control modern DCC seeks to address.

DCC first entered the field as long ago as 1972, when Hornby in Britain introduced their Zero 1 system – the ancestor of all modern commercial digital systems. At that time, Zero 1 was promoted as offering two-wire control, with the chief advantage being seen as the elimination of the sectional wiring associated with traditional dc systems such as cab control. In the event, this attribute of the system proved to be something of a blind alley, as a model railway of any size wired 'all of a piece' without sections becomes almost impossible to manage in the event of a fault. Modern thinking about DCC recognises that, if anything, it makes greater demands on the wiring of the layout, but this is more than compensated for by what are now recognised as its four great advantages over conventional control.

DCC – the train control advantages

The first of these is the 'onboard' nature of the system, where each locomotive is controlled by a discreet decoder circuit board or 'chip' located within the model itself. The chip is commanded by digital signals sent from the master controller and transmitted via the track. What this effectively means is that there is a dedicated controller for each individual locomotive – a controller, moreover, that can be precisely tailored not only to the electrical characteristics of the particular motor fitted but also to the job the engine is required to do on the layout. This ability to optimise factors such as the point in the control sweep at which the loco starts to move, its maximum speed and rate of acceleration or deceleration and the finesse of control, makes it possible to endow each locomotive with a unique set of operating characteristics. As on the prototype, a shunter will behave in a total different manner to a suburban tank engine or an express passenger type.

The second major advantage of DCC is that it is always consistent. Once a locomotive has had its chip programmed, it will always behave in the same way; 'forwards' will always be the same direction, the top speed will always be the same, and a given controller setting will always give the same rate of acceleration or progress. These characteristics will remain constant even if the locomotive is used with a different DCC controller or run on a different layout. They can be altered at will by re-programming, but otherwise are independent of all other factors.

A third key advantage of DCC is that such systems maintain a constant voltage level on the track irrespective of the number of trains operating and their speed, direction or loading. As this power level has been standardised at 15–20V ac, factors like dirty wheels and track, poor pick-up contact and other electrical gremlins that have long been the bane of traditional dc systems – with their much lower on-track voltages – cease to be so significant. DCC thus offers greater reliability with a lesser maintenance requirement. It also offers far greater power reserves than conventional dc systems, with as much

Above: DCC decoders as a breed are very small and often very boring too look at. Here is one, installed in the chassis of an 00 gauge 'Castle'; it's the sort of flat silvery thing tucked beneath the motor …

Below: Here's a typical DCC loco installation – in this case, in a Bachmann 57XX pannier tank fitted with a Comet chassis. The actual 'chip' is mounted inside the body, connected to the motor and pick-ups via a wiring harness routed through a sub-miniature four-way plug which enables the chip to be readily removed if required. Use of a simple 'blanking plug' in place of the chip enables the loco to operate in normal DC mode for mechanical/electrical trouble-shooting or running on non-DCC layouts. Some decoders now incorporate this last facility in the form of an inbuilt 'switch out' function.

as 5 amps of current available compared with the typical 1 amp of dc power systems.

The final trump card in the DCC hand is its enormous potential. Essentially, DCC is a fully-fledged digital computerised control system and thus, as with all modern computers, it has a huge range of capabilities that permit it to do many things at once. DCC-linked control of accessories like lighting, motor-driven fans on diesel locomotives and, of course, on-board sound systems, are already well established. The latest, third-generation, systems now incorporate 'talk back' and can 'report' information to the master control computer – information such as speed, load, direction, status of ancillaries and – most significantly – the train's position on the layout. The potential uses to which such information can be put are almost limitless, and things like integrated onboard video systems and a whole range of sophisticated special effects are now real possibilities. We ain't seen nothing yet!

Subsidiary DCC functions
As well as controlling the actual trains, DCC also has the capacity to control other aspects of the layout such as turnout direction, signalling and lineside accessories. This was originally seen as a great virtue of the system, as it offered the potential to have a wide range of power-operated functions with a minimum of wiring. The drawback has proved to be the rather cumbersome method of control, usually necessitating the entry of a multi-digit 'address code' followed by the use of command keys to activate the function. The need for a complete alphanumeric keypad plus a set of function keys has made for rather complex controllers that do not naturally replicate any aspect of real railway control and can be confusing to non computer-orientated folk. However, more recent developments in computer systems generally now offer a far greater range of control methods, and this objection may soon be overcome by control options that take advantage of the potential of the digital system in ways which are not only more convenient and approachable, but also replicate prototypical railway control systems.

Earlier DCC systems attempted to combine all the running, programming and accessory operating functions into a single control unit, resulting in complex units that required considerable dexterity to operate accurately. More recent thinking suggests the various functions of DCC are best kept separated, with aspects such as decoder programming or point operation segregated from running control. Many people now see the ideal DCC train controller as having only those functions that a real engine-driver has to play with – speed, direction of motion, power delivery and braking, plus the operation of ancillaries such as lights, whistles or horns. The only other addition might be the selection of the particular locomotive being controlled. All other aspects of layout operation are combined with the 'signalling' controls on a separate panel, in accordance with the prototypical operating philosophy that seeks to separate the train driving and signalling/route setting functions.

How DCC works
Although the actual electronics of DCC systems are quite complex, the underlying principles on which they operate are actually straightforward. The heart of the system is the master controller and its associated power supply. The master controller is the computer that generates the digital signals upon which the whole control process depends, while the power supply is just that, providing the constant 15–20V ac track voltage which powers all aspects of the DCC operation. The other key component is the decoder or chip which responds to the digital signals and controls the actual locomotive or other device such as a signal, point motor or accessory.

Each decoder has a unique address code, enabling it to determine which commands in the digital codes sent out by the master controller it needs to respond to. These commands are sent as 'packets' of digital data superimposed as pulses over the straightforward ac of the track power supply. Each packet of information includes the address code of the decoder to which it applies, plus instructions such as changes in speed, rate of acceleration or direction, or a command to stop or start. The decoders incorporate integrated circuits having memory and processing capacity. This enables them not only to respond to new commands, but to continue to carry out the last set of commands received until these are superseded. Thus, even if no commands are being sent or received – perhaps due to momentary breaks in continuity, or because a controller has been temporarily unplugged or assigned to another function – the decoder will continue to control the locomotive or other device and will carry on doing whatever its last set of instructions told it to do.

DCC choice

The galloping progress of contemporary micro-electronics allows the necessary processing power, memory and solid-state power and switching circuitry for DCC to be incorporated in ever-more-compact devices. There are now decoders small enough for Z scale locomotives, while the latest top-flight H0 or 0 scale units sport a bewildering array of features – usually representing far more capability than most of us can hope to use. Making an informed and relevant choice from among the plethora of DCC products now offered is somewhat akin to negotiating the sort of technophiles' minefield that Hi-Fi audio used to be. Bombarded with complex information, extravagant claims and (to the average buyer) more-or-less-meaningless techno jargon and mumbo-jumbo, it's difficult to decide what you actually need and what just looks impressive on the spec. sheet!

If I tried to present any sort of run-down of the current DCC market here, by the time it made print it would be well out of date. All I can realistically offer is a few broad guidelines – starting by reiterating the old chestnut that, by and large, you get what you pay for. Cheap DCC (leaving aside the DIY kits from the likes of MERG) is usually cheap because it either has very limited capabilities or it is made using lower-grade components. That is not to say that some of the more expensive stuff is as good as its price-ticket suggests – my own experience being that some of the smaller makers charge high prices but don't offer too much in the way of technical back-up – or reliability.

My own DCC product evaluation checklist goes something like this:

1) Does the system/product conform to the NMRA standards? If not, I don't want to know – no matter how clever it is, I don't want to be restricted to a non-compatible product or a single supplier.
2) Is it suited to what I actually want to do or am I buying a lot of capacity I don't need?
3) Does it use 128-step speed control? (This makes for much finer control.)
4) Is the accompanying literature/instruction manual written in plain, clear English or is it either techno-gabble or badly translated Korean? Is there a technical helpline and a decent guarantee? Or a helpful dealer/shop? In other words, someone to *talk* to when you hit a problem.
5) Is there a choice of suitable chips, especially those including a feedback feature? (This is a slightly rhetorical question as – if the system is NMRA-conformant – then you can use any make of NMRA DCC chip and someone, somewhere will have what you need. The only problem then is finding that someone!)
6) Does the actual controller have good, clear ergonomics that form a natural way of driving trains or is it either just an undesigned mess of more-or-less random knobs and switches or – worse still – an intimidating mass of close-spaced push-buttons and tiddly LCD screens? If it's a hand-held unit (and I hope it will be) then does it lend itself to easy one-handed operation?

Of these various requirements, No. 4 is, I feel, the most crucial. No matter how good the equipment is, if you don't understand how to use it properly then it's a total waste of money. This is where the quality of information – including back-up – can make all the difference.

DCC for all?

The spread of DCC seems as relentless as the advance of digital electronics in every other sphere. Decoders are already inbuilt in many RTR models in the USA, where if you *don't* want DCC it's a 'delete option'. Even here, a few RTR locos are available ready-chipped while most of the more recent RTR introductions have NMRA sockets to take plug-in decoders. So it's here to stay, rapidly getting cheaper and thus set fair to become the new standard, just as the CD replaced the vinyl disc and 'engine management' ousted a distributor and a pair of carefully-tuned SU carburettors. The advantages are manifold and undeniable. The drawback, as with all things electronic, is that if it goes wrong with it there's usually no way Joe Modeller can fix it.

Whether or not DCC is an apt choice depends greatly on individual circumstances. On my own small layouts, where everything has been optimised for conventional DC control and good, reliable running is the norm, then the DCC case is not so pressing as the benefits would not be that great and the cost – pro rata – not inconsiderable. But for a larger, more complex layout, with a larger loco stud and more complex operation, then the story would be very different. My own conclusion is that, while DCC is not *essential*, to start a new project without it would to turn your back on a lot of present and future potential. For that reason alone it's worth the investment.

Above: This is ZTC's hand-held control unit, which is far more accessible, to my mind, than the usual 'TV remote-control' format. The big red button is the 'panic stop' which freezes the whole layout when you realise disaster is imminent!

Opposite: The British semaphore signal – one of the most characteristic aspects of our railways throughout most of their history. This splendid example is preserved at the Didcot Railway Centre; it is a GWR wooden-post bracket signal fitted with later-pattern GWR steel lower-quadrant arms. It has also acquired a track circuit – denoted by the diamond plate on the main post – and a train crew telephone in the small cabinet on the left of the post. The small arm marked 'CO' is a calling-on arm that could be lowered to permit the main arm to be passed at 'danger' for shunting purposes. The free-standing case beside the signal is an outside equipment box (OEB) containing the relays pertaining to the track circuit and any other associated electrical components. Plenty to model here.

Chapter 6

SIGNALLING AND POINT CONTROL

If ever there was a minefield awaiting the aspiring railway modeller, signalling is it – for this is a subject of a breadth and complexity which merits not just one book, but a veritable library. There are indeed, some impressively weighty volumes out there, usually dealing in detail with the signalling practice of one of the old pre-Grouping or 'Big Four' companies – so at least there's no shortage of prototype information! Modern signalling is, oddly enough, less well covered – but you can at least go and study the real thing, which is never a bad option. It will come as no surprise that these notes can form but the briefest of introductions to the topic.

The first thing to say about signalling is that virtually no British model railway with any pretensions to authenticity can do without it. Unlike many overseas networks, the entire British railway system – with the sole exceptions of purely mineral and industrial branch lines – has always been entirely

controlled by a very comprehensive system of signalling, applying to all lines on which general traffic is carried. This is based on the concept of the 'block section' – a length of running line, entry to which is regulated by a lineside signal and on which only a single train may be permitted at any one time. True, in very recent times a few lightly trafficked routes have dispensed with such traditional lineside signals in favour of radio-based control systems (Radio Tokenless Block), while the latest generation of very high-speed trains are now being equipped with onboard signals triggered by lineside transmitters. But for the vast majority of Britain's railways throughout virtually their entire history, nothing moved without the say-so of a signal of some sort standing sentinel beside the track.

A very potted signalling history

In the earliest days, this signal would have been nothing more than a hand, lantern or flag shown by the railway policeman or 'Bobby' standing shivering at the lineside. As speeds rose this hand signal gave way to various combinations of balls, assorted shapes, lamps and even baskets of flaming coals, all hauled up a tall post to make them visible at a distance. These makeshifts were in turn soon replaced by the first semaphores, with or without lamps – a wondrous variety of designs including rotating discs and crossbars, fantails, vanes, butterflies and boards – but still under the control of the lineside Bobby. This worthy despatched the trains on the 'time interval' system, which relied on them making steady progress through the section without any untoward halts. This somewhat chancy method – effectively, 'see and avoid' – originated in the days before the electric telegraph arrived on the scene. This was invented in 1837 and was first employed for railway work about 1840. Many companies only installed telegraphs on their main lines, however while lesser routes stuck with time interval working well into the 1870s.

Once the Bobbies were in communication with one another by telegraph, things became much more certain; they at least knew that the train they had despatched had reached the end of their jurisdiction in one piece! Soon, they were able to retire to the relative comfort of telegraph huts, then graduate to signal cabins – often with the signals mounted on the roof before this arrangement gave way to the long-lived system of remotely worked semaphore arms on lineside posts acting in conjunction with coloured lights. These illuminated semaphore signals were gradually refined, becoming fail-safe, so that any derangement of the operating linkages caused the signals to show danger, and settling down – after a period of often over-complicated multiple aspects – to the simple, unequivocal binary system of 'on' (arm horizontal) or 'off' (arm inclined or hidden in a slot in the post). Almost all older semaphore signals were lower-quadrant, the 'proceed' indication being given by the arm inclining downwards

from the horizontal at somewhere between 45° and 90°. The arms were usually pivoted at one end, but some railways used centre-pivoted somersault arms which dropped at a very steep angle to show clear.

As train speeds increased still further (but train brake power remained negligible) it became desirable to increase the warning of the need to slow or stop, leading to the introduction of advance or 'distant' signals that presaged the indication of the main, or 'home' signal. These early distant signals usually had a 'V' notch in the end of the arm but were otherwise the same as the home signals, both types being painted red with a white stripe or dot at the outboard end. Illumination came from oil lamps shining through a spectacle glass attached to the arm and moving with it. With the arm 'on', a coloured glass – violet or ruby-red for 'home', green for 'distant' – was held in front of the lamp; when the arm was 'off', the lamp was uncovered and showed a white (well, dull yellow) aspect for 'proceed'.

Opposite: An early pre-semaphore signal of a type common in the 1840s that survived on the former North British Railway branch to Jedburgh until 1949! This is a 'rotating board' signal – face-on to the track (as here) for 'danger', edge-on for 'proceed'. In this instance it serves simply to protect the level crossing, playing no part in the block signalling arrangement, which is probably why it survived so long. Author's collection

Right: Early GWR slotted-post semaphore signals on the mixed-gauge line at Didcot Railway Centre. As with many early signals, these only gave a positive 'danger' indication, with the arm horizontal and the spectacle glass in front of the lamp (unfortunately, the lamps were missing when I took the picture). When the signal was 'off', the arm dropped into the slot in the post out of sight, and the spectacle left the lamp uncovered, so a bare post by day and a single white light at night were the only 'proceed' indications. Later semaphores gave positive indications for both states.

Right: A typical pre-Grouping lower-quadrant semaphore signal, in this case LBSCR, seen in BR days. This has all the characteristic features of the breed including a tapered wooden post, probably 14in square at the base reducing to about 10in with a cap (some had a finial) to keep the water out of the top, and a slightly tapered wooden arm about 4ft long bolted to a heavy cast-iron spectacle casting, driven by a push-rod from a balance arm on the post. In this instance, this is quite high up, and in turn takes its movement from the pull-wire from the signalbox. There is an oil lamp mounted on the post which is fitted with a backlight blinder (the fork-tailed crescent seen just below the lamp) and an access ladder on the front of the signal post, although rear-mounted ladders were probably more common.

The green spectacle glass is missing – presumably broken – so it appears as it would probably have been when new, before green replaced white as the 'all clear' colour. The track circuit diamond and OEBs denote the date of the picture, c1960. Author's collection

Below: The other main type of signal arm was the centre-pivoted 'somersault' pattern, favoured by the Great Northern Railway and a number of minor railways including, here, the Midland & Great Northern Joint. The spectacle was not attached to the arm, but linked to it by an operating rod. Somersault signals gave a very clear 'off' indication. F. G. Hepburn

The next important step was to arrange the levers controlling the various signals together in a common frame, which soon came to also include levers controlling the points, or at least those sited in a running line. This then enabled the great signalling science of mechanical interlocking to develop, where a complex system – usually made up of sliding notched bars, into which slid shaped steel bolts called tappets – 'locked' the various levers together to prevent conflicting signal indications being given or unsafe routes being set up. Further refinements – usually electrical – took things a stage further, detecting the positions of trains on the track (track circuiting) and monitoring the indications of signals, the state of the lamps and the settings of the various block instruments connected to the telegraph. The whole set-up was complex, sophisticated and largely fail-safe. Accidents there still were – but now almost always due to human error rather than shortcomings of the apparatus!

By the time of the Grouping in 1923 the art of semaphore signalling had reached

Above (left and right): Distant signals in their later, familiar form, with fork-ended yellow-painted arms and amber glasses for 'on'. The 'ordinary' distant perched on the cutting-side shows the normal movable version with spectacle-plate having a green glass for the 'clear' indication. It also shows how signals are adapted in form to suit the situation required.

'Fixed' distants (top right) are used where a permanent 'caution' indication is needed, as on the approach to a junction or terminus. The arm has no spectacle plate and is permanently mounted in the 'on' position; the lamp has an amber lens.

Right: In pre-Grouping days, the alternative to a solid wooden post was the metal lattice. Lattice signals could readily be made far taller than wooden-post types, and the GNR had some very lofty 'sky arms' on posts more than 60ft high. This more modest example, on the North British Railway, is still somewhat taller than many wooden signals. Author's collection

Left: Typical of the earlier pattern of signalbox – small and simple, with relatively modest windows – is this Highland Railway cabin modelled in 7mm scale by Simon de Souza for Laurie Griffin's 'Cluny' layout.

Opposite: The final evolution of the semaphore signal – a BR LMS-pattern steel-post upper quadrant dating from the 1950s. The upper quadrant arm was really an American innovation which was only adopted in Britain after the Grouping – and then not by the GWR! Steel signal posts like this were sometimes made out of old boiler tubes – thrifty but not, apparently, very long-lived. This example was at Inverness on the Highland line; the engine is an ex-Caledonian Pickersgill 4-4-0, heading a train of LMS Stanier 'Period 3' coaches.
Author's collection

maturity. Arm shapes and colours had become standardised, with square-ended arms painted red and carrying a white stripe for the 'home' signals, and notched 'fishtail' arms coloured yellow with black chevron markings for the 'distant'. Lamp colours too, had evolved, with red displacing violet for 'stop', green replacing clear for 'proceed' and amber replacing green for 'caution' on distant signals. Other than these commonalities, however, the detail of signal design was left to the various railway companies and their signalling contractors, resulting in an amazing variety of equipment, much of it distinctive and highly characteristic of a particular railway.

Full interlocking of signals with points became the norm, and most main lines had track circuits for train detection. The telegraph block instruments by means of which the signalmen communicated and forwarded the trains from block to block also became more sophisticated, capable of being interlocked with the signals themselves, so that these could not be cleared unless the appropriate telegraph codes had been sent. Signals were also often backed up by detonator placers worked by fogmen. These were trackside devices which could be used to slide a small explosive capsule on to the railhead when the

signal was at 'caution' or 'danger' in times of bad visibility. The resulting 'bang' (slow down and prepare to stop) or 'double bang' (stop NOW!) left the driver in no doubt that he'd passed an adverse signal!

After the Grouping, the semaphore signal continued in use, with upper-quadrant arms being introduced in the 1930s, along with power operation, all-steel posts, full track-circuiting with electrical interlocking and the introduction of AWS warning systems which reinforced signal indications by giving the driver an on-board audible warning triggered by track ramps. Large mechanical frames gave way to miniature power frames on control consoles, often fitted with train describers and signal repeaters at important signal boxes. Also in the mid-1930s the first pure colour-light signals appeared, dispensing with the signal arm altogether and using 'searchlight' beam of intense light focused on the driver's sight-line to show a red, green or amber aspect. This was produced by coloured glasses being moved in front of a bulb backed by a parabolic mirror and projecting through a Fresnell lens to concentrate the light into a very narrow beam. A searchlight signal could thus show any indication – making for greater flexibility in the signalling system, especially

at busy times or where trains were travelling at high speeds. It could also be seen from a greater distance than a semaphore, especially at night or in poor visibility.

The combination of full track-circuiting to detect train positions with electric colour-light signalling paved the way for modern automatic signalling systems, where the trains themselves control the signal aspects behind them. The three aspects possible with single-lamp searchlight signals have now been superseded by four-lamp multi aspect signals, which add another stage to the advance warning given. A 'green' now means more than two blocks beyond the signal position are clear; 'double yellow' indicates two blocks clear but the third occupied; 'single yellow' indicates one block only clear, and 'red', as always, means 'do not pass'. The advent of this system spelt the death knell of the traditional block post signal cabin, and these have now been largely replaced by a combination of trackside relay cabinets and 'district control centres', mega-signalboxes controlling hundreds of miles of track and really only concerned with route-setting at junctions, management of route occupancy and stations, and an overall monitoring role. And even much of that is done by computer!

What we need to model

As I trust will be apparent from the foregoing potted history, signalling apparatus forms a very prominent and important part of the railway scene – which means that we need to represent it on our models if these are to look right. Most modellers accept this need, but many are at a bit of a loss to know what type of signal to use and where it should be positioned. To answer the 'what' part of the question fully a bit of background research will almost certainly be needed, although if you stick to the generalities outlined here you won't be too far adrift. Positioning is a more complex matter, but some general rules plus a bit of common sense can go a long way towards the production of a credible signalling set-up on the model. This is where modelling an actual location to scale pays off – you simply copy what the prototype did!

Most of us, however, are trying to fit our signalling in either with a totally fictional layout or in the context of a prototype that has been adapted and compressed. So we have to be a bit more creative. To start with the choice of hardware, here are a few conclusions I've drawn from years of trying to get it right – starting with choosing signals of appropriate vintage for the period being modelled. The

Left: A modern multi-aspect colour-light signal. This is a three-aspect head on the West of England main line near Taunton; it can display a single green for 'clear' (block ahead and block following clear), a single amber (block ahead clear; block following obstructed) or red (block obstructed: stop). The traffic density on this route does not justify the extra amber indication used where trains run on short headways.

This particular signal is offset on a bracket to improve sighting and also carries a divergence indicator and associated describer panel, in this case protecting the entry to a station avoiding line/loop.

Below: Modelling signals form a fascinating and challenging branch of the hobby, and it doesn't get a lot more challenging than this: a superb LSWR-pattern lattice-post three-doll bracket signal modelled by Bill Rankine – in 2mm scale! Fully working, of course, it has been fitted with Southern Railway upper-quadrant arms. It was very common for older signals to receive new arms and lamps on the original posts.

key observation to make here is that signals, by and large, are long-lived things and – providing the track layout isn't altered or they don't get skittled over by some mishap – they can stay in place and in use for decades. Thus, it's quite in order to have, say, a BR-period model planted firmly in the 1950s but running under pre-Grouping signals installed half a century or so before. Many such signals saw the railways out, even if in their old age they took on an air akin to the Irishman's famous shovel; thus, a pre-Grouping tapered wooden or lattice post might sport a post-Grouping steel upper-quadrant arm in place of a lower-quadrant wooden original, lit by a new lamp incorporating electrical flame detection and perhaps displaying a track-circuiting diamond or train crew telephone of BR origin. Of course, this venerable veteran could find itself standing next door to a late-Grouping or BR semaphore with a tubular steel post, upper-quadrant arm and all-electric lighting – or even an armless colour-light.

Signal anatomy

The actual detail design of a signal would depend upon the company that originally installed it. Most pre-Grouping signals were lower-quadrant, but there the similarity ends; arm size and shape, type of post, arrangement of balance weights and operating linkages, shape and size of the lamp, positioning of access ladders and, of course, the design of the distinctive finial that capped the post – all could vary. This is where all those signalling books come in so useful; they describe and illustrate signal design in great detail. As is so often the case, as things progressed diversity became less and the type of metal-posted upper quadrants introduced by three of the 'Big Four' companies during the 1930s were all-but identical; the odd man out was, of course, the GWR, which remained resolutely lower-quadrant to the last, tubular steel posts notwithstanding. As a general rule, the most modern signals would be found only on the most important lines, or on lines newly built or remodelled. The less important the route, the older its signalling would generally be, and

even if signals were replaced due to accident or alteration, it would often be with reclaimed equipment rather than new; the railways were nothing if not thrifty in such matters.

If you're modelling a pre-Grouping scene then determining your signalling hardware will need to be part of the background research that forms such an integral (but fascinating) aspect of historical modelling. Fortunately, these days, the subject is very well-documented and, between the various books and specialist journals, the publications and technical advice available from the various individual line societies, the National Railway Museum archives and the actual signals preserved on the many heritage railways that abound in this Isle as nowhere else on the planet, it is usually possible to amass the required data needed to make accurate model signals.

Coming forward to the present day or the recent past will call for colour-lights, hopefully working – something that modern miniature LEDs have made possible even in the context of scale-sized signals. Searchlight signals – which proliferated in the 1950s and 1960s and are still in widespread use today – can also be made to scale and working, thanks to the winning combination of LEDs and fibre-optic threads. So there's no excuse for a diesel-era layout bereft of signals, unless it represents one of those barren 'extended siding' branch lines devoid of any pointwork and terminating at a weed-grown platform punctuated by a vandalised bus-shelter. How depressing!

Signal placement

Here we reach the heart of the signalling minefield, for this is a topic of bewildering complexity. I couldn't hope to produce a definitive essay on the subject – even had I the space to do so! Thus I shall concentrate on some general rules and a few typical examples. I will also repeat my number one modelling mantra at this point: if in doubt, consult the prototype. If you're at a loss as to how to signal the particular track arrangement of your layout, look for pictures of similar situations in reality and observe

Above: Realistic signalling on a model railway, this being the EM gauge 'Pixton Hill'. The signal cabin is the Wills Saxby & Farmer type, cut down in length to suit this minor location. The starter/block signal is from a Ratio kit for an SR upper-quadrant on a rail-built post and there is a similar signal facing the opposite way at the far end of the station. The turnout to the siding has a facing point lock – the protective wooden ramp can be seen in front of the signalbox between the rails. There is also a trap point on the siding – hidden behind the PW hut in this view. The trackwork is C&L.

what the full-size signal engineer has done in the circumstances. (However, it doesn't take too much such study to realise that full-size practice is not as consistent as many armchair experts would have you believe!)

Starting with the general rules, I'm going to break down signalling installations into the basic situations in which they occur: plain line block signalling for double and single-track, loops and lie-byes, junctions, through stations and terminal stations. In practice, of course, these various signalling requirements often overlap, resulting in signals which fulfil more than one role, or in arrangements that appear odd until you understand what is going on! Before any signalling gurus jump on my neck, I'll stress that the following is about as boiled-down a summary of basic signalling practice as can still be useful; much is unsaid and many special situations or matters of detail are, perforce, ignored or glossed over.

Block signal working

So, the plain block section on a normal line of double-track with no stations, junctions, sidings, loops or other complications is the most straightforward signalling installation and is the foundation-stone of the whole mighty signalling edifice. Such a section might be anything from a few hundred yards to many miles long, depending on the nature of the railway and the density of its traffic; generally, the busier the line the shorter the block sections. The traffic over each section will be regulated solely by a signalman manning the signal box dedicated to controlling that particular block section of track, known as a block post. On a double-track line, the up and down track sections controlled will not coincide; rather, they will be staggered so that each of them *finishes* adjacent to the signalbox and extends away from it 'to the rear'; that is, the signalman is positioned at the *end* of the section he controls. This is because a key function of the signalman is to examine each train passing his box to ensure it is in good order and – most importantly – that it is all there. Until he has 'seen the tail-light' he will not send the message that the train is complete and entering the following section.

The line in each direction – 'up' and 'down' – will have a home signal controlling the exit from the section and hence the entry to the following block section. This signal is normally positioned within sight of the signal box and some little way in advance of the actual start of the following section – a distance known as the 'clearing point'. The home signal will be preceded by a distant signal at the required interval, which, depending on the line speed, is usually at least 440yd. Such sets of signals would be described as the 'up home/up distant' and 'down home/down distant' to distinguish the direction of the traffic they regulate. On a plain block section with no loops, stations or junctions, these 'end of section' signals are

the only ones under control of our signalman; there is no 'block entry' signal as such, progress down the line being governed by the exit signals of each block permitting the train to enter the succeeding one. And so on, ad infinitum, or at least 'ad terminus'.

The signalboxes would be linked by the block telegraph. This consists of pairs of instruments – one set of them for each line, in the case of double track – which give the status of the block under control and its relationship to those either side of it : the 'block in rear' and the 'block in advance'. Such block instruments could be of several patterns, but the most common was the three-position type, which had two dials. One of these dials had a 'key' by which the position of the pointer could be altered; the corresponding dial in the box in rear or advance would show the same indication as that set by the key. The second dial was the repeater that showed the setting of the corresponding instrument in the adjoining boxes. Each dial displayed three indications: 'line blocked' (the 'normal' reading); 'line clear', which meant a train could be accepted on to the relevant section, and 'train entering section' or 'train on line', to indicate that a train had left the preceding section and was now occupying that being controlled.

The signals guarding entry to a succeeding block section normally stand at 'danger' with the telegraph instrument reading 'line blocked'. On the approach of a train, our signalman (let us call him Smith) will be notified by a descriptive bell code (giving the type and status of train) sent over the telegraph system by the man (Jones, naturally) in the signalbox controlling the preceding

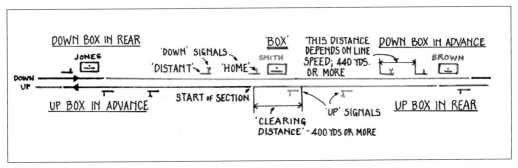

block section – the 'box in rear'. Provided there are no obstructions of any sort, no trains standing at his signals or otherwise occupying the tracks in his section, Smith will accept the oncoming train by repeating the bell signal and altering his telegraph instrument so that it (and the repeater in Jones's box) moves from 'line blocked' to 'line clear'. This enables Jones to pull off his signals to permit the train to enter Smith's section.

By the same use of bell codes, Smith will meanwhile 'offer' the train to the next block post in the direction in which it is travelling – the 'box in advance' – manned, of course, by Brown. Only when that message has been acknowledged by Brown and the appropriate block instrument indication for Brown's section changed to read 'line clear' does Smith 'pull off' his own home and distant signals; if Brown *cannot* accept the train (the bell signal is not repeated and instrument remains at 'line blocked'), then Smith's home and distant signals remain 'on' and the oncoming train will be brought to a stand at the home signal. If it overshoots, it still has the distance to the 'clearing point' (usually at least 400yd) to pull up in before violating a 'blocked' section – the big 'no-no'. The train will be held at the home signal until 'line clear' can be given for Brown's section. However, if Brown's section is given as clear when the train is offered then Smith can lower his signals and let the train pass unchecked.

As the train passes Jones's home signal and enters Smith's section, Jones will change the position of his block instrument – repeated in Smith's box – to read 'train entering section' (or 'train on line'). Having inspected the train and 'seen the tail light', Jones restores his signals to 'danger' and turns the instrument for his own section to read 'line blocked' – which is how it will remain until the next train is offered. Smith and Brown will do the same as the train passes their signals and signalboxes. All these telegraph signals and actions and the times at which they were made will be meticulously recorded in a ledger known as the 'train register' – the Victorian equivalent of a cockpit voice recorder for when things went awry.

Single-track block

On single-track routes, the same basic arrangements and signal descriptions apply, although the signals will all be sited beside, and relate to, the same line of rails and the 'up' section of one signalbox would overlie the 'down' of the next. In this case – for obvious reasons – line occupancy is governed by a further layer of protection in addition to the signal indications. This usually takes the form of a 'track authority' – a staff or token, or a specific written authority which must be in the possession of the train crew before they can enter the single-line section of track to which it refers. The boundaries of such a section usually coincide with those of the signalling block – but not always; a lengthy single-line section can contain several signalling block sections, or (rarely) vice-versa. For most modelling purposes – where we'd be jolly lucky to be modelling even one block or single-line section in its entirety – we can treat them as the same thing. In terms of the physical plant we need to model, to the signals we need to add provision for staff or token exchange: a walkway, post or simple lineside platform where this was accomplished by hand (slow speeds only!) or some form of automatic exchange mechanism where this was in use on the prototype.

In model terms, on all but the largest layouts only part of this system (single or double line) is likely to need to be modelled – usually the signalbox itself and its accompanying home signals. Occasionally, the distant may get a look in as well; 440yd is a bit over 17ft in 4mm scale, but allowing for the usual compression we can get away with 12ft or so – half these distances in N. Of course, where sections were short, it was by no means unknown for the distant for a following section to be mounted on the same post as the home for the immediate section – a very characteristic and charismatic type of signal that is often modelled.

Junctions

After the basic block working, the next most important function of signals is to protect and control junctions. Any junction is going to involve conflicting routes and track occupancy rights, so junction boxes often controlled traffic over several sections rather than the single pair of 'up' and 'down' that fell to the lot of a normal block post. The actual junction itself was protected by junction signals which, as well as being block signals in the normal sense, had the subsidiary functions of indicating the route set and preventing conflicting moves through the junction pointwork.

The typical positioning of these signals at a basic double junction is shown in the picture. A junction signal having two arms mounted on brackets is described as a 'splitting' signal; the arm on the taller post refers to the principal route, the shorter post carrying the arm relating to the diverging or subsidiary route. This type of signal indicates to the driver which route is set through the junction, which will determine his speed through the formation as well as telling him where he's going. You might think he'd know that in advance, but diversions and the use of alternative routes due to traffic hold-ups, engineering works, accidents and so on might well mean a different routeing to that normally followed. Or at least, it did before all the alternative routes were shut down!

Refuge loops and lie-byes

Thus far, what I've been attempting to describe is the *absolute* block system, under which only one train was allowed on any block section at any given time. This was all well and good when routes were relatively lightly trafficked and all the trains were going at roughly the same speed and stopping at the much same intervals. But applying absolute block working to a busy railway carrying a wide variety of train

Below: Signals at a junction, protecting the different routes. The apparently odd track arrangement conforms to the normal rule that where a single line joins a double track, the single line will split to give separate connections to the 'near' and 'far' lines. The diamond crossing in the foreground takes the 'far' connection over the 'near' line, while a trap point is inserted in the connection to 'near road' to protect the main line should a train overshoot the signals. The turnout forming the split would normally be set for this near connection and the trap would be 'open', but here there is some out-of-the-ordinary jiggery-pokery going on. The NBL Type 2 diesel is running 'wrong line' and the picture was taken from a train negotiating the junction 'wrong way'. Author's collection

Above: A special signal within station limits: a rare SR upper-quadrant 'shunt' arm on a Southern rail-built post which also carries a ground disc (rather far from the ground in this case!). Rail-built posts – fabricated from two lengths of worn-out rail bolted together with spacers – were typical of the economical way the railways reused and recycled material. Here, the signal post also doubles up as a telegraph pole. This wonderful specimen is on the preserved Bluebell Railway in East Sussex. Author's collection

types – some stopping at every station, some at a few stations and others not stopping at all, and running at speeds ranging from 60+mph for express passenger down to 25mph or less for heavy, loose-coupled mineral trains – was a very different proposition! In practice, it meant that when things got busy everything was soon reduced to the speed of the tardiest train. It was obviously necessary to make provision for faster, non-stop trains to overtake those going more slowly or making more frequent stops. This flexibility was achieved by the 'permissive block' system.

The 'permissive' arrangements allowed for a slower train to be run into a siding, loop or other side track which allowed it to come to a stand entirely clear of the main running line. Once it was safely stowed in such a refuge loop or lie-bye siding, held under subsidiary signals and with the points once more set for the running line, the section could be cleared to accept other trains as the sloth was no longer blocking the line. The slow train could then sit tight in its refuge until a gap in the

more important traffic allowed it to creep out once more on to the running lines – a move controlled by those subsidiary signals, which would be worked from the block post within whose section the lie-bye was situated. This whole process would be repeated at intervals, so that the faster traffic was not held up – a tedious process which often meant that the slowest goods trains took all day to cover a few tens of miles. To ensure that the signalman didn't forget about trains held in loops or lie-byes, these were either located with their exit/entry pointwork in sight of the signal cabin, or provided with a track circuit giving an indication on the track diagram to show that they were occupied. The crews of trains held at signals or in refuges also had a duty to report their presence to the signalman, usually by the fireman going into the signalbox or, later, by phone; that's what the telephone-boxes often seen mounted on signal posts were for.

Station limits

Stations were also special cases under the permissive block system, for things went on in them that would be unthinkable out on the open line. Each station was a sort of subsidiary section, known as 'station limits'. These limits were protected by a home signal at their commencement with a second home signal – a 'starter' – controlling the exit from station limits back on to open line. These 'station' signals might also double up as block signals, or – where the station limits lay entirely within a single block section – they might be additional to them.

How extensive the station limits were depended upon the layout of the station and the type of working that went on there. In many cases, they were sub-divided by additional subsidiary signals to facilitate all manner of shunting moves. Some railway companies – the old North Eastern Railway was famous for it – provided a separate signal for just about every conceivable move, resulting in veritable forests of posts and arms and workings of fearsome complexity. Fortunately, this was the exception rather than the rule;

most lines opted for the minimum that would do the job. These subsidiary signals included a number of specialised types: 'splitting' arms to indicate diverging routes into loops or bays, 'calling on' and 'shunt' arms that allowed a home signal to be passed at 'danger' for the purposes of a given shunting or operational move, and 'ground' or 'shunting signals' to cover set back moves, routes into and out of sidings or loops, crossovers and the like. It's very difficult, within the context of a book like this, to be proscriptive about the positioning and purpose of all these secondary signals. If I had to sum up the basic rule, I'd suggest that any move that formed part of the regular working of the station would have a signal of some sort controlling it.

However, what one can be fairly definite about is the basic sequence of signals found at a typical through station. These, taken in order from the direction of approach (whether that be up or down) were: station distant; station home (start of station limits) and starter – the latter normally being at the departure end of the station platform and marking the end of station limits. Larger or more important stations might add a couple of extra signals – a second home on the approach to the station proper, giving an 'outer' and an 'inner' home.

Similarly, at the other end of the layout, where shunting called for trains to pass the starter at the platform end to perform certain moves, a second or 'advanced' starter might be placed some way ahead of this so that the shunting moves could take place within station limits. Bay platforms leading on to the main running line would also have their own, discrete, starter signals.

Termini

The great thing about terminal stations is, as the wag remarks, that nobody gets to run straight through without stopping. This simplifies things somewhat from the signalling point of view. As for a through station, the sequence of signals approaching a terminus is the normal one of distant, followed by the home signal controlling the entry to station limits. At branch line or other small terminals, the station distant is often fixed in the 'on' position whatever the position of the following home, to remind drivers that they are approaching the end-of-track and caution is thus needed! At larger termini having several platforms, the station limits signal might be a splitting signal indicating to which

Below: Signals at a simple terminus.

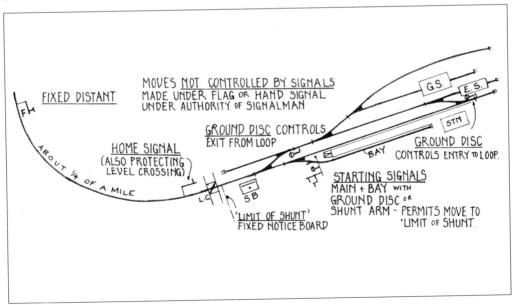

Above: Sighting requirements could see signals placed almost anywhere – even at a considerable distance from the track. Here, a home signal and a call-on arm stand at the side of a country lane, albeit one that just happens to lead over the top of a short tunnel! This fairly extreme example of remote sighting was at Midford, on the old Somerset & Dorset line. Author's collection

part of the station the train was routed, or it might be followed by splitting signals closer to the actual station entry pointwork. At major stations, these splitting signals might also carry platform road indicators – mechanical or lamp signs displaying the actual platform number into which the train was headed; vital information where braking distances varied!

Terminal stations are obviously signalled

for outbound as well as inboard traffic. Once again, the starter is the key signal, a home arm mounted at or in sight of the platform ends. Larger stations would also possess one or more advance starters to extend station limits, the outermost of which would normally also control entry to the ensuing track block section. Within the station, the same sort of subsidiary and ground-signals would be provided as at a through station, to control the regular moves needed to work the station. Any emergency or other out-of-the-ordinary moves would be handled by flag signals which, when given by the signalman, have the same authority as a semaphore signal indication. At smaller branch line terminals where 'one engine at a time' was the norm, the subsidiary signalling might be entirely by flag, or otherwise be restricted to a very simple and basic set-up.

Signal sighting

Given the fundamental role of the visual signal in safe railway working, it was obviously vital that the signals themselves be clearly seen under all conditions. Good 'sighting' thus determined the design and positioning of signals and governed the addition of repeater arms which gave an alternatively located or reinforcing signal. Curves, bridges and tunnels were the great problems for the signal engineer when positioning his signals, and many special designs of signal were evolved to ensure clear sighting in difficult locations. Among the most characteristic of these were the very tall post carrying two co-acting arms; one high up – the 'sky arm' – and one at eye level, often found where there was an overbridge on the approach to the signal and installed so that the signal indication could be seen both above and below the bridge. Also common were signals with brackets offsetting the signal arm from the post to locate it on a natural sightline, signals mounted on the 'wrong' side of the track on a curve, signals with extra-tall posts to raise the signal above distracting backgrounds, or signals backed with white-painted 'sighting boards'.

To site signals appropriately on a model railway, it is necessary to 'think yourself in' to this fundamental requirement, to try to visualise what view the crew of your miniature locomotives would have of the signals. This is the guiding principle used by the real signal engineer, so you won't go far wrong if you place your signals where they would be most readily seen – even if this means that they are 'out of position' when judged by the convention that says signals should be normally to the near side of an approaching train with the arm facing away from the track. T'aint always so, as studying a few photos will soon reveal; many an odd arrangement makes sense when the sighting criteria are taken into account.

Sources of model signals

Signals have formed part of the stock-in-trade of toy and model train-makers more or less since the beginning – usually grossly over scale and often of somewhat unlikely design. Hornby-Dublo was the first to produce 4mm scale model signals that were somewhere near scale and of reasonably realistic design. These were upper quadrants on square,

'wooden' posts – not a particularly common combination. They also produced a bracket signal with a distant arm on both 'dolls' (a splitting distant) – a very rare beast on the prototype. Hornby-Dublo went on to produce working colour-light signals of two-aspect design which weren't too over-scale – even if they didn't really represent a type of signal often seen on the real railways, where searchlights or three-aspects were more likely. Today, the modern Hornby range includes a few upper-quadrant semaphores on LNER-style lattice masts – plain home and distant, and a junction bracket as well as a somewhat chunky two-aspect colour light.

The first true scale commercial model semaphore signals for 4mm were produced

Below: Signal modelling is almost a hobby-within-a-hobby, especially when it comes to more specialised examples like these 4mm scale LMS upper quadrants on lattice posts, built by Graham Warburton from some of the wide range of etched and cast components available.

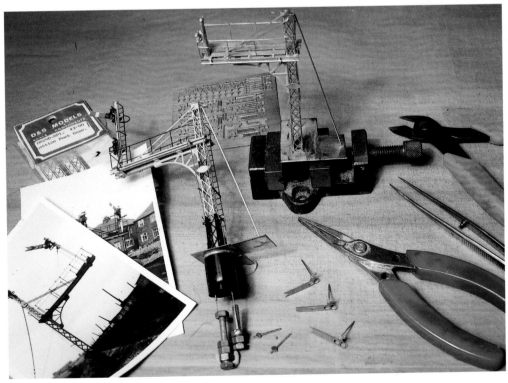

in the 1950s by Scalesig – lovely things that came in kit form, all in brass with stamped arms for upper and lower quadrants, turned finials and lamps and all manner of brackets, cranks and pulleys. They weren't cheap, mind you, but they did facilitate the provision of model signals that both looked the part and worked properly. However, it took the advent of plastic moulding in the early 1960s for

Below: Signal components – for 4mm scale, in this case, although 7mm is equally well provided for. There is a bewildering variety of parts to be had, covering not just mainstream signalling of the Grouping and BR eras, but also pre-Grouping and specialised signals for a plethora of different companies. MSE are the specialists, but signal parts feature in many makers' ranges and are also produced by some of the specialist societies.

popularly-priced but accurate model signals to appear, in the form of the Ratio signal kits that are still around to this day. Initially for GW tubular-post (i.e. late 1930s) lower-quadrants, the range has expanded to include LMS steel-post, LNER lattice-post and SR rail-built post upper-quadrants as well as LNWR and older-style GWR wooden-post lower quadrants. These excellent and economically priced kits provide for plain signals and a variety of bracket designs, and the range also includes a Pratt truss 'signal bridge', laddering, levers and various other accessories. A few of these types (the basic, simple home and distant signals for GWR, SR and LMS) are now available in ready-to-use pre-built and painted form. Ratio GWR pattern lower-quadrant semaphore signals with wooden posts and LMS style upper-quadrants on tubular posts are produced in kit form for N, as are the junction brackets

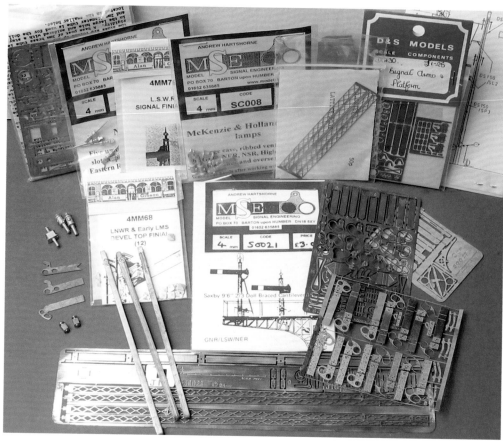

and the Pratt truss gantry/signal bridge. These N scale signals can be built up in working format, although it must be admitted this is a tad fiddly.

Plastic mouldings like these have to sell in large numbers to be viable, which meant that the Ratio range has perforce to concentrate on the more common types of signal – those that were seen in large numbers on the main 'Grouping' railways and on BR. This in turn meant that the huge variety of signal designs produced by the various pre-Grouping railways and the signal contracting firms like McKenzie and Holland, Railway Signal Co., Saxby & Farmer, Dutton and Stevens were unrepresented. This all changed when Derek Munday set to and used the etched-brass and white metal casting processes to produce a huge range of components that enabled almost any type of pre-Grouping or 'Big Four' railway signal to be modelled. This Model Signal Engineering (MSE) range is still available today and is a key resource for the historical modeller (and in a signalling context, anyone modelling the railway scene prior to about 1980 is a historical modeller!).

Making them work

There used to be long debates in the model railway press and in the bars of numerous pubs after club meetings as to the difficulties and advisability of trying to make scale model semaphore signals function as their prototypes. 'Dummy' (i.e. non-working cosmetic) signals were quite prevalent on many layouts – the theory being that as signals were only cleared when a train was approaching, a non-working signal modelled in the 'on' position was right for most of the time. The sight of a train gaily waltzing past an adverse signal was lumped in with other such model railway inconsistencies as wagons that never got unloaded, passengers standing rooted to platforms who never got on the trains, road vehicles frozen to the highway and so on; all things that were supposedly covered by 'suspension of disbelief'.

There were always those who either had dysfunctional disbelief-suspension, or who were more concerned with the operational rather than cosmetic role of signals on a layout, or who took the view that if something *could* be made to work, it *should* be. After all, all those toy-train signals all worked; why should scale models not function equally well? So working scale signals became more widespread and most modern modellers would not consider relegating such an important visual and operational aspect of the railway scene to the status of a mere static stage-prop – certainly not in 4mm scale, although working N scale semaphore signals are naturally somewhat rarer.

There are several ways in which model signals may be animated, but the basic construction of the moving parts is usually consistent. The arms are fixed to a pivot pin or wire, which revolves in a bearing fixed to, or drilled through the post. The exact position of the pivot depends on the arm design and which quadrant it works in. The arm pivot is secured by the 'backlight blinder' – in reality a cast component which moved with the arm and which, when the arm was pulled off, concealed the backlight – a small lens in the rear of the lamp which enabled the signalman to monitor the status of signals for which he could not see the actual aspect, as well as confirming to linemen and train crews that signal lamps were lit.

The movement of a real signal arm is made by the 'drive rod', the linkage which joins the arm to the vital balance weight at the foot of the post. Although signal arms were made so that their natural balance, aided by gravity, would always return them to 'danger' should the drive rod break or become detached, on their own they didn't have enough mechanical advantage to overcome the friction in the wires and pulleys by which the signal was connected to the signalbox. Hence, to ensure that the signal always returned to danger, a hefty weight on a lever was fitted at the base of the post, arranged so that 'pulling the signal off' raised the weight and kept the signal wires under tension. Thus, should the wires break, the weight would restore the signal to danger immediately; even the

Above: A simple 4mm scale LNER upper quadrant tubular-post signal built from brass tube and etched brass components for 'Cade's Green'. The arm is vintage Scalesig, the laddering is by Alan Gibson and the balance weight is MSE. This is an illuminated signal using a miniature, grain of rice bulb fed by a fine flex running up inside the post, with return via the metal structure. There is a hefty below-baseboard operating crank and return weight, and like the prototype, the signal is arranged for pull for 'off' actuation.

signalman putting the lever back in the frame would cause the weight to drop sharply on to its 'stop' – the cause of the famous 'bounce' that many semaphore signals exhibited when returning to danger.

On a model, the drive rod is represented by an operating wire working in a hole in the arm offset a little way from the pivot position. This wire runs up the front or side of the signal post. Some modellers can't resist the temptation to ignore the balance weight, but I reckon if you're going to make your signals work, they may as well do so in their entirety!

In the system I use – which I poached from my old friend Graham Warburton – the signal linkage (which includes the cosmetic model balance weight) is held in the 'on' position by an actual weight (usually a small fishing weight) hanging on the bottom of the linkage and resting against a 'stop' to take the load off the linkage. To 'clear' the signal this weight is simply lifted by a crank, cam, solenoid, piece of string or some other means, when the drive is transmitted via the linkage to raise or lower the arm as appropriate. More on operating systems in a moment.

Things get a little more complicated when we need to take the drive out from the main signal post to subsidiary dolls and arms on bracket signals. There are two ways of doing this; either by means of cranks and rods, as the prototype does, or by using a stiff bent-to-shape operating wire. The first method is prototypical and satisfying, but it must be admitted that it takes a bit of doing. The second method is a subterfuge which is surprisingly discreet if done cannily using a suitably fine wire. Either is a great deal better than a non-working signal!

The ultimate refinement on model semaphores is working lamps, definitely something of a 'wow' when you come across them. Again, there are two ways of achieving this, both much easier to do with the components we have available nowadays. You can use a fibre-optic thread (one of those trendy 'illuminated hedgehog' lamps will provide loads of these; whenever I build a signal I just nip in to my No. 2 daughter's bedroom and give her lamp a discreet haircut) with the light source mounted below baseboard level. The fibre optic can be laid in a groove filed or carved in the 'woodwork' of a timber signal post or inserted up the middle of a tubular one. It is fine enough to be bent through tight angles and fed into the lamp either from the rear or the bottom. The alternative is a sub-miniature grain of rice' bulb or a 'golden-white' LED inside the lamp, fed with fine wires disguised in the same way. Only one wire need be hidden if you use the signal post (if metal), or its ladder, as an electrical return.

Model colour-light signals

There has never been much debate about whether or not model colour-light signals should be functional. Even the first examples from Dublo worked, while the advent of tiny, 1.5V grain of rice bulbs and even smaller, sub-miniature LEDs now makes it possible to produce model colour-light signals where the lamp and housing sizes are very close to true scale, even in N scale. There are several comprehensive ranges of ready-to-use colour lights of UK, US and European origin. However, most of these are for multi-aspect types; searchlight signals are more of a problem, as a single lamp has to show two or three colours. In Britain, the best-known colour-light signal range is by Eckon and includes prototypical four-aspect types suited to contemporary layouts featuring automatic block signalling. Eckon also make two-aspect (found on the Underground in London) and three-aspect (older installations, particularly suburban electrified lines) types as well, with a good selection of junction brackets and colour-light ground signals to round things off.

Searchlight signals have always been more of a problem. The traditional approach for home-made signals was to use a 'light box' containing red, green and amber grain-of-wheat bulbs as required. This was fitted to the base of the signal for below-baseboard mounting, the light being carried up the tubular post to the signal head by a length of fibre optic thread. More recently, the advent of bi-colour LEDs – which change colour when the voltage polarity is reversed – has made possible a two-aspect searchlight with the light source in the signal head. Tomar Industries in the USA make a nice H0 scale searchlight signal that certainly wouldn't look out of place in a 4mm scale British context. On the prototype, many such signals used here and in the USA were from the same source, the Westinghouse Brake & Signal Company.

For those who are happy to 'brew their own' colour lights, the various sub-miniature bulbs and LEDs are available from model railway electronics and component suppliers, while brass or plastic tube and suitable sheet materials are to be found among the stock of the specialist materials suppliers like Squires or Eileen's Emporium. Etched signal laddering – just as applicable to colour-lights as semaphores – can be bought from MSE. Articles describing colour-light signal construction – from simple single-head designs to complex brackets with route indicators, platform number displays and all manner of other bells and whistles – feature in the model railway press from time to time, while the Model Electronic Railway Group (MERG) produce lots of material and componentry for signalling purposes.

Signal linkages

Any linkage or motor that can change a point can also be used to work a semaphore signal, so most of the set-ups described below for turnout operation can equally well be used with signals. A possible exception is slow-action motor-drive point actuators, which would move the signal arm at a rate which would look a bit odd. Given that such devices are anyway far from cheap, they would also represent a rather extravagant method of merely moving a semaphore.

What is positively parsimonious, on the other hand, is a method of working model signals that has long been used and, to boot, is very close to what the prototype does. I refer, of course, to the use of thread to pull the signal 'off', working against a weight or spring that is set up to return it to danger. The thread can be anything that is strong enough and doesn't fray – carpet thread and fishing line have long been favourites, usually running through ordinary, small screw-eyes fixed as needed below the baseboard. The return can be a hanging weight (my own preference) or some form of spring – really dedicated penny-pinchers use rubber bands. At the control end, you need a lever with a lock of some sort to hold the signal 'off' against the pull of the return weight or spring. If you don't want to go the trouble of brewing all this yourself, you can buy just such a system ready-to-install from Ratio as their Remote Control for Signals, product reference number 250.

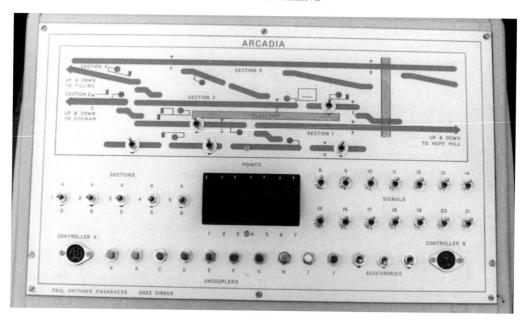

Above: A very well-executed layout control panel by the late Martin Brent, with an engraved diagram and a mix of geographically located and banked switchgear for sections, cab control, signals, points (by levers) and electro-magnetic uncouplers.

Below: Fascia-mounted 'dispersed' control on 'Cade's Green'. This separates the turnouts that would, in reality, have been worked from the signalbox, making them electrically operated via switchgear on the panel seen here. All the other turnouts – the ones that would have been worked from trackside hand levers at full size – are manually operated by simple push-pull 'buttons' located in the fascia adjacent to the points they control; a pair are seen either side of the switch panel. The remaining switches are the track sections. Not terribly elegant, I fear – but workable.

Control options

Like the prototype, we have three basic options when it comes to controlling points: direct manual operation by means of the good-old trackside lever; remote manual operation using combinations of cranks and rodding; and remote power operation which is normally by the agency of electricity, although the prototype went in for pneumatics as well. Also as on the prototype, we can use a variety of methods in combination, each selected for their suitability for a particular application.

However, before worrying too much about the actual means by which a given turnout is to be thrown or a signal cleared, it is a good idea to think through the way you intend to operate the layout and to manage the various control functions. The traditional approach was the master 'control panel' on which everything was grouped and from which everything was worked. On larger layouts, the result would often have done the flight deck of a Jumbo proud – serried ranks of switches, a fairground's-worth of coloured lights, banks of push-buttons and levers, frowning rows of meters and dials, and a bevy of knobs for the actual controllers. This is what I like to think of as the 'Super Wurlitzer' school of model railway control, where hands flit over switches and buttons and twirl knobs like some demonic organist playing a monster fugue. Some people just love this sort of thing, which is great, but it bears very little resemblance to the way a real railway is run.

More recently, there has been a move towards a far more prototypical form of control, aided by the advent of DCC which has eliminated the need for the elaborate section switching which was a prime function of the traditional 'master panel'. This approach follows the clear division that lies at the heart of real railway operation, between the signalling/route-setting function and the actual driving of the trains. The engine driver may be lord of his locomotive, but he's always subservient to the signalman, whose commands he must obey unfailingly. The same separation of control can be applied to a model railway, in the form of local 'signalbox panels' – replicating the jurisdiction of the signalman – in conjunction with hand-held loco controllers giving the driver access only to the functions he would control on a real engine: direction, acceleration, braking and speed.

It is the signalbox part of this divided control approach which concerns us here. There are several forms that this can take: traditional-style control panels with the switches neatly ranked and labelled, perhaps served up with a garnish of indicator lights; 'geographic' panels, where the point, signal and section switches are installed at the relevant locations on a track diagram; a 'lever frame' format which sets out to replicate as far as possible the equipment that would have faced a real signalman in the situation being portrayed, and a 'dispersed' set-up that simply locates levers and switches on the layout fascia at a logical spot in relation to the point or signal being controlled. This last approach is very popular on 'walk-around' layouts in the USA, where block signalling is rare and British-style signalboxes almost unknown. It also works well on small layouts and in situations where the real railway would have used trackside hand levers to throw points rather than connecting them to a lever frame.

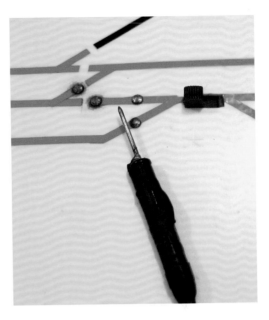

Above: Solenoid point-motor operation by live probe – or 'electric pencil' – and studs, all mounted on a geographic track diagram.

Which of these approaches you go for depends on personal inclination and, particularly, how intensive you like your operational involvement with the layout. There's no doubt that it takes greater concentration to work a lever frame than it does to cope with a geographical panel. (Which is one of the reasons why the real railways have replaced lever frames with geographic panels!) It is also quite possible (and logical) to mix control methods on the same layout, as in the combination of a lever frame system for the main line pointwork and signals, in conjunction with dispersed control for the sidings in the goods yard, which would in reality have been worked by the shunter or train crew, and not connected to the signalbox.

The type of control set-up you opt for determines to a considerable extent the nature of the actuating system needed to work the actual signals and points. Obviously, the panel approach usually starts from the presumption of electric actuation controlled by a switch or – on geographic diagrams used in conjunction with solenoids – by stud-and-probe (sometimes termed 'electric pencil'). A lever frame, on the other hand, can be made purely mechanical, wholly electric or a combination of the two. Dispersed control, too, can be electrical or mechanical or a mixture. Whichever of these possibilities you choose, do take the time to think through all the implications, both operationally and practically. Having the point controls on a panel remote from a part of the layout – such as a goods yard – that you will want to operate from close to can be a real pain if you have to cross the room every time you need to throw a point. Taking mechanical point linkages across baseboard joints on sectional layouts can also involve all sorts of complications that, while they can be eased with a solenoid and a plug, are best avoided by using dispersed control to eliminate the need to cross the Rubicon in the first place.

Mechanical point-actuating systems

The systems devised and used by modellers to operate pointwork mechanically are many and varied and range from the comparative sophistication of torque-rod systems through wire-in-tube and rod-and-crank to wondrous confections involving fishing line, rubber bands, screw-eyes, and string – devices of which W. Heath Robinson would have been proud. No matter; so long as it does the job, there's no 'right' way of going about things. The only one of these mechanical methods to have been 'productionised' into a range of off-the-peg components is the Mercontrol wire-in-tube system, which uses spring-steel wire running in fine copper capillary tube, all activated by a simple lever frame.

This is the easiest type of mechanical system to install and for that reason is the most widely used. The only real essential is to anchor the tube properly so that when you move the lever the wire slides within the tube rather than the whole ensemble wandering around the baseboard. Although you can bend the tube around quite sharp curves – certainly down to a couple of inches radius – this will increase the friction in the system

considerably; far better to plan a route for the tube that keeps all the bends as gentle as possible. The tube can be mounted above or below the baseboard surface as it is only ⅛in in outside diameter, so it is pretty simple to disguise even when surface-run.

To work such wire-in-tube or other mechanical systems there are a variety of lever frames available, from the comparatively straightforward ready-to-use Gem item sold as part of the basic Mercontrol system to sophisticated affairs in kit form, accurate models of real signal levers fitted with working catch-handles and even available with working mechanical interlocking for those who enjoy 3-D chess. Typically, these full-feature lever frames are quite large and consequently need a suitable location for mounting 'off scene', either below the front edge of the layout or at one end. The Gem frame, by contrast, is small enough to be hidden by a structure or be inset into the layout fascia. For this reason, the all-singing types are a bit more troublesome to install and, of course, have to be built up in the first place. MSE, the Scalefour Society, Brassmasters and Ambis Engineering are the main suppliers.

At the other extreme of the manual point control spectrum is the simple push-pull operated device shown in the sketch, which is ideal for fascia-mounting for local or 'dispersed' control. This is very easy to make, costs virtually nothing and has almost nothing to go wrong! It uses stiff wire (piano wire, bought from model aircraft shops), a block of wood, a slot in the baseboard surface and a chunky lever which I normally make out of PCB sleeper strip or suitably sized brass strip from the K&S Metal dispenser you'll find in nearly every model shop. With live-frog turnouts needing external switching (i.e., pretty much anything other than Peco), it will be necessary to fit polarity switching of some kind, such as the microswitch suggested in the illustration.

Manual polarity switching

The switching system of a manual linkage can take one of several forms. It can be readily incorporated in the 'point lever' end of

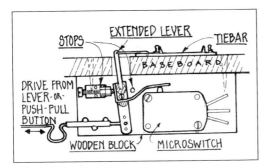

things – fitted into a lever frame or otherwise connected to the point lever. Indeed, it is quite a common arrangement to fit it in *place* of the point lever, neatly despatching the proverbial avian duet with but a single switch. This is usually of the simple DPDT slide variety – a very useful, cheap and quick solution especially suited to dispersed or local control. Both slide and toggle switches work well in this application, as they incorporate a definite 'over centre' locking action that serves to hold the point blades firmly in place once thrown.

At the other end of the linkage, it used to be the fashion to build a simple form of changeover switch into the throwbar arrangements of, particularly, PCB-sleepered turnouts – a set-up still suggested by SMP in their point kits. It's a method I don't care for – partly because it's visually obtrusive, and also because it is somewhat vulnerable to dirt and damage. Far better, I feel, to use an enclosed SPST microswitch, either driven from the end of the point throwbar off the linkage at some suitable location between lever and turnout. Such a microswitch is easily hidden and very reliable, while the faint 'click' it emits as it operates I find a useful indication that the point-change linkage is functioning correctly.

Solenoid point motors

There are two types of point motor in common use: traditional solenoids and the new generation of motor-drive units. Solenoids nowadays are really confined to the Peco design and the very similar 'Seep' – although if you're old enough or lucky enough you may have a stock of vintage Hammant & Morgan

Above left: A design for a manual point actuator, including changeover microswitch for live-frog turnouts.

Above right: Turnout polarity switching – an SPDT micro-switch driven directly from the point throwbar, which is normally hidden beneath the ballast bin seen on the left.

Below: Solenoid point motors: the non-latching, switchless Peco, bottom left, with the similar Hornby unit above. Top right is an old H&M SM3 – powerful, robust, self-latching and incorporating a changeover switch and a user-friendly output crank. This has been out of production, alas, for more than 20 years, but is still highly sought-after! Bottom right is the nearest present-day equivalent – a Gaugemaster/Seep PM4 – powerful and self-latching, with an inbuilt changeover switch but, unfortunately, no crank.

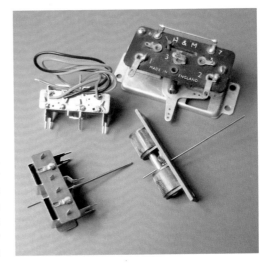

SM3 units, the 'hobby standard' for many a year but no longer, alas, available. The Peco and Seep are both really only intended to work with Peco pointwork which – as described in Chapter 4 – incorporates its own over-centre locking spring to hold the switch blades in the position selected, together with an inbuilt power-routeing switch.

Peco motors are designed to fit directly to the underside of the actual point using a simple twist-tag mounting system; with typical Peco ingenuity, they have managed to arrange things so that the same basic PL10 motor will fit any Peco turnout from N up to Gauge 0. The actual movement is purely linear, being transmitted by a vertical drive pin direct from the mid-point of the armature to a hole in the centre of the point throwbar. Look Ma – no linkage! This direct drive enables the point motor to do without any locking of its own while leaving it free it to develop just the right degree of travel to operate the particular point to which it is mounted. The only real snag with this overall package is the size of the hole you need to make in the trackbed to accommodate a motor mounted directly beneath the toe of your turnout.

Over-centre locking and power-route switching are necessities, however, for any live-frog turnout without Peco's built-in arrangements. Such locking and switching – together with cranks allowing for different drive directions and travels and extensions to permit above or below-baseboard mounting (by means of ordinary small woodscrews) – were features built-in to 'universal' point solenoids like the SM3. The Seep motors (made by Gaugemaster) share the linear design of the Peco and are configured in the same way with a central drive pin to engage directly with the point throwbar. The Seep design is, however, intended for normal below-baseboard mounting by means of screws through a baseplate, with an extended drive pin to cope with any normal thickness of trackbed. It is available in three variants: the PM2, which, like the Peco has neither locking nor switching; the PM1, which (confusingly) *does* have a changeover switch, and the PM 4,

which has both a switch and a locking system, and is thus the nearest thing to a general-purpose solenoid point motor currently available. Provided, that is, you can come up with a suitable method of taking the drive off to a non-Peco turnout.

But no matter! Peco have ways around all these drawbacks… Firstly, to allow the motor to be mounted below the baseboard *à la* Seep, there's a version with an extended drive pin (PL11), which gives a much longer reach, enough to allow for up to an inch or so of baseboard thickness. For more universal use, the lack of locking is addressed by the provision of an Adaptor Base (PL12). This is a moulded plastic assembly basically designed to permit screwed-to-the-baseboard mounting, to which the point motor clips by the same twist-tag system used to attach it beneath a turnout. The mount itself can be fitted above or below decks and incorporates a similar over-centre spring to that used on the turnouts, thus producing a self-locking motor. The PL10's lack of power routeing is addressed by fitting add-on switches (PL13, a straight SPDT changeover, and PL15, a DPDT version to give an extra accessory circuit). Thus accoutred the PL10 is certainly more belle of the ball than kitchen drudge, but the SM3's glass slipper still doesn't quite fit. No cranks, you see – the drive is still strictly linear and the actual take-off is a plastic slider with a large 'eye', intended to clip on to the moulded stud at the end of a Peco throwbar. This plastic eye does not at all suit the sort of wire link typically used to drive a normal point throwbar, although you can fix that with a little brass-tube bush. The cost of a PL10 with all the add-ons also tots up to rather more than the Seep equivalent.

Switching solenoids

The switchgear and power supply used to control solenoid point motors also needs a bit of consideration. The coils are designed to work on a minimum of 15–16V ac – the traditional 'accessory supply' – using a short-duration burst of power to fire them. Even though the standard 16V is often only just enough to kick the motor over, leaving the solenoid coils energised for anything more than a second or two will result in a nasty smell, swiftly followed by a wisp of acrid smoke, and a dead point motor.

Traditionally, the required brief shot-in-the-armature was delivered by a passing-contact switch, a spring-loaded push-to-make pushbutton or an electric pencil. More recently, however, the normal way of powering solenoids has been by means of a capacitor discharge unit (CDU) delivering a far heftier but very accurately controlled pulse which fires a point motor (or even several motors at once) in no uncertain manner. But this method, too, has drawbacks; for a start, the capacitor takes several seconds to recharge after each firing – which can be tedious when you want to change several points in quick succession. Also, the whopping electrical 'spike' which puts such zest into the action of the solenoids is equally effective at frying the innards of any associated switchgear, which thus tends to have a short life and a gay one. Even electric pencils emit more sparks than Harry Potter's wand and erode away before one's very eyes when used with a CDU, although in that case one can at least polish the resulting pitting off the studs and the business end of the 'pencil' when things look too black.

However, this is the 21st century – so we now have a natty gadget designed to do the exact job required in controlling solenoids. This is the Masterswitch, designed by Richard Johnson of DCC Concepts in Australia and now available here in the Old Country. Rather than using one thumping great capacitor to power all the solenoids on the whole layout, the Masterswitch incorporates two tiny hi-tech capacitors – one for each coil of the solenoid. These capacitors recharge in a few hundredths of a second (faster than you can operate the switch) but still deliver more than enough 'poke' to fire several Peco motors at a go! The switchgear is totally unaffected by all this power because it can now be on the 'input' side of the capacitor circuit – where there are only minute power levels and no spikes – rather than the output as hitherto. The transistorised Masterswitch circuitry also incorporates a double-pole changeover switch for point frog and accessory switching and comes with LED point-position indicators for panel-mounting. It can be triggered by a normal SPDT toggle switch (supplied), by a microswitch on a lever frame or by a DCC accessory decoder. Any dc supply from 4V to 12V will suffice to power the device; one of those cheap plug-mounted power supplies is sufficient to run a whole layout's worth of Masterswitches. Each switch costs about the same as a full-feature solenoid point motor – well worth it, in my opinion.

Motor-drive point motors

These are the new general-purpose devices, with a number of important advantages over solenoids. Unlike the abrupt 'shock' action of an electro-magnet prodded into a sudden burst of life by a capacitor, a motor-drive unit is far slower and more progressive in its movement – and thus far kinder to the linkages and point components attached to it. Solenoids are notorious for fracturing soldered joints of all sorts, most particularly those holding point-blades to throwbars. The motor-drives

Below: Open-frame motor-drive point motors by Fulgurex. These are powerful and effective but rather noisy; the travel is set by limit switches, while further reed switches provide changeover facilities.

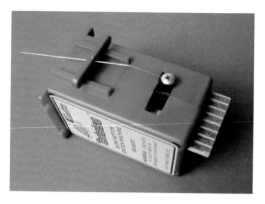

Above: The fully enclosed American Tortoise motors are quiet and smooth with the travel adjusted by an ingenious sliding pivot block. They are designed for vertical mounting beneath the turnout, where they take up rather a lot of space, but if this causes a problem there is now a horizontal mounting kit available.

also produce a far more realistic movement for point blades, which in reality go over quite gently, especially when manually operated. Even Charles Atlas as signalman would fail to match the vigour shown by a typical solenoid! Motor drives are also powerful and reliable, with adjustable throws and plenty of inbuilt switching capacity.

There are two basic designs of motor-driven point actuators: the 'open' type that uses worm-and-pinion gearing to drive a nut along a spinning thread (Fulgurex, Lemarco) and the enclosed variety with a gear-and-quadrant drive (the American Circuitron Tortoise). Both cost about the same and both need a dc power supply of between 6 and 12 volts (the exact voltage is not usually critical unless you need ultimate power). The point drive is actuated by reversing the polarity of the dc supply (using a cross-wired DPDT switch – exactly the same set-up as reversing the motor in a locomotive) when the motor will cut in and move the drive to the opposite end of its travel. The 'open' designs use limit switches which cut the power off once the motor has thrown; the Tortoise doesn't bother with such shenanigans and simply stalls at the end of its travel. Its current consumption is

so low that it can stay 'stalled' indefinitely without suffering any ill-effects.

The required travel is set by adjusting the cut-off switches on the screw-drive motors or by moving the pivot point of the throw arm of the Tortoise, which also incorporates a spring action to take up over-travel and hold point blades in place. The screw-drive motors need a suitable linkage to connect them to the point throwbar (see next section); the Tortoise can drive the turnout directly. Disadvantages? Well, the screw-drive designs can be horribly noisy in operation, while their open design makes them a little vulnerable to dirt and damage. The Tortoise is much quieter in operation, though it does hum to itself when in stalled mode. It's very bulky and is only suited to below-baseboard mounting, where it needs at least 3½in clearance in its normal vertical position. You can get a special mounting bracket which will turn it sideways, but even then it still needs a good 2in. The Fulgurex and Lemarco versions are far more compact and can be readily mounted above or below decks.

Over-travel

One tricky aspect of point actuation is the actual connection of the drive to the point throw-bar (aka tie bar), as this needs to take account of any 'over-travel' in the system. This is the amount by which the 'throw' of the controlling lever or motor exceeds the distance the point blades actually have to move. Most actuating devices – be they lever frames or motors – are universal in application, and hence have to provide sufficient travel for any scale or turnout type. Which means that in many – most? – cases they will develop a greater throw than is needed – especially for fine-scale turnouts in 4mm scale and below, which typically only call for a millimetre or two of movement. This excess travel is not all a bad thing, mind you; it allows for slack in the linkages, flexing tubes and other losses of movement en route. But the chances are that it will be necessary at some stage to match the travel to the turnout to avoid overloading the actual point blades and their attachments to the throwbar.

There are two ways of doing this: one either inserts a spring of some sort into the linkage to accommodate the additional travel, or provides an adjustment-cum-compensating device – a lever or crank with unequal pivot-to-centre distances on either arm – to match the final travel to the throw required, as shown in the diagram. Best of all is some combination of the two, as a *little* spring pressure is useful to hold the point blades firmly in contact with the stock rail. The usual form of spring used for point-connecting purposes is the omega loop, but a 'Z' spring bent into the actuating wire will also do the job, as will the springy drive rod of a Tortoise. Indeed, this last is often a tad *too* springy – any friction in the linkage or the flexure of the point blades will see the Tortoise arm flexing rather than the blades moving; not very helpful! Stiffen its resolve by slipping some fine tube over it for at least part of its length.

Signalling summary

Proper working signalling is probably second only to trackwork in terms of its complexity in mechanical and electrical engineering terms and the work entailed in installing it properly on a layout. For this reason, I suspect, a lot of modellers fight shy of providing a proper signalling set-up for their layouts, either settling for non-working cosmetic signals or ignoring them altogether. It's certainly an

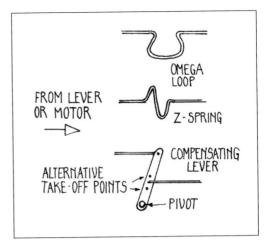

Above: Over-travel linkages.

area in which the trade could help more – we have nothing comparable to the ready-to-use working signals offered elsewhere in Europe and the USA. I expect that the endless variety of the British prototype is at least partly to blame for this, but it's a pity nonetheless.

That said, my own experience is that a full installation of working signals is one of the most worthwhile additions to any model railway, whatever its scale, gauge or subject. It adds so much to the general realism, atmosphere and operational potential of the model that the effort involved is well repaid. Give it a go, is my advice.

Chapter 7

MODELLING THE
LANDSCAPE

There's one big difference between real railways and models when it comes to scenery; in reality, the railway came along a long time after the scenery, whereas on models the railway usually comes first and the scenery somewhat later. Or, in a good few cases, never at all! So the great trick with model railway scenery is to make it *look* as if it was there before the tracks, rather than being added as an afterthought. This means that the nature and features of the landscape – together with the positioning and size of structures and civil engineering works – need to be conceived and planned as a single operation alongside the development of the track plan. Scenic considerations form a major part of the 'complete layout design' approach advocated in Chapter 2.

To conceive and execute convincing scenery you need, as in other areas of railway modelling, to make a careful study of the real thing. If you're trying to model East Anglia, you won't convince anybody if you include hills shaped like juvenile Alps or red-soiled fields bounded by dry-stone granite walls! Creating a realistic model railway is all about selecting elements – landscape, buildings, colours, lighting, accessories – that live naturally together to produce a cohesive whole. Taking the trouble to get this right can really 'lift' a layout and give it atmosphere and character – even where the railway side of things is relatively straightforward in subject or in the use of common commercial models.

Scenic inspiration

A lot of modellers (your author included) tend to choose to set their model railways in landscapes that are familiar to them – often the place in which they grew up or in which they now live, or a favourite holiday destination. In my case, these areas have been East Anglia – where I spent my youth – and West Devon and North Cornwall, where I have lived for the last 36 years and where many a childhood holiday was enjoyed. Mind you, that hasn't stopped me dipping a toe into the other, more exotic settings with which I've become acquainted over the years – Holland, Brittany,

Opposite: 'The landscape was there before the trains.' Few people have captured the essential relationship between the railway and its setting better than Barry Norman, whose ground-breaking 'Petherick' layout was one of the first layouts to shift the balance from the pure railway model towards the railway-in-a-landscape setting.

Traditionally, most model railways had consisted of a mass of trackage with a sparse fringe of 'scenery' around the edges; with 'Petherick', Barry presented a substantial tract of countryside with a relatively modest stretch of railway embedded in the middle of it. The result was this wonderful evocation of high summer in North Cornwall just after the First World War.

parts of New England and Ontario. Oh yes – and Yorkshire. This variety is one of the joys of building a series of small layouts rather than one larger effort.

Personal knowledge of a landscape – its peculiarities and features, vernacular architecture and traditions – is a great starting point in creating a realistic model. Books, sketches, notes, photographs, maps and magazine articles can all help, while if you are setting out to model a landscape not familiar to you then making a personal visit or two is well worthwhile and usually very enjoyable. You can even dignify such jollies with the title of 'field trip' or 'research' to impress friends and family! Apart from recording 'modellogenic' features by photography or drawing, you can really only get the 'feel' of a place by going there and simply absorbing your surroundings. To round out this personal observation, postcards, local history books and maps (especially the 1:25000 Landranger OS maps) can all contribute to building up a mental picture on which to base your layout design.

It is very difficult to produce a definitive checklist of things you need to know about a landscape in order to model it effectively, but certain key things must be right if it is to be convincing. These include the nature of the topography – hilly, flat, steep, rolling, rocky or just plain mountainous – as getting the lie of the ground right is a key signature element of any landscape. Other such signatures are soil colour, native vegetation types, tree species and the way they occur in the landscape, the shaping and size of fields and the nature of their boundaries, the type of farming, and – particularly – the nature of the watercourses. Not too many rocky mountain streams in Lincolnshire…

'Imagineering' landscapes

Obviously, if you're setting out to model an actual location, then the landscape surroundings are determined for you, but many model railways – (the majority?) – owe more to fiction and imagination than to strict fidelity to a specific prototype. Some of the most revered and imitated of scenic model railways have as subjects places that are, to a

Above: Pendon Museum is world-renowned for the authenticity and realism of its model landscapes, but in point of fact, they're all fictional scenes. Their stunning effectiveness is due to careful observation and understanding of the subject matter, with as much as possible taken from real life and everything else made as typical as possible of the area being modelled. That, and superlative modelling standards … Here is the 'Dartmoor' scene, representing the landscape on my doorstep; it convinces me!

Below: Part of the 'Vale' scene at Pendon, with elements – buildings, gardens, domestic details, vegetation, trees and landscape parameters like ground slope and soil colours – taken from life and carefully blended into a cohesive scene that is utterly convincing.

greater or lesser extent, fictional. You won't find the village of Pendon Parva on any map of the Vale of the White Horse, but few people would argue that this in any way detracts from the stunning realism and atmosphere of the 'Vale' scene at Pendon Museum. (If you've never been to Pendon – go, and soon; it'll show you just what is possible in the field of landscape and architectural model making.)

The recent annals of British railway modelling are marked by a series of just such remarkable fictional-but-convincing scenic models: Barry Norman's 'Petherick', Jas Millham's 'Yaxford Branch', Tom Harland's 'Bramblewick', the Model Railway Club's 'Copenhagen Fields', Steve Hall's 'Halifax Kings Cross', Martin Brent's 'Arcadia', the *Model Railway Journal*'s 'Inkermann Street', the Manchester Club's 'Chee Tor' and Vincent de Bode's 'Flintfield' all spring to mind. The success of models like these is due in large part to the observance of two basic rules: take as much as possible from real life, and aim to model the typical rather than the exceptional. Masterpieces like Pendon are created by combining structures, landscape features and scenic elements that are accurately modelled from actual prototypes then brought together in as natural a way as possible, grouping them carefully into an apposite and highly-typical environment free of any freakish features – for all that these might exist somewhere in reality.

'Tis the season …

'Surely it was always summer when we made our first railway journeys …' wrote Hamilton Ellis at the beginning of his classic of railway literature, *The Trains We Loved*. Walking around the average model railway exhibition, you'd have to agree with him; almost all the journeys made by the miniature trains on view will be through picture-postcard summer countryside, perpetually green and smiling and often (to judge by the multiple shadows)

Below: Autumnal trees, dead vegetation, plenty of puddles and fallen leaves, an overcast sky and low-level lighting help define the late-October setting of my Dutch-prototype layout 'Bodesmeer'. The effect I'm trying for here is 'sunshine between the showers'.

Above: The popular option – the lush greenery of early summer in the Kentish Weald, as recreated by Bill Rankine on 'Baldown' in 2mm scale. This scale offers the scenic modeller great scope as it facilitates landscape modelling in the broader sense – representing a whole tract of countryside in a relatively modest area.

do so because they incorporate seasonal anachronisms. One comes across bare winter ploughland alongside crops ready for harvest, shaded by trees in pale, spring-like greens but bordered by hedges heavy with the growth of a long season. Sheep graze unshorn under a blazing August sun amid gambling new-born spring lambs, while not so much as a blade of grass ever gets dry and sun-bleached…

Summer, with the trees lushly canopied, the hedges and verges rampant and the world generally in full bloom, is certainly an attractive proposition for a layout setting, but it is far from the only option. Representing other seasons can also offer rich dividends in atmosphere, creating an effective and less-usual setting for the actual trains. Choosing to eschew summer can also pose some rewarding modelling challenges – a wet day in midwinter is no sinecure in modelling terms, be the subject rural or urban. My own view is that the intended season is a part of the overall concept of a layout, just as fundamental as period or location. Like these factors it is a consideration that, for realistic results, needs bearing in mind at all stages of the design; trees that in full summer foliage will block a view in winter will frame it nicely with their bare limbs.

The pillar of salt syndrome

This is one of the fundamental dichotomies of scenic railway modelling, where the trains run realistically but everything else that should be mobile – vehicles, figures, animals, birds – is frozen into a quite unnatural rigidity. The same stasis persists, unfortunately, with the many aspects of our miniature landscape that should also involve subtle and constant movement of one sort or another; where are the rippling streams, wind-ruffled tree-tops, swaying grasses and corn-stalks or clouds scudding across the sky? Let alone roaring waterfalls, waves crashing on the shore and trees leaning to a gale? Model railways exist in a world of utter calm and inertia, where the weather is never ever anything other than a dead calm, all is silent, and nothing living ever so much as twitches.

This sort of thing is all supposed to be dealt with by 'suspension of disbelief' – which,

basking in the warmth of several suns! So prevalent is this unrelentingly green and sunny setting that it is quite a relief to stumble across a layout portraying a bit of grubby urban grot or, even rarer, one set on a dull day in December rather than high noon in June.

Well, it is understandable that most of us – for whom a model railway is to some extent an *escape* from reality – should seek to create something to some extent idealised, a setting redolent of balmy summer days in some favoured nook in this green and pleasant Isle (but without the bugs that bite, less-than-idyllic rural smells, noisy farm machinery and other downsides of reality!). Choosing to portray summer, however, doesn't mean that a model has to be unrealistic; as with any other aspect of scenic modelling, it just needs to be well-observed. Alas, many summery layouts that strike a false note in the eye of the viewer we're told, allows us to accept or ignore howling anachronisms like toppling waves that curl but never break, horses arrested in mid-gallop and the patient fireman on the footplate with his shovel-full of coal poised perpetually in mid-air; poor fellow must have awful arm-ache by now! My disbelief obviously has faulty springing, as I find all these things worse than irksome; unacceptable, in fact. So I go out of my way to avoid them, by – as far as possible – 'designing them out' of my model landscapes. I only incorporate still or very gently-flowing waters, while I try to create backdrops and scenic settings suggestive of a calm day. Vehicles are relatively few (an advantage of modelling earlier periods, when the roads were far less busy) and those that do appear are parked or otherwise sited so that they can remain stationary without looking silly. But, most important of all, people and animals are in attitudes of repose; my horses, sheep and cattle graze, lie or stand patiently, while the population sits, stands or leans in postures they could, in reality, comfortably maintain for some time. Nobody, ever, breaks into an amble, much less a run…

Scenic animation is an area of railway modelling where there is still a lot of scope for experiment. Thus far, the odd revolving windmill, oily-smoking chimney, jerkily-waving figure or speeding road vehicle is about all we've managed in the way of movement, although providing realistic ambient noise should not be a problem in these days of solid-state sound chips. Wind would also appear to be possible, as would effects generated by moving or changing lighting. The powered model road vehicle situation is getting better, with smaller and more refined drivetrains, smaller batteries and even miniature radio control systems. No, the big problems are running water and inert people and animals. But who knows what the future may hold in terms of sophisticated fluid technology, computer control of special effects, miniature animatronics and other micro-mechanisms? Much technology we now take for granted would have seemed equally far-fetched a decade or so ago.

Above: Avoiding 'frozen' poses helps realism in figures and animals. This cheery 7mm scale chappie taking his ease on 'Alexandra Yard' looks quite natural as he is in a pose that would, in reality, be static.

Below: Vehicles can also be modelled in attitudes where the fact that they are not moving doesn't jar. Here, on my old 'Tregarrick' layout, Uglow's fish-cart, with shafts to the sky, awaits the return of the crabbers and line-boats working the rocky North Cornish coast. The awful majesty of PC Trewenna awaits – well, anything really; for the vigilance of the law is ceaseless…

Display height

The 'feel' of a particular landscape is often determined as much by how we see it as what we're actually seeing. For instance, much of East Anglia is 'big sky' country. When you stand on the bank of the Old Bedford River and look out over the flat expanse of the fens, the actual landscape only occupies the very bottom of your field of vision; most of what you see is sky. And – unless you're up in an aircraft or perched on the top of Boston 'Stump' – that's the only way you'll ever see this countryside; you look *across* it, not down on it. So, for a model to capture this feel, it too needs to be viewed across, not down – which means that it will need to be displayed at a height that puts it in the right relationship with the viewer. Pretty high, in other words – particularly if it's being viewed from a standing position.

Life is a little easier when it comes to hillier territory, where the landscape can in reality be perceived from viewpoints of different heights. Thus, looking down into a valley as from an adjacent hillside is an entirely natural way of seeing such an undulating landscape. The more mountainous the scenery, the wider the range of possible viewing heights and the easier it is to capture the feel of the landscape. Does this explain the popularity of often positively precipitous settings for model railways? Certainly, in the USA there seems to be a preponderance of layouts that go in for what I term 'Rocky Mountain Whoopee' scenery – although much of it owes more to Walt Disney than realistic observation!

Choosing the right display height has a major influence on the effectiveness of any landscape modelling. This is a context in which the traditional 30–36in 'table top' height – although a lot better than the nursery trainset on the floor – is very limiting. It is still too low to present a natural view of the model, even from a seated position. Display heights for layouts have been going up steadily in recent years, however, with a nominal track level set 3ft 9in (45in) from the floor now being a popular compromise. This gives most people of average height a nice natural viewpoint when seated on a normal chair, while being low enough to work on comfortably from a standing position. And, crucially, such a display height is compatible with the use of an effective backscene. For model railway viewing/operation, a roll-around office chair is ideal as it enables you to scoot around the layout while still seated and will usually incorporate height adjustment so you can set it appropriately to give yourself the best viewpoint.

Backdrops – the great space expanders

A trick question: how can you model umpteen square miles of rolling countryside in any scale within the thickness of a sheet of paper? Answer – by painting it on a backdrop. In this country, we are very bad at backdrops, something no self-respecting American scenic model would be seen without. This reluctance to make use of one of the simplest and most effective aids to realism has long puzzled me; I conclude that it has a lot to do with the influence of the British exhibition layout, traditionally sited at table-top height or a little more and operated from the rear. If there is any attempt at a backscene on such a layout, it is usually only a few inches high, far too low to incorporate an eye-level horizon and is thus hopelessly unconvincing. To my eye, this sort of display simply serves to set off nicely the operator's midriff, usually enhanced by that stylish purple-and-lime-green pullover his aunt Daisy knitted him for Christmas.

Creating a truly effective backdrop is nowhere near as difficult as a lot of people assume provided you obey a few more basic rules and don't try to outdo Michelangelo. The first rule is to make it high enough. In the real world, the horizon is always on your eye-level – which is why tall fellows see further than the likes of Rice! So, for a truly 'natural' look the backscene needs to be high enough up to get the horizon-line at the eye level of the viewer and the 'top of the sky' some way above this – preferably right out of the natural field of view. The ideal is to get this horizon level exact, but as different viewers

Above: Backdrops can be enormously effective at expanding the visual dimensions of a model without calling for extra real-estate. In this example the actual modelling is only a few inches deep; the backdrop provides the rest of the setting.

Below: The author – no beauty, he – operating 'Trerice' and showing the viewing relationship to the layout with the latter at its normal display height with a track level of a shade over 54in from the floor. This gives a reasonable, if not perfect, relationship to the horizon-line within the backdrop and results in a fairly 'natural' view. From square-on, you don't see the lighting and top bracing bar, visible in this view. The fascia has been rubbed down ready for long-overdue painting and it is now a neutral sage green colour.

will have different eye levels this is obviously not possible. In point of fact, an error of plus or minus four inches or so does not jar too much, which gives quite a bit of leeway.

I have the benefit of moderate stature (a tad over 5ft 7in) which puts my eye level at about 47in seated and around 62in standing. So those are the 'target' heights for my backdrop horizons. In which context, that popular 45in display height works very well for seated operation; my East Anglian layout 'Cade's Green' is mounted thus. At exhibitions and other situations where a layout is operated while standing (or while lounging on a bar stool or other similarly elevated perch), I go for a much greater display height. 'Trerice' – which lives on shelf brackets on a bedroom wall – has the track level 54in above the floor, and this is a figure widely used for walk-around layouts in the USA.

The other rule concerning backdrops is to keep them simple and to ensure that the colours used match and blend with

or otherwise complement those in the modelled scene – something that can take a little experiment. There's normally no need for detail on backscenes and perspective on structures, etc., is also best avoided. In fact, in a large number of cases, simple sky with perhaps the barest outlines of hills or other basic landscape features is all that is needed. Even a plain background of neutral colour

Below: Backdrops don't need to be complex or detailed to be effective. On Andrew Duncan's 'Maiden Newtown' layout, the Dorset downland setting is very simply represented. The backdrop is rendered in a restrained and limited palette of colours using emulsion paint on hardboard, but the result is a real feeling of open countryside with the railway running along the floor of a valley. Once again, figures in repose avoid the freeze-frame look.

can be effective at cutting out distracting background, the other chief function of a backdrop. When 'blending' the backdrop with the modelled scene, the best bet is to make use of features – landforms, trees, hedges, walls, buildings and so on – that are part of the scene to hide or disguise the point where 3-D modelling meets 2-D paint.

Things to avoid as far as humanly possible when creating backscenes include abrupt changes of direction (i.e. angles or corners, concave or convex) and, of course, visible joins; the real sky is a uniform, continuous surface that is visibly 'flat', while it certainly doesn't have dead-straight cracks running up and down it at regular intervals! Likewise, shadows of modelled objects cast on the backdrop are a dead giveaway that can be difficult to avoid. One way of preventing the problem is to place trees, structures, telegraph poles and the like

in actual contact with the backdrop, so they cast no shadow at all. Otherwise, such things need to be positioned well in front of the plane of the drop, in a relationship to the light source that ensures any shading falls on the 3-D part of the scene and not on the 'sky'. A further enemy of convincing backscenes is unwanted and obtrusive texture like prominent brush-strokes, uneven paint surfaces, a coarse base material or dirt, hairs and other stray bits of the environment sticking to or caught up in the paintwork.

Contriving seamless backscenes for sectional portable layouts certainly isn't easy. The most elegant answer is a continuous theatrical-style 'backcloth' that can be detached from the layout and rolled up for transport. Vincent de Bode has done this on 'Flintfield' using roller blind fabric as a basis, clipped to and supported from an overhead 'raft' that also carries the layout lighting; I've done much the same thing in the past – but more prosaically, using heavyweight reinforced (scrim-backed) wall-lining paper with the edges further reinforced with self-adhesive carpet binding tape. But I must admit the paper doesn't 'hang' as nicely as Vincent's fabric and is more prone to creasing and transit damage. For permanent layouts, I generally make backdrops from hardboard or thin MDFB, which can be formed to quite tight curvatures. As coved (i.e. curved) corners are always the aim, a material that bends easily and smoothly is essential.

To avoid brush marks – which can show like the devil on plain sky – it's best to apply paint by means other than a brush. Vincent's backscene was created by Len de Vries, who is a wizard with the airbrush; he used fine acrylic paints working on blind fabric that was already dyed a suitable shade of sky blue. I use a small paint roller (the sort made for painting radiators and the like) to roll out and blend emulsion and acrylic paints initially applied by brush, dropper or by being dabbed on with a bit of sponge. Using the roller blends the colours, taking away any hard edges, and results in an even overall texture that doesn't show under the layout lighting.

Probably the ultimate in realistic display is to combine a backdrop with the use of ply or MDF side 'wings' and a proscenium arch/lighting beam 'top' matching the fascia 'bottom' to form an all-round frame for the model, just as an appropriate picture-frame is used to set off a painting; the pictures of 'Trerice' should give an idea of this. Aptly positioned, such a framed presentation can cut off the line of sight to hide things (like the 'top of the sky' or the 'edge of the earth') that are best not seen. This sort of display framing is best finished overall in some contrasting neutral shade that sets off the colours used in the modelled scene. Personally, I try to avoid the matt black sometimes suggested for this as it is rather 'dead' visually and doesn't give a very natural effect; greys, browns, beiges, dark greens and some blues can all work well – much depends on the colour balance and shades contained in the scene. While you certainly don't want a high gloss finish on your display framing, it doesn't have to be dead flat and featureless either; rather than using paint, you can stain the ply or MDF with wood dyes and finish with a satin varnish, cover it with a suitable fabric, or even a fine grade of carpeting.

Landscaping

Model landscaping comes in two halves: creating the basic landform, and dressing it with suitable textures and colours to represent vegetation and other ground surfaces. The first thing to say about this fascinating process is that there's no one 'right' way to do it, experience having shown that equally effective results can be obtained by widely differing means. It has always been an aspect of railway modelling offering great scope for experiment and innovation, producing some ingenious uses of materials and a whole range of original techniques. The only point that needs making in this regard is that, while different combinations of material and technique can be used to reproduce any given landscape texture or feature, it is best not to mix these alternatives within the context of a single layout. Consistency and homogeneity are more likely to produce a realistic result.

As with the other aspects of constructing a model railway, the landscaping benefits greatly from a bit of pre-planning and thought. Traditionally, it came at a late stage in the layout-construction sequence; you built the baseboards, laid, painted and ballasted the track, wired and tested the layout – and then thought about making it look like the real world. Experience has shown that this order of business isn't always such a good idea, as some landscaping techniques are pretty messy and can have a decidedly deleterious impact on that immaculate finished trackwork! It's impossible to generalise as to the best order in which to tackle the job as much will depend on the nature of the layout, but considering the When? of landscaping might suggest a different approach to the How?

For instance, some landscaping techniques lend themselves to a piecemeal approach, enabling the overall landscape – landform and texturing – to be built up as a series of small units rather than as a single, large-scale whole. The choice of material is important here, in that some are only really suited to an all-in-one-go type of operation. For instance, in my experience, choosing to base landscaping on laminations of solid material – such as expanded polystyrene sheet carved to shape – means doing the job in one big hit, whereas fabricating landscape over card formers with some form of 'shell' surface makes it easy to tackle small and discreet areas. In fact, there are so many possible ways of creating model landscapes that it would not really be practicable to describe them all here, even in outline. In over forty years of building model railways, I've had a go at most of the more popular methods; so what follows is what works for me! Other brands are available…

Creating the landform

Over the years, railway modellers have attempted to make model land forms out of just about every likely material and quite a few unlikely ones – solid concrete, hessian sacking and old nappies, to name but three! Traditional techniques came to rely on such staples as scrap wood, crumpled newspaper, card, brown paper, papier-mâché, glue size, chicken wire, sawdust and builder's plaster, while more recently other materials have been used – plaster bandages, Artex, expanded metal lath, plastic mesh, expanded polystyrene, polyurethane foam, resin, and glassfibre.

There are two basic approaches to creating landform; you either start with something solid and sculpt it to shape, or you fabricate the required contours over formers with a thin 'shell' surface. Both methods give you relatively precise control over the final topography, although they entail very different techniques. Solid landscaping used to be much in vogue, often executed in large volumes of plaster on substantial timber-and-chicken-wire frameworks. The result was solid all right; several well-known classic large American layouts are documented as consuming several full-sized tons of Gyproc in this way – not so good for portability! Nowadays, solid landscaping is usually based on laminations of expanded polystyrene structural insulation sheet 50mm or 100mm thick, stuck together with an inert adhesive and carved to shape. This job can be accomplished either with some form of hot-wire tool, or the styrene can be cut and abraded with saws and surforms – a spectacularly messy process involving little balls of styrene that get *everywhere*! Once the desired landform has been attained, the surface of the sheet is sealed, usually with a skin of plaster bandage or a coat of textured emulsion paint.

Fabricated shell landscape is constructed over a series of formers, cut from ply, thin MDF, hardboard or card. Usually, it is sufficient to use formers set at approximately right-angles to the direction of the main slope of the land and 4–6in apart, but more precise control of the final contours can be achieved by closing up this spacing or by building an egg-crate grid of formers running across the slope as well as up and down. These formers are topped with some form of surface support/reinforcement – a role in which many materials will serve. Popular alternatives include chicken-wire, expanded metal lath, old net curtaining, plastic mesh or a lattice of thin card strips.

The actual landscape surface is laid over this supporting material; it can be made of plaster bandage or kitchen towelling soaked in soupy plaster (hardshell) or thick paper towelling stuck in place and impregnated with diluted PVA glue (glueshell).

The glories of glueshell

My own preference is very much for the glueshell approach, using a mix of ply, thin MDF and thick card (normal double-skin card carton material) to build the formers – all fixed together right speedily with a hot glue gun. I do often go for the 'full grid' approach, as working with card and the glue gun makes this so quick and easy. Over the formers I normally opt to build a lattice of thin card strips – in which role the ubiquitous corn-flake packet is invaluable; once again, the glue gun serves to secure these. When it comes to the surface, I'm a dedicated PVA-and-paper towel man. The PVA I use is 'school white glue', which you can buy from educational suppliers or good craft shops in five-litre plastic cans for only a few pounds. It's relatively low-strength and washable – perfectly adequate for the job. My towel of choice is the coarse-textured grey, green or buff Cresco stuff you often find in public loos or on garage forecourts. This is surprisingly tough and, being designed to be absorbent, soaks up the glue well. If you get your PVA from an educational suppliers, they'll almost certainly stock Cresco towels, too; a single pack is a lifetime's supply!

To make glueshell, you simply tear the paper towel into small irregular pieces – the more intricate and convoluted the landscape feature you're modelling, the smaller the pieces of towel need to be. The only implements you need are a cheap, stiff hogs hair paintbrush about half-an-inch in diameter (the educational supplier again), a jam-jar full of water and a container of some sort to pour a modest measure of PVA into; individual yoghurt pots are just the job. The technique couldn't be simpler; brush some PVA over a few square inches of your card lattice or other sub-surface support, then pick up a piece of towel with the tip of the brush and lay it in place.

Above: Card landscape formers in place on 'Pixton Hill', ready for the surface supports (a card strip lattice, in this case) and then glueshell surfacing and ground texturing. Note that this 'messy' scenic work is being carried out before the track is laid – often a better order of proceeding.

Below: Laying glueshell – paper towelling soaked in diluted PVA white glue. Here, I'm adding some additional foreground terrain to 'Corrieshalloch' by sticking the towelling to a supporting lattice of card strips laid to match up with a new layout fascia. Simon de Souza

Dip your brush in the water to thin the glue a bit then work the PVA well into the towel until it is saturated. Simply repeat this process until you've covered the desired area with a skin of PVA saturated-towel several layers thick. Then prime your next section of support lattice (I find about 4 x 4in a convenient sort of area to do at a go; small enough that you can apply all your layers before the glue starts to go off) and carry on. You can do as much or as little as you want at a go, and the technique is precise enough to allow you to carry the landscape surfacing right up to structures or to the edge of the trackwork.

The advantages of glueshell made like this are manifold; it is versatile, quick to execute, light in weight, very cheap and – once it's gone off – incredibly strong. You can cut into it easily with a craft knife or scissors, patch it or alter it with ease, and stick things to it with almost any adhesive. Unlike plaster skin hardshell, finished glueshell remains resilient and flexible and is very resistant to damage. It doesn't chip or flake like plaster, and even if it is exposed by accidental abrasion of surfacing materials its grey-green or buff colour is far less obtrusive

Below: Rockwork on 'Trerice' uses the real thing – tiny frost-shattered fragments of genuine Delabole slate gathered on the edge of Bodmin Moor, set into hot glue on the paper-towel landform before the vegetation textures were added.

than the staring white of plaster. You also don't have to wait until the glueshell dries before you go on to add the scenic texturing, as the same PVA adhesive is the basis of this process and you can simply 'plant' your vegetation straight on to the wet and sticky surface of the shell. I very often go from bare baseboard to finished scenery in one seamless process, and, best of all, it's a process that's not particularly messy. You could carry out glueshell construction attired in your best Armani without deleterious effects, and it's certainly a lot kinder to track, carpets, structures, inquisitive children and family pets than dribbly, soupy, messy plaster or lots of clingy little beads of expanded polystyrene.

Rockwork

All sorts of things have been used to represent rock in miniature landscape modelling, from the real thing to layered, torn wood-fibre board or crumpled paper. For many years, raw cork bark was advocated; it looked OK if you were modelling the Cheddar Gorge or somewhere similarly precipitous. Nowadays, things have become a little more authentic; rock is no longer generalised, and attempts are made to recreate the stratification, form, texture and colouring of the specific rock appropriate to the area being modelled. The usual raw material for rock-modelling is plaster of some sort, either modelled or carved in situ, or produced as rock castings that are then set in place on the layout. Self-setting modelling clays such as DAS can also make good model rockwork – it all depends what it is you're trying to reproduce. You *can* buy pre-cast and even pre-coloured rockwork in plaster, resin or expanded foam – although I have to say I've rarely seen any such off-the-peg rock that was truly convincing.

As with so much else, realistic rock-modelling starts with observation. Good colour photographs of real-life rock formations can be invaluable reference – although taking such pictures can get you some funny looks! When I was planning my H0 scale New England harbourside layout 'Roque Bluffs', I spent a few days happily bumbling about the relevant bits of the Maine coastline gathering reference material of this kind – an activity regarded with incredulity, amusement or (in one instance) acute suspicion by the locals. Fortunately, the Sheriff's deputies were very understanding…and the resulting snaps were invaluable when it came to reproducing that characteristic low-lying rocky shoreline from 3,000 miles away!

The Americans are the great masters of model rockwork, so it is no surprise that the best rock-modelling products are of US origin. Probably the most useful to UK modellers are the range of rock moulds made by Woodland Scenics; there are 15 of these covering a wide assortment of different rock types, so it's usually possible to find something appropriate. Although made for use with hydrocal lightweight plaster, I've found that ordinary plaster of Paris (which you can get from craft shops or at most chemists) works as well; just mix *gently* to a soupy consistency and pour in. (If you mix the plaster vigorously you're more likely to entrap air, resulting in bubbles in the mix and pockmarks on the castings.) On larger castings, I lay a strip of gauze bandage into the rear surface of the wet plaster for reinforcement.

Rock castings are best installed on the layout using a decorator's filler like Polyfilla, which has good adhesive properties as well as filling in any gaps. You can break the plaster castings up and combine the pieces in different ways, perhaps using fragments of castings from different moulds, to produce rockwork of a nature and extent appropriate to the situation; the Polyfilla will blend everything together. The same material – or a textured filler like Artex – also forms the usual basis for modelled or carved rockwork, when the basic shape of the rock formation is built up in the filler then either 'modelled' with a palette-knife or similar tool while it is still 'plastic', or allowed to harden before being carved and incised to give an appropriate texture. This is an intuitive sort of process, quite satisfying and very relaxing; after all, if you make a mistake or you don't like the result, you simply bung on another layer of filler and have another go. You can carve the filler with knives, sharpened

screwdrivers, lino-cutting tools or just about any other implement that seems appropriate.

Modelled rockwork can also be executed in purpose-made modelling clays including DAS Pronto, which have the advantage of staying plastic for far longer than most plaster-based fillers. You can build up such rockwork from individual lumps of clay, or shape and incise

Above: Some very effective rockwork in DAS modelling clay on the Norwood Club's 'Ulpha Light Railway'. Keen observation coupled with some skilled carving (although, let it be admitted, it took several attempts) arrived at this result.

Below: Raw cast-plaster rockwork in place on 'Roque Bluffs', bedded and blended with decorator's filler. Loose stones in this case are from cat litter. The rock mould used was 'washed rock' from the Woodland Scenics range.

a layer of the material spread over the basic scenery shell. You can also impress textures into DAS; try making a ball of crumpled aluminium foil and rolling it over the surface of the clay to get an irregular stone texture, or simply prodding the surface with a piece of rough tree-bark or broken wood. As with so many aspects of scenic modelling, experiment costs virtually nothing but can often yield highly satisfying results

I always get my rockwork in place and coloured before trying to add any ground texture or vegetation detail. To colour plaster rocks you can use watercolours, poster colour, diluted matt acrylic paints or – probably best of all – the water-based 'rock stains' from Woodland Scenics which are very effective and easy to use. It is well worth viewing the 'How to use rock moulds' video clips on the Woodland Scenics website, or you can get the *Scenery Handbook* from them which covers techniques relevant to all their various scenic products. DAS rocks are basically self-coloured pale limestone grey which can be highlighted and have its texture enhanced using washes of stain or pale grey matt acrylic paint brushed dry on to high points with a stiff brush.

Basic ground cover

We live in a fertile and temperate isle with a more-than-generous rainfall (especially on my bit of western Dartmoor, where we get nearly 80in a year!). This means that there is very little bare soil to be seen in the predominantly verdant English countryside, where the native vegetation is profuse and varied. Keeping lineside growth in check was one of the chief preoccupations of the PW department – even in the heart of urban areas, where every scrap of waste ground soon acquired a thick covering of rough grass, nettles, brambles and scrub trees if untended. This type of growth is a great characteristic of the typical railway environment, where it covers any cutting-side not laying bare the rock, together with every embankment or piece of made ground. Once you get over the boundary fence, the same families of plants will be found busy colonising the field-margins, the banks of waterways and

roadside verges. Representing this type of rough and varied vegetation is a fundamental aspect of modelling the British scene.

There are many other types of ground-cover to replicate of course, and much of the challenge and skill of landscape modelling comes in getting the right mix of textures and colours to represent the various different prototype possibilities. Tackling arable farmland, for instance, might call for newly-ploughed soil still standing in furrows – although not as often as you might believe. Such fields will soon be harrowed to a tilth, then drilled and rolled – shortly leading to sprouting corn, green crops of various heights, standing corn ready for harvest and, finally, to stubble. I've seen plenty of (usually unconvincing) ploughed fields, and a quite a lot of standing corn. The odd harvest-in-progress sometimes figures, but I don't think I've ever come across any of the other stages! Not all crops are cereals, either; you can't model East Anglia without getting to grips with sugar-beet, turnips, kale and swedes, while modellers of the modern scene need to find some way of dealing with vast tracts of eye-searing oilseed rape.

Then there's pasture – in reality far from the tame-and-tidy affair that figures on so many models. Sheep-cropped turf on chalk downland may result in the sort of uniformly green and even surface so often seen in miniature, but elsewhere such ground cover is only found on golf-courses. Even these are predominantly rough – or where would lie the challenge? Most pasture is both taller, lusher and a good deal coarser than downland turf, with a good mix of thistles and docks and clumps of taller grass in the wet spots, while in winter (or bad summers!) the areas around gateways, water troughs or feeders will be poached and muddy. Boggy areas and riverbanks may sprout reeds and rushes, while the hedgerows that surround so much British pasture will be a dense mix of species – hazel, ash, thorn, holly, beech and hornbeam – close-laid, banked or ditched or both, with occasional mature trees.

I could go on, but I think that I've made the point that there's a good deal more to

producing realistic ground cover than simply
sprinkling on a bit of green sawdust. We need
to employ a range of different materials both
individually and in combination to create the
right mix of textures and colours. As usual,
there are lots of possibilities, with many well-
known scenic modellers having favourite
'brews' for the different types of vegetation.

*Right: Highly convincing limestone rock on
Phillipe Moniot's H0 layout, set in the Ardennes
region of Belgium. This rock is modelled in
a wood-fibre and plaster mix that is readily
carved with a palette knife during setting;
Artex fibre-reinforced filler can be used in much
the same way.*

*Below left: 'Corrieshalloch' grows some high-
speed rough grass – sprinkling the basic foliage
texture mix of chopped-up carpet felt, acrylic
grass fibre and ground foam on to PVA-coated
glueshell. The hair-stylist had the afternoon off
when we took these pictures…* Simon de Souza

*Below right: Fortunately, she left her hairspray
behind – just as well, as it's a vital last stage in
securing scenic textures in place.* Simon de Souza

Materials commonly used include carpet felt, surgical lint, plumbers hemp, sisal string, dyed sawdust, ground foam, rayon or nylon flock, 'polyfibre' filament, rubberised horsehair, foliage matting, dried tea leaves, sand, bristles and natural root or foliage armatures such as some types of lichen or 'sea foam'. Glues include PVA, contact adhesives such as Bostik, UHU or Evo-Stik, spray carpet or photo-mounting adhesives, artist's fixatives, acrylic matte medium, and cheap hairspray.

To explore all these alternatives would obviously take more space than I have here, so I'm once again going to content myself with describing my own methods, materials and mixtures, together with the techniques I use to apply them. I don't do much painting of landscaping, preferring to rely on a mixture of appropriately pre-coloured materials to achieve the shades and effects I'm after. These combinations produce the results seen in the various pictures illustrating this book – which cover quite a number of different British landscapes ranging from East Anglia to Cornwall via Dorset, the Welsh Borders, the Scottish Highlands and the Yorkshire

Below: Rough grass texture on 'Hepton Wharf', made and applied as described. Leafy shrubs are a mix of Heki foliage matting and ground foam, and the stunted trees are based on sprigs of Dartmoor heather. The rockwork is in Artex plaster. The solitary figure is well-and-truly in repose!

Pennines – not to mention those side-trips to Holland and the State of Maine. These methods work for me, but you may well come up with something better!

So – to start with rough ground cover for embankments, cuttings and other similar situations. I use a mixture three ingredients to produce a basic rough grass-and-weed 'mix', which I use alongside and in between materials chosen to represent specific plant types. The basis of the 'basic rough' mix is pale-fawn coloured felt carpet underlay – not laid as it is, but merely used as a source of suitable fibre. I pull the felt off the usual plastic mesh backing in small 'sheets', then cut strips of about a quarter of an inch or a tad wider off the edge of these with scissors. I place these strips of felt in a suitable container (margarine tub) and rub them between my fingers until I've reduced them to a sort of coarse fluff. To this I then add quantities of ground foam (Woodland Scenics turf, medium grade) and rayon flock ('grassfasser' in German – which is where mine comes from, being either Heki or Silflor). The shades I use depend on the season being portrayed; I judge the amounts and colour balance by eye – you can always adjust these by sprinkling on extra material.

The rough grass mix is applied in conjunction with the materials I use to represent specific plants: chopped sisal string for rushes, fine plumber's hemp for tall dried grass, small chunks of torn rubberised horsehair with fine foam foliage for brambles, fragments of scouring pad for thistles and scraps of foliage mat for leafy weeds like docks or stinging nettles. None of this material is scattered on to an evenly glued surface; rather it is 'planted' into a thick final layer of all-but-undiluted PVA, usually the final coat painted on when laying the top layer of the glueshell scenery skin. As with building up the skin, I work on a smallish area at a time – the grass mix and other plant materials being applied as a series of small clumps or bunches 'planted' using my fingertips or a pair of cheap plastic tweezers to build up a characteristically uneven growth.

Once the basic vegetation is in place over a reasonable area, I adjust the colour balance

Above: The tranquil waters of the harbour at Roque Bluffs consist of a considerable number of thin coats (30+) of polyurethane gloss yacht varnish on a base of heavy wall-lining paper painted a dark green-blue shade with hints of brown using artist's acrylics. The slightly uneven texture of the paper gives a subtle but convincing sub-surface ripple effect.

to get the effect I want by gently sprinkling on ground foams or acrylic fibres of the appropriate shades. I'll also adjust textures, perhaps adding more 'leafy' material or building up the height and density of the vegetation in some places. Any colour highlights or other details of the vegetation – such as flowers, dead or contrasting leaves, bare branches, fallen wood, rubbish, individual pieces of stone or 'slides' of scree – also go on now. Finally, the whole area gets a generous 'blat' of cheap hairspray to hold everything in place. The same basic techniques will work for any scale, but you do need to adjust the texture of the mix accordingly. I chop the felt much shorter for N scale, using the finest grades of ground foam and foliage mat and easing up on the acrylic fibre. Fine dyed sawdust and sand are also useful in the smaller scale. For 0 gauge, longer felt, coarser ground foam and more acrylic fibre/hemp/sisal make an appropriate brew.

Water

Now, here's a tricky customer in scenic modelling terms. Why? Well, the big problem is that, in most instances, water in the landscape is constantly moving – something we simply can't replicate using our static materials; the old pillar of salt scenario. My own approach

to the problem is, as far as possible, to avoid it – by not trying to represent what I can't convincingly model – which includes moving water, especially violently disturbed water – waves, rapids, waterfalls, weirs and foaming torrents of all kinds. That's because I know the result will just jar my perception every time I look at it – although I have to say other folk don't seem so worried by such anomalies.

Still or gently moving water, on the other hand, can be realistically and readily reproduced, with the resulting reflections adding greatly to the atmosphere and veracity of the modelled scene. Virtually all my own layouts have incorporated water of this nature, some of them extensively. If you study a placid stream from close to, you'll see that the surface exhibits subtle changes in level, gentle eddies or undulations caused by features on the stream-bed interrupting the flow. But these surface features stay in

Above: 'Calm as a millpond' – as here, fronting the Upper Mill at Pendon Parva. The limpid 'water' in this situation is absolutely flat and still – so has been modelled using a sheet of Perspex painted a very dark green-brown shade (almost black) on the underside. The result is totally convincing, helped by the careful, well-observed work around the banks.

Below: Mountain streams are not all foaming torrents rip-roaring over rocks; in dry weather, they can present a far more tranquil face, with 'quiet' ripples and relatively calm stretches between the boulders littering the streambed. This is the River Lyd on western Dartmoor.

the same place, unlike waves or spreading ripples, so that from a little way away they are seen simply as slight surface irregularities that are, to all intents and purposes, static. That's an effect you *can* model…

Still or limpid water lies completely flat and level, so the first essential in modelling it is a base that is likewise. I like the smooth face of hardboard or MDF for its total lack of texture and dead-true surface. Real water doesn't exhibit too many seams or gaps, either – so if at all possible avoid carrying watery areas over baseboard joints. If this is unavoidable, disguise the join with a bridge, jetty, weir or other feature that can hide the 'impossible crevice'. I also try to make the water surface from a piece of material big enough not to need any joining; any cracks, dimples or other imperfections need to be filled with fine Polyfilla and sanded very smooth.

Having created a smooth base, the next step is to paint the surface a suitable colour which – for still or slow water of any depth – I make a dark green-brown, slightly lighter towards the edges and tending almost to black in the middle; matt acrylic paints are my choice for this job, as for most scenic work. Once the base colour is dry, it is varnished to a very high gloss to make it look truly 'wet'. To achieve this, I've found that by far the best material is traditional oil-based polyurethane gloss yacht varnish or similar; original Ronseal is my usual choice. For mill-ponds and similar oases of still and calm, I carefully brush on a great many thin coats to build up a deep but completely smooth layer of varnish; 30 to 50 coats is not uncommon. For slow-flowing or slightly troubled water exhibiting gentle surface eddies or undulations, I use fewer but thicker coats of varnish – still brush-applied and aiming at much the same overall thickness (at least 1–2mm). However, rather than brushing-out the varnish to a smooth finish I 'puddle' it on to get a slightly dimpled finish. Understatement is the key to the right look. I never, *ever* pour varnish on to create a water surface, as sometimes advocated; it is far too uncontrollable a process and always creates a give-away curved meniscus where the 'water' meets banks, bridge-piers or other verticals.

Trees

Trees are among the most dominant features of much of the British landscape. Unless you're portraying the bleaker bits of Northern Scotland, the High Pennines, the North Wales Mountains or the middle of Dartmoor, you're going to need to model them, and probably quite a few of them at that. British arboriculture exhibits terrific variety (except for those dour forestry plantations made up of monotonous, crowded ranks of Sitka spruce or Douglas fir). Native deciduous trees and characteristic conifers like Scots pine or larch are the great determiners of landscape character as well as unequivocally defining the season. Nothing this side of a 10ft snowdrift says 'winter' more eloquently than a bare-branched oak.

A perennial problem for the modeller, realistic miniature trees are not as rare as they once were – but they are not yet that commonplace. There are now some tolerable ready-made specimens to be had – such as the K&M range distributed by Peco – but they're not cheap and are still nowhere near as good as handmade trees. Almost invariably, they're far too small – an oak or elm of average habit should come out 8–10in tall in 4mm scale, where most commercial trees are little more than half that height. As is always the case

with off-the-peg scenic items, you get the twin drawbacks of ubiquity (everybody else has the same tree on their layout) and inconsistency of texture and colour with the other elements of your modelled scene. Certainly, a ready-made tree is better than no tree at all, but as you'll probably have gathered from the foregoing, I'm an advocate of 'growing your own'.

It's an uncomfortable fact that there's probably more work in making a truly effective 4mm scale tree than there is in, say, building a modest structure or an item of freight rolling stock; several hours-worth, in other words. Life gets a little easier in N scale, although the small size brings a few textural problems of its own, but move up to 0 and the problems multiply by leaps and bounds. This may be the detail-freak's scale par excellence for locos and stock, but when it comes to trees – especially if they're in the foreground – that degree of fidelity could call for individually applied leaves and a fully modelled branch structure. Pretty daunting when you realise a typical English hedgerow elm in 7mm scales out at the better part of 2ft tall and should have something in excess of 200,000 leaves!

Mind you, life these days is rosier than it used

Below: The ultimate scenic modelling challenge? Creating a convincing reproduction of this typical group of English hedgerow trees in their winter garb (or lack of garb!) would be a considerable undertaking in any scale and all-but-impossible in 0 gauge.

Above: Mature trees – elm and ash – in full summer foliage on 'Petherick'. The models have a basic armature of stranded soft iron wire covered in a mixture of Polyfilla and PVA glue to give the trunks and main branches. Barry used ground foam (Woodland Scenics coarse turf) over clumps of rubberised horsehair to produce the twig structure and foliage.

to be as there is a far better selection of materials available to aid the tree-modeller. In particular, the advent of 'teasable' foliage matting has made that aspect of miniature arboriculture, at least, considerably easier and more effective. There are also flexible plastic tree armatures, a wide range of ground-up-foam foliage materials giving different textures and colours, and fine-stranded green or brown-dyed Polyfibre netting to bulk out foliage. New natural materials have also come into use, most notably sea foam – a low-growing, fine-structured plant native to the Dutch sand-dunes and heaths which provides a very good source of fine and convincing branch structure material. The combination of sea foam branches, a trimmed-twig trunk, spray painting and teased-out foliage matting

held with hairspray is probably the easiest way to make a halfway convincing tree in N scale or 4mm.

As with all other scenic elements, realistic trees need to be based on the real thing. All trees are different and it is well worthwhile taking the trouble to decide what sort it is you're modelling and at least getting the general characteristics of that species – overall shape or 'habit', foliage density and colours and bark texture and shade – right on the model. Again, photos of suitable subjects are a great aid, while keeping an eye open while out and about or working in the garden can often throw up useful bits of natural material. Some plant root material can bear an uncanny resemblance to branch structures, while certain plants and shrubs can yield surprisingly effective tree armatures. The big sycamore trees on my Dutch layout are based on Spirea twigs bulked out with sea foam, while the leaning, stunted and wind-sheared blackthorns on 'Trerice' were very simply made from small pieces of old, gnarled heather gathered high up on Dartmoor, topped with a sparse thatch of Heki foliage mat.

Truly authentic tree modelling, however, calls for a more controlled approach and is usually based on a handmade wire armature. The real challenge is, of course, the bare winter tree – that thick thatch of summer foliage can hide a multitude of sins, but a late-November elm does not have any place to hide anything. However, such things *can* be effectively modelled using techniques pioneered back in the 1950s by the man widely regarded as the father of modern scenic modelling, George Illiffe Stokes. George's stunning winter trees were made from plaited steel-wire rope, usually the fine 49-strand cable used for control wires on light aircraft or for boat rigging. This has seven entwined 'bundles' each containing seven twisted strands. What George did was to heat this wire to red heat in a flame to burn off grease and to soften the stiff steel strands, then combine several differing lengths of the cable – usually five or more – to form the raw tree armature. The cable was then 'unpicked' to form branches (from one or more of the seven-strand bundles) and finally 'twigs' of individual strands, always working from a photo or drawing of an actual tree to ensure the 'habit' was authentic. Bark was made with papier-mâché or modelling clay, and each tree was subtly painted and detailed with just a few dead leaves clinging on, or growths of ivy or mistletoe. If you want to try your hand at this method, some scenic suppliers like Green Scene sell short lengths of suitable cable.

It has to be said that few modellers have followed in George's winter footsteps – the most notable being Bob Barlow, founding editor of the *Model Railway Journal*, some of whose model trees are illustrated alongside. However, the principle of the wire armature has been adopted and adapted in a simplified form for in-leaf trees by other scenic modellers including Barry Norman and the Pendon team. Here, the wire used is single-strand copper of various thicknesses liberated from normal household wiring cables, while the object is to produce an armature restricted to the trunk and main branches of the tree. This is relatively simple to achieve by twisting or soldering the various wires together to

Above: Winter trees in wire by Bob Barlow on the East Suffolk Light; a hedgerow elm, a neglected and ivy-swamped willow and an alder. These convincing replicas were made in the Illiffe Stokes manner from lengths of 49-strand aircraft control cable, softened, joined, unravelled and formed to shape, with 'bark' added from DAS Pronto modelling clay.

Below: Modelling in 2mm scale favours large, mature trees like this impressive specimen oak created by the late Roger Littlejohns for the Launceston MRC's 'Lydtor' layout. It has a basic wire armature with foliage from teased-out horsehair and fine ground foam.

Above: The boscage which disguises the 'end of the track' at 'Trerice' is partly modelled in 3-D and partly painted on the backdrop – effectively, these are low-relief trees. The foliage uses a mix of Heki and Woodland Scenics mattings over 'sea foam' branches, with added colour and texture from applications of ground foam held with hairspray. The objective was to achieve variegation in the foliage, suggesting different species of tree.

Below: A length of characteristic Cornish summer hedgebank on 'Trerice'; the bank is faced in herringbone stonework (scribed card and DAS) topped with a mix of carpet felt fibre, rubberised horsehair, 'sea foam', Heki foliage matting and ground foam. The rough grass is sisal and plumber's hemp. A surprising amount of work went into this minor scenic feature.

form the basic shape, once again following a prototype photo. This basic wire form is then covered in modelling clay, car filler or hot glue to build up the correct degree of 'bulk' to give a good impression of the underlying structure of the tree. The fine branches are represented by a filigree 'bulking' material, usually rubberised horsehair or Polyfibre, and the foliage then built up using foliage matting or loose foliage held with spray adhesive or hairspray. This method is relatively quick and does enable the reproduction of models authentic to species; it can even produce a recognisable portrait of an individual tree.

Hedgerows

Much of what I've written about tree-modelling applies equally to hedgerows – or at least, some of them; for, like so many of the subtler aspects of the British countryside, hedgerows show distinct regional variations. Many hedgerows are actually hedge banks; that is, the hedge itself is planted on top of a raised earthen bank. In some areas – most notably, the West Country – these banks are stone-faced in distinctive local styles. In parts of the Midlands and East Anglia – especially on arable land – hedges are far thinner and more open, made up of distinctly separate species and often having gaps filled by fencing. These variations are just the sort of detail you need to get right to create a convincing model, so take a good look at what is appropriate.

However, the hedge is one feature of the countryside which has undergone substantial change in recent years, so looking at a modern hedge in many parts of the country will mislead rather than inform. This is due to the advent of mechanical hedge-trimming and, particularly, the use of flail cutters. These are brutal but very effective, giving the hedge a far more severe haircut than was formerly possible and promoting very vigorous re-growth. The result is a far denser and more regularly rectangular affair, substantially different in appearance to the open texture and irregular outline of the traditionally laid hedge that bounded the steam-era railway. Old photographs are more of a help here, therefore.

Given all these differences, there's no one sure-fire method of modelling hedgerows. The dense modern stock-proof hedge is easiest – a square-edged strip of rubberised horsehair covered in a layer of uniformly coloured foliage matting does very nicely. Older hedges are best represented by irregular torn clumps of the horsehair planted in a row, with a variety of foliage colours and textures applied to give a more variegated effect. For an even more 'straggly' hedge, sea foam, Polyfibre or lichen can be used in place of the horsehair, with post-and-rail or wire fencing in the gaps. Hedges are normally cut back in late winter and then left until well into the autumn, so the later in the growing season your model is set, the thicker the foliage layer you need on your hedgerows and the 'shaggier' the outline should be.

Fences and gates

As with flail-cut hedging, much of the stock proof fencing seen on modern farms is of recent origin and owes more to enclosure methods developed in the American mid west and Australia than to British tradition – strained barbed wire, round tanalised posts, square mesh sheep-wire and split-round fence rails are not native to our countryside!

In fact, fencing per se has never been that common a feature on British farms, where the ditch-and-bank, the hedge and the wall have long formed the usual field boundaries. Where fencing does figure, it's usually of a basic timber post-and-rail construction or lightweight form of railed fence all in metal. These cast iron (posts) and wrought iron (rails) 'estate railings' were much in vogue in the late Victorian period, when they were mass-produced in panels that could be erected quickly and needed little maintenance; even a piece of quarter-by-inch-and-a-half iron bar (a size commonly used for the rails) takes a long time to rust away to the point where it won't keep stock in. Iron fences were particularly common in Ireland and some Highland areas of Scotland, where timber or suitable walling stone were not readily available.

Railway boundaries where lines bisected

Below: Traditional and natural boundaries of all sorts beautifully observed and modelled at Pendon – where else? Picket and board fences and hedgerows bound the cottage gardens in this captivating scene from Pendon Parva – probably my favourite Pendon picture. Pure scenic artistry.

farmland were the great exceptions to the 'no fence' generalisation, as here fences were the norm from the outset. Timber and iron structures – often of a superior, substantial or decorative nature – were used in the early days, but this generous provision soon gave way to more economical methods of keeping stock off the tracks – usually strained wire on posts of timber, old rail, cast iron or, later, concrete. This wire was plain galvanised, kept taught by screw tensioners at intervals. The wires were usually no more than 6–8in apart, and the fences usually stood about 4ft 6ins or 5ft tall. Ratio make timber and concrete posts for this type of fencing. Many modellers fit the posts but ignore the wires, which even in 7mm scale should be very fine. For foreground fencing, at least, I like to fit them, using either single strands of 40 gauge copper wire (from deconstructed layout wire) or fine Lycra thread, which is very elastic and makes for a fence that looks realistic, but is not easily damaged.

Some types of timber post-and-rail are also available from Ratio and Wills in moulded plastic format, mostly representing fencing with mortised-in rails – a rather superior form which few farmers could contemplate, but which some railway companies adopted for

their more important boundaries along main lines. Unfortunately, it is difficult to adapt this rigid moulded fencing to accommodate much in the way of undulations in the topography. The fence posts should be vertical no matter what the slope of the ground, with the rails following the contours; nothing looks odder than that old model railway chestnut, the whole fence on the tilt. The only ready-made model post-and-rail fencing I know that can be adapted to follow contours in a realistic fashion is Peco's flexible plastic type – although this is still a rather grand and substantial affair. I prefer to knock up my own somewhat rougher wooden farm fences from Plastikard microstrip or fine wood sections. Field gates can be made by the same methods, and here again, it is worth working from picture references if at all possible, as traditional gate design is another aspect of the rural scene exhibiting considerable regional variation. The iron 'estate' fencing is no problem – it's available in etched form from Scale Link and others, and – with its short panels and the easily bent form of the etchings – can readily be tailored to follow almost any slope of ground.

Dry Stone walls

In upland parts of Britain, where fieldstone is plentiful or where exposure to unfriendly weather means hedges grow slowly, fields are usually bounded by stone walls (or 'dykes' in parts of Northern England and Scotland) built dry – that is, without any mortar. The results differ between regions even more

Below left and right: Dry stone walls come in many forms; here are two extremes, a neat, close-textured Cotswold wall in creamy-grey limestone and a rather more rugged Dartmoor example, with one of the moor's better-known buildings in the background ...

than is the case with hedges – there's a world of difference between the tight texture and neatness of outline of a Cotswold wall composed of nice regular slabs of grey-gold oolite and the sort of shaggy assemblages of irregular, lichen-encrusted granite boulders you find on Dartmoor!

A Cotswold wall, with its neat, narrow courses and relative lack of texture, can be modelled in the same way as ordinary stonework, but the more open and 'loose' type of wall calls for a different technique altogether. Fortunately, we have readily at hand the ideal material for the job – good old DAS Pronto modelling clay. This is great stuff with many uses in scenic and structure modelling and has the advantage of setting hard at normal room temperatures, unlike Femo and similar clays that need curing in an oven. To make a rough dry stone wall with DAS, simply break off and shape small pieces appropriate to the type of wall you're modelling – and build the thing, exactly like the prototype. This is neither as slow or as tedious as it sounds (I find it quite relaxing and therapeutic, in fact) and the results are well worth the effort. Apart from all other considerations, a wall built like this can hug the contours of even the roughest of terrain, a very distinctive characteristic of the real thing.

Probably the best ready-made dry stone walls are the cast-resin ones produced by Harburn Hobbies, which are a pretty good representation of a rough-stone wall of the type typically found in upland country – they'd pass for Dartmoor, parts of Wales, the Lake District, the rougher parts of the Pennines and the Scottish Highlands. These walls come in sections that interlock together and include horizontal and vertical curves, corners, level and inclined wall sections and contoured lengths of wall designed to be 'built in' to the landscaping.

Rural roads, tracks and pathways

The British countryside is riddled with roadways of one sort or another, from deep hedge-set green lanes dating back to prehistoric times to the noisome banality of modern multi-lane highways. Fortunately, I suspect, very few people elect to model

Above: A Pennine dry stone wall on 'Hepton Wharf', modelled with individual DAS stones built up while tacky. Laborious, but not as bad as it sounds; a couple of feet of wall took an evening.

the latter – just as well, given that a typical contemporary dual carriageway trunk road scales out at over a foot wide in 4mm scale and would need to be populated with literally hundreds of vehicles hurtling along at breakneck speeds and amid a deafening howl of tyre-noise! A typical traditional rural single-track byway, in happy contrast, can be modelled comfortably to scale in less than a quarter of this width, needs few if any vehicles and would be aurally accompanied only by a little birdsong.

In these days of almost-universally asphalted roads plastered with signs, bollards, markings and stark orange sodium lighting, it's easy to forget how different things were only a few decades ago, when many model railways are supposedly set. Most country lanes then would have a hard gravel surface if they had any surface at all, usually with a grassy strip up the middle and a plentiful supply of potholes. They varied in width, had irregular verges, erratic drainage and a paucity of signs. Minor roads as seen on many 'period' model railways are, to my eye, far too smooth and regular, and almost always the wrong colour, being far too dark. Real roads are never, ever 'black'.

As with every other aspect of scenic work, the best starting point for modelling a road, track or pathway is a quick look at the real thing

Above: An old-fashioned country lane with a traditional gravel surface and a grassy centre. A lot less pristine than many model back roads.

– in which cause, I offer a picture that might help. A lot of country roads and trackways are of medieval or earlier origin, incorporating bridges, fords, curves and gradients quite unsuited to much modern traffic; they were engineered for packhorses, not Porsches… The usual width of a single-track country lane is between nine and twelve feet, although in Devon they can be a lot narrower; six feet is about the minimum – the width required for a packhorse with 'crooks' for carrying bulky loads. It is worth remembering that in many rural districts, there was little if any wheeled traffic much before the early 19th century – so most roads weren't suited to it. A horse is the ultimate 4 x 4 off-roader!

'Made' roads – even minor ones – usually have a raised crown to aid drainage, often with a gulley, gutter or ditch along the margins. A traditional Macadam road had a pure gravel surface on a stone substrate; from the 1920s onwards, these roads were often 'bound' by spraying with hot tar then rolling on fresh gravel chippings, which sealed the surface and – in theory at least – stopped water penetrating the road metal. So to model such a road convincingly, we too need a raised crown – simple enough to arrange with a bit of corn-flake packet card, some carton board for packing and a hot glue gun to stick it all down. I then coat it with a layer or two of glueshell to cover up the joins and blend the edges with the surrounding landscaping.

For a surface dressing, I represent the gravel chippings with fine sand – the dry silver sand sold in DIY centres for brushing into the gaps between concrete paviours is ideal, as is best Cornish beach sand dried out in the slow oven of the Rayburn. The sand is laid into a coat of thinned PVA tinted a grey-brown colour with acrylic paint and brushed on. I use an old, fine coffee-strainer as a shaker to apply my sand, not worrying too much about the odd bald patch. This results in a finely textured surface of a nice grey-brown hue. The last job is the grass down the middle and the rougher vegetation along the verges or at the hedgefoots. Farm tracks, public byways and pathways didn't even get this much roadmaking; here, ruts, stones, mud and scoured gravel are the hallmarks. Polyfilla tinted a suitable soil shade with powder colour, some model railway ballast, suitably coloured ground foam, and dyed sawdust are all useful ingredients for 'byway goop', stippled on with a stiff paintbrush to give the effect of hoof prints, and liberally supplied with puddles of varnish or clear acrylic.

Scenic details

There is a long tradition of producing small detail castings to enhance model railways that, once again, goes right back to the early days of tinplate. No vintage Hornby 0 gauge station could be called complete without its serried ranks of cast-mazak milk-churns and colourful array of platform barrows, luggage, penny-in-the-slot chocolate machines and 'speak your weight' scales. Such charming accessory ranges soon spread to 4mm scale, with die-cast platform fittings, luggage, signs, churns, fencing, seats, figures and animals all appearing from either the big RTR firms like Hornby Dublo or independent makers like Britains or B. J. Ward, whose offerings came to include such unlikely items as cast-metal flowerbeds and even solid lead trees!

These items were all die-cast in metal moulds, so the ranges were never other than limited owing to the tooling costs. The subjects and the amount of relief were also restricted by the limitations of the process, which didn't permit undercuts or much in the way of fine detail. With the advent of whitemetal casting using easily made rubber moulds in the later 1950s, the way was opened for an explosion in the variety of scenic detail castings available, with a commensurate improvement in the fidelity and sophistication of the models. By the mid-1980s, ranges like Gem/S&B, Springside, Langley, ABS, Dart Castings, Mike's Models, Scale-Link, Chris Leigh and W&T between them produced just about anything you might need in 4mm and 7mm scales, although N has never been so well-served. The widespread adoption of photo-etching from the mid-1970s on added another valuable medium for the production of scenic items. Scale Link were at the forefront of this, with Dart Castings/Shire Scenes, D&S, Chris Leigh and Langley all chiming in to add etched components to their existing cast ranges.

Plastic soon got a look into the accessory market; George Slater was a pioneer in the use of polystyrene for modelling, and in the later 1950s he produced some early figures in 4mm scale, as well as fencing, station valencing and moulded alphabets for making signs. Merit also introduced plastic accessories in the late 1950s, a range which grew to be quite extensive and is still around today, once again being subsumed into the Peco empire. Airfix too were quite early in the field, with the inevitable set of 'platform accessories' – trolleys, barrows, chocolate machines et al – and figures for railway staff and passengers, soon joined by farm animals, post-and-rail fencing and telegraph poles. A few of these items are still being made by Dapol.

Another material now being increasingly used to produce small scenic details is filled polyester resin, cast in rubber moulds which give very fine detail. The largest such range in 4mm scale is that produced in Scotland by Harburn Hobbies under the Harburn Hamlet label. This covers an eclectic and extremely varied selection of subjects – everything from Victorian tombstones to Portaloos. Among all manner of wagonloads,

Above: Figures and accessories in 7mm scale are big enough to incorporate much fine detail. Careful painting - as here by John Dale - is needed to get the best from these exquisite castings. Graham Baseden.

walls, small structures, crates, stacks, barrels, boxes, drums and sacks one finds such esoterica as statuary, garden features (pond, rectangular, with koi carp), fishing boats and gear, old-style AA and Police call-boxes and cruising narrow boats. More prosaic items include traffic islands and bollards and a comprehensive selection of rubbish in various forms, together with the accompanying skips and bins. There are also some very telling agricultural items such as round-baled hay – vital for contemporary rural landscapes. All these models are pre-painted – presumably by hand – and are thus 'ready to use' – which is reflected in the prices, often a bit more than an equivalent whitemetal casting.

Figures and animals

Miniature figures have been part of the model railway scene from the very start, but have often smacked more of caricature than accurate modelling. They have also always been one of the prime sufferers from the 'pillar of salt' syndrome already lamented; only in comparatively recent times have we seen a move toward really well-modelled figures in natural-looking static poses rather than the usual arrested capers. There are now some truly excellent whitemetal figures for

Above: Nowadays you can get some exquisite cast whitemetal model figures in 4mm and 7mm scales. These 4mm examples from the Monty's range are among the best – realistic modelling, natural, restful poses and believable and characterful subjects. They come 'raw'; these examples being painted by the author using Humbrol matt acrylics. Monty also has many other excellent accessories.

4mm and 7mm scales from ranges such as Phoenix, Omen and Monty's. Careful painting (an area in which we railway modellers can learn a great deal from our military-modelling confrères) results in miniature people who look truly convincing and can really bring the modelled scene – figuratively if not literally – to life.

Apart from the various die-cast figures of pre-war origin or from big makers like Hornby, it was George Slater's Huminiatures that set the model-figure ball rolling. Alas, George's figures were rather 'flat' and very stiffly posed – probably a consequence of the somewhat-limited manufacturing process. The first really realistic 4mm scale figures came from Airfix – their railway staff, passengers and miscellaneous civilians (including a very

splendid 'Hello, hello. What do we 'ave 'ere, then?' Bobby with hands clasped behind back in approved fashion). These all arrived with the mandatory 'paving slab' cast on their feet and were moulded in a rather unfortunate 'soapy' grade of flexible plastic that was difficult to stick – either to itself or anything else, and almost impossible to paint; even Airfix's own enamels soon flaked right off! Which was a pity, because the actual models were really good, well observed and covering a good variety of ages, heights and physiques and modelled in mostly lifelike and relaxed poses – although the 'man running for train' always looked ridiculous, frozen in mid-sprint.

What goes for people applies equally to animals; the relaxed pose of a contemplative cud-chewing cow lends itself to modelling – the lack of movement of the jaws is unapparent from normal viewing distances. Sheep nibbling downland turf can likewise be portrayed convincingly, as can animals lying down, which they do quite a lot, if you look; cows, sheep and horses can't sit. Pigs can, though, but better still they like to lie on their sides in a nice muddy puddle. Cats and dogs are great sitters and very fond of curling up or stretching out in a suitably sunny spot. Hens will brood, ducks float idly and birds of prey perch unblinking and motionless on poles, posts and branches. All these things are very modellable. A horse at full gallop, on the other hand…

Both plastic and metal figures can be relieved of any cast-on 'stands' or bases and kept upright and in position by drilling into the base of the figure to insert a pin or short piece of stiff wire. A corresponding hole in the landscape or structure where the figure is to be sited is all that is needed, with a touch of suitable adhesive (I use UHU) to keep them in place. I prime figures – plastic or metal – using white car primer, which sticks pretty well to most things, even Airfix's soapy brew. (The Dapol figures are in normal polystyrene, thank goodness). Unless you're modelling Carnaby Street c1966 and Beatle-girls in PVC mini-skirts, figures need painting in absolutely matt paints as very few clothes

throw any reflections. My choice for many years has been Humbrol's excellent acrylic range, which has a wide selection of matt colours. For figure work, it is well worth investigating the paints and finishing materials available for military modelling, as the range of colours and effects are often far wider than in other paint ranges.

There is a lot more to say about the minutiae of landscape modelling, but it'll have to wait on some other occasion; for now, we need to take a look at the other main element of the scenic setting for our model trains – buildings, bridges and ancillary structures of all kinds.

Below: Figures, animals, vehicles and accessories – the final touch in bringing the landscape to life. Pendon again, of course; Bradbury Farm, but I won't go on about the poses…

Chapter 8

STRUCTURES

Second only to the landscape in defining the geographical setting, nature and period of a model railway are the structures, both railway and – particularly – vernacular. One of the characteristics of the British landscape is that many of the man-made aspects are very old, especially in the more rural areas. In other words, they pre-date the railways, often by several centuries. Unless you're modelling a town or city scene ravaged by ruthless redevelopment, even the most contemporary of model railways will usually still call for the

representation of period features and historic buildings. This mix of styles and periods in the infrastructure and architecture is, to me, one of the fascinations of modelling the British scene. It is a stark contrast to much of North America, where you could accurately recreate vast tracts of the country using the same half-dozen or so structure kits.

It was a further aspect of the individuality of the old pre-Grouping railway companies that they employed highly distinctive civil engineering solutions and architectural styles

Above: Distinctive railway architecture. One of the London & South Western Railway's characteristic station buildings, as found all over the lines west of Exeter – modelled in Wills moulded plastic sheet stonework by Barry Norman for 'Petherick'. Without a train in sight, this architecture defines the railway being modelled. Barry Norman

Opposite: The start of it all – probably the first layout to be graced with a full complement of realistically modelled structures was John Ahern's immortal 'Madder Valley'. This is 'Madderport', conjured into being out of cardboard combined with great artistry, keen observation and a deep affection for the subject – all leavened with an impish sense of humour. You can see this wonderful model at Pendon – another reason to make the pilgrimage. Pendon archives

Right: At the opposite end of the country to 'Petherick', the Highland Railway's board-and-batten timber structures were unmistakable. Here is the station building at 'Corrieshalloch' – clean, crisp 4mm scale structure modelling in Plastikard by Simon de Souza. In the context of Simon's pre-First World War Highland Railway layout, this represents a newish structure, hence the lack of weathering and the fresh colours.

to produce bridges, retaining walls, tunnels, lineside structures and buildings of real quality and originality. And – it goes without saying – of enormous variety. Take station buildings as a case in point; you can find them in the style of Jacobean country houses, Palladian villas, Greek temples, Scottish baronial castles, Swiss chalets, demure country cottages, seaside pavilions, French chateaux and mock-Tudor 'superior residences'. Some wayside stations were mean and basic, while others (such as Alton Towers in Staffordshire) were of apparently inexplicable splendour – usually due to some local big-wig demanding they be built in a style to match his country pile!

Above: Unexceptional but accurately observed vernacular buildings are a key element in the setting for a model railway. This typical small West Devon farmstead has been beautifully observed and convincingly modelled by Roger Littlejohns for the Launceston Club's 2mm scale 'Lydtor' layout. Plastikard is the basic material, combined with commercial door and window mouldings from Dornaplas. Other important factors in making this model so convincing are the grouping of the structures, the realistic hedgerows (not too straight or angular) and the apt choice of vehicles and accessories.

Below: Just as much an example of vernacular architecture – albeit an industrial structure rather than a domestic one – are the clay dries on 'Trerice'. Again, closely based on a prototype dry (Crugwallins), this rendition of a typical pan dry cements the location of the layout; you won't find a building like this anywhere else but Cornwall. The model is in paper and card over a structural shell of foam-cored board.

Some railways went in for an architecture of the plainest severity, while others broke out in riotous explosions of Victorian gothic revival at the least excuse. A few – the LNWR springs to mind – made a lot of use of prefabricated structures of standard design, which might turn up at any point on the system, while others seemingly had no overall policy and built no two stations alike. But usually, the buildings of a given railway exhibited at least some 'family resemblances', which is a key element in capturing the character of the lineside.

Vernacular variety

Whatever is true of the railways in the matter of architectural variety is even more the case with the traditional vernacular. For a compact island, Britain exhibits an extraordinary range of domestic building styles, often strongly associated with particular landscapes. Cob cottages under thick straw thatch go with Devon as much as pargetted plasterwork under peg-tiles with East Anglia and crow-stepped gables and Roman tiles with Fife. A lot depended on local materials, of course; by and large, traditional buildings were made out of whatever was most readily to hand, or what could be most easily obtained. For instance, pantiles from Holland and Belgium turn up on roofs all over the east of England and Scotland, where they made a good return cargo for ships exporting coal and wool to the Low Countries; but you don't find many in North Wales or Cornwall!

So choosing the right sort of non-railway buildings to model is an important aspect of creating a believable and realistic setting for a model railway, especially in a historical context. It's a regrettable fact that the nearer you get to the contemporary, the greater the spread of architectural conformity and banality becomes. We are now at the point where a new estate house or industrial unit is likely to look much the same be it anywhere from Cornwall to Caithness. As always, no matter what the subject or period, observation and the representation of the typical is the key – yet it is so often just the sort of humdrum, everyday buildings we need to create our authentic settings that are

Right: Beautifully observed and detailed architectural modelling is seen in this row of unremarkable cottages in 7mm scale, the work of the late Martin Brent. The basic material is once again foam-cored board, overlaid with Howard Scenics embossed-card brickwork coloured with wax crayons and then finished with a matt varnish. The windows, however, are plastic – and transatlantic plastic at that: Grandt Line mouldings in quarter-inch scale (American 0). The keen-eyed will note an oblique 'Madder Valley' reference in the signage. The figures are by Phoenix and Omen.

hardest to come by commercially. Finding a factory, warehouse, or public building in ready-built or kit form is usually easier than coming up with, say, a convincing selection of ordinary suburban three-bedroom semis or humble artisan's cottages.

Sources of model structures

To provide a model railway with a due complement of structures, there are three basic options: you can buy your buildings over the counter and ready-built; use kits of one sort or another, with current choices embracing printed card, embossed card, moulded plastic, vacuum-formed plastic, cast resin and cast plaster; or you can make your own, using a variety of materials and techniques. Most people, of course, don't put all their eggs in any one of these baskets, with the result that the majority of model railways incorporate structures of differing origins. The big difficulty then is getting them all to *look* as if they had the *same* origin – the problem being that the various different approaches to structure modelling yield results that, while fine in themselves, often don't sit happily alongside each other.

Scale has a big influence on the choice of structure-modelling approach, due to the degree of texturing needed to produce a realistic result. The larger the scale, the greater the depth of relief needed to model the surface textures of buildings effectively. In N, the depth of the mortar courses on brick structures would, if reproduced to scale, be

so slight as to be unnoticeable; at 0 scale, though, it would be very obvious. Conversely, the smaller the scale, the more important it is that things be sized properly; overscale brickwork on an N scale model completely destroys the proportions of the building while over-emphasised textures just look false and clumsy. Printed flat finishes – or their hand-produced equivalents – work just fine for N, but 0 calls for the full-relief of moulded or carved surfaces. The eternal compromise – 4mm scale – sits right in the middle of this conundrum; you can go either way without it looking obviously 'wrong' – one of the features of this size that keeps it as the most popular choice. In 4mm/1ft, more than ever, the key to realism is consistency – something often made more difficult by the wide-range of choices and possibilities available.

One of the most respected 4mm modellers and elder statesmen of our hobby, the Rev. Peter Denny – creator of 'Buckingham' – was once asked why he didn't make more use of modern embossed or moulded-plastic materials in his structural work. 'Ah well,' he said, 'if I were to do that, I might indeed have a few buildings that were better detailed; but, you see, they would just make all the others look wrong. I've always found that making everything blend together is the greater part of realism. So, if I went 'plastic' I should have to start all over again – and it's a bit late for that, don't you think?' As parts of 'Buckingham' were by then more than half a century old, one could see his point! Sticking to traditional methods was not without its problems however and Peter would often ask new visitors to Buckingham, wistfully and more in hope than expectation: 'I don't suppose you have any old Merco building papers tucked away anywhere? I'm particularly anxious to find a few sheets of 'smoky brick'…'

Peter's point about consistency as a prerequisite for realism is perfectly valid of course, and a very good reason for sticking with one set of structure-modelling techniques even though 'better' methods and materials may have arrived subsequently. 'Better' is very much a relative term in this context anyway; there are plenty of full-relief, all-singing-and-dancing, fully detailed model buildings about that don't look even half as convincing as Buckingham's acutely observed and lovingly modelled structures, for all their 'flatness' of surface. All of which is a rather long-winded way of saying that mixing 'flat' printed finishes with painted relief surfaces – especially in representing similar prototype building materials – kills consistency stone dead, and, with it, overall realism.

Achieving a convincing homogeneity of finish for the buildings on a model railway really comes down to making a fundamental choice of approach: printed card kit-built structures can be happily married to scratchbuilt card-based efforts using matching building papers and a similar degree of relief in the detailing, while models with full relief detail – be they moulded or embossed plastic, cast resin, cast plaster, embossed card or hand-carved or built-up textures – can likewise live equably together *provided they have a common standard of finish*. That is, they're painted in the same way, using the same palette of colours, and the same techniques to represent all the various prototype surfaces and building materials. What never seems to work is a mish-mash of modelling methods, finishes and materials, mixed together without any unifying factor.

Ready-made buildings

Buildings and such characteristic structures as footbridges, cranes and water tanks are elements of the railway scene that have always lent themselves to production in ready-built form. Stations and engine sheds – often of fanciful grandeur or great charm – formed an important part of the traditional tinplate toy railway in 0 gauge and above, as did footbridges, level crossings, water cranes and tanks and goods-yard cranes (usually working). Basic railway buildings – a station or two, signalbox, goods depot and engine shed – also featured from the outset in the main ready-made ranges in 00, progressing from the crude wood-and-printed-paper of early Hornby-Dublo buildings through cast-metal Dublo and early Tri-ang moulded plastic to the sophistication and comparative realism of the cast-resin Skaledale range of today.

Tri-ang was the first RTR maker to go into the business of producing vernacular buildings as well as pure railway structures. Their moulded-plastic Model Land pre-built and plastic-kit structures of the early 1960s were actually rather good, based on very believable and workaday prototypes surprisingly well-observed. With careful work in finishing and painting (they came in pre-coloured plastic, inevitably with a hard and shiny finish), a bit of extra detailing and weathering and some internal partitions to stop daylight showing through the structure from windows in the opposite side, you could finish up with quite convincing models.

However, these Tri-ang models were an exception, as most ready-built structures (and quite a lot of kits) don't really hack it as scale models. For a start, to keep costs moderate and packaging sizes within bounds, they have tended to be on the unrealistically small side (or are made substantially under-scale). Also, they rarely seem to follow actual prototypes and sometimes incorporate improbable architecture or awkward proportions. One recalls two-storey houses with no possible location for a staircase, or window arrangements that aligned with no feasible floor plan – the result being models that just look plain wrong. There have also been some fairly unhappy combinations of materials – Hornby, for instance, went on (post Model

Land) to marrying flat (and shiny!) printed brick and stonework with moulded relief detail. A few such structures remain in their current catalogue; they have a certain doll's house charm, but realistic they ain't.

Hornby's current Skaledale range – together with its N scale equivalent, Lyddle End (ugh!) – is a much better bet. These models are produced in China, being either cast in filled resin or moulded in full-relief plastic, with the resin examples being realistically hand-finished in matt colours. Some of these structures are quite large and ambitious – recent introductions including such trifles as a complete gasworks – and most of them are based on credible and fairly typical designs. But they are a good deal more expensive than traditional pre-built structures and cost several times the price of an equivalent kit.

The big plus of ready-built structures is their 'instant' nature; open the box, and you can transform that blank bit of baseboard into a desirable piece of real-estate in a matter of moments. The trouble is, so can everybody else; the biggest drawback to using ready-built structures is their ubiquity. You end up having exactly the same 'look' to your layout as every other Tom, Dick or Harriet – not much help if you're after a bit of individuality. Very often, such off-the-peg buildings also don't quite fit the site or application you need them for, leading to awkward arrangements that rarely look other than odd. And, of course, you're stuck with the textures and colours chosen by the manufacturer, which may well not live happily alongside other structures or scenic elements on the layout. Yes, you can alter and adapt ready-built models and you can certainly re-finish and weather them to blend them in to the overall scene, but if you're going to that much trouble, you may as well start with a kit in the first place – or even create your own structure from scratch.

Card structure kits

Structure kits were amongst the first aftermarket products to be introduced to the scale model railway hobby when it gained momentum following the end of the Second World War. The usual materials for these early kits were wood and card, with printed celluloid glazing and brick and slate building papers to finish the exterior. In skilled hands, these materials produced very effective results and a lot of these early building kits by Anorma, Modelcraft, Ballard, Ratio and Bilteezi made up into respectably realistic models. The last-named, in particular, were beautifully observed and produced to a very high standard from the exquisite artwork of Charles Vacey-Ash, but with their printed-on windows and general lack of relief they cried out for that bit of extra work that could transform them into something quite special. Take the trouble, and models made from many of these older kits were often a lot more convincing than the trains they were meant to complement!

Something of a revolution occurred when the Superquick range of card building kits first appeared about 1960. These were well-observed scale models of very typical British structures, cleverly designed and beautifully

Below: The Bilteezi range of card structure kits first appeared in the late 1940s – basically, just full-colour artwork by Charles Vacey-Ash printed on thin card, to a very high standard. There was no relief detail, windows were simply printed on and the structures needed reinforcing, but they were authentic, well-observed models and the artwork was exquisite. Many modellers put in the effort to upgrade them with glazing and by laminating them on to layers of card to produce relief detail. This is the low-relief housebacks, which was very popular on 1950s layouts.

Above: Probably the most influential range of card structure kits was Superquick, which came out in 1960 and are still going strong. These models were printed in full colour on thick card which was die-cut, with relief detail and 'proper' glazing printed on clear plastic film. Straightforward to assemble – all you needed was a knife, glue and some watercolour paint to tint the cut edges – the range was soon very extensive, giving a modest selection of (non-specific) railway structures and a wide choice of vernacular buildings. This is the island platform building, one of the earlier offerings.

printed in realistic and subdued colours on high-grade cardstock about 1mm thick. Use of this substantial material allowed for considerable relief as well as making for a robust model – one which also avoided the somewhat tedious and time-consuming two-stage process of cutting out and assembling the shell of a building then having to apply the finish as extra layers of paper glued on. A Superquick structure did both jobs in one go. To make them even simpler to build, the card parts were die-cut to shape with the door and window openings ready-pierced – which all meant that, compared with the older 'chop-it-yourself' kits, they really were 'super quick' to put together.

Superquick buildings soon became extremely popular – leading, it must be said, to an element of *déjà vu* when the same structures featured on almost every layout. At least the range soon grew to be large and varied enough to avoid too much monotony,

while many of the kits were capable of being built in differing configurations. Superquick were also not afraid to tackle more complex structures, and many of the kits featured angled corners, irregular footprints, overhangs, interesting and varied rooflines, all manner of recessed porches, bow and bay windows, gables, dormers, skylights, proper chimney stacks and similar authentic details. Subjects were very varied, ranging from half-timbered Elizabethan to contemporary 1960s structures – presumably intended for 'Modern Image' modellers. (Although exactly what a 'modern image' might be has always rather escaped me!) Crucially, Superquick also offered a range of matching building papers, which made it possible to extend or re-work the basic kit models or to scratchbuild structures with similar finish and colouring.

The Superquick kits are still very much around – although it's salutary to realise that many of those 'modern image' 1960s buildings would in reality be overdue for demolition by now! The Superquick approach has been adopted by two other major ranges, Metcalfe and Townscene. As with Superquick, the Metcalfe models take as subjects very typical and workaday British structures, using the same die-cut thick card and matt-printed finish. To my eyes, though, the colouring of the Metcalfe buildings lacks the restrained subtlety of Superquick, although a bit of toning-down and weathering with washes of watercolour paint help to blend models from the two ranges, while adding considerably to the realism and individuality of the structures. Townscene sit somewhere in the middle, but can be adapted to blend with both. Metcalfe's range comes in three groups of subjects: Railway, industrial, and town and country. Townscene's more limited range lives up to its name, being mostly urban in character. Between them the three ranges offer well in excess of a hundred different kits, enough variety and choice to equip even a large layout with structures benefiting from commonality of texture, detailing and finish.

When it comes to authentic railway buildings, one other long-lived range of card kits deserves special mention: Prototype Models. As the name implies, these differ from the vast majority of model railway structure kits by being accurate models of actual structures. Ian Wilson, their creator, was an enthusiast for the old Great Northern Railway, so unsurprisingly the range includes a good selection of GNR buildings, including Stamford signalbox and engine shed (a delightful structure), the goods shed from Little Bytham and the station building from Horncastle. Other railways to feature in the range include the LNWR, GCR, GWR and SR. As with Superquick, these models are printed on thick high-quality card, although using the screen rather than litho process; the thicker layer of ink thus applied gives a very slight relief effect. Cutting-out was down to the builder, however, while the considerable amount of relief detail incorporated often makes for multi-layer construction that could get a little involved. The results, however, are worth it, and with care you end up with a pretty classy model. Most of these kits are 4mm, but some have appeared in 7mm scale with a good few in N.

More recently, Peter Howard's 4mm scale Howard Scenics range has revisited the basic card kit technique but endowed it with a far higher degree of sophistication, using etched windows, high-grade glazing and full relief detail to go with some very subtle printing and first-class artwork. The subjects chosen were also truly valuable – an absolutely typical pair of Edwardian semi-detached houses and a row of traditional shops, beautifully observed, accurately to scale and capable of being made as models of the very highest quality. As a spin-off, we also had some superb, highly authentic brickpapers, embossed paper and card brickwork, and some really convincing signs. I only wish the range was bigger…

Card kit building techniques

All these printed-card kits share the same properties, and hence call for similar constructional and finishing techniques. There are three main areas to address: cutting out, assembly, and edge-tinting. The tools needed are few and straightforward: a steel ruler or straight-edge, a good, sharp modelling knife and a suitable surface to work on – a nice flat off-cut of MDF or hardboard or, better still, a self-healing rubber cutting mat. My knife of choice has always been the brass-handled Swann Morton with the curved No. 2 blade. Suitable adhesives for card work include medium-strength PVA 'white glues' such as Speed Bond or clear contact adhesives including Bostik Clear or UHU. For tinting cut edges – as well as general weathering and toning-down of finishes – ordinary artist's watercolour paints are ideal – see the 'Painting' section at the end of this chapter for more details.

As already noted, some card kit ranges are die-cut, which means that cutting out comes down to simply freeing the individual parts from the sheet. You *can* just push them out, but this can often result in little ragged 'nibs' due to tearing of the tiny attachment points left by the cutting process to retain the part in the sheet. Far better is to use the tip of a sharp craft-knife blade to run around the outline of the part and cut through these attachments cleanly. 'Uncut' kits like Prototype Models or Bilteezi require rather more effort and care, as clean, accurate cutting out is the key to good card structures. Never stint on new knife blades for this job – change them as often as needed to ensure that you're always working with a really keen edge. (Don't throw the discarded blades away, though; keep them for use in less-demanding applications. I fit them in a second handle so I always have one knife for 'best' and one for 'rough' use – distinguished at a glance by coloured tape wrapped around the end.)

Plastic structure kits

Full relief detail was the main advantage of the first British plastic structure kits, the ubiquitous Airfix 'two bob' models that first appeared in the early 1960s. Although offering texture and relief, however, these kits had their drawbacks. They needed painting, for a start, and painting plastic structures realistically is actually quite a tricky business, especially with the very limited selection of suitable paints then available. One shudders at the memory of all those Airfix thatched cottages with roofs finished in bright yellow gloss! Many of these buildings were also slightly under scale or unrealistically small, a reflection of tool-making limitations and packaging considerations, while details like glazing bars in windows were often far too thick and chunky. Somewhat better were Tri-ang's competing Model Land and Real Estate building kits, which were at least pre-coloured – although far too shiny and garish for realism. However, for the most part the new plastic buildings generally looked less convincing than their card equivalents, while the two styles of model – flat printed and moulded/painted – never sat happily together.

Plastic structure kits never took off in Britain to the extent that they did elsewhere, especially Germany. Firms such as Kibri, Faller, Pola and Vollmer were soon offering ranges of Teutonic model buildings that incorporated a far greater level of detail and refinement than the old stagers from Airfix. In spite of the fact that these structures were H0 scale and followed mostly German prototypes, many found their way on to British layouts – leading to that strange phenomenon, the Great Western branch line set in a sort of slightly-shrunken Schlesswig-Holstein. Many were the lamentations over the lack of British-prototype structures of equivalent quality, but the high tooling costs and the restricted nature of the British market have always dictated against this route to producing the wide range of different building styles needed.

The two main sources of home-grown plastic structure kits have been Ratio and Wills, both still going strong. Ratio started out in the early 1950s producing surprisingly refined 4mm scale railway buildings and rolling stock from milled wood and card. They switched to plastic moulding in about 1960 – at first for wagon kits and signals, then graduating to small structures and accessories. The Ratio range is biased toward complete kits, rather than components or materials, and centres on prototypes of mostly Great Western provenance, very often scale models of actual structures: Castle Cary station building, Buckfastleigh goods shed and Yeovil Pen Mill cattle dock all feature. Bigger and more sophisticated moulding and die-sinking machines gradually improved Ratio's capabilities and the size and complexity of the subjects they could tackle, to the point that they now produce models – such as the Midland signalbox – that are equal in quality and sophistication to anything found in Europe or the USA.

Ratio's range spans the scales, with plenty for 2mm and 4mm models and a limited selection in 7mm. However, they limit themselves almost entirely to railway subjects, offering very little that is of use in modelling the scene beyond the lineside fencing – of which, however, they do offer a wide choice! A few Ratio kits are 'hybrids' – that is, they combine two or more manufacturing processes in their production. The odd N scale structure features etched windows, for instance, while whitemetal castings are also used where appropriate – the signalbox interior fittings springing to mind. They also offer some useful general sprues of architectural details – guttering and downpipes, platform canopy valencing, various window mouldings, brick window arches, wooden staircases, laddering, ventilators and skylights.

Wills were initially known for their extensive Finecast range of 4mm scale whitemetal locomotive kits – still out there today as South-Eastern Finecast. They also had a non-model-railway side to their business which, quite early on, became involved in plastic injection moulding. Inevitably, once they had the technology available it wasn't long before Bob Wills was looking for ways to apply it to model railways. The main problem with plastic moulding at that time was the very high cost of machining the necessary dies, but Wills' toolmaker Ron Platt devised an ingenious and relatively cheap way of making simple flat mould tools. This process inevitably had limitations – the mouldings could only be relatively shallow and were usually only single-sided, while the maximum size was limited by the capacity of the small-bed

machines available – but it also had distinct possibilities in the field of model structures and accessories.

So Wills went on to produce their Scenic Series. This was a mix of complete kits for small structures, fully-textured architectural materials sheets that were thick enough for structural use, and a range of plastic architectural and detail components. The series eventually totalled some 30 different materials sheets and well over 100 different kits and detail packs. All these products are intended for 4mm scale, although some of the materials sheets do have uses in other scales. A range of Craftsman's Kits producing relatively sophisticated models of larger structures is based on the materials sheets, used in conjunction with a mix of 'standard' architectural details (like gutters, downpipes and bargeboards) and dedicated mouldings specially produced for each kit to provide appropriate windows, doors, brackets, signs and other details. Templates are provided for the various wall and roof panels, but – as with traditional wood or card 'craft' kits – the actual cutting out, trimming and assembly of the parts is down to the individual modeller, as is the painting and finishing. Detailed instructions in all aspects of this work are provided in a booklet that comes

*Above: **Plastic structures from the Wills moulded building Material sheets; this is the station building on 'Pixton Hill', Wills' own EM gauge showroom layout. The original handbuilt structure seen here later formed the basis of one of the more complex of the Craftsman series. The PW hut is a straightforward Wills Scenic series structure kit, but the water tower has gained a brick plinth in place of the rugged stone original, to blend it in with the Sussex setting.***

with each kit and most modellers find that, once they've tackled one of these Craftsman structures, they have acquired the necessary skills and confidence to go on and produce their own original models in the same fashion.

I must confess that I was quite heavily involved in the development of many of these Wills products – especially the Craftsman's Kits – so I'm probably a little biased in their favour! However, they do have some outstanding virtues – none of which are anything to do with me! Of these, the most important – homogeneity – arises from the nature of their manufacture. The complete kits, Craftsman's Kits or structures self-built from the materials sheets and architectural components and accessories, are all made in the same way and so all possess the same

Above: More 4mm scale plastic structure kits from the Wills Scenic series. The barn on the left is a regular, complete building kit, but the cottage is one of the cut-it-out-yourself Craftsmen series – a halfway house between kit and scratch-building. Bob Wills

Below: The Wills Scenic series Materials sheets greatly facilitate the scratchbuilding of structures with the full-relief surface detail offered by the plastic moulding process. All the structures use Wills sheet together with door and window mouldings from the Wills and Ratio ranges and cast whitemetal and etched details from Scale Link.

quality of detail and surface texturing. The only real drawback to the Materials sheets is their limited size – roughly 5 x 3in – which can make for some tricky joining work on larger structures. The range is wide enough (covering both railway and vernacular structures) and versatile enough to enable virtually all the buildings and civil engineering features on a layout to be made in essentially the same way, thus ensuring an even standard. Only basic and conventional modelling tools – a craft knife, files and abrasive papers – are needed to work with the plastic, while the adhesives and solvents used for assembly and fillers and paints used for finishing are exactly the same as those used for normal plastic kits or with sheet plastic, pre-cut strip or extruded sections. Although the Craftsman's Kits do call for more skill and input than a conventional kit, if you make a mess of a wall or roof panel then identical moulded sheet comes in the relevant Materials Pack so you can have another go!

Peco – which now controls both the Ratio and Wills ranges – has also marketed a limited range of plastic structures (and the odd card one) under their own banner, although this has never been a very significant area for them. Of the big European plastic kit manufacturers, the only one (so far as I'm aware) to dip a toe into Britannic waters has been Heljan of Denmark, which has produced a few 'British' building kits – albeit to H0 scale, which somewhat limits their usefulness! The range includes a Great Western country station, a wayside halt, a covered footbridge and a goods depot together with an English church, suburban villa and a country pub – the latter three subjects perhaps chosen as an ironic commentary on England as seen from a Nordic perspective? There was also, for a time, a neat 7mm scale brick engine shed that was well received but seems to have disappeared now. Heljan has recently introduced some very fine 4mm and 7mm scale RTR British diesel locos, so hopefully their increasing involvement in the UK market might result in a few more building kits – to the right scale this time!

The other significant home-grown plastic-kit range is Dornaplas, an offshoot of Springside Models. In 4mm scale this includes a wide range of building parts – window frames, doors, rainwater goods, valencing, bargeboarding, fencing and so on, equivalent to the similar items in the Ratio and Wills ranges – plus accessories as diverse as tombstones and point levers. Dornaplas also produce some complete 4mm scale structures – mostly fairly small buildings, although they have a station building, platform shelter, signalbox, crossing cottage, goods warehouse and a loco shed. All these are rather plain models of generic designs, which can nevertheless form a useful basis to work on. As assembled 'straight out of the packet', I find them a little bland and lacking in character. There's a similar but smaller range in N scale – far fewer railway buildings, but the building components are very useful and the accessories include road vehicles.

Cast plaster kits

These are well-established in the USA, where they've always liked their plaster, but, as yet, they're very much a minority here, with – at the time of writing – only one substantial range, Townstreet (not to be confused with Townscene!). In terms of relief detail, texturing and so on, plaster is a very versatile medium that produces results to equal the most refined plastic and resin mouldings. It is obviously a very suitable and sympathetic material for reproducing masonry, particular coarser and more heavily textured stonework, but the very fine-grade plaster used by Townstreet can also be surprisingly effective at replicating woodwork and even smooth metallic surfaces. Plaster cast into flexible rubber moulds will reproduce very fine detail and accommodate a considerable degree of undercut, which makes it possible to incorporate features like rainwater downpipes and guttering integrally with walling without undue loss of finesse and effective 3-D relief. Combined with etched-brass windows and details, cast-plaster structures can produce extremely realistic results – provided they're well painted.

This is where the main difficulty lies. Cast plaster is, by its nature, highly absorbent, and soaks up paint thirstily – which can make it very difficult to control the colouring, particularly the intensity of shade. Techniques like dry-brushing, widely used in structure painting, just don't work on raw plaster. The answer, therefore, is not to try to paint plaster models 'raw', but rather to thoroughly fill and prime the surface before attempting to apply the desired finish – a job for which ordinary household emulsion paint seems to serve perfectly well. I use a basic matt white emulsion tinted to a sort of pale grey-brown using matt acrylics (acrylic and emulsion paints are more-or-less the same thing and usually mix without a problem). This priming paint is thinned slightly with water so that it penetrates the plaster without filling the modelled textures and obscuring or softening the detail. It is simply brushed on with a

Below: Close-up detail of one of Townstreet's stunning cast-plaster structures. This garage (a railway arch 'infill', so characteristic of the urban scene), is a one-piece moulding; brickwork, corrugated iron, doors and windows, window display, petrol pumps, air-line – pretty much everything except the car itself (a 1949 Ford V8 Pilot from an ABS kit) is incorporated in the casting. Painting is in Humbrol acrylics over a sealing coat of ordinary household emulsion paint; in this case, matt white tinted slightly with acrylics to give a mortar shade.

normal decorator's half-inch paintbrush, working it well into the textures. I apply two or three coats, at intervals of around an hour, until the plaster doesn't want to absorb any more paint. The model is then allowed to dry thoroughly for several days, after which it can be painted in the same way as a plastic building – using the techniques detailed later in this chapter.

Self-built: materials and methods

There is a long-established tradition of railway modellers producing their own buildings from scratch – even when most other items on their layouts came straight off the dealer's shelf. For a long time, this was a matter of necessity, as with the meagre choice of structures available commercially – kit or ready-built – it was mostly a case of 'if you want it, build your own'. But the popularity of DIY structure modelling was also a reflection

Below: Dutch modeller Renier Hendriksen made the pilgrimage to Pendon and was so bowled over by what he saw there that he resolved to have a go at structure-modelling Pendon-style himself. This is the result – the exquisite west country village of 'Moor's End', scratchbuilt in scribed card, paper, plaster and wood, all painstakingly and subtly painted in watercolours and muted acrylics. Notice the wonderfully convincing mossy tiles on the roof of the station building in the foreground.

of the relative ease with which the job could be done, using readily available, cheap materials and simple tools and techniques. Many modellers also chose to create their own structures for less prosaic reasons; for a start, they can then produce *exactly* the building they want, rather than making-do with the nearest available kit. Better still, they soon discover that structure-modelling is a very satisfying pursuit in its own right, allowing ample scope for craftsmanship, experiment and (most important!) individuality. Once mastered, the basic techniques can be applied to any prototype in any scale, while the results invariably equal – and usually surpass – anything the trade has to offer. The downside – if that is what is – is that brewing your own buildings invariably takes longer than assembling a kit; how much of a drawback this can be considered to constitute in the context of a pastime is debatable.

In the context of a general book like this, it is obviously not possible to give chapter and verse for every set of materials and techniques used for structure modelling. I have, perforce, to content myself with a quick round-up and review of the main alternatives, with a few choice examples of each. There are more specialised books – many devoted entirely to a particular material or approach – which cover the topic in far greater detail. These are well worth acquiring if the whole business of being your own builder appeals.

In the early days card, wood, celluloid glazing and printed building papers were the stock-in-trade of the DIY structure modeller – usually the same building papers as found in contemporary kits, which made for a pleasing homogeneity between kit – and self-built models. Printed building papers may have gone out of fashion a bit these days, but they are still around and they still have some virtues. They are self-coloured, for a start – and if hand-painting large areas of brick or stonework isn't your cup of tea (and it *can* be pretty mind-numbing, let me tell you...) then that can be a boon. They're also cheap, easy and quick to use, can be applied to wood, card or plastic sub-structures and come in good-sized sheets (cutting down on the need for joins). And, by their nature, they offer the all-important consistency of appearance.

The other main set of structure-modelling techniques is based on the use of plastics materials. Here, there are three basic approaches: 'kitbashing', working with moulded sheet material, and using Plastikard sheet styrene, either in the raw flat form, embossed or vacuum-formed to give texture. These options overlap to a considerable extent, and all three can be employed even within the context of a single structure. This is greatly helped by the commonality of the basic material – polystyrene. This is a family of plastics that can be joined by effectively welding them together with solvent adhesives. Plastic structures, whatever their provenance, rely to a great extent on appropriate painting and finishing for realism; whatever messrs Pola, Kibri and co. might think, self-coloured unpainted plastic is only good at representing buildings made entirely out of self-coloured plastic...

Scratchbuilding in card

The great advantage of card is its enormous versatility and there are very few building types, building materials, finishes and structural details that you can't use it to replicate convincingly. It can be laminated and de-laminated, embossed, scribed, incised, distressed, torn, carved, bent, distorted, folded and formed. It's easy to stick to itself or a huge range of other materials, using a wide variety of different adhesives, from office gum to cyano-acrylate superglue. It comes in a huge variety of thicknesses and surfaces to which you can easily apply all manner of materials – plaster, gessoes, grits or powders, modelling clays – to create many different wall textures, or, if need be, varnish to a glass-smooth surface. You can paint and finish card in that subtlest of all media, artist's watercolours. No wonder it has long been the material of choice for dedicated structure modellers, from pioneers like John Ahern up to the Pendon modellers of today.

Card on its own can't do everything, however, so it is combined with other

Above: The master at work: Roye England, founder of Pendon, evolved and developed the disciplines and techniques which raised the whole business of small-scale architectural and landscape modelling to something between an art-form and a scholastically accurate record. This is the Chapel Group, centrepiece of Pendon Parva, one of the most important artefacts of our miniature heritage. **Pendon Museum**

sympathetic – often natural, rather than synthetic – materials: papers of all sorts, modelling woods including balsa, obechi and spruce; wood veneers; plumber's hemp for thatch, threads of various sorts, fine fabric, cotton fibres, sawdust, plaster, glass or clear plastic for glazing, wire, strip and metal sections for rainwater goods, metal foils, sheet and strip plastic and fine plastic or metal tubing. There are, of course, plenty of enticing bits to buy to help create realistic card structures: etched metal or moulded plastic panelled doors and all manner of window frames, etched brackets and fancy ironwork,

Above: Here is the real McCoy – a Pendon card structure (the 'extension' of the Ashbury group, to be precise) more or less ready to be incorporated in the Vale scene. Note the deep 'foundation' which enables the building to be seated home in a socket in the landscaping – both a sound and secure way of locating the structure and of seating it visually into its setting; no chance of a give-away 'crack around the bottom'. Scribed card painted with watercolours. **Pendon Museum**

ridge-tiles and wall-plates, cast whitemetal chimney pots, corbels, rainwater goods and interior fittings. The possibilities are almost endless!

There are two basic approaches to making a card building: you either start with the outer surface and work inwards – 'finish flat then fold' construction – or, build a card shell to which you apply your finishes, working from the inside out. Both methods have their advantages and drawbacks. Starting with the outside is the Ahern method, adopted and refined by Roye England at Pendon Museum. A relatively thin card – somewhere about 20thou thick – is used, one that has a good white surface, cuts cleanly, can readily be embossed and takes paint well; Apsley pasteboard is a recommended choice. The structure is marked out in detail with the card flat on the workbench, with the walls laid out in continuous opened-out form – the corners in this method being formed by scoring and

folding. All the door and window openings are cut out and the various surface textures scribed or cut into the card or applied to it. Still with the building 'in the flat', the walls are painted – probably the most critical part of the process, and something that can't be hurried.

Once the wall surfaces are textured and painted, the windows and doors, together with any necessary reveals (the portion of the wall thickness showing between the outside of the wall and the face of the window or door-frame) are fitted from behind, complete with window curtains, interior and exterior sills, plinths, lintels, cornices and so on. These too are painted and finished. Only when all this work has been completed are the corners folded and the walls assembled around the interior floors (or even a completely modelled interior, for the truly dedicated!). The insides of the thin card walls are reinforced and braced with card or stripwood stiffeners to make the resulting structure more robust. The roof is then made, fitted, slated, tiled or thatched as appropriate, and painted. Lastly, the fine exterior details – gutters and pipes, porches or lean-tos, buttresses, pumps, lamps, water-butts, signs, date-plaques, weathervanes, TV aerials, creepers, flowers, mosses and so on – are added and painted. The results can be stunningly realistic, but it must be said that buildings constructed by this method are rather delicate and vulnerable to handling damage; not, perhaps, ideal for portable layouts.

With the shell-first method, the basic structure is constructed out of stout card (or laminations of card) of a thickness appropriate to the type of wall being modelled, chosen to create window or door reveals of the appropriate thickness. The various walls are marked and cut out separately, with all doorways and windows pierced out and with due allowance made for material thicknesses at the corners. The walls are then firmly stuck together with a strong contact or resin-PVA adhesive to form the shell of the structure. This should incorporate any internal floors or partitions and any necessary reinforcements, roof supports and so on; the idea is that it provides a truly robust framework on which to build up the cosmetic finishes of the model. This finishing can then be accomplished in a variety of ways, from applying individual paper-cut bricks or stones (real hair-shirt stuff!) to making your own scribed-card or paper wall surfacing, applying ready-made embossed sheet plastic materials or commercial, printed building papers. Personally; I make great use of artist's watercolour papers as a basis for my own wall finishes, using very similar embossing and painting techniques to those described above for flat-and-fold construction, except that I usually add the door and window details and do the painting with the building 'in the round'. But this approach, while it results in a realistic and individual building – is scarcely speedy; quicker results can be accomplished by using commercial sheet finishes, pre-printed glazing, etched or moulded windows, and so on.

Printed brickwork, in particular, can be very effective; the bricks are usually of scale size, where a lot of plastic structures appear to be built from rather over-fed specimens; modern litho printing also gives a good range of appropriate colours and a nice matt finish. Some printed brickwork – such as that by Howard Scenics – is very subtle, with beautifully observed variations in the shades of brick colour used. As for them being too 'flat', it is worth pointing out that a well-built, properly pointed brick wall has very little relief detail anyway. If this does worry you, it is possible to buy building papers that are screen-printed in a thick 'filled' ink (ink to which talc or china-clay is added), which results in a very subtle and realistic brick texture. Even using normal flat building papers, it is easy enough to add at least some of the missing relief by laying tiles or slates in overlapping courses and lightly scribing the mortar-courses into the paper brickwork with a darning needle or defunct ballpoint pen. Only when it comes to irregular surfaces with pronounced relief – coarse stone rubble walling, old and crumbling brickwork with deeply incised mortar courses and the like – do building papers really fall down.

Above: A rather more prosaic card model, a 4mm scale version by the author of the stationmaster's house at Maiden Newton, GWR as it was in about 1930. This is an all-card structure, with a basic shell of thick grey backing board (off-cuts from a local picture framer) overlaid with watercolour papers for the slate-hanging and the rear wall, which is cement rendered. The doors and window frames are fabricated from Plastikard, while the elegant chimney pots are once again whitemetal castings from Scale Link. Watercolour paints were used for the slates, but the woodwork is finished in Humbrol acrylics.

Shell and overlay structures

These are made on the same principle as the card-shell structures just described, except that the shell is even more robust, being made of ply, thin MDFB, foam-core board or the like, glued together with a high-strength woodworking adhesive, while the overlays can be chosen from a huge variety of materials. This method is thus especially suited to very large buildings, structures being modelled in large scales, or those which need to be handled a lot. Unlike a simple card shell – which, although quite strong, is still vulnerable to damp – a shell fabricated in something like ply or MDF can use a 'wet' finish, such as a layer of plaster or modelling clay, applied thickly enough to create the most heavily-textured of surfaces by direct modelling, scribing or carving. This makes it a technique especially valuable in the larger scales, where

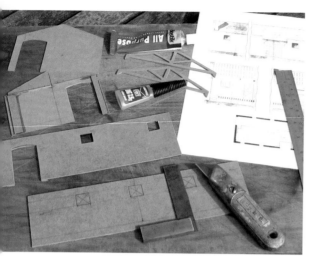

Above left and right: Creating a building shell – in this case for a goods shed – in 2mm thick MDFB. This versatile material can be cut with a Stanley knife and glued together with PVA, hot glue or, as here, with cyano-acrylate 'superglue' – quick and strong. Note that the internal roof trusses have been incorporated into the shell, where they brace the sides and provide support for the roof. This shell was overlaid with scribed paper stonework, with woodwork in plastic and metal details.

relief detail is obviously more pronounced. Modellers in 7mm, like Gordon Gravett, create stunningly realistic buildings using DAS modelling clay applied over a thick layer of strong PVA (such as Unibond) painted on the surface of a ply shell. This results in a finish which is not only realistic but truly robust.

For smaller scales, or where relief is not so pronounced, then all the methods already described can be used to add realistic finishing surfaces to the basic structural framework, which can actually be quite crude in its construction. I make extensive use of a rather less substantial form of this approach for 4mm scale work, building the shell out of 6mm thick foam-core board or 2mm MDF sheet assembled with a hot glue gun, which I then overlay with a wide variety of materials to get the effects I'm after. The great advantage of the 'shell' in this instance is that none of

these finishes has any structural role and can be chosen simply for the way it looks. I can therefore happily mix all manner of materials and methods in finishing my buildings.

Kitbashing

This is the noble art of ignoring instructions. The whole basis of 'kitbashing' lies in using whole kits or parts from kits – alone or in combination – to create something completely different to whatever it was the kit-designer intended them to be. A kit is regarded not as an entity in itself, but merely as a supply of useful parts and possibilities with which to get to work with the imagination. This may seem a haphazard way of building anything, but – coupled with a due measure of prototype observation and a dose of common sense – it is a surprisingly effective way of producing original and convincing buildings, but with all the detail and texture characteristic of a kit. It's worth noting that most of the models for the *Star Wars* films were, effectively, kitbashed, being created out of the contents of innumerable plastic kits – for aircraft, ships, military vehicles, buildings, bridges and who knows what else – which were simply sorted into bins of similar bits: flat panels, girders, pipes, wings, wheels and so on. The modellers sifted through these parts at random to find something suited to their purposes; most of the time, they hadn't a clue what it actually was!

Above: Classic kitbashing, American style, on my H0 layout 'Roque Bluffs'. Ma Tylick's soup factory started life as Walthers Golden State Fruit Cannery, but somewhere along the line it got shipped from California to Maine, gained a flat roof in place of the pitched original, and was turned into a low-relief model. The boiler house came from something else, and a water tank (Rix), perches on the roof. The plethora of structure kits on the US market makes this type of operation simple and painless; British modellers don't, alas, have as many starting points or potential 'donors'.

Architectural kitbashing is usually practised on plastic kits, although I can see no reason why you shouldn't bash card ones in much the same way. Reworking plastic-kit buildings is something that American modellers have long excelled at, to the extent that some ranges, such as Design Preservation Models and Pikestuff, are specifically *aimed* at the kitbasher, being merely a generic starting point – usually in modular form – to which matching panels and parts can be added. The versatility of this approach, combined with the huge selection of kits and bits available, enables whole layouts to be kitted out with structures exclusively made out of something they are not supposed to be! My 'Roque Bluffs' is one such; the fish meal processing plant, for instance, started out as a Pikestuff 'modern warehouse' to which I added a pair of Con-Cor steel grain hoppers, structural steelwork pinched from Central Valley bridge kits, some pipework, stairways and sheds from a Walthers oil depot and various vents, lamps, ducts and other excrescences trawled from the scrapbox into which I throw all the left-over bits of plastic kits – whatever they might be for. Virtually every other building on the layout has a similarly mixed genesis.

Scratchbuilding in plastic

Structure modelling from scratch in plastic sheet, strip and sectional materials has certain similarities to card modelling in that there are two basic approaches that equate, broadly, to the 'skin inwards' and 'shell outwards' ways of going about things. Essentially, the embossed or pre-scribed plastic sheet materials are, like the pasteboard used for flat-and-fold card modelling, too thin and flimsy to form a structure unless firmly braced on the inside with thicker plastic or other materials such as card or stripwood. Plastikard brickwork, for instance, is only 10thou thick and very flexible. Buildings made from it need extensive bracing and the lamination of additional layers of material at window and door openings to give the walls a realistic degree of 'visible thickness'. So, in this instance, the walls are normally built up, surface detailed, doors and windows added

Above: Straightforward scratchbuilt structures in sheet styrene on 'Bodesmeer'. Although the layout is to H0 scale, the brickwork uses a mix of 4mm, 3mm and 2mm scale brick Plastikards, representing the different prototype sizes of brick seen in Holland. The plastic brickwork is finished with Berol 'Karisma' coloured pencils used brass-rubbing fashion over a base coat of mortar-coloured Humbrol acrylic. The windows are clear plastic sheet with the glazing bars drawn on in thick acrylic paint using a draughtsman's ruling pen.

Right: Sometimes plastic is better mixed with other materials for part of the structure. The model of Maiden Newton signalbox on Andrew Duncan's layout is not quite what it seems; although all the brickwork is Slater's Plastikard, the basic shell of the structure is actually made of thick card. The roof is also in card, with watercolour-paper slates to match the other all-card structures on the rest of the layout. The windows, however, are entirely made of plastic, using American Evergreen styrene strip material and clear plastic glazing sheet. The characteristic roof vents are a whitemetal casting from Chris Leigh. The lack of point rodding is horribly obvious!

and even painted 'in the flat' before being assembled into the finished structure.

The alternative approach sees the shell of the building cut out from moulded plastic sheet and assembled – and often painted – before any of the finer detail is added. Moulded sheet materials like those made by Wills are quite thick and rigid enough to be structurally independent, so a building shell constructed of these materials should be quite strong enough to do without bracing and will possess a wall thickness sufficient to give good depth to door and window reveals. That it will also possess realistic surface texturing means

that the use of such materials is a very quick and efficient way to create model buildings. The main drawback of the moulded sheets is their limited size, which can cause problems on larger structures and often calls for a little ingenuity in disguising joins between sheets – especially on roofs or large expanses of unbroken wall. They are also rather more difficult to cut than the rolled sheet materials, particularly when it comes to piercing window openings.

Ease of working is one of the main attractions of styrene as a modelling material. In straightforward sheet form it is very easy to cut, either by 'score and snap' for straight lines, or repeated passes with a craft knife for curves. It can be filed and sanded, carved, incised, bent, textured and laminated. It is extremely quick to glue together – see below – and it takes acrylic and enamel paints well (but not cellulose or xylene-based paints like Floquil, which will attack the surface). The tools needed to work styrene are few and straightforward: the usual modelling knives with a cutting mat, a steel straight-edge and square, a good-sized pin vice and a selection of drills in the 0.8–3mm range, a handful of small files and abrasive papers and a cheap wee paintbrush to apply the solvent, are the basics.

Cutting the thicker and more heavily-textured moulded sheet can sometimes call for a saw rather than a knife – especially when it comes to piercing out curved-top window openings and the like. An ordinary modeller's piercing saw or small coping saw will do the job, but don't use too fine a blade or it'll snag. Lubrication with washing-up liquid can help. The other truly useful tool is an Olfa Plastic Cutter – a purpose-made hook-bladed draw knife that will score or cut through styrene really cleanly and without raising a surface burr. It is ideal for scoring planking or mortar-courses.

One of the key advantages of styrene plastics as modelling materials is the speed and ease with which they can be glued together by using liquid solvent cements to 'chemically weld' them – a process which

the volatile nature of the solvents makes the next-best thing to an 'instant' joint. The fact that all these materials – whether moulded, embossed, extruded, machined, hot-rolled or vacuum-formed – are essentially the same thing chemically speaking means that they can all be used and welded together with equal facility, so in structure modelling you have a very wide range of options. In one building you could combine moulded sheet masonry walls from Wills with injection moulded windows by Ratio, extruded-styrene steelwork from Plastruct, vacuum-formed corrugated sheet and embossed brickwork from Slaters, moulded pantile roofing from Vollmer, milled-styrene weatherboarding from Evergreen and internal partitioning or detailing from hot-rolled flat sheet from any number of sources in any thickness from 80thou/2mm down to 5thou. All stuck together with a single solvent like Slaters Mek-Pack, Plastruct's Plastic Weld, Humbrol's Liquid Poly or De-Luxe Materials Plastic Magic, to name only the commoner brews.

Below: Simon de Souza is one of our finest exponents of the art of modelling in sheet plastic. This absolutely exquisite GW weighbridge hut has hand-scribed brickwork that is absolutely correct in coursing and bond, with proper 'closers' at the corners and prototypical brick-arch lintels. Painting is in Humbrol enamels – one brick at a time.

Here, I must add a few words of warning. All of the above are potent organic solvents, so not too good for your well-being if inhaled; work in well-ventilated surroundings, use sparingly and *DON'T SMOKE*. Not only are these solvents highly flammable, but they can also produce toxic gases when drawn through a cigarette. Especially, guard against accidental spillage, which will have disastrous effects for the model and many tools and workshop fittings, not to mention damaging your health and that of most domestic furnishings and floor coverings. So keep the bottle stoppered when not in use and sit it in one of the special 'anti-tip' stands available, or at least anchor it to the workbench with a good-size blob of Blu-Tack.

Bridgework

The trouble with bridges in the real world is that, by and large, they have been designed

Below: This set-piece was inspired by a 1950s photo taken in Ipswich. I made this simple 4mm scale road overbridge with girders scratchbuilt (very simply) in Plastikard sitting on Wills abutments (available in the Scenic series). The large advertising sign was a common feature of railway overbridges at this period. The Eastern Counties bus is an EFE model, the Ford van and Vauxhall car are from Scale Link kits and the AEC tanker is a Cooper-Craft kit built and detailed by Bob Barlow. The figures are Monty's.

individually for a specific location and set of circumstances, so they're all different. This isn't 100% true, as where the same circumstances recur – such as the standard minor road or occupation overbridges crossing a normal line of railway, or very basic underbridges as those used to span minor roads, small waterways or cattle creeps – then standard designs can be used. But anything more complex than these basic bridge types – a skewed or inclined span, a bridge on a curve or of larger span – would call for a custom design. To make our life more difficult, the type of bridge chosen in each set of circumstances would depend on a lot of considerations of which we modellers remain largely (if not blissfully) ignorant.

I have a retired friend who earned his crust as a civil engineer. When he needs a bridge for his model railway, he sits down and designs it exactly as he would have done the real thing, taking account of all the necessary parameters: axle-loads, speeds, gross-weight-per-foot-run, hammer-blow, clearances, deflections, drainage, permissible skew angles, material weights, windage, soil stability and a dozen-and-one other factors that would never occur to lesser mortals. He applies the technical solutions and chooses the materials favoured by the prototype he's portraying (the former LNWR lines of the LMS) and then simply builds a model of the resulting design – a model which never fails to be other than utterly convincing because it is a 'proper' bridge. Unlike, I fear, a great number of the improbable-looking affairs too often seen on model railways, many of which in reality wouldn't even stand up under their own weight! Popular howlers include steel girders curved in plan, impossibly long spans with no intermediate support, lack of adequate deck thickness and fundamentally flawed proportions. However, not everyone has upwards of forty years of professional experience to draw upon.

I'm a great one for creating fictional settings for model railways – but I'd certainly never contemplate a completely fictional bridge. I'll happily wing my way through the odd bit of landscaping or minor vernacular

Above: The old Great Eastern Railway was famous for its timber-pile bridges. Vincent de Bode has modelled one for 'Flintfield', using spruce and obechi stripwood bought from a model shop catering for aeromodellers.
Len de Vries

architecture using natural features, materials, stylistic and structural elements with which I'm pretty familiar – but faced with the need to take my tracks o'er river or road or beneath a byway, highway or canal, I'm off scouring books, pictures and the real world in search of a suitable prototype to model. I might call upon a kit as a basis or make use of ready-made components like bridge girders or piers – provided they were suitable – but I'd be taking spans, widths and clearances, general proportions, materials, basic dimensions, pier types and placements, wing and retaining walls, decking, railings or parapets and similar structural details from real life. It's the only sure way of producing a believable model. The trouble is, there are very few general 'rules of thumb' that one can look to when pondering an apposite choice of structure. Perhaps the most useful generalisation is the fact that, whereas a masonry bridge or viaduct can be built on a continuous curve of any desired radius, a steel or iron bridge can follow curves only as a series of straight sections of appropriate length. Thus, curved bridges, especially if built to tight radii, are more likely to be masonry structures.

Model bridges

There has never been a particularly great selection of good, prototypical model bridges – especially the typical, workaday sort – available on the British market in any scale, more's the pity. Things have improved, but there are still many traps for the unwary and some howling gaps. The toy-train makers have produced very few likely candidates – and a lot of thoroughly unlikely ones, such as Hornby's Victorian chain suspension bridge – a type of structure almost never used to carry a railway, as the harmonics of a moving train would soon have the whole thing dancing a merry dance as a prelude to total collapse! Steel truss girders of fairly substantial mien have long been a popular and more plausible subject – Hornby Dublo did a peach of a bowstring girder in die-cast metal which was actually a pretty good model, for all that it was finished in near-Dayglo orange.

Above: The Wills Scenic series includes a good selection of bridges, such as this workaday brick arch with wing walls – about as plain Jane as they come.

Tri-ang, too, offered a hefty truss bridge – rather too hefty, in fact; the structural members were more in proportion with 0 scale than 4mm. Masonry bridges fare little better; Hornby again perpetrate an improbability in their brick viaduct, which has piers which are wider at the top than the bottom – the exact opposite of the normal taper on a real masonry pier and structurally almost impossible!

A lot of the better bridges available from the British model trade follow relatively small prototypes. The card ranges have few useful candidates: Prototype Models' GC plate girder/brick arch combination overbridge is a good and very typical road overbridge which can be adapted to a number of situations. But, of course, it's nowhere near hefty enough to represent a railway underbridge. Metcalfe Models make some printed-card viaduct kits that are realistically proportioned, a low, urban-style brick or stone affair in double-track width and a tall and elegant single-track design in brick. Alas, these kits are designed to be built unrelentingly straight, so are difficult to adapt as a basis for a curved viaduct. Peco have offered a low stone-arch bridge in card for donkey's years, but it looks more like a road-over-water bridge than a railway structure. They also used to produce a card plate-girder bridge which was a bit more substantial, but

it seems to have vanished from the current catalogue. South-Eastern Finecast has some realistically-proportioned vacuum-formed plastic bridge and viaduct walling that can form a good starting point, while there are some very authentic bridge piers, abutments, wing walls and arches in the cast-plaster Townstreet range. What is lacking is a decent selection of actual bridge structures.

In 4mm scale moulded plastic, the real old stager is the Airfix/Dapol 'girder bridge'. Although accurate in constructional details, as it comes this is not a particularly convincing affair. The prototype represented is quite a modern and substantial double-track through-truss steel bridge of relatively short span. The trouble is that for a *single-track* bridge – as supplied in the kit – the steelwork is far too hefty; the size and proportion of the girders accord with the requirements of a somewhat longer span. Combining two of these kits to make a single-line bridge at least one-and-a-half times as long as standard produces a better-proportioned and more realistic model, as does widening the bridge for double track – when the weight of steelwork makes more sense in relation to the span. The main drawback however, is really that through-truss girder bridges of this sort are relatively rare in Britain, where plate or lattice trough girders are the usual choice.

The Wills Scenic series includes quite a useful selection of small bridges, including the short-span single and double-track occupation underpasses, a small and relatively modern curved-top girder span on stone or concrete abutments, a stone-arched culvert or creep, and that old favourite, the decorative Victorian cast-iron bridge. This is fine for carrying a modest roadway or occupation crossing over the railway, or as a minor road bridge over a stream but – as it comes – it is nowhere near substantial enough to support any but the lightest of narrow gauge railways. Cast iron railway bridges are rare beasts at the best of times, and are usually of very short span. The Wills bridge needs a lot of 'beefing up' before it can convincingly hack it as a rail underbridge.

For normal standard-gauge main line bridgework, Wills do have some useful modular brick-arch structures of typical railway proportions – suited for use as underbridges, continuous urban viaduct or a basis for heavy arched retaining walls. To go with these arches there are matching brick abutments with piers and wing walls, plus the Vari-Girder – a series of square girder 'panels' that can be assembled to produce a typical railway-proportioned riveted plate girder of variable but moderate length. Generally, with all metal bridges, the greater the span the deeper the girder, and the 4ft depth of the Wills effort would in reality be good for railway bridges of up to around 40ft or so in span (a bit under 7in at 4mm scale). Longer bridges would call for intermediate piers, or heavier girders. Step forward Peco, which makes some usefully hefty bow-topped bridge girders of a somewhat more substantial depth with a span of just under 60 scale feet in 4mm scale (about 9in). They also do a steel truss girder side, but it is no longer and rather oddly proportioned falling somewhat into the same category as the Airfix girder bridge kit. These Peco bridges are also available for N scale. The thing that is really missing in either scale is a characteristic British diamond-pattern lattice girder; there's nothing in ready-to-use or mass-produced kit form, although there are a few very nice etched bridges.

Railway bridge kits of overseas origins are of limited use. Axle loadings in much of Europe are far higher than the UK (up to 36 tons in Germany, against our measly 22), so German bridges – on which the majority of kits are based – are usually much more massive than equivalent British structures; even allowing for the difference in scale, they rarely look convincing. The Americans have high axle loads, too – but they have always run at slower speeds and tolerated bigger bridge deflections than are usual here, so their bridgework tends to look quite spindly in comparison to the trains. (This can be alarming to ride over, to boot; much more 'sway' and general movement than we're used to!) However, this relatively lightweight construction, coupled

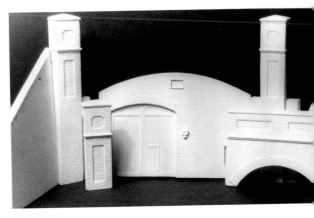

Above: One excellent source of masonry for model railway civil engineering in 4m scale is Townstreet's cast plaster range. Here are a few sample mouldings.

with the reduction in size due to H0 scale rather than 4mm (or 1:160 N in place of 1:148) means that some American model bridges can look OK in a British context. In particular, the ranges of bridge parts – steel, concrete and masonry piers, and various plate girders – made by Central Valley for both H0 and N are a useful source of components.

Below: One aspect of railway bridges that often gets overlooked is the deck, which is usually far from flat and featureless. Here's a correctly modelled bridge deck with the rails on massive timber baulks supported by cross-bearers resting on the main girders, with wooden decking between the rails. The girders are from the Wills occupation bridge, lengthened and deepened to suit a longer span.

Retaining walls/tunnel mouths

My comments in relation to bridges also apply in large part to those other two stalwarts of the railway civil engineering scene, tunnel mouths and retaining walls. A lot of the foreign offerings are wrongly sized and proportioned to convince as British structures, while the home market offers only a very limited choice. The Peco/Merit moulded-plastic stone tunnel mouth is a real old modelling chestnut, having been around since the Ark tied up, and anyway has over-generous clearances to accommodate sectional track and over-tight curves. Wills offers a brick tunnel mouth as part of their 'brick arch' range, which also includes retaining walls, and there are likewise a few candidates

Below: Tunnel mouths and retaining walls – not difficult to model if none of the commercial offerings suits. This is Potter's Bluff Tunnel on the old North Cornwall Minerals Railway layout, built using Peco vacuum-formed embossed stonework. **Chris Chapman**

in the card ranges. Probably the most convincing off-the-peg source for both brick and stone tunnel mouths and retaining walls is Townstreet, whose cast-plaster offerings look very convincing and match the proportions and finish of their bridgework.

Fortunately, all that said, scratch-building tunnel mouths and retaining walls is far from being the most demanding aspect of structural modelling – which is just as well, as very often a spot of DIY is the only way to come up with something appropriate to the situation on the layout. I tend to use a shell-and-overlay technique, making the basic structures from 2mm MDF sheet and adding the textures and detailing with overlays of embossed or moulded sheet plastic or hand-scribed masonry on thick watercolour paper. And, of course, working as closely as possible to the prototype – fortunately, this sort of basic railway civil engineering is, for the most, still intact and in place (whether in use or abandoned), which means you can at least go and study the real thing. However you go about the modelling, the worst part of the job is painting the finished result – especially if you're committed to 'one stone at a time' over a large area. A good programme on the radio and a large glass of a decent malt may be needed to retain your sanity!

Painting and weathering

One of the most critical aspects of realistic modelling – be it buildings or almost anything else – is painting and weathering the completed model. A good paint job can 'lift' even a relatively mediocre effort, while bad finishing has all-too-often been the ruination of otherwise excellent work. So it is something deserving care and consideration, not a 'quick lick of paint and a slosh over with some dirty thinners', as I've seen suggested more than once! As well as adding the final touch to an individual model, painting and – especially – weathering have an important role as blending a model in with the other elements of the layout to present a cohesive and convincing scene. Even where structures on a layout use a diversity of materials and

modelling techniques, skilful painting and subtle weathering can unify their appearance and help blend them together.

As always in railway modelling, there are a number of ways of going about this task, with different people swearing by particular brands of paint or alternative weathering techniques. As usual, I'll reiterate my mantra about consistency: it doesn't so much matter *how* you do the job so long as you always do it the *same* way (at least within the context of any given layout). If you're going to experiment with some new way of going about this sort of work, I'd suggest trying it first on some scrap models or in the context of a 'test-piece' diorama of some sort rather than on your latest prize model!

Once again, constraints of space don't allow me to ramble around all the many alternatives – which is probably just as well, as there quite a few techniques with which I have had either no success or which didn't appeal so I haven't tried them. So, unapologetically, I'm going to round off this chapter with a brief description of my own preferred methods and materials for finishing structures. There are alternatives…

Above: Realistic structure painting often calls for careful, time-consuming work with fine brushes and subtle colours that will need mixing rather than being used straight from the pot. This is the station entrance at Maiden Newtown, a scribed-paper over MDF shell structure painted (a flint-sized dot at a time!) with Humbrol acrylics, which were used for both masonry and woodwork. The slates on the roof, however, are in watercolour.

Water-based paints and plastic pencils

When it comes to *painting* buildings, I'm basically a watercolour-and-matt-acrylic man – both water based, but differing in their opacity, adhesion and covering power. The watercolours – I use the artist's tube variety – are ideal for the subtler aspects of structure painting, especially working on card, paper, bare wooden or plaster surfaces. I use these paints to pick out individual bricks, tiles or stones in walls, and as basic colour washes for things like stone walling or slate roofs made out of paper, with individual stones or slates picked out in variations of the basic shade. Watercolours are also the best medium for touching-in cut edges on card – particularly relevant to die-cut card kits. I find the most useful colours for structure work are: Ivory black, Chinese white, Payne's grey, burnt umber, raw sienna, yellow ochre, red oxide and Terre Verte (a sort of blue-green-grey 'neutral tint'). To go with these, you need a small plastic or china palette.

The acrylics come into play where a more 'solid' body colour is needed and, of course, for plastic buildings – ordinary water colours won't take on non-absorbent materials. Even on a card structure, I use acrylics for some 'denser' types of stonework, for colour-washed walls, most woodwork, corrugated iron and similar materials. For very many years now – since they first appeared – I've used the Humbrol acrylic range, which I have always rated as the best brushing acrylics bar none, and that includes all the fancy US brands! Humbrol acrylics became very hard to find for a while, but following the take-over of Humbrol by Hornby, they have become freely available once again.

The Humbrol range is very wide and includes matt, satin and gloss finishes and some excellent metallics. For structure work, I stick mostly to matt with very sparing use of satin. My must-have acrylic paint list runs thus (numbers given are from the Humbrol shade card; add an 'AC' prefix for acrylics): matt white 034, matt black 033, matt crimson 060, matt yellow 024, matt blue 025, matt dark earth 029, matt sea grey 027, matt dark grey 032, matt dark green 030, matt brick red 070, matt ochre 083, matt varnish 049, satin varnish 136, metallic silver 011, and metallic gold 016. With this basic selection I find I can mix almost any shade I want. Also useful are metallic gunmetal 053, matt sand 063, matt cream 103, matt rust 113, matt flesh 061, matt forest green 150 and satin mid green 131. These paints mix very well (I use foil cake cases as palettes) and can be thinned with tap water. Water also cleans the brushes – no smelly solvents!

A swift word here about paintbrushes for use with these paints. First, keep dedicated brushes for the two types of paint; a brush that's been used for acrylic won't be up to snuff

for watercolour work and anyway, the same type of brush doesn't suit both; watercolour calls for a decent sable or a top-flight synthetic artist's brush, whereas for acrylics a mid-range synthetic such as Daler's Dalon is quite adequate. Better, in fact; a Dalon will stand up to use with acrylics a lot better than any sable. The old advice about not skimping on brushes holds good, but there's no need to go over the top. For watercolour, Rowney series 34 Student or Series 40 Kolinsky sables or Windsor & Newton's Cotman watercolour synthetics are fine and not too expensive. I find a No. 0, a No. 2 and a No. 3, plus a ¼in flat-ended 'wash' brush, do all I want. Look after these brushes carefully; wash 'em thoroughly in warm, soapy water and twizzle them to a point before you put them away, heads in the air; never standing on the bristles! For the acrylics, I stick with the Daler nylon Dalon range, in sizes 0, 1, 2, 3 and 4. Wash them in hot water and washing-up liquid and rinse them frequently while in use and they last surprisingly well.

Not all aspects of structure colouring are, I feel, always best represented by paint. I also make a lot of use of the modern breed of blendable, plasticised artist's colour pencils – specifically, the excellent Berol Karisma range – as well as powders, usually ground-up artist's pastel colours. The Karisma pencils are my favoured method of colouring masonry – especially brickwork – made from moulded or embossed plastic; they work particularly well on Slater's Plastikard brickwork – which I use extensively both as a structural material and as an overlay. I give the whole area of the masonry a coat of mortar colour in acrylic, then build up the brick colours using a small range (three or four) of suitable shades applied diagonally and lightly to build the colour up gradually. This is a very controllable process and very subtle and pleasing effects can be readily achieved.

Weathering such as water or soot stains can also be applied using these pencils. All the brickwork for the 30+ structure models on my H0 Dutch layout 'Bodesmeer' were coloured thus.

Pastels, powders and paint mist

For weathering/toning down/blending in, I use a two-pronged approach: weathering of an individual structure is usually carried out on the bench using a mix of dry-brushed matt acrylic or watercolour paints and weathering powders, whereas the blending and toning are undertaken with the model in its final location on the layout as to be effective, this work needs to be done with reference to the tonal values already in place on the modelled scene. 'Drybrush' weathering is just as it sounds; the brush – a small, stiff hog's hair or a worn-out Dalon – is used dry. As is the paint, being kept in paste form – either neat tube watercolour or thick 'gunk' dredged up from the bottom of a pot of acrylic with a bit of bent wire. The brush is dipped lightly into the paint and all excess is wiped off on a piece of paper towel, until the merest trace of paint is left when the brush is dragged over the texture of the model surface. The technique is used for highlights and to represent features like moss or lichen growth on a roof or wall. Powder weathering is also brush-applied, either scrubbing the powder into a texture with a stiff brush for staining or drifting it with a soft one for general toning or colouration. Either way, once a satisfactory result has been achieved, the powder is held in place with artist's matt fixative or hairspray (which is much the same thing, but smells nicer!).

For toning down and blending-in structures, I drift on an overall light 'mist' of well-thinned acrylic paint in a very pale neutral grey-brown tint, using an airbrush. I spray from a good way back – around 12–18in from the model – with the airbrush set to give a very fine spray

*Above: **Subtle weathering and detailing by Vincent de Bode on the station building at 'Flintfield', based on the GER structures at Eye, Suffolk. These again are card models, surfaced with Howard Scenics brickwork painted with Humbrol matt enamels. Weathering – in watercolour and pastels – includes water staining and bird droppings.** Len de Vries*

pattern; the idea is simply to take the 'sting' out of colours and finishes and to give the effect of a building viewed from a distance rather than close to. Thus, the further back in the overall scene a structure is, the greater the degree of such 'distance dimming' I apply. It's a subtle business, but one that can make a surprising difference.

Chapter 9

MOTIVE POWER

Having chomped our way steadily through all the bread and butter of railway modelling, now it is time to chew over the bit everybody loves: locomotives. There are many railway modellers whose interest extends no further, for whom the building or acquisition of motive

Below: This is the sort of loco many railway modellers would really like – well-polished top-link express passenger power. Alas, few of us have the space for layouts that can do justice to this sort of engine – although you have more of a chance in N gauge, as here. This is a Graham Farish A4, subtly reworked by Steve Earle and refinished to represent No. 60032 Gannet. *Telling but straightforward improvements include scale-diameter bogie wheels in place of the undersized originals, close coupling of loco and tender, glazing the cab windows, provision of loco lamps, bufferbeam hoses, a fall-plate and a crew on the footplate, and some real coal on the tender.*

power is all that they ask of the hobby – or at least forms the main point of it. It matters not to such motive power devotees that the mixture of models that they muster is, at the end of the day, a nonsense in prototypical or operational terms. They just love locos – all locos, or a heterogeneous selection of favourites – and considerations of realism and authenticity don't enter into their selection.

However, such an approach doesn't really marry too well with the aims underlying this particular tome, realism and authenticity. For the modeller pursuing these objectives, the choice of apt motive power is a vital piece of the whole jigsaw. However, as with most other aspects of realistic railway modelling, you won't go far wrong if you base your motive power stud firmly on prototype considerations. Which means picking the right kind of locomotives not just for the sort of trains you'll be running on your layout, but

also for the nature of the line you're modelling, its period and geographical situation. And, as with so many aspects of realistic railway modelling, if you want to paint a convincing picture it's the *typical* items of motive power you want, not the oddball exceptions.

I'm not going to say that you never saw a large passenger tender engine or a hefty diesel on a branch line goods train, because such things did happen on occasion. But such instances are rare – and you would certainly never see a big, heavy main line engine running over lightly laid or sharply-curved track, or crossing bridges too weak to support its weight. The results of doing so on a model might not be as dire as they most certainly would have been in reality, but such an inappropriate mixture of train and setting will never look other than odd. Similarly, while it is true that – for instance – GWR pannier tanks worked in the Scottish Highlands and ex-GE 'Buckjumpers' saw service in North Wales, neither of these classes could be described as *typical* of the area or the railways concerned. Choosing a collection of locomotives that are truly at home in the geographical setting and historical context you're portraying goes a long way towards creating a convincing picture.

The right loco for the job

Under the Parliamentary legislation which authorised them, the vast majority of Britain's railways were 'Common Carriers'. That is, they *had* to accept and convey whatever traffic was offered to them, whether it be passengers,

Above: This is more the type of loco most steam-era model railways really need – the common-or-garden general-purpose 0-6-0 tender engine, in this case an ex-SECR Wainwright C class. This EM model was built by the author from a South-Eastern Finecast whitemetal kit. Notice the fireman's push-bike perched atop the tender – the kind of detail that adds character to an otherwise workaday model.

Below: The Great Western has always been well-served by the model trade in all scales. Here is one of the best (and most useful) of the current crop in 4mm scale, Bachmann's well-detailed 45XX 'Small Prairie' of the later 4575 series, pretty much straight out of the box. Just about every GW layout can use at least one of these versatile and widespread locomotives.

urgent mail and parcels, perishables like milk, fish or fruit, general merchandise of all kinds, bulk minerals including coal, stone and ore, flammable liquids, livestock, heavy materials such as steel, bricks or pig-iron, and exceptional loads like giant transformers or ship's propellers. Providing for this enormous variety of traffic resulted in a wide range of different sorts of train, and a corresponding diversity of design in the locomotives provided to haul them. In selecting locomotives for a layout, we need to ensure that we assemble an appropriate mix of types to cover the different duties offering; if you're modelling mineral operations in a hilly coal-mining area, for instance, a stud of high-stepping Pacifics won't be a lot of use to you!

Broadly speaking, the 'middle ground' of railway workings – encompassing such everyday duties as general mixed or pick-up goods, transfer or trip workings, stopping passenger trains, secondary and branch line workings of all sorts, non-urgent parcels traffic, empty stock workings, cross-country passenger services, permanent way trains and so on – called for much the same capabilities as to power, speed and tractive effort. So these jobs could be handled by a basically similar type of all-round locomotive, usually described as a 'general purpose' engine. As these commonplace tasks formed the bulk of all traditional railway workings, the general-purpose locomotive was by far the most common type and are thus the sort of engine most fundamental to any model motive power stud. Not that you would ever have known that from studying model railway manufacturers catalogues, at least until recently…

The omnipresent 0-6-0

Leaving aside the earliest and final days, throughout the whole period in which our railways were steam-operated, the inside-cylinder 0-6-0 tender engine was by far and away the most prevalent general-purpose type. It is a safe bet that for most of this period – a full century – there were probably at least half-a-dozen such 0-6-0s for every example of any other wheel arrangement. The LNWR 'DX goods' – designed by John Ramsbottom in 1858 – effectively formed the prototype of the breed, establishing a format and set of general

Below: The omnipresent 0-6-0 – and none was more omnipresent than the MR/LMS 4F, of which there were no fewer than 768 examples built. The LMS reckoned you could do just about any job with a 4F including – as here – working an express passenger train.

Below: The 4F has, understandably, long been a popular subject for modellers, with a number of kits in scales from 2mm to 7mm, and RTR models in 2mm/N and 4mm/00 scales. Here is the 4mm RTR version by Airfix (now Hornby), but fitted with a scale chassis for P4 standards. This was built from a Perseverance kit and uses 'conventional' drive – with the motor in the loco, in place of the original set-up of a powered tender pushing a freewheeling loco. Above the footplate, the body has had very little modification.

dimensions that remained current for over 75 years. The DX was such an outstanding success that it eventually became the most numerous of all British locomotive classes, with no fewer than 943 examples being built over a quarter of a century. Although classified as a 'goods', it was the archetypical British all-rounder; like many such, it was so described to distinguish it from engines suited *only* to passenger work. The DX had driving wheels 5ft 2½in diameter on a modest wheelbase of 7ft 3in + 8ft. 3in, 17in cylinders and an overall length with tender of 46ft. Tellingly, one of the last 0-6-0 general-purpose engine classes built, the 1930-vintage GWR 'Collett goods', had driving wheels of 5ft 2ins diameter on a wheelbase of 7ft 3in + 8ft 3in, cylinders of 17½in diameter, and was a bit under 54ft long over its (much bigger) tender.

Well-known and numerous examples of this general-purpose goods genus include the 'Dean Goods' and the Collett 2251 class on the GWR, with the LMS boasting the ex-LNWR '18-inch goods' or 'Cauliflower' (successor to the DX), the legions of ex-Midland 3Fs and 4Fs and a hoard of ex-Caledonian 'Jumbos'. On the LNER, one found the ex-GE J15 and J17 classes and their first cousins, the Worsdell family of J21s and J25s from the NER. The GNR contributed the Ivatt J3 and J6, while from the GCR came the handsome Robinson J11 'Pom-Poms'. North of the border, the North British had the comely

Above: Another railway to make great use of the general-purpose 0-6-0 tender engine was the old GER, which built no fewer than 289 examples of the basic Y14 design, most of which survived into BR days as the J15 class. This is my 4mm scale P4 model of No. 65454 as running c1954, when it still carried a 'utility' stovepipe chimney fitted during the Second World War. The model was built from an Alan Gibson kit; the J15 has, as yet, not made it into the ranks of 'Ready-to-Run'.

J36 and the powerful J37 'Superheater'. Post-grouping, Gresley added nearly 300 thoroughly modern J39s to this already substantial stock.

Below: Here is the 4F as rendered in 2mm scale RTR by Graham Farish; apart from a crew, lamps and some real coal, plus a modicum of judiciously applied dirt, Steve Earl's example is just as it left the factory. This has to be one of the most useful N gauge locos available.

Above: The last of the breed: the Southern Q1s, introduced in 1942, were the last, largest, heaviest, most powerful, most modern and least conventional examples of the 0-6-0 tender engine to run in Britain. Hornby do an excellent RTR model in 00; this EM version was built from a South-Eastern Finecast whitemetal kit by Louis Baycock.

Below: A less-common example of that widespread breed of general-purpose 0-6-0, the Great Western pannier tank family. This is a 4mm scale version of the 1076 class or 'Buffalo' series, built for 00 gauge from an Alan Gibson whitemetal kit by Andrew Duncan.

Right: Over on the other side of England, the Great Northern Railway favoured the 0-6-0ST for general-purpose and shunting duties, once again building the type in large numbers. This is one of the later types, LNER and BR Class J52, a stalwart of Hornby's 00 range. The body moulding is excellent, the chassis not quite so good, having an error in the wheelbase. Once again, the combination of the Hornby body with an aftermarket chassis (from Mainly Trains in this instance) results in an accurate model. This one has new, finer handrails, sprung buffers and a cast-brass injector (the latter items supplied with the chassis kit).

The Southern Railway also built modern 0-6-0s, including the last, least conventional and most powerful, the wartime Q1 class – an odd contrast with the conservative Q of 1938, a design derived from the LMS 4F. The Southern's pre-Grouping inheritance included the LSWR Drummond/Urie 700 class – the famed 'Black Motors' – along with Billinton's C2 and twin-domed C2X from the LBSCR and Harry Wainwright's handsome and efficient C class from the SECR. Within all four groups, there were many other similar 0-6-0s in small classes originating with minor pre-grouping railways, while many of the classes mentioned in my list were several hundred examples strong; the MR/LMS 4F (more than 760 engines in all), being the most ubiquitous.

The second large type of general-purpose locos were the legions of six-coupled tank engines, usually 0-6-0Ts but sometimes using the 0-6-2T wheel arrangement to allow a bigger coal bunker. These versatile locos usually had driving wheels a size or two smaller than the tender engines, with 4ft 8in or thereabouts being the most common diameter. A few prolific 0-6-0T classes – such as the ex-NER J72s and the ex-GER 'Buckjumpers' had even smaller (4ft) wheels, but the J72 was really a shunter, while the 'Buckjumpers' (LNER Classes J67, J68 and J69) started out thus before being developed for working suburban passenger trains making many stops at close intervals, a duty calling for rapid acceleration but no great top speed. (Although no-one seems to have told the drivers that; a frantic

60mph was not unknown!) The really great user of 0-6-0Ts was the GWR, with many series of 0-6-0 saddle and pannier tanks, including the 842-strong 57XX class – and the LMS, which added 412 Class 3F 'Jinty' 0-6-0Ts to the large fleet of similar engines inherited from the Midland Railway. The Southern, on the other hand, apparently had comparatively little use for the 0-6-0T, with all its examples being pre-Grouping engines of which the Brighton 'Terriers' are the best known. The largest class was the ex-LSWR G6 designed by William Adams, with the E1 and E2 types also representing the 'Brighton' and the P and R/R1 series the SECR.

Mixed traffic

A second broad group of duties – still of a general and secondary nature, but calling for a greater power and speed capability than offered by the 4–5ft-wheeled 0-6-0 – was met by a second large category of locomotive, the Mixed Traffic type. The work for which such engines was intended included the more demanding local and cross-country passenger services, fast main line freight, parcels and perishables traffic, secondary main line workings and the less-demanding express passenger trains. The archetypal British mixed-traffic engine was of the 2-6-0 or 4-6-0 wheel arrangement with driving wheels of 5ft 6in to 6ft 2in diameter and a power classification of 4, 5 or 6. Many of the best-known types of the 'Big Four' and BR eras were just such mixed traffic locos, led by the

Above: 'There is nothing made that cannot be made better' goes the old saying – although with some modern RTR you need to look very hard to spot the scope for improvement! However, older models from the big makers did incorporate fundamental errors or manufacturing compromises that were worth correcting in the cause of greater authenticity or better appearance.

This Bachmann GWR 93XX Mogul – a model dating from the mid-1990s – came with a front end that was too long and had undersized cylinders. Some simple 'plastic surgery' has eliminated the excess length (the join is just visible behind the loco lamps) while correct-sized castings from Comet have solved the cylinder deficiency. Other refinements include an etched-brass pony truck (Comet again) in place of the original solid plastic block, together with a little thinning-down of the rims of the chimney and safety valve. Add on a touch of weathering and some etched-brass cabside plates, and the result is a model that is far more realistic and individual than the factory effort.

Below: One of the most successful of prototype mixed-traffic types was the LMS Hughes 'Crab' 2-6-0. Bachmann have a superb RTR version in 4mm, and Farish make this neat and powerful 2mm version. This one has been 'got at' by Alex Hodson.

Stanier Class 5 of the LMS – another design built in very large numbers – together with the GWR 'Grange', 'Hall' and 'County' 4-6-0s, the LNER V2 2-6-2s and B1 4-6-0s and the Southern's S15 4-6-0s and Bulleid 'Light Pacifics'. Even the BR 'Britannia' and 'Clan' Pacifics were technically mixed-traffic designs.

Once again, there were tank engine equivalents, often very closely related to the tender locos. The most common mixed-traffic tank type was the 2-6-4T, which appeared on the LMS, LNER and Southern; the GWR sticking with the slightly smaller 2-6-2T. The BR Standard 4MT 2-6-4T, derived from the Fairburn and Stanier LMS designs, was an outstandingly successful engine – powerful, sure-footed yet easy to drive, fire and maintain. Many of these fine locos have been preserved and often form the backbone of heritage railway operation.

Specialised locomotive types

Once you get outside the middle ground of general-purpose and mixed-traffic duties, steam locomotive types became more specialised and less adaptable. At one extreme, deep in the shadows amid the grit and grime, toiled the real workhorses of the railway – the heavy freight locomotives. Also lost and unsung amid the drudgery and dust of freight working were the many shunting engines, just as vital to the flow of commerce. In slightly more salubrious circumstances one found a large group of passenger tank engines, mostly engaged on short-haul suburban workings or on branch line passenger duties. On the high sunny uplands of long-distance, high-speed work sparkled the 'Prima Donnas' of the railway world, the top-flight express passenger classes – few, fey and famous.

Far from famous were the dedicated freight locos, which ranged from doughty 0-6-0s up to the biggest eight and ten-coupleds and a handful of Beyer-Garrett articulateds. No shakes at all in the speed stakes, most of them, but serious, husky low-speed haulers, the drudges of the railway world. Their work lay in shifting the serious tonnage of minerals – a thousand tons of coal, limestone or iron ore at a time, a few hundred of china-clay or quarry products

– together with the raw materials and produce of industry and agriculture: oil, chemicals, steel, metal ingots and castings, grain, malt, sugar-beet, potatoes and timber. Other freight ran mixed in general goods or merchandise trains, carrying everything from groceries to gunpowder and manure to mattresses. Fruit, flowers, flour, fertiliser, furniture, machinery, manufactured goods of all kind, raw and finished wool and cotton, jute, fabrics, carpets, linoleum, glass, tanned hides, personal effects and luxury goods, canned foodstuffs, horse-feed and household necessities like Sunlight soap and Zebrite grate polish – all were grist to the general goods mill.

In the steam era, throughout every day and night and in every corner of the network, rumbled the long rakes of slow-moving wagons: 20mph for mineral, 25mph for general freight, 40mph fast freight. But it was the heaviest bulk mineral traffic that was – and to a considerable extent still is – the foundation of the railway's freight operations. To work this traffic there were built the largest and most impressive of British locomotives, the LMS Garrett articulated engines, as well as smaller but outstanding designs like the GWR Churchward 28XX series, GCR Robinson 8K, LMS 8F, LNER O1, O2 and O4, and BR 9F. Freight working also gave employment to many hundreds of those ubiquitous general-purpose 0-6-0s; the Midland, for all that it sat astride the heartland of British industry, never moved a goods train with anything bigger – even its heaviest mineral trains struggling along behind nothing stouter than a pair of panting 4Fs.

Heavy freight engines

The Midland aside, the most common type of British heavy freight engine was the 0-8-0 or 2-8-0 with driving wheels of around 4ft 7in diameter and a power classification of 7F or 8F. These 'monster' engines first appeared on the LNWR in 1892 in the form of the Webb Type A 0-8-0 coal engine. The 0-8-0 really became popular during the early 1900s, and although some designs – the LNWR compounds and the Caledonian 600 series spring to mind – weren't a great success, the type soon gained wide acceptance. Notable pre-Grouping examples

Above: Specialised types 1 – heavy freight.
British motive power doesn't come much
heavier than this – an LMS Beyer-Garratt in
2mm scale for N gauge. Steve Earl's model is
from a whitemetal kit by Skytrex/Fleetline,
using a pair of Graham Farish LMS Class 5
chassis – only one of which is powered, but it'll
still walk off with 50+ wagons.

were the D and 'Super D' on the LNWR, the fine Aspinall and Hoy engines on the L&Y, Robinson's lumbering 8A on the GCR (ironically known as the 'Tinies'), Worsdell's T series on the NER and Ivatt's 'Long Tom' GNR engines. There were also a few mighty hefty heavy-freight 0-6-0s introduced at this period, of which the massive GER J20s (as long and heavy as many an 0-8-0) were the most powerful.

Other lines favoured the 2-8-0, first introduced *as a design* by Churchward on the GWR with the 2800 class of 1903, an outstandingly successful engine. I draw this distinction because a few LNWR compound 0-8-0s had had their overweight front-ends propped up by extempore pony trucks to become effectively the first British 2-8-0s, but they were lame ducks in either version. The 28XXs became a Churchward 'standard' engine, and spawned a 2-8-0T derivative, the 4200 class. Also early in the field with another fine 2-8-0 design was Robinson on the GCR, his superheated 8K engine of 1911 being selected

by the ROD as their standard locomotive during the Second World War, with several hundred built for military purposes. Ironically, another successful 2-8-0 design was that produced in 1914 by the Midland to work on the Somerset & Dorset railway, a joint line it co-owned with the LSWR. Why they didn't go on and build themselves some as well – to give all those overworked 4Fs a break – is an abiding mystery. Last of the pioneering 2-8-0s were the two- and three-cylinder types introduced by Gresley (succeeding Ivatt) on the GNR. The LSWR also dipped a tentative toe into eight-coupled waters, with a quartet of massive 4-8-0Ts built by Urie for hump-shunting and transfer work at its Feltham marshalling yard in South London.

With the exception of the Southern – which had relatively little bulk mineral work, being mostly concerned with perishables, ferry traffic and other less-weighty matters – the 'Big Four' grouping companies and BR all found the need for large numbers of heavy freight engines. The GWR continued to build 2-8-0s, Collett updating the Churchward 2800 design into the 2884 class and rebuilding some of the 42/52XX 2-8-0Ts into monstrous 2-8-2Ts (the 7200s) for working coal trains through the Severn Tunnel. After a false start with a duff 0-8-0 that was effectively a stretched 4F, the LMS under Stanier went on to produce – in the 8F 2-8-0 – the most outstanding example

Above: The GWR was unusual in having a large stud of heavy 2-8-0 and 2-8-2 tank engines, the 42XX/52XX/72XX series, totalling 150 locomotives. Here is a 3mm scale model of one of the later 42XX engines, built by the author from a Worsley Works etched kit. Kits for these engines are also available in 4mm and 7mm scales.

of the type to run in Britain. Indeed, in a lot of other places as well; its adoption as a War Department standard design during the Second World War saw 'Stanier 8s' working as far afield as the Adriatic, Turkey and Middle East, as well as in Europe after D-day. The 8F eventually formed one of the largest of all British locomotive classes, with well over 800 examples built; BR inherited 624 of them in 1948, gaining a few more later while many remained overseas.

The only dedicated freight engine boasting larger numbers was the 'Austerity' 2-8-0 designed in 1943 by R. A. Riddles for the War Department. The 'WD' was intended as a universal lightweight 2-8-0 that could run anywhere and was cheap and quick to construct; it was an outstanding success, with no fewer than 935 being built during the latter part of the war – of which some 730 finished up in British Railways stock after Nationalisation. The remainder – minus a few combat casualties – were still serving with the military or on the railway systems of Holland, Belgium, Sweden and Hong Kong, among other places. At the same time as the 2-8-0, Riddles designed a 2-10-0 variant with the same tractive effort but a lower axle-loading, 150 of which were built, and of these 25 came to British Railways. The WD kept a few and the Dutch had most of the rest, with a handful ending up in Greece and Syria.

Shunters

In many ways, the lot of the humble shunting engine is one of the hardest on any railway, real or model. Constant stopping, starting and reversing, the need to start and move heavy loads and the ability to negotiate indifferent and often sharply curved trackwork are all part of the job, often performed under cramped and dirty conditions with the minimum of maintenance and the maximum of availability. Small wonder this was the first prototype role to be assigned to the diesel locomotive, where the low-maintenance requirement and instant 'turn of a key' availability were most valuable.

Real shunting locomotives can usually be placed in one of three categories; they can be purpose-designed and built for the role and have no other duties; they may be small, general-purpose types that include shunting among their range of abilities; or they can be pensioned-off examples of other types, working out their days in the role, which is an expedient resorted to by railways suffering a shortage of more suitable motive power. Familiar examples of these three

Above: Specialised types 2 – shunters. Here's a classic purpose-built shunting engine, the GWR 1366 class or 'Collett Dock Tank'. Small wheels, a very short wheelbase, modest overall dimensions, and not much speed capability. My P4 model of No. 1369 is mostly scratchbuilt, although the chassis is from the Peter K kit for the 1361; the two classes having identical running gear.

Below: Cast-off. The other common type of shunting engine was a more general type that had seen its best days on more salubrious duties and had been 'handed down' to a semi-retirement in the shunting role. The ex-GER 'Buckjumpers' worked smartly timed suburban passenger trains in their heyday, but most ended up amid the wagonry. No. 68499, here seen resting at Cade's Green, was a Stratford engine, one of the wide-tank engines of Class J69/1. My model was cobbled together from a very old Wills whitemetal kit on a home-brewed chassis. The current South-Eastern Finecast version of this kit is much-refined and includes an etched chassis.

categories would be the ex-L&Y 'Pug' 0-4-0ST or Hunslet 16-inch 0-6-0ST (LNER/BR Class J94) as true shunters, the GWR 57XX pannier or LMS 'Jinty' as suitable, general-purpose types, and the ex-L&Y 23 class 0-6-0STs (rebuilt from 0-6-0 tender engines) as an older type relegated to shunting duties.

Passenger tank engines

Often handsome, sometimes surprisingly speedy, but always frenetically busy were Britain's plethora of short-haul suburban and secondary passenger tank locomotives. The 2-4-0T, 2-4-2T, 0-4-2T and 4-4-0T types were the usual Victorian answer to this need (except on the LBSCR and GER, where small 0-6-0Ts were initially favoured), evolving into the 0-4-4T , 4-4-2T or 0-6-2T in Edwardian days before their final metamorphosis into 2-6-2T or 2-6-4T after the Grouping. Some railways, such as the North London, Metropolitan, District, and London, Tilbury & Southend railways – possessed loco studs almost entirely made up of such engines, while all the major pre-Grouping lines serving large cities had extensive fleets. They were found, too, on the teeming branch lines of the South Wales coalfields and in the industrial heart of the Midlands and North. Only railways such as the Cambrian and Highland – whose systems were essentially long, straggling main lines with a few branch lines in sparsely-populated countryside – knew them not.

The typical suburban passenger tank had wheels between 5ft 3in and 6ft in diameter, was relatively compact, carried water and coal supplies adequate only for a shortish trip, and could run equally well in either direction. Early specimens of the type included the 'Metro' 2-4-0T and 517 class 0-4-2T on the GWR, the classic Beyer Peacock 4-4-0Ts of the Metropolitan and District, Stroudley's famous 'Terrier' 0-6-0Ts on the LBSCR, the Beattie 2-4-0WT 'well tanks' on the LSWR and Kirtley 0-4-4WTs on the MR, 2-4-2T radial-axle tanks on the LNWR, LYR and GER and 4-4-0T and 0-4-4T by Drummond on the NBR and Caley in Scotland. And, of course, in the later 1880s came the Adams 4-4-2 'Radial tanks' on the

Above: Specialised types 3 – passenger tank engines. This splendid Victorian example is an 1865-vintage Adams 4-4-0T of the North London Railway, a scratchbuilt 4mm scale model by the author. This must have been one of the raciest suburban tank engines of its day.

Above: The last word in suburban passenger power – a BR Standard Class 4 2-6-4T; an outstandingly successful design. I built this 00 version from a DJH whitemetal kit, but nowadays Bachmann have a superb RTR version in 4mm scale that puts this effort in the shade. Chris Langdon

LSWR and the fabled 'Buckjumpers' on the GER. Edwardian examples were a lot sleeker and usually a size or two larger: Billinton 0-6-2Ts and 0-4-4Ts on the LBSCR, Drummond M7s on the LSWR, Johnson 0-4-4Ts on the MR and Hill's N7 0-6-2Ts on the GER, the Ivatt C12 4-4-2T and the 0-6-2T Ivatt N1 and Gresley N2 on the GNR, 'Precursor' 4-4-2Ts on the LNWR, Aspinall 'Superheater Radials' on the LYR and Pollitt and Robinson 4-4-2Ts on the GCR. Scotland went big early on, with the handsome Caledonian Railway 4-6-2T 'Wemyss

Below: Far more typical suburban power of the late 19th/early 20th century – an ex-GER 'Gobbler' 2-4-2T, LNER and BR Class F5. This is typical of the older examples of the suburban tank type, for which the 2-4-2T, 4-4-0T, 4-4-2T and 0-4-4T wheel arrangements were usual; later engines being 0-6-2T, 2-6-2T or 2-6-4T. By the early 1950s, most of the four-coupled passenger tanks had been relegated to branch line duties, as here. My model of No. 67217 was built from an old Jidenco etched kit.

Bay Tanks' and the brutish Whitelegg 4-6-4T 'Baltics' on the G&SWR, as did the GWR with the Churchward 'Large Prairie' series of 2-6-2Ts.

The final flowering of the suburban tank was mostly limited to the use of suitable mixed-traffic types for the longer and heavier runs. Stanier did design a 3-cylinder variant of his handsome 2-6-4T especially for the Tilbury line, while Gresley produced the V1/V3 series of (also 3-cylinder) 2-6-2T for Edinburgh and Tyneside suburban workings. On the LMS, the Fowler, Stanier and Fairburn 2-6-4Ts displaced a lot of the older LNWR and MR engines. Elsewhere, though, the Edwardian engines – especially the more modern, superheated specimens like the GER N7 and GNR N2, Churchward 'Large Prairies' and LSWR M7 – saw out steam working. Where there *was* a need for new steam power, the

Below: High Victorian branch line power: a Hudswell Clarke 4-4-0T of the Midland & Great Northern Railway, which ran east–west across Norfolk. Finished in the M&GN's unique 'Golden Gorse' livery, this delightful 4mm scale model was built by the late Frank Watts, mostly from scratch but incorporating a few bits of a Jidenco kit.

BR Standard 4 2-6-4T was a complete answer. However, electrification had long been seen as the future of suburban working, the long process of change starting on the LBSCR, Metropolitan, LYR, LNWR and NER in the early 1900s. The Southern Railway went electric in a big way between the wars, and the former GER network started to go under 1,500V dc wires in the late 1940s. The early 1960s saw the extensive 25kV ac north London, Manchester and Glasgow electrifications, and everywhere else the DMU took over. Steam suburban trains were all-but extinct by 1962.

Branch line passenger power

Most branch line workings came within the remit of the general-purpose types or formed the province of the suburban passenger types just described – often older specimens 'bumped down' from their original status. Some railways, however – most notably the GWR – preferred to provide at least some motive power specifically designed for the role. The prolific series of 517 class 0-4-2Ts were staple branch line passenger power on the GWR from the end of the broad gauge onwards, later augmented by pensioned-off 2-4-0 'Metro tanks'. Then, in 1906 Churchward, as part of his 'standard engine'

Above: Top-link refined RTR. This is a Hornby Stanier Pacific as re-worked for fine scale 00 standards by Tim Shackleton, finished and detailed to represent the engine named for the great man himself, as it appeared in the final years of steam.

policy, introduced a light but powerful loco specifically for such workings, in the form of the 'Small Prairies'. These took on the heavier or longer-distance duties, relegating the old four-coupled engines to the less-important lines. However, when these older engines were worn beyond the point at which even the GWR felt they were worth patching up, they were replaced – not with more suburban retirees (there were anyway no suitable candidates) – but with new engines built for the job. Thus arrived the push-pull fitted 48XX (later 14XX) 0-4-2T – the only 20th century examples of this wheel arrangement ever built – and the 5400 class large-wheeled pannier tank. These, together with the 'Small Prairies' and abetted by a sprinkling of 57XX and 64/74XX series general-purpose panniers, worked the many GWR branches from the early 1930s until the diesels or Dr Beeching swept them all away.

The model retains the original Hornby tender drive system, but has a completely new unpowered locomotive chassis built using a Comet 'chassis pack' (a kit containing etched nickel silver frames, bogie and valve gear and cast whitemetal cylinders). It is fitted with Markits & Gibson wheels, closer to scale than the Hornby originals. The body has been refined with new handrails and extra details, and the whole model has been repainted and lined out in the final BR maroon livery with electrification markings; the diagonal stripe on the cabside indicates the engine was banned from working beneath 25kV overhead catenary.

Express passenger locomotives

At the other extreme to the plodding freight haulers and shuffling shunters were the racehorses, the high-stepping top link express passenger types with their large-diameter driving wheels, exotic names and thoroughbred lines – real rail-born glamour. There were never all that many of them by comparison with other types, and most *premier* passenger classes – the GWR 'Kings', LMS Stanier Pacifics, LNER A4 streamliners, Southern 'Lord Nelson' 4-6-0s and Bulleid 'Merchant Navy' Pacifics – only amounted to thirty or so examples each. Far more numerous were the second-rank express types: the GWR 'Castles', 'Stars' and 'Saints', LMS 'Compound' 4-4-0s and 'Royal Scot', 'Patriot' and 'Jubilee' 4-6-0s, the

LNER non-streamline Pacifics and 3-cylinder 'Sandringham' 4-6-0s, and the Southern 'King Arthur', 'Schools' and 'Light Pacific' classes. Taken all-in, though, express passenger engines made up only a fraction of the total locomotive stock of the steam-era railway.

Working fast non-stop or limited-stop express passenger workings was the prime duties of all these types – but these were not their only uses. Mail and express parcels trains often rated front-rank power, as did important perishables workings; milk would come up from the West Country behind a 'Castle' on the Western or a Bulleid Pacific on the Southern; West Coast postal specials rated a Stanier Pacific, and the famous 'Blue Spot' express fish trains from Aberdeen often sped south behind a hard-pounding A4. Some quite unimportant local trains also had express passenger power as 'fill in' turns between main-line duties, while lines connecting with the major locomotive works would often see top-rank power on local passenger or parcels workings, the engines being road-tested and run-in after overhaul. Some premium fast freight trains – duties where the ability to keep a tight schedule were more important than ultimate load-shifting – were also hauled by express passenger classes.

In the later years of steam, when the availability of express passenger locomotives was greater than the need, many front-line types worked out their declining years on quite humble duties: local or semi-fast passenger trains, fitted freight and parcels, and even branch line turns. The ultimate in such sorry degradation was the sight of filthy, neglected

Below: The general-purpose diesel was the backbone of British Rail from the demise of steam through to the dawn of privatisation and the appearance of the Train Operating Companies. This Class 37 epitomises the breed, here in Transrail colours at Exeter, working stone hoppers from Meldon Quarry. Hornby, Lima, Bachmann and ViTrains all offer '37s' in 4mm scale, and Farish in N. This particular paint scheme – setting off the ultimate in uninspiring names – will probably be down to you and some Fox transfers.

Edinburgh A4s, displaced by the new D200 series and 'Deltic' diesels on the East Coast Main Line, working pick-up goods trains on the Waverly route. Painful, but, I suppose, a good prototype for someone!

Diesel locomotives

When considering internal-combustion motive power, the situation becomes much more straightforward. One of the virtues of the diesel-electric or diesel-hydraulic locomotive over the steam engine is its greater versatility and adaptability. Speed capability and pulling power are no longer dictated by the size of the driving wheels, while the 'slippage' allowed by the electric or hydraulic transmission systems allow the same locomotive to develop maximum tractive effort at low speed for freight working or similar tasks, as well as the high ultimate horsepower needed for fast express working. Thus, the vast majority of British Railways diesel locomotives fell into the general-purpose or mixed-traffic categories. There were a few dedicated passenger designs – the Class 55 'Deltics' and the InterCity 125, later Class 43, HSTs come to mind – but most diesels could turn their hand to a wide range of duties when called upon. While large, main line diesel types may not have been that much lighter overall than the steam types they superseded, the weight was usually spread much more evenly over their wheelbases,

Above: If there was a diesel top-link express passenger-only 'glamour queen', then this was surely it: the prototype 'Deltic' in its original English Electric colour scheme. At 3,300hp this was the most powerful single-unit locomotive in the world at that time (and for some while afterwards) and also among the fastest of internal-combustion locos. Not much could match a 105mph service speed in 1955! Steve Earl's 2mm version has been modified from a Farish model of the Class 55 production 'Deltic'; the special transfers being from B+H Models.

Below: The opposite end of the diesel loco spectrum to the 'Deltic' was the BTH Type 1 800hpBo-Bo for 'secondary duties' – a short-lived and unsuccessful (if handsome) design. Steve Earl's N version has a Parkwood Models cast-resin body on a Farish Class 20 chassis. A surprising number of first-generation and 'out of the way' diesel types are available in kit form for 2mm scale.

resulting in a lower maximum weight on any single wheelset – which usually gave them a surprisingly wide route availability. The load carried by steam locomotive driving axles, on the other hand, was often quite high and was further exacerbated by the 'hammer blow' resulting from the oscillating movement of the machinery; this is an effect entirely absent in the diesel locomotive, which has an all-rotary geared final drive.

Although the 1955 BR Modernisation Plan that saw the switch from steam to diesel power did produce a relatively large number of different first-generation diesel designs, many of these were extremely short-lived or never went into series production. The end result – established by the later 1960s – was a selection of perhaps twenty or so basic types, several of which were propagated in very large numbers. Some of these designs – like

the D8000 series Class 20 Type 1, D5500 series Class 31 Type 2, D6700 series Class 37 Type 3, D1500 series Class 47, or the 350hp Class 08 0-6-0 shunter – were outstandingly successful and have seen service lives of nearly half a century, considerably longer than many steam types. The combination of a limited range of prototypes having widespread usage makes the choice of suitable diesel power much easier than is the case with steam. All the principal classes of BR diesel locomotive are available as RTR models in both 2mm and 4mm scales, with one or two now appearing in 0 from Heljan.

Electric locomotives

Electric traction is an altogether more specific business. Most older-established British electrification schemes have been associated with a specific type of traffic – usually high-density suburban working or heavy freight. Even on the main line routes now electrified on the modern 25kV ac system, electric locomotive traction is largely reserved for a few main line passenger workings. Diesel locomotives handle the freight traffic and multiple unit stock – either diesel or electric – is used for passenger services. Some electrified networks – such as the Southern's third-rail 650V dc system – have long used electric multiple unit

Below: Electric locomotives are far from being 'boxes on wheels'. This 4mm scale BR class 87, modelled by Jim Smith-Wright for his Birmingham New Street project, uses a Lima body on a Bachmann mechanism (with Hornby sideframes!) and a Hurst Models pantograph. Creative cross-kitting like this is an American approach with many British applications. Jim Smith-Wright.

(EMU) operation for virtually all passenger workings, and this trend is now spreading to other types of passenger working including long-distance expresses. A Virgin 'Pendolino' is simply a souped-up EMU.

This situation means that there have never been any truly widespread classes of British general-purpose electric locomotive equivalent to the German 101-series or French B-B16000. The differing nature of the various electrification schemes have resulted in three specific 'families' of motive power, none of which can operate on any of the other systems. The oldest are the 600V dc outside-third rail types associated with the Metropolitan Railway in London (the fourth rail on London Transport tracks merely provides a return circuit independent of the running rails). There were also a handful of electric locomotives or dual-working 'electro-diesel' designs built for work on the 650V dc outside-third rail routes of the Southern Railway and BR's Southern Region, of which the best-known and most numerous were the 600hp 'electro-diesel' Bo-Bos, Class 73.

The second main group of electric locomotives stemmed from the pioneering main line electrification schemes of the North Eastern Railway, based on a 1,500V dc overhead system. This was the system later adopted and developed by the LNER for the post-war Sheffield–Manchester electrification through the Woodhead Tunnel, a busy trans-Pennine route with heavy freight and mineral traffic. To work this line, the LNER engineers designed two very distinctive and successful locomotive types, the 1,750hp EM1 Bo-Bo and the 2,700hp EM2 Co-Co. As with the Metropolitan locomotives, these engines didn't stray from the specific line for which they were built and – due to the non-standard electrification system – when that line was closed there were no other British routes on which they could be used, although some EM2s saw service in the Netherlands.

Under the BR Modernisation Plan already mentioned, it had been decided that all future main line electrification not linked to the existing third-rail network would be on the 25kV ac overhead system as successfully adopted in France – a far-sighted decision now vindicated by the opening of the Channel Tunnel linking the two systems. The first British main line to be electrified on this system was the West Coast Main Line from Euston, originally to Crewe and subsequently extended over Shap Summit to Carlisle and on to Glasgow. At much the same time, 25KV electrification was applied to outer suburban routes in north London, Manchester and Glasgow. Subsequently, the 25kV main line network was expanded to take in the East Coast Main Line from London, King's Cross to Edinburgh via York and Newcastle, and the former Great Eastern route to Colchester, Ipswich and Norwich in East Anglia. The newest section of 25kV electric railway comprises the routes linking London to the Channel Tunnel, including the new high-speed link being completed at the time of writing.

To serve the 25kV main line routes, the only general design of British electric locomotives was developed. These were the 'AL' type high-power Bo-Bo electrics which started with the AL1s and extended through several series and variants to the AL6 and Classes 87 and 90. Different groups of locomotives within this series were geared for high-speed passenger or mixed traffic/freight duties, and the various sub-classes saw a process of continual modification to fit them for varying roles, including multi-unit and push-pull operation. With some three hundred engines in total, these are the largest group of British electric locomotives, joined in more recent times by the Class 91s on the East Coast route as well as the special articulated two-unit locomotives developed for Channel Tunnel use. However, with the switch to multiple unit or self-contained trains – such as the 'Eurostar' and 'Pendolino' – for passenger working and the use of high-horsepower diesels for freight, it is unlikely that further general-purpose electric locomotives will be built for British operation in the near future.

Contemporary motive power

On the contemporary British railway network, the multiple unit train in either diesel or electric forms now predominates passenger working, with locomotive-hauled passenger trains almost extinct. Most development is centred on new examples of the multiple unit genre, both in the familiar local-passenger application and also for long-distance high speed work. These multiple-units are taking over from the locomotive-at-each-end fixed-formation trainset configuration pioneered by the BR 'Blue Pullmans' and successfully developed in the HST sets that have formed the backbone of passenger workings on many main lines since they were introduced some thirty years ago.

Freight traffic is now largely hauled by modern, six-axle diesel types, augmented by updated examples of some older designs from the BR Modernisation Plan. Many of the BR locomotive types that have been familiar in recent years are now disappearing fast or have already become extinct. The hugely

Below: Twenty-first century diesel super-power – although it's worth noting that there's not a lot between this and a 'Deltic' when it comes to raw horsepower; comparing the tractive efforts, however, the Class 66 has it hands down, thanks to modern computer-controlled anti-slip technology. This superb 2mm RTR model is by CJM Models; Dapol and Graham Farish have subsequently introduced their own versions.

successful Class 59 and 66 Co-Cos – a design derived from the American General Motors SD40-2 and originally developed for the heavy Mendip stone traffic – is becoming the standard freight locomotive not just in Britain, but across much of Europe too. Only in the liveries applied by the various operating companies is the variety and interest in the modern motive power scene expanding.

Sources of model motive power

In assembling a representative power stud for a model railway, there are a number of sources to draw on for the necessary models. Most accessible are ready-to-run models in 4mm scale/00 gauge and N scale, with a few such models now appearing for 0. These can be augmented by detailing or conversion kits intended either to improve the authenticity of the basic RTR model or to produce a different variant of the same general design. Alternatively, the RTR plastic superstructure can be mounted on more refined finescale chassis – a combination known as a 'hybrid' model. The other side of the same coin is a complete superstructure kit – traditionally made up of whitemetal castings – designed to fit on an appropriate RTR mechanism. This used to be a popular approach in 00 but is

now largely confined to N; 4mm scale today prefers complete loco kits, including the chassis but usually supplied without wheels, gears and motor. This permits the models to be constructed for fine scale standards like EM or P4 and enables the modeller to specify his own drivetrain. Such complete kits can use whitemetal or lost-wax castings, etched brass and nickel-silver etchings, milled or machined brass or steel components and resin mouldings. The various types of complete loco kit are described in more detail later.

If you don't have the time or inclination to tackle locomotive kit construction yourself, there are a number of professional craftsmen who will do the job for you, and there is no doubt that the combination of a state-of-the-art loco kit in 4mm or 7mm scale and a good builder can produce a model of the very highest quality. However, the cost will also be high, several times the price of a good-quality RTR model of a similar-sized prototype. Even more costly will be the commissioning of a model completely hand-built from scratch, but the end result will, of course, be unique. Nowadays, with a huge choice of kits from a wide variety of sources, there are relatively few prototypes for which scratchbuilding will be necessary. Most scratchbuilt models are made

for the love of the craft by individual modellers rather than as a commercial proposition.

While commissioning a high-quality kit-built or scratchbuilt model represents a considerable investment, such models don't generally depreciate and, if by a well-respected maker, may well increase in value. As a result of this trend, there is now an established investment market in good quality, handmade models, particularly in 7mm scale. However, these tend to be bought more for showcase display rather than as working motive power for a layout, and often exhibit a

Below: The hybrid loco stud. The four engines that work regularly on my 'Trerice' layout typify many model railways, in that they each have a different origin. The 57XX pannier tank at the rear uses the excellent Bachmann plastic RTR body, mildly reworked and sitting on an aftermarket scale chassis; the small-wheeled 16XX pannier in front of it is from a cast whitemetal kit (by Cotswold, now available via Autocom) with a chassis of my own making; the Beattie 2-4-0 well tank is based on an etched-brass kit by Jidenco (now Falcon Brass), and the 1366 class 0-6-0PT at front right is scratchbuilt. A common standard of detailing and finish (i.e., weathering!) gives them a common feel.

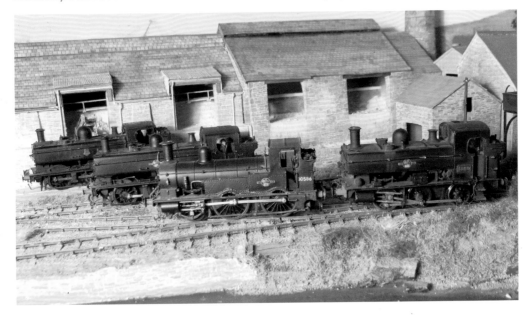

degree of 'exhibition finish' rather than being realistic representations of locomotives in everyday service.

The art of model locomotive construction is almost a 'hobby within a hobby', and there are a good few modellers who don't actually get any further than simply building engines from kits or from scratch. There is no doubt that there's a good deal of satisfaction to be had from 'hatching your own', and such a model will often be more individual than a purchased engine, whatever its provenance. However, in the context of providing a balanced stud of locomotives to work a layout, it is accepted practice to combine RTR, hybrid, kit-built and scratchbuilt models as needed to achieve the desired mix of prototypes. The trick is to work on the various models to bring them, so far as is possible, to a common standard of appearance – certainly, in respect of matters such as degree of detailing, type of paint finish, degree of weathering and so on. With the quality of so many modern RTR models, the problem often lies in making the handbuilt models look as good as the bought ones!

Locomotives for finer scale track

Thus far, I've really only touched on model locomotives in the popular-but-compromised scale/gauge combinations, 4mm scale/16.5mm gauge (00) and 2mm scale/9mm gauge (N). Once you move to finer standards in either of these scales, things become a little more complex, at least so far as the use of RTR models is concerned; most kits can be built to suit finescale standards readily enough. Given that the chief advantage of RTR power in 00 or N is that it can come straight out of the box and go straight on to the layout, how much more work and cost is involved in making 00 RTR locos suitable for EM or P4 standards, or N scale ones for 2mm fine scale?

The answer depends to a large extent on the particular model. By and large, diesel locomotives in either scale are simply not a problem, as all that is involved is the swapping of the wheelsets for the appropriate fine scale replacements, which are readily available. This is a straightforward process that often

takes only a few minutes, and given that the replacement wheelsets are not particularly costly, need not be a great obstacle. Steam engines are considerably more difficult to convert, as the need to remove and refit coupling rods, cylinders and connecting rods, valve gear and so on inevitably makes life harder. In N scale, only one or two steam-outline models (such as the Farish 57XX pannier tank) can readily be converted to 2mm fine scale, using components supplied by the 2mm Association. Otherwise, it is a case of extensively modifying the RTR mechanism or building a new one to fine-scale standards.

In 4mm scale, it used to be very much the done thing to simply re-wheel standard 00 RTR steam engine mechanisms for fine scale 00, EM and even – in the early days at least – for P4. This resulted in some pretty big compromises, and such conversions could also be tricky to carry out as the typical older mechanism didn't come apart in a user-friendly fashion. They often used axle diameters that varied from scale standards while gear ratios were often far too 'fast' for scale use – and re-gearing posed all sorts of problems. The limited selection of driving wheels available meant you often ended up with the wrong diameter, wrong spoke number and wrong crank configuration. Unless you really rolled your sleeves up you still had a model with chunky rods, simplified or overscale valve gear, and no chassis detail.

The current generation of RTR mechanisms are, thankfully, far more sophisticated and dedicated to a specific prototype – unlike the older approach of using the same basic chassis under a variety of different bodies, whether or not it had the right wheelbase, wheel-size or configuration! The modern 00 RTR mechanism generally conforms to fine-scale 00 needs as it comes, with excellent chassis detail, correct-pattern wheels and nice fine rods and accurate and delicate valve gear. The widespread adoption of 'keeper plate' assembly and multi-stage gearing makes these chassis easier to dismantle and adapt, while the rods and valve gears need little or no modification. EM and P4 RTR conversions are now catered for by 'drop in' or tailored replacement wheelsets from makers like Ultrascale or Alan Gibson. Using these dedicated conversion kits eliminates the need for bushing bearings for smaller axles, re-fitting and sleeving gears and a lot of other tomfoolery that used to be necessary; and the result is a super scale model in the matter of a few hours. Fine scale never had it so easy!

Ready-to-run locomotives (RTR)

One of the most significant developments of recent years has been the immense broadening of choice when it comes to the steam locomotive types for which good ready-to-run models are available, especially in 4mm scale. Time was when most proprietary ranges offered only the extremes – several large, glamorous express passenger engines with the odd tank loco for all other duties. The Hornby Dublo 00 gauge range, for instance, offered you a choice of top-flight power: streamlined LNER A4 or LMS 'Duchess' and 'City' Pacifics, the GWR 'Castle' and, latterly, the rebuilt Bulleid 'Light Pacific'. To go with these express passenger types were a solitary mixed-traffic loco – the BR 2-6-4T – and the LMS 8F 2-8-0 for heavy freight. For every other class of duty – shunting of all kinds, suburban work, pick-up or lighter main line goods trains, branch line workings of every sort, pilot duties and work trains, there was the ubiquitous N2 class 0-6-2T, a sturdy if plain diecast model of which well over a quarter-million examples were made. Every one of them modelled on Sir Nigel Gresley's fleet-footed suburban tank engine, a type quite unsuited to most of the duties for which it had to suffice in model form!

The situation for the diesel enthusiast in 4mm or N scales has long been much better-balanced, with a realistic and reasonable selection of types available as accurate models. All the common types needed to model the post-steam BR scene through the 'green' and 'blue' years up to Sectorisation and Privatisation are out there in RTR form, with many prototypes being available from more than one source. In 4mm now, just about every likely diesel locomotive can be had in just about any variant or period, often in the

Above: A typical example of an RTR-based hybrid model. This LNER J71 class 0-6-0T combines the old Mainline (now Bachmann) J72 body moulding with a purpose-designed etched chassis and body conversion kit from Mainly Trains; Brassmasters and Comet also specialise in similar 'RTR rework kits'. As well as a new chassis – seen unadorned in the second picture – the kit includes new bufferbeams and sprung buffers, cast details and etched replacement splashers, the J71 having larger wheels than the starting-point J72. The chassis has been completed with a modern drivetrain – a Mashima 1420 motor and a High Level gearbox. The wheels on this EM model are from the Sharman range.

form of a smooth-running, super-detailed, highly accurate state-of-the-art model. The latest arrivals from Bachmann, Heljan and Hornby run like a Rolex, are DCC-ready and incorporate refinements like fully working lights, working radiator fans and now, onboard sound. N scale isn't *quite* so well-served, although the revitalised Farish/Bachmann range now includes virtually all the necessary types, fitted with vastly improved wheel profiles and more refined mechanisms.

Many of these RTR locos tend to 'come and go' in the various maker's catalogues, so not everything is available brand-new off the shelf all of the time. However, there is – and always has been – a brisk trade in used RTR models. Between swapmeets, 'table traders' stands at most model railway events, the small ads in the various magazines and the many hundreds of items listed every day on eBay, it is not usually too difficult to come up with virtually any recent-production RTR model. Only limited editions and older models acquire much by way of rarity value, while bargains may often be had, particularly if you're prepared to take on a model needing a little remedial attention.

Hybrid models

The introduction of accurate, realistic and well-detailed moulded-plastic 4mm scale RTR loco bodies in the early 1980s opened up a new way of producing locos suited to particular layout requirements, particularly for EM and P4 modellers: combining the plastic body with a new chassis built to finer-scale or more refined mechanical standards. In fact, given that a lot of the older 'new-generation' RTR Models by Airfix, Mainline and Hornby used mechanisms – often tender drives – that didn't run or pull too well, this approach also commended itself to 00 workers wanting an engine that ran as well as it looked. The usual 'hybrid' combination was to sit the plastic body on an etched chassis, which could be a plain straightforward replacement for a poor-running RTR original, but was usually a very much more sophisticated affair altogether, allowing for suspension, a refined drivetrain and lots of extra detail.

This hybrid model became a very popular way of assembling a stud of good-looking locomotives that had refined performance and followed fine-scale wheel and track standards, but neither cost a fortune nor took an age to build. The fact that the necessary RTR body mouldings were often widely available very cheaply as spares also helped! These older bodies, good though they were, could readily be improved with finer handrails, extra detail and better fittings; they

were an excellent basis to work on to produce a very high-quality model. Building just such hybrid engines became the accepted way of entering the general field of model locomotive construction, as the skills acquired during chassis construction and body reworking were a good foundation for moving on to complete loco kits in whitemetal or etched brass. This is still a popular approach, although the current generation of RTR loco superstructures are much more difficult to come by as spares and are certainly not cheap. Given the quality of modern RTR mechanisms and the relative ease with which they can be converted to fine scale wheels and track gauges, however, the hybrid philosophy is anyway less relevant to the current generation of RTR.

However, there are still plenty of suitable starting-points out there among the serried ranks of the older swapmeet RTR engines, often with defunct mechanisms and hence available for knock-down prices. Perfect hybridisation material! Prime candidates include the Airfix/Dapol GWR 14XX, 61XX, 'Castle' and 'Dean Goods', plus the LMS 4F and rebuilt 'Royal Scot' and that evergreen, the LNER N2. From Mainline (later Bachmann) came locos fitted with the original split-frame 'pancake motor' mechanisms: the GW 2251 goods, 43XX Mogul, 56XX 0-6-2T, 57XX pannier and 68XX 'Manor', together with the LMS 'Jubilee', LNER J72 and B1. Hornby had quite a few possibilities, too: almost anything with a tender drive – which included some crackers like the GW 28XX, the LNER 'Shire' and the SR 'Schools' – plus old favourites like the 'Jinty', LNER B12 and 'Britannia' and newer arrivals such as the LNER J52 and LMS Fowler 2-6-4T. Aftermarket chassis are available for virtually all these types from Comet, Perseverance, Branchlines, Mainly Trains, High Level or Dave Bradwell.

Locomotive kits

Nowhere else in the world is there a selection of locomotive kits which even comes remotely near the variety of those available to the British modeller. Today, even allowing for the enormous prototype diversity, virtually every railway (no matter how obscure) is represented by at least one – if not a selection – of locomotive kits, while more popular choices are available in a range of versions, qualities and formats. Whatever engine it is you want to model, in 4mm and 7mm scales, it is a better-than-even chance that someone, somewhere, makes a kit for it! Only in N scale is the choice limited – mostly by the availability of suitable mechanisms on which aftermarket bodies can be mounted. Not many people feel able to tackle chassis construction in this small size and there are anyway almost no suitable components available; only in the realms of 2mm fine scale will you find much 4mm-style loco building going on. That said, what is achieved in this size is sometimes little short of the miraculous; normal mortals can only gape in awe!

Back in the earlier days of the hobby, when mass-produced RTR models were few in number and rude in outline, if you wanted a halfway decent model locomotive the only way to get it was to roll your sleeves up and build it yourself. The first loco kits that appeared in 4mm or H0 scales were simply designed to aid this DIY process, either by providing a complete loco body die-cast in zinc or lead alloy, or a set of stamped-out metal parts together with a few useful castings or turnings. The cast loco bodies were often generic rather than following a particular prototype, as with the ubiquitous Steward-Reidpath 0-6-0T that turned up in any number of guises either side of the Second World War. The stamped-sheet kits – most notably the Jamieson range – did follow specific prototypes, at least in outline; they saved a bit of work in marking, cutting-out and forming, but the success of the finished job – including the quality of the running gear

Right: A typical modern 4mm scale whitemetal kit from South Eastern Finecast, which comes complete with an etched chassis and vacuum-formed flush glazing for the cab spectacles. Note the very clean, smooth castings and the lack of flash or mould-marks; only the footplate casting will need much in the way of preparation – and that mostly in the matter of trimming off the 'feeds'. Cast kits weren't always this good! The E1R illustrated here is also typical in that the choice of wheels and drivetrain is left up to the modeller.

Right: A state-of-the-art etched locomotive kit, the Peter K GWR 1361 0-6-0ST, available from Agenoria Models. Complex, yes, and not cheap – but replete with every conceivable detail and fitting together with astonishing accuracy. The cast fittings are all in lost-wax brass and are very complete. Kits like this sit at the top of the loco modelling tree; they are most usually in 4mm and 7mm scales, but there are now some pretty astounding examples in 3mm and even 2mm scales. Many etched kits are far more basic and some – often described as 'scratchbuilding aids' – provide only a set of basic etched parts without fittings. All have their place, but do check what you're buying!

and any detailing – was very much down to the skill of the builder.

The user-friendly 4mm scale loco kit first appeared in 1957, when K's released their cast-whitemetal kit for the GWR 48XX/14XX 0-4-2T. This loco, assembled from fully-detailed interlocking castings that could be glued together and including a chassis with pre-mounted and quartered wheels and gears that needed only basic 'screwdriver assembly' skills, set the trend. Over the ensuing thirty years, many hundreds of similar cast-whitemetal locomotive kits were introduced to the market, and models built from these enabled railway modellers to 'spread their wings' and tackle subjects previously 'off limits' due to lack of suitable motive power. Wills joined K's in the whitemetal business in 1959, introducing their evergreen GER 'Buckjumper' 0-6-0T – 35 shillings (£1.75) for the loco with a separate cast chassis (to take Romford wheels, gears and motor) for a further 15 bob (75p). A year later, Wills introduced the GWR 94XX pannier tank as a superstructure-only kit to fit the Tri-ang 'Jinty' 0-6-0T chassis, and this 'bodyline' approach – a new cast body to fit an existing RTR mechanism – became extremely popular. Kits of this kind were intended to make available loco types for which no RTR model existed, but without the need for chassis construction; the assured performance and convenience of using a mass-produced mechanism made such kits a far less daunting proposition for many modellers.

Alongside the new cast kits, the sheet-metal offerings continued to appeal to the more skilled and experienced modeller. In the early 1950s, Sayer-Chaplin and S&B Productions had taken the sheet-metal format a stage further by using photographic block-maker's engraving techniques to produce sets of 'building plates' with rivet and beading detail fully-formed. Models built from these parts – which had to be cut out by hand with a jeweller's saw, filed, fitted, formed and assembled – attained fabled status in their day. In the early 1970s, George Pring (George Allen Models) and Fred Blackman (Mallard) took the newly developed precision photo-etching or 'chemical milling'

process and used it to produce the first etched kits. These not only included all the detail of the engraved plates, but were also fully cut out from the sheet. This introduced a genre of locomotive kit which, refined and improved over the next thirty years, and allied to other production processes such as high-speed precision turning, brass and nickel casting by the lost-wax method, high definition whitemetal casting, vacuum-assisted resin moulding and now laser-cutting or CNC (computer numeric control) milling and turning, has led to locomotive kits of great sophistication and superlative quality, from which models equal to the finest hand-built productions can be made.

Loco kits today

The situation today has seen the number of loco kits on offer for 4mm and N scales decline considerably, with several well-known ranges either disappearing altogether or becoming very restricted in availability. This reflects to a considerable extent the advent of high-quality new-generation RTR locomotives covering a much wider range of subjects than hitherto; the arrival of one such usually sounds the death-knell for any mass-market kit based on the same engine. RTR products have always formed the benchmark for kit models and the running quality, detailing and, particularly, standard of finish of modern RTR set a standard that it's very hard for kits to come up to. Add on the cost factor – the pre-built loco from China often costing no more than the raw parts for the kit-built alternative – and it is not hard to understand why kits no longer find the popular favour they once enjoyed!

Except in N scale, the easy-to-build bodyline style of loco kit is long gone. In 00, most of the standard Tri-ang or Hornby Dublo underpinnings around which they were designed are as extinct as the Dodo, while modern 4mm RTR mechanisms are specifically tailored to a particular model and don't lend themselves to adaptation. Complete loco kits require the builder to tackle the construction of the mechanism as well as the superstructure, so the running quality of the final model depends very much on the competence with which this is done and the quality of the 'bought-in' components used – something that has always worried many modellers. Many of the older whitemetal and sheet-metal loco kits are also lacking in detail and refinement when compared with modern RTR productions, and certainly can't stand comparison with locomotives built from the current generation of 'super kits'. To bring such models up to scratch requires a lot of extra time and effort – and not a little skill.

However, the loco kit still occupies an important place in the modern hobby. Traditionally, one role of the kit was to extend the range of prototypes it was possible to model without resorting to bare-metal scratchbuilding – and that remains the case. Although modern toolmaking techniques and low-cost hand-assembly by the skilled artisans of China has made it viable to produce high-quality RTR models on short lead-times and in production runs of only a few thousand rather than the tens of thousands formerly needed, the range of prototypes for which there will be an adequate demand is still limited. Other newly developed origination and production techniques make it economically feasible

to produce loco *kits,* on the other hand, in quantities as small as a couple of dozen – and there are very few prototypes so obscure that it's not possible to find two jury's-worth of takers. So the loco kit still forms an essential resource for historical modellers, or those modelling offbeat light-railway, industrial or narrow-gauge subjects.

Modern technology has also made possible the current trend towards 'Super kits'. These are extremely complex and sophisticated, being designed to produce an 'ultimate' model of a particular locomotive type rather than simply plugging a gap in the loco stud. Normally designed around fine-scale wheel standards and track gauges, they often have custom-designed drivetrains using very high-quality components and incorporate mechanical refinements such as springing or equalisation of the wheels. Cosmetically, every detail will be present, inside and out, above and below. We used to talk about 'super-detailed' models – which were locos that actually had things like brake gear or lamp-irons. Well, by that yardstick a Finney, Brassmasters or Mitchell super-kit is 'hyper-detailed'; if you can see it on the real thing (or even if you can't, a lot of the time!) it's there on the model. The results – given a due allowance

Below: One of the principal virtues of the etched kit is that it is very versatile and lends itself to small production runs – batches of twenty or thirty kits are not untypical. This means that the more offbeat prototypes can be catered for, often through the specialist 'line societies'. This HR 'Medium Goods' is one such, a kit produced by the Highland Railway Society.

of skill – are unimpeachable; but building such a model consumes hundreds of hours and the exercise will set you back the price of two or three top-flight RTR locos. These kits are really intended for modellers whose interest lies in loco construction rather than layout building. For a lone worker to create a model railway of any size to this sort of standard he'd have to be richer than Croesus and longer-lived than Methuselah!

There's a third very good reason for choosing to build loco kits rather than simply buying RTR: the satisfaction of 'hatching your own'. There's no doubt that building a good-quality, well-designed kit is a very pleasant and rewarding way of spending your leisure time. To a large extent, that's the intent of the super-kits, but the same is also true of more modest offerings from the many specialist kit makers. There is a wide selection of reasonably priced, well-designed, good quality loco kits available, not just in 4mm and 7mm scales, but also in 3mm and 2mm fine scale. The cost of a mainstream kit-built model compares favourably with an equivalent (in terms of size and complexity) RTR model. With modern high-quality Mashima can motors and multi-stage gearboxes from High Level, Comet or Branchlines and using chassis designs that facilitate sprung or equalised suspension (although it's not compulsory!), the potential is there for achieving running of the highest quality. You can also build a kit loco to suit your chosen gauge/standards, adapt the kit to follow a chosen prototype engine and add any details or refinements you desire. The end result will be individual rather than ubiquitous – far more 'personal' than anything imported *en masse* from the Far East, no matter how good it is.

Whitemetal cast or etched brass?

There are still a good few cast-whitemetal models to be had, most notably the South-Eastern Finecast range. Some of these kits are based on the Wills models of old but now greatly refined, with much added detail in the superstructures and state-of-the-art etched chassis designed around modern drivetrain components. Many others are all-new and take the whitemetal kit to new levels of refinement. The skill level called for in building a typical whitemetal kit is less than needed to tackle an etched model, as forming and fitting are taken care of by the castings rather than being down to the modeller. The parts can be assembled using adhesives or special low-melt solders, and filling and finishing can be carried out with plastic putties and stoppers. Whitemetal locos can be readily adapted and modified, refined, super-detailed and generally souped-up. A well-built whitemetal kit will produce a very fine model – with the added bonus of inbuilt mass (the castings being nice and weighty in themselves) and usually a nice, quiet quality of running as the cast superstructure won't resonate like brass or plastic.

The other main media are kits etched in brass or nickel-silver, often also including parts lost-wax or whitemetal cast and – increasingly – boilers, fireboxes and similar complex assemblies moulded in one piece from resin. Etched kits can range from the very basic – you get a selection of etched bits, a few castings or turnings, and a single scruffy photocopied sheet of near-illiterate instructions – through user-friendly kits with tab-and-slot construction, lots of pre-formed parts and instructions a toddler could understand, to sophisticated Origami in sheet brass and nickel, accompanied by bags of gleaming gold and silver castings and a beautifully-illustrated manual the size of a small telephone directory. As in so many walks of life, you get what you pay for! All of these levels of kit have their place; the 'basic' affairs save the experienced modeller some (often tedious) work in cutting all the bits out, while the easy-build variety enable a model to be produced in relatively short order with limited facilities and experience.

Loco kits in 0 and N

In 7mm scale, where there has never been very much in the way of scale-model RTR equipment available (although it is now starting to appear, mainly in the form of good-quality metal models made in China and the odd plastic diesel), kits are still the main source of motive power. Due to the large size, cast whitemetal has never been that popular in 0, being generally restricted to kits for small locomotives. Most 7mm kits are sheet-metal based, originally stamped but now almost universally etched. Many modern 0 gauge kits are extremely sophisticated and offer the potential for showcase-quality museum models. However, such things aren't cheap; a top-flight 7mm kit from a maker like Finney, Just Like The Real Thing, DJH or Shedmaster, taken together with a suitable drivetrain and a set of Alan Harris' superb machined cast-iron wheels, can easily stretch into four figures. Custom-built by a good craftsman, such an 0 gauge model will set you back the price of quite a presentable second-hand motor car.

Locomotive kits in N scale have always tended to be body-only efforts designed to utilise some pre-existing mechanism, for reasons already touched on. The vast majority of such kits are cast whitemetal and comparatively unrefined, with detail like handrails and pipework cast on rather than being separately applied as in the larger scales. Many N gauge kits also incorporate fundamental errors of proportion or dimension, needed to fit them to one or other of the very limited choice of available mechanisms. Carefully built and painted, however, models that will live happily alongside RTR N scale models can result, and there is no doubt that these kits are a boon in the traditional role of increasing the range of prototypes available. Within the general context of N scale, often chosen for its ability to represent an overall view rather than a tightly focussed microcosm, most of these kits serve their purpose well – and are usually comparatively straightforward to build. The most difficult job is usually modifying the mechanism as needed to take the new superstructure.

3mm scale locomotive kits

As adherents to a minority scale with virtually no mainstream trade or RTR support, 3mm modellers enjoy an amazingly wide selection of kits and components. This is in no small measure due to the splendid efforts of the 3mm Society, supported by a small but resourceful band of specialist traders and aided by a higher-than-usual level of hands-on skill and experience among the scale's adherents. In terms of locomotive kits, most 3mm efforts are etched – often using artwork originally drawn for other scales, either 'fired down' from 4mm or 7mm or 'pumped up' from 2mm finescale. This may sound like a somewhat compromised and flawed way of doing things, but in fact the results are often surprisingly effective and can be stunning; the J&M LMS 'Jinty', for instance – which started life as a 2mm fine scale model – is an amazing piece of work; even the cab doors are hinged! There are a few older and cruder whitemetal loco kits still about, mostly bodyline efforts designed to sit on a Tri-ang TT chassis. But the majority of 3mm offerings from the likes of Worsley Works or Chris Thane are complete etched kits and are comparable with a typical 4mm scale production, while 3SMR make extensive use of resin moulding for their offerings.

Technically, 3mm scale locomotive modelling is pretty much on a par with the skill levels needed to build a 4mm etched kit, increased 'fiddliness' due to small parts being offset by the number of details you can leave off in 3mm because they're simply too small to see! The way a 3mm loco chassis goes together is very much in line with normal 4mm practice and uses many of the same components – motors, gears, pick-up-systems, wheel types – whereas 2mm locomotive mechanism building uses a radically different approach and demands a higher skill level.

Kit-building skill requirements

Which brings us neatly on to consider briefly what skills you need to tackle locomotive kit construction. These really come under two headings; small-scale mechanical work and basic metalwork. The mechanical skills needed range from basic jeweller's screwdriver and tweezer work up to obtaining accurate alignments, mounting and quartering push-fit driving wheels, gear meshing, fitting and adjusting coupling rods and valve gear and the making and fitting of pick-ups – a very critical task. Even the simplest chassis kits will call for at least the odd soldered joint, but many of the more straightforward examples use screw-assembly techniques to erect the basic frames. The more advanced kits *will* call for solder assembly of the chassis framing – but, that said, the better examples include plenty of alignment aids and often go together very 'true'. Most modern kit chassis – even on the more sophisticated offerings – give you the choice of a simple 'rigid' set-up or an all-singing compensated or sprung suspension system – so you can, to some extent, tailor the model to your skill level and aspirations.

Whitemetal loco superstructures can be built up with a suitable adhesive – a rapid-cure epoxy resin being the usual recommendation, with cyano-acrylate superglue used to attach small details. Before assembly, however, the castings will inevitably need a certain amount of preparation to drill out any holes cast 'blind', to remove any feeder pips or 'flash' and to smooth away the mould part lines – careful work with small files, a scraper and fine abrasives such as wet-and-dry paper or glassfibre burnishers. There will also be a certain amount of finishing work – filling in any gaps or cracks where parts don't quite mate perfectly, or hiding surface blemishes such as slightly porous castings or accidental tool-marks. A fine resin-based filler such as Plastic Padding or Milliput epoxy putty can be used, with more careful work with files and abrasives to blend in the filler. Alternatively, whitemetal castings may be soldered together using a suitable soldering iron (often of the temperature-controlled variety) and special low-melt solders and fluxes. Done right, this approach joins the parts and fills the gaps and cracks in one operation, but it is a ticklish business as it is all-too-easy to melt the casting as well as the solder!

Soldering is the key technique for working in etched brass. Soft soldering (which is what we're doing in small-scale modelwork) is really just a form of hot gluing, the solder bonding to the metal in much the same way as a good glue joins wood. It is a key skill that is invaluable across the whole sphere of railway modelling – and it is one which is nowhere near as difficult to master as many would have you believe. Like most skills, it is best acquired in the context of simple tasks that don't matter to much, rather than setting out to learn as you build a top-flight loco kit! Start with simple assemblies and work your way up to multi-level overlays, fine beading and tiny details.

'Fitting' – adjusting parts so that they locate accurately together – is the other key skill in kit building. The best kits will need very little such adjustment, but tolerances in the various manufacturing processes and slight inconsistencies in the build process makes a modicum of fitting almost inevitable. Wise kit designers take account of this by providing 'fitting allowances' – making parts a tad oversize in critical areas on the basis that it is a lot easier to file a bit off than it is to stuff up unsightly gaps! Careful checking and the restrained use of files are the basis of good fitting work. Other kit-building techniques revolve around finishing work such as the removal of excess solder, filling of small gaps and cracks and the addition of fine detail. Fine files and abrasives are the finishing tools,with careful use of a soldering iron accomplishing both the filling and detailing functions.

Then, of course, you have to paint the thing! Another whole discipline in its own right… Modern aerosol primers and paints can go a long way, aided by lining transfers and enamel and acrylic brushing paints. For serious loco-painting work, sooner or later you will arrive at the point where you need to obtain an airbrush and master its use. Once you have that under your belt, the world is your oyster; the same skills have wide application in many areas of railway modelling, from toning-down scenic work to weathering wagons. (They can also be very handy for making good any minor transgressions in the paintwork of the family transport!)

Narrow gauge motive power

Narrow gauge railways have always exhibited a rather more cosmopolitan aspect than their standard gauge equivalents, with locomotives and rolling stock originating in a number of countries operating on the same system. This means that RTR models of European narrow gauge engines can be employed in a British context without looking too far out of place, which is just as well, as if you're stuck with using RTR power you'll look in vain for any British prototypes! The main source of motive power for the most popular narrow-gauge standard, 009 (4mm scale on 9mm gauge N track – corresponding to a prototype gauge of 2ft 3in, but widely used to represent prototype gauges from 2ft to 2ft 6in) is the combination of a cast whitemetal kit-built superstructure on an adapted N gauge mechanism. These models vary considerably in authenticity, from totally freelance efforts like the Peco Vari-kit to surprisingly accurate affairs like the Chivers Finelines range. In terms of building technique and detailing, they lie between the simple N scale superstructure kits and a normal 4mm model with separate handrails, plumbing and other details.

However, more recently, some rather more sophisticated 4mm scale narrow-gauge locomotives have arrived in the form of complete kits using the full range of state-of-the-art etching, casting and resin-moulding techniques to produce very accurate and super-detailed models with custom-designed mechanisms of excellent quality, running on prototypically-correct track gauges. Initially, there were kits for Isle of Man and Irish 3ft gauge prototypes by Branchlines, but you can now buy a veritable multi-media 'super kit' for such 2ft gauge esoterica as the Himalaya-Darjeeling Class B 0-4-0ST and the Tasmanian K 0-4-0 + 0-4-0 Beyer Garrett (as now on the Welsh Highland Railway), from Backwoods Miniatures. Such a kit is, however, a challenge for the experienced rather than suitable territory for the novice!

Narrow gauge modelling in 7mm scale using 16.5mm gauge 00 or H0 track is also increasingly popular, as it permits the use of the huge selection of 4mm drivetrain components to produce the running gear. The prototype track gauge works out at 2ft 4½in – not exactly

Above: There are many superb kits for NG locos; this is a Backwoods Miniatures Cavan & Leitrim 4-4-0T, being built by Simon de Souza. Simon de Souza

the most common of distances to spike the rails apart, but once again used to represent prototypes in the 2ft–2ft 6in gauge range. As the narrow gauge prototype is very variable in these matters and most narrow-gauge layouts follow essentially freelance themes, this comparative approximation rarely looks out of place. The 7mm narrow gauge loco modeller can choose between cast whitemetal or etched superstructure kits, either to fit on 00 gauge RTR

Below: Narrow gauge motive power comes in a great variety of forms, including esoteric examples like this Motor Rail 'Simplex' loco-tractor, a whitemetal kit by Saltford Models for 4mm scale on 9mm gauge track (009). Built by Renier Hendriksen for his 'Moor's End Light Railway'.

Above: Wide though the choice of kits is, there are still many prototypes that have been passed by – most notably, the earlier steam locomotives of the pre-1870 era. If you want a model of one of these, then it's out with the brass sheet, snips, files and piercing saw for a spot of DIY. This is Lion *of the Grand Junction Railway, a veteran of the 1840s modelled by Mike Sharman in 4mm scale.*

Below: For these older and smaller prototypes, 7mm scale is a natural size to work in. This diminutive engine is Needlefield, *an old Nielson engine acquired by the Highland Railway when they took over the Inverness & Aberdeen Junction Railway. Laurie Griffin built this charismatic model for his 0 gauge 'Cluny' HR layout.*

mechanisms or using dedicated scale chassis. There are some stunning complete whitemetal loco kits with their own etched chassis, to all-singing, all-dancing etched and composite kits that are as fully sophisticated and accurate as the best 4mm and 7mm loco kits.

A garden of delights?

Taken all-in, the current state of the model motive power market across all the scales is the best it has ever been. Provided your bank account can stand it, there is almost nothing you can't source, to a quality that would have been but a dream only a decade or so since. This commercial cornucopia should not be allowed to obscure the very real satisfaction that can be had from building at least some of your own engines – an area of the hobby that has long been regarded as the pinnacle of railway modelling achievement. The difference today is that DIY locomotives are now a matter of choice rather than of necessity.

Opposite: A crack passenger train like this features high on many a modeller's 'wish list' – but assembling the ingredients is rarely an easy proposition, even in the popular scales and for popular prototypes. If you lust after a gorgeous pre-Grouping train along the lines of the GER 'Restaurant Car Express' – all beaded panels, plush seats and varnished teak – you're in for a mammoth (but rewarding) task, and the investment of a substantial sum.

Chapter 10

PASSENGER ROLLING STOCK

Assembling a realistic and individual selection of rolling stock for a model railway is one of the most varied and enjoyable tasks in the hobby. In these days of abundance, with comprehensive and reasonably well-balanced RTR ranges and a bewildering choice of kits, it's nowhere near as difficult as it once was. Indeed, the biggest problem facing today's modeller is working out what to choose from the tempting cornucopia facing him!

Striking the balance

Every piece of rolling stock that runs on a real railway does so for a purpose. Railway managements don't buy coaches or wagons because they like the look of them or because

they're the latest thing from Hornby; neither are they seduced by bargains on eBay nor by special-offer adverts in the *Railway Modeller*. They buy them because they *have* to in order to run the trains needed to carry the traffic offering. In the cause of realism, then, we need to do the same (although the odd flight of fancy or 'just because I like it' item is never ruled out; it's only a hobby after all!).

Most model railways have far too many engines and nowhere near enough rolling stock. In some ways, building up an appropriate selection of the necessary everyday vehicles might be regarded as a rather 'bread and butter' aspect of the whole railway modelling business, with the icing and the cherries all

coming in the motive power department. Given the usually limited contents of the modelling piggy-bank, it's always tempting to blow the available booty on another loco (no matter how unlikely or unnecessary) rather than adding the three or four coaches or dozen or so wagons the same money might buy. In terms of the overall picture, however (not to mention the operational scope) either of the latter might be the better investment. And, I'd also suggest, the 'stock option' is not always the less-interesting choice – for the world of rolling stock is full of fascinating byways and opportunities for rewarding modelling.

As with most aspects of the realistic model railway, half the battle in achieving a really relevant roster of equipment is determining what it is you need to model. In other words, a spot of research is usually

Below: Crack passenger trains may have (sometimes!) featured complete rakes of coaches matched in style, colour and outline – as in the GER example – but more often than not the exigencies of the traffic and the different types of carriage needed to provide for it resulted in far more of a hotchpotch. In this example on the Southern, the rule seems to be more like 'no two carriages the same and as old as possible'! The result looks a bit incongruous behind brand-new 'King Arthur' class 4-6-0 No. 798 **Sir Hectimere.** **Author's collection**

called for. 'Research' somehow sounds rather dry and academic, redolent of poring over the pages of ponderous tomes in some dim and dusty library, but when it comes to train formations it's not remotely like that. Pictures – still and moving – are the principal source of information; books, certainly, usually of the album format; postcards, photographs, paintings and prints; and – best of all – old film clips depicting trains, preferably on DVD so you can slow things down or freeze-frame and see clearly what it is you're looking at. Written sources – magazine articles and, rarely, text references or tables in books – are the least likely to yield the required data.

The second stage of the campaign is hunting down the appropriate models to build up this stocklist. As with the locomotive stud, acquiring the ingredients for the 'stock pot' mix might well involve a marrying of items from a variety of sources: RTR models, either 'as bought' or reworked in some way; kits of various sorts, including a few kitbashings or other lesser modifications, second-hand models trawled from eBay or the small ads, and even the odd scratchbuild; all is grist to this particular mill.

It's a big topic, this, as not only does the prototype offer a very wide field for study, but there are a positive plethora of providers when it comes to procuring the necessary models. Not only is there the whole gamut of the various RTR ranges to consider, but an absolutely vast choice of kits. These are models produced by of all manner of means, from sophisticated etched-brass paragons through injection-moulded plastic, pre-printed plastic, cast resin, cast whitemetal, milled wood and stamped-aluminium offerings to composite kits containing a mix of any (or all) of the foregoing. They range in difficulty from five-minute shake-the-box efforts to projects that take big bites out of your life and cause strong men to weep. This chapter and that following attempt to steer a course through this modelogistic minefield, starting with what our American cousins call 'The Varnish': passenger stock.

Prototype passenger stock

In these days of multiple units, HSTs and other fixed-formation trains, it is easy to overlook the terrific variety of passenger stock running on our railways until comparatively recently. The last decades of the steam era were particularly rich in terms of the designs and eras of the stock to be seen – vintage, wood-panelled pre-Grouping coaches with gas lighting, clerestory roofs and button-back horsehair upholstery mixing it with classic 'Big Four' designs and the latest BR standard all-steel Mk 1 stock, all 'brave new world' in Formica and aluminium. Trains of the 1950s-era, particularly, often had extraordinarily variegated formations, with coaches of very different origins and outlines coupled together, exhibiting a variety of liveries and ranging in condition from near-derelict to new and sparkling. It was all a stark contrast to the uniformity of outline and colouring seen in each multiple unit train today!

In the pre-Grouping period, of course, the coaching stock was as diverse as all the other facets of the 'Old Companies'. Much of it was very distinctive in design and the best of it was, as Hamilton Ellis memorably put it, 'of more than palatial splendour'. Some of the paintwork and detailing was positively sumptuous, especially on Pullman coaches and on special stock built for the principal trains. The two big joint stock groups, on the West and East coast main lines from

Above: Still on the Southern, although now early in the BR period, this is an example of the sort of distinctive and somewhat mixed express passenger train you hardly ever see on model railways. Almost certainly a boat train hurrying up from the Channel ports, the as-yet-unnamed Bulleid Pacific is tailed by a pair of four-wheeled 'general utility vans' (GUVs) (presumably for luggage), followed by a pair of the flat-sided steel-panelled SECR coaches built for the Hastings line, then a solitary Pullman car, with a further pair of Maunsell coaches tailed by what looks like a second Pullman – and that's just what you can see in the picture! A train like this makes a great modelling proposition. Author's collection

London to Scotland, produced coaches of a quality found virtually nowhere else in the world. They offered gilded accoutrements, wonderful inlaid woodwork and panelling, acid-etched decorative glass, upholstery to equal the most luxurious Gentlemen's club (with service to match), steam heating of Turkish-bath effectiveness and, of course, the electric light. The West Coast used the LNWR livery of blue-white upper panels over dark plum, lined throughout in golden ochre and finished to a flawless sheen by countless coats of the finest copal varnish. The East Coast settled for natural teak panelling varnished to a rich golden shade, lined in lemon and

Above: The GWR could scale the heights when it came to passenger trains, as witnessed by this superb ensemble of a shiny new 'Saint' hustling a matched set of 'Toplight' coaches along the estuary wall at Teignmouth on the eve of the First World War. Newton Abbot Museum

crimson with wonderful seriffed 'Railway Roman' script. Roofs on both sides were finished in white and *kept* white – don't ask me how!

The more everyday coaches often fell well short of this magnificence; the GWR – for all that it had fine, new stock on its premier trains – carried its humbler passengers in a remarkable variety of antiques, often converted from carriages originally built for the broad gauge. An unheated South Eastern or North London Railway suburban compartment third was widely reputed to be considerably less comfortable than the average prison cell, and even the mighty LNWR had some coaches – sans toilets, heating and just about every other amenity – about which the less said, the better. The beacon of rectitude in all this was the Midland, which abolished second class and upgraded the third to provide all its passengers with an upholstered seat, decent lighting, heating, ventilation and access to lavatories – all in coaches of uncompromisingly handsome outline finished in a rich crimson

and fully lined. Other companies, like the LYR, preferred a more austere paint scheme (tan over chocolate) on stock devoid of much in the way of external panelling, lining, fancy woodwork or other decoration – but made up for it with exceptionally spacious and substantial coaches with comfortable seats and steam heating of commendable efficiency.

During the pre-Grouping era, coaching stock grew steadily in size, weight, strength and amenities. Four- or six-wheeled rigid underframes gave way to bogies towards the end of the 19th century, and carriage lengths went up steadily from 30ft or so to around 50ft for earlier bogie stock. With the adoption of bogies, the wooden underframing of the old rigid-wheelbase coaches gave way to steel, allowing not only longer stock with stronger, heavier bodywork and a much wider range of amenities, but also leading to a far greater degree of safety in the event of mishap. The old all-wooden coaches disintegrated horribly in accidents and were distressingly prone to catch fire. Some companies, such as the Great Central, Caledonian, GWR and the East and West joint stock companies, were soon going in for even larger coaches, the longest being the 70-footers on the GWR. But by the Grouping in 1923, most main-line coaches were at least 57ft long, with many at the 60–63ft surviving as the 'standard' British

main line coach length up to the mid-1970s, and the introduction of BR Mk 2 stock.

The coaches that appeared on the 'Big Four' grouped companies between 1923 and the BR takeover in 1948 were also surprisingly varied in design and very distinctive. Steel underframes and electric lighting were universal for new stock by 1923, but most coaches still had bodies basically framed in wood and built in a very traditional manner. The first 57ft main line and compartment carriages built for the LMS (described by LMS carriage experts Jenkinson and Essery as 'Period I' stock) still had full panelling! Even when Stanier on the LMS followed the GWR and the Southern and clad the post-1933 'Period III' coaches in flush-sided steel, they were still *painted* to look as if they were panelled, with full lining-out. Maunsell did much the same thing on the SR in the 1920s. The real 'odd man out' was Gresley on the LNER, who stuck with wood cladding (specially faced ply), panelled out with a half-round beading; his main line coaches were 61ft 6in long, had a domed-end profile with white-painted roof and a glorious finish of varnished teak, thus perpetuating the classic features associated with the East Coast Joint Stock. Even when later LNER stock appeared with steel cladding, it was still artfully painted to *look* like varnished teak!

*Above: **Probably the most distinctive of the 'standard' coaching stock designs of the Grouping era were the wood-panelled, bow-roofed Gresley coaches on the LNER. Ex-GE B12 class 4-6-0 No. 8508 hurries a boat train made up of new Gresleys out through the East London suburbs.** Author's collection*

All-steel coaches first appeared in the late 1920s, but it wasn't until after the Second World War, that steel framing began to replace the traditional wood structure in most coach bodies. The Southern's 'Bulleid' stock used steel throughout, as did the new 'Hawksworth' coaches on the GWR – handsome vehicles with a Gresley-style dome-ended roof and very large windows. Thompson on the LNER produced some rather austere all-steel stock, which made no pretence at being 'faux teak'. These designs of the later 1940s influenced the development of the all-steel BR Mk 1 coaches introduced in 1951 – truly excellent vehicles built in larger numbers, with more variants, than any other single coaching stock design before or since. They were intended to replace the older main line stock of all four companies, so had to cover a very wide range of requirements as to accommodation and facilities. Many BR Mk 1 coaches had working lives of over 40 years and several hundred still survive as the staple passenger stock on most heritage railways.

Pullman cars

'The Quality of Service is Remembered Long After the Price is Forgotten' – so ran the mantra of the Pullman Car Company, an American institution that operated both here and in Europe as well as in the USA. Pullman cars were introduced in the 1860s to offer greater comfort and amenities to well-heeled passengers making the long, slow and tedious journeys that characterised rail travel in the USA at that time. They offered comfortable armchairs, civilised dining and sleeping accommodation, and even an upright piano in the parlour cars. Pullman sleeping cars were first introduced in Britain by the Midland Railway, which put them on their new Anglo-Scottish night expresses by the Settle and Carlisle route from 1876. You paid a supplement over first class to travel in spacious, well-padded high-Victorian splendour, amid more fancy gilt scroll-work than you could shake a stick at.

The success of these first Pullmans (characteristic American vehicles assembled at Derby from kits of parts shipped from the Pullman works in Chicago) led to the Pullman company setting up its own operation in Britain and in Europe (the ponderously-titled

Below: The all-Pullman 'limited' train – in this case, the 'Devon Belle' in its later years under BR. With six regular cars and the famous observation car bringing up the rear, this is a modest and modellable sort of train in any scale – although certainly not without a touch of glamour! Author's collection

Compagnie Internationale des Wagons-Lits et des Grandes Expresses Européens, thankfully shortened to CIWL, or just Wagons-Lit). Pullman provided a fleet of its 'superior carriages' which could be attached to regular express services or, later, run as complete 'Pullman Limited' trains offering luxury travel at premium fares. Many of these 'Pullman Limited' trains achieved legendary status, with the best-known being the London–Paris 'Golden Arrow'/'Flèche D'Or' and the Continent-wide convolutions of the fabled 'Orient Express'.

British Pullman trains reached their zenith in the inter-war period, and by the later 1930s there were a good few such workings in Britain, especially on the LNER and Southern; the former had the 'Eastern Belle', 'Harrogate Pullman' (later extended northwards as the 'Queen of Scots') and the 'West Riding Pullman', the latter the 'Bournemouth Belle', 'Devon Belle' and the all-electric 'Brighton Belle' as well as the 'Golden Arrow'. Pullmans were also used for premium luxury workings such as race specials, and were attached (singly or severally) to regular express or tourist trains, often as 'Club Cars' for regular travellers; one such ran regularly on Metropolitan Railway electric trains from Baker Street out to the heady Chiltern heights of Chesham. The LMS ran Pullman observation and dining cars over the former Highland lines, and the LNER did the same on the West Highland. If you were rich enough, you could even hire a Pullman yourself and have it attached to a normal train for your personal indulgence! After the war, most of these Pullman workings were revived or renamed, and several more added: the LNER's 'Sheffield Pullman' became the 'Master Cutler' and the 'West Riding' became the 'Yorkshire Pullman'.

BR went on to extend Pullman service to lines that had never previously seen it, using their own Pullman-specified stock built and operated under licence from the Pullman company. This included individual carriages and special purpose-built all-Pullman diesel train sets with a power car at each end – the fabled 100mph 'Blue Pullmans'. These handsome, specially liveried trains were put on to the former MR route to Derby, Sheffield and Leeds (the 'Midland Pullman') and the GWR routes to Bristol ('Western Pullman') and Cardiff ('South Wales Pullman'). They also formed the springboard for the later development of the all-conquering InterCity 125 'HST' high-speed train sets. Loco-hauled Pullman trains were introduced to the ex-LMS West Coast Main Line when this was electrified to Crewe and Manchester. These were made up of the individual stock that had appeared in the 1960s using the basic Mk 1 and later Mk 2 coach architecture but with Pullman interiors and very distinctive windows – large double-glazed panes with a stainless steel frame on the outside and no ventilators; air-conditioning had arrived! Initially painted in traditional Pullman 'Jersey cream over umber' livery, these 'BR Pullman' cars soon appeared in 'reverse' corporate livery, with grey as the main body colour relieved by a blue upper panel around the windows; 'Orrid!

Traditionally, Pullman cars were a completely separate fleet of vehicles designed, built and owned by the Pullman Car Company and bearing no relationship to regular coaching stock. They were very distinctive, being built to the limits of the loading gauge and hence taller, longer and heavier than ordinary carriages. They were distinguished not just by their livery and superb paint finish, but also by their characteristic flat sides and dome-ended roofs. The generous-width corridors were accessed from 'end vestibules' having tall, oval-windowed doors, rather than using the normal British arrangement of disposing doors along the length of the vehicle. Even the corridor connections were bigger and better than the rather constricted affairs found elsewhere – although the large, square-shouldered 'Pullman Gangway' was later adopted by the LNER and SR, and subsequently used by BR for the Mk 1 stock.

Non-passenger coaching stock

This extensive classification describes vehicles that were numbered in the coaching stock series, had coaching stock running gear, could be coupled to passenger trains and be run at express passenger speeds – but didn't actually have any seats! The description thus embraced a wide variety of different types, from 'full brakes' (a brake coach with guard's compartment/lookouts and stowage space taking up the rest of the vehicle) through 'baggage vans' (same thing without the

Below: Non-passenger coaching stock (NPCS) is a wonderful field for the modeller, as it is full of variety and interest. The trains of some railways – the Highland was notorious – had as much NPCS as regular coaches. Here is a gorgeous 4mm scale SECR horsebox built from a Branchlines etched kit by Simon de Souza, sandwiched between an open carriage truck and a guard's van.

Below: More 4mm/P4 Highland NPCS on Simon de Souza's 'Corrieshalloch': a delightful 1860s-era luggage van from an etched kit by Peter K and a prize-winning pair of open carriage trucks, scratchbuilt in Plastikard. The carriage – a 'Brougham' – is from the Shire Scenes/Dart Castings range, suitably modified.

Above: On the GWR, a distinction was drawn between carriage stock without seats – such as this luggage van, finished in normal coaching stock livery – and true non-passenger stock, which was painted 'plain chocolate' and hence were known as 'Brown Vehicles'. This one is an express fruit van, built from a David Green whitemetal kit; the diagram K4 luggage van is an etched kit from D&S Models. Both models were built and painted by Andrew Duncan in 4mm scale for 00 gauge.

Above: Non-passenger coaching stock of a slightly later period; an LMS covered carriage truck (CCT), built from a Parkside-Dundas plastic kit by Graham Warburton; 4mm scale, 00 gauge.

Below: One of the most distinctive and well-travelled items of NPCS was the Southern GUV already noted. Always a popular subject across the scales, this pair of 2mm scale GUVs was built by Steve Earl from some excellent plastic kits by Chivers Finelines. Note how fine the rivet and underframe detail is even at this tiny size.

guard's compartment) to GUVs (general utility vans), CCTs (covered carriage trucks, the same as a GUV, but with end-loading doors), milk vans and milk tanks, general perishables vans, fruit vans, fish vans, 'Special Traffic Vans', horseboxes, mail coaches, postal sorting vans, bullion vans, sealed ferry vans, gas tank vehicles, car-carriers, and open carriage trucks.

Such vehicles formed an important part of the railway's revenue fleet; few passenger trains of any consequence ran without a non-passenger vehicle or two somewhere in the formation, while even the humblest branch line train often had such a vehicle – usually a milk van or something similar – tacked on as 'tail traffic'. Express parcels trains, made up entirely of NPCS vehicles, ran at high speed over main-line routes, hauled by first-rank express passenger locomotives. On the ex-GER lines in East Anglia, a very characteristic sight was the 'stock train' – a combination of express parcels and perishables/milk behind a 'Claud Hamilton' 4-4-0 or a B1 4-6-0. Many items of NPCS became familiar components of the railway scene; the Southern's characteristic wooden 'Utility Vans', GWR 'Siphons' for perishables and 'Monsters' for bulky items, 6-wheeled 'Stove Vans' on the LMS, and the BR 4-wheel and bogie GUVS and CCTs. No model railway can do without a selection of such vehicles.

Brakes on passenger trains

Subsequent on the passing of the Regulation of Railways Act of 1889, all British passenger stock was required by law to have automatic power brakes. An automatic brake is one which, in the event of any mishap or failure, automatically *applies* the brakes; the 'power' part of the system was thus basically dedicated to keeping the brakes 'off'; springs, air pressure or gravity (falling weights) providing the emergency braking force. There were two types of power brake used in Britain – the vacuum brake and the Westinghouse air brake. The vacuum brake was the simpler and cheaper system of the two and hence the most widely-used.

With an automatic vacuum system, all the vehicles in a train are connected together via a 'train pipe' and flexible hoses, in which extensive plumbing an exhauster (an air pump or steam ejector on the engine) maintained a vacuum. Beneath each coach or van there was one or more large-diameter brake cylinders in which a heavy piston was moved upwards against the vacuum by atmospheric pressure. (Often things were arranged so that the piston was fixed and the cylinder – which was even heavier – moved.) The weight of the piston or cylinder was thus 'sucked' up to release the brakes. If the vacuum was reduced or lost for any reason – the driver or guard operating a brake valve, a passenger pulling the emergency cord or a hose coupling parting – then the weights of the cylinders or pistons would fall, acting through the brake linkage (which used leverage with mechanical advantage to generate the necessary force) to apply the brakes. The more completely the vacuum was destroyed, the harder the brakes were applied. The system was simple and fail-safe, but the gear was heavy and cumbersome, with high-volume cylinders and large-diameter pipework; once the vacuum was destroyed, all this pipework and cylinder volume had to be 'pumped out' before the brakes could be released, which could take some time. The maximum pressure available to act on the pistons and release the brake was a lowly 1 atmosphere – about 15psi.

The Westinghouse air brake worked in a totally different way. Once again, it was a 'continuous' brake – all the vehicles in the train were connected together by a train pipe and flexible hoses – but instead of a vacuum in a large-diameter pipe the system used air compressed to about 4 atmospheres/60psi in much smaller pipework. The compressed air was supplied by the loco, which would carry a steam-operated Westinghouse brake pump. Under each coach was an air reservoir divided into two halves; 'train air' – connected directly to the train pipe – and 'brake air', at the same pressure, but fed through a special one-way valve. The brake air normally held the brakes *off*, but the valve was so arranged that this

Above: A Westinghouse air-braked train on the London, Brighton & South Coast Railway. The air pump is clearly visible in front of the cab, and the bufferbeam hose connection is a small-diameter pressure fitting rather than a larger, wire-wound vacuum hose. Author's collection

only occurred when the pressure in the two parts of the circuit was equal. A drop in the air pressure in the train pipe – from any of the same causes listed for the vacuum brake – would result in the pressure in the brake air reservoir *applying* the brakes. A Westinghouse brake cylinder was double-acting, with air pressure on both sides of the piston; loss of pressure on one side resulted in the pressure on the opposing side forcing the piston along the cylinder and applying the brakes with a force proportionate to the pressure imbalance. The brake air reservoirs normally held more than enough air at pressure to stop the train completely, although springs also acted to help apply the brakes and provide braking effort even when there was no air in the system.

The Westinghouse was thus a true power brake, using positive pressure to produce braking effort – and with smaller, lighter and faster-acting components, a very potent and precise system. Under normal service conditions, it would stop a train in considerably less distance than a vacuum brake, and it was very much quicker to release. For this reason it found great favour with railways – like the Great Eastern and the London, Brighton & South Coast – operating intensive suburban passenger services with frequent stops, as well as on lines with a lot of gradients to contend with. The two biggest Scottish railways – the North British and the Caledonian – used the

'Westainhoos' exclusively, as did the smaller Great North of Scotland, together with the North Eastern, London, Chatham & Dover, South Eastern, and the Tilbury lines.

The problems came with through trains running from one railway on to another, or where stock from railway A – a vacuum line – was required to operate on railway B, a Westinghouse user. You can't, of course, mix air and vacuum-braked stock in a single train, or haul air-braked stock with a vacuum-fitted loco or vice-versa. This led to some stock being built 'dual-fitted' – having both vacuum and Westinghouse cylinders acting on a common brake shaft and linkages. Dual-fitted stock could happily run with either system. Many railways also fitted at least some of their locomotives with both vacuum ejectors and Westinghouse pumps, resulting in two sets of hoses on the bufferbeam. This was a great characteristic of Great Eastern, North Eastern and Brighton engines, as well as those on the Caledonian and North British. Even the resolutely vacuum GWR had a few locos coyly sporting alien-looking Westinghouse pumps. Most BR diesel locos were also dual-fitted for air and vacuum, although nowadays air reigns supreme on all passenger workings; virtually all BR coaches from the Mk 2 onwards have been built dual fitted or straight air-braked.

Passenger train formations

Just as the passenger stock wasn't purchased at random, it wasn't *run* haphazardly either. The precise mix of accommodation and facilities needed for each service was carefully assessed, and train formations devised to offer what was required in the most efficient possible way. 'Deadweight' – weight in a train that had to be hauled (at a considerable cost in fuel and power) but did not contribute to the earning of revenue – was the ultimate anathema of the Traffic Department. Offering the required accommodation at the least cost in capital and weight was the starting point of passenger stock design, determining the fundamental layout of individual carriages as well as the numbers of each type built.

Leaving aside the earliest period, it soon became the rule that any journey involving a run of an hour or more's duration between stops warranted corridor stock with lavatory accommodation. Trains whose journeys took two hours or more, or whose running times embraced principal meal times, would probably rate a restaurant car or at least a buffet. It would be necessary to provide a suitable balance of accommodation for each class (and there were three classes on many railways until the 'group' period); not only that, it would be necessary to provide smoking and non-smoking seats in each class and to ensure an adequate provision of 'ladies only' compartments. Every passenger train would need to offer guard's accommodation in a brake carriage (where the guard's compartment contained a vacuum brake valve enabling the guard to stop the train in an emergency), as well as luggage accommodation and space for express parcels travelling by passenger train, urgent perishables like milk, and the carriage of the Royal Mail in the days when this went sensibly by train and not wastefully by road. Some of these extra traffics were of considerable importance and often called for dedicated vehicles, such as mail or milk vans, horse-boxes or carriage trucks.

The core formation for a given service was usually provided by a basic rake of vehicles offering the right mix of accommodation, including any necessary catering facilities, and having one or more brake vehicles. A typical five or six-coach formation for a secondary express or cross-country working in the 'Big Four'/early BR period would be a brake compo, all-first, buffet car, compo, all-third and brake third. After 1949, third class was done away with and thirds became seconds – all BR coaching stock being built thus. The core formation would be strengthened as necessary with additional ordinary carriages – usually composites – and any required special NPCS. Precise train formations can best be determined by studying the pictorial references already mentioned. I've found old cine films a very good source of this type of information, while an ultimate written record of actual train formations can be found in guard's logs, which are held in some library collections or occasionally come up for auction.

Some of the things one discovers about particular formations can be less than obvious. For instance, trains serving Navy towns like Plymouth or Portsmouth often had extra baggage accommodation for naval dunnage, while afternoon and evening down trains from London to major provincial centres would convey a 'GUV' or two for newspaper traffic; the London evening editions were always traditionally available first from the station bookstall. Early-morning up workings had corresponding vans for newspaper returns – also used for milk traffic and by those skilled in the art of 'railway hitch-hiking'; the various GWR 'Siphons' were extensively employed in this way.

When devising the make-up of trains, the Traffic Department could, of course, only draw upon what rolling stock was available – which is one of the reasons why British passenger trains (particularly of the post-Grouping and early BR periods) often offered such a glorious mixture of styles, periods and origins. Nicely-matched formations of coaches of common ancestry and livery were usually only found on a few principal trains – often those warranting the provision of dedicated stock, such as the 'Flying Scotsman' or 'Coronation' on the LNER, the 'Coronation Scot' on the LMS and the 'Cornish Riviera Limited' and 'Channel Islands Boat Train' on the GWR.

Apart from the managements of those pre-Grouping companies who set great store by the appearance of their passenger trains – the Midland, the Great Central and the two joint stock companies spring to mind – the other

Above: The GWR was famous for the amazingly varied outlines of its lesser passenger workings. 'Duke' class 4-4-0 No. 3277 Isle of Tresco *has netted a very mixed bag on this working over the South Devon line, including a through coach from the LNWR and sundry non-passenger vehicles. The train is just leaving Dawlish to embark on the famous sea wall section of the line.* Newton Abbot Museum

progenitor of homogeneous formations was the wholesale replacement of old carriages with new vehicles of standard design. This happened mostly on the LMS and SR and, of course, later on BR, where the advent of ruthless standardisation – in the shape of the Mk 1s – led to the wholesale scrapping of pre-Nationalisation 'company' stock, much of it relatively modern.

Coaching stock descriptions

The classification of coaching stock employs a rich – if sometimes rather obscure – terminology that baffles many railway modellers. There is not only the straightforward technical

Right: Main line express workings on the LMS were a bit more orderly in the matter of their carriages. It had been pretty ruthless with the older pre-Grouping carriages it had inherited, so a train like this – composed entirely of new LMS-built stock – was not uncommon. All the coaches built by that railway were of similar outline even if the construction, cladding and lining-out varied. Author's collection

description, based on factors of construction and accommodation, but also often a generic term denoting the origin of the stock and sometimes a telegraphic code as well! That's where names like 'Siphon', 'Monster' and 'GUV' come from. Nowadays, the initial-letter codes associated with BR stock are widely use as a general shorthand abbreviation to describe the basic layout of a coach; more on these codes in a moment.

Some coach descriptions can get pretty involved; when you come up against convolutions such as a 'GW Toplight s/s 70ft 7 cmpt/2 lav corr bk compo Dia E98 Lot 1240 w/multi-bar and 9ft fishbelly' you might well be forgiven for wondering whether you had strayed into the lesser-known works of Lewis Carroll! In fact, it is all quite logical: GW was the owning company, 'Toplight' indicated the design type and 70ft was the nominal length (actually 69ft 11¾in in this case, but a '70-footer' could be up to 73ft long). This is a coach having steel sides (s/s), seven compartments and two lavatories, a through corridor, a brake/guard's compartment and first and third class (i.e. composite) accommodation. It was built to works diagram E98 under order lot number 1240, had a variant of the standard

Below: Passenger coaches with a raised lookout for the guard were often described as having a 'birdcage roof'. The old SECR was very fond of this arrangement, and much of its passenger stock was known by the generic title of 'Birdcage Stock'. Here is a vintage panelled 'Birdcage' brake end complete with lookout – typical of some of the older pre-Grouping stock that survived into the BR era. There are etched kits for these coaches in both 4mm and 7mm scales. Author's collection

underframe design using twinned round-section truss-rods and known as a 'multi-bar', it rode on 9ft wheelbase bogies with pressed steel sideframes, nicknamed the 'fishbelly' type on account of their shape.

Probably the most important part of this description from the modelling point of view is the 'design type'. The majority of coaches belonged to families of designs having certain distinguishing features, and so could be grouped under a generic title. Sometimes, these titles derived from the actual designer, as with 'Bain' and 'Clayton' stock on the Midland. More often, however, the presiding CME got the credit, as the Carriage and Wagon department lay within his purlieu. Thus, one gets 'Webb' coaches on the LNWR, 'Dean', 'Collett' and 'Hawksworth' stock on the GWR, 'Gresley' and 'Thompson' on the LNER, 'Stanier' (but not Fowler, for some odd reason) on the LMS and 'Maunsell' and 'Bulleid' stock on the SR. Some families of coach design were also known by a descriptive title or familiar nickname: 'Dreadnaughts', 'Concertinas', 'Toplights' and 'Centenaries' on the GWR, 'Barnums' on the GCR, 'Grampians' on the Caledonian, 'Birdcages' on the SECR, 'Ironclads' on the LSWR and 'Balloons' on the Brighton, to offer but a random sample!

Until the arrival of the BR Mk 1s in 1951, there were no 'standard' sets of passenger stock configurations. However, all the Mk 1 stock used a common body architecture and underframe, so were all the same length/width/constructional type, with similar route availability, running speeds, braking and heating systems and accommodation standards. It was thus possible to devise very concise descriptive/telegraphic codes for these vehicles, using the class, seating format and facilities in initial form, with the oddity that 'K' was used for corridor to distinguish it from 'C' for composite. Thus one gets common types like 'CK' (corridor composite coach) 'FO/SO' (first/second open), 'BSK' for corridor brake second and 'RB' for buffet car (restaurant car with buffet). There were a few inconsistencies: 'RB' was a restaurant/buffet, whereas 'RB(R)' was a restaurant car with kitchen. The code was also quite specific; a 'TSO' (tourist second open) was distinct from an 'SO' – it had more loos, I fancy – while an 'RMB' was a restaurant *miniature* buffet where, presumably, you got smaller sandwiches …

Model coaching stock

As I hope will have become apparent from perusing the foregoing, British coaching stock exhibits the tremendous variety and individuality so characteristic of the railway scene here. Which means that assembling a suitable selection of vehicles for an authentic layout will usually involve mixing RTR models with kits of various sorts; these days, few people scratchbuild coaches – at least in the smaller scales. Adopting this catholic approach, there is a huge range of prototypes to choose from. The problem, as always, lies in achieving a uniformity of appearance – particularly in terms of finish and detailing – between models built in very different materials and by widely varied techniques.

As a subject, coaches offer the model manufacturer a number of challenges. Leaving aside the complexity and bewildering variety of the prototype for a moment, reproducing the intricacies of panelling on older coaches and the flush-glazing on newer ones pose manufacturing conundrums of no small order – especially the latter. An important characteristic of steel-sided coaches from the modelling point of view is that their glazing only lies back from the face of the coach-side by a quarter-inch or so at full size – about 0.003 of an inch in 4mm scale! This is a characteristic that's difficult to represent in miniature, especially where moulded plastic sides are used. In all-steel coaches like the Mk 1s, there's also the lack of overall thickness in the sides to contend with. Only the latest generation of RTR models, with their thinner precision-moulded sides and accurately-fitting flush glazing, manage to look truly convincing in this respect.

All this is before you come on to consider the sheer amount of *detail* involved in the average coach: ventilators, hinges, door handles and handrails on the sides; cover strips, ventilators, periscopes, light fittings, plumbing and rainstrips on roofs; steps, corridor connections, lamp brackets, grab-irons, pipework and communication-cord gear on the ends; footboards, steps, brake rigging, gas cylinders, battery boxes, dynamos and truss rods on the underframes, and longitudinal and lateral partitions, doorways, seating and fittings in the interiors. Experienced modellers will often tell you that there's as much work in building the average coach as in many a loco.

4mm scale RTR coaches

Time was – and not so long since – when mass-produced ready-to-run (RTR) coaches from the big makers in 4mm scale were poor runts of things, universally short of true scale length (and hence woefully disproportioned) with running gear that at best only approximated to the prototype arrangement and at worst bore it no resemblance whatever. Interiors were either missing altogether or very basic, glazing was usually ill-secured and far too deeply inset (except on Hornby Dublo's tin-sided stock, which looked all the better for it, in spite of the handrails and door handles being merely printed on rather than modelled in relief).

Below: The glazing conundrum, or how flush is flush? Steel-sided coaches, like this GW Collett 60-footer, in reality have glazing that is inset from the face of the coach side by half an inch or less; around 6 thou. in 4mm scale. So even the 25 thou. or so that Bachmann have achieved here is a bit on the chunky side, although a great deal better than the 40+ thou. common on older plastic-sided coaches. The separately applied ventilators and roof-grabs and the general level of detail and finishing of these scale-length coaches is excellent.

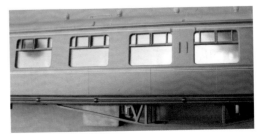

Detail was crude and basic – where it wasn't absent altogether – and such things as roof ventilators were usually incorrectly positioned, a consequence of the same roof moulding being used for different coaches. The other traditional drawback with all RTR coach ranges has been lack of variety, the choice usually being restricted to an 'ordinary' carriage, a brake-end and a restaurant car. It was thus impossible to replicate prototype train formations.

With only Graham Farish producing anything approaching 'scale' 4mm RTR coaches – in the form of their matchboard-sided Pullmans and some presentable 57ft steel-sided suburban stock – there was an obvious opening in the market for something better than Tri-ang or Hornby. This 'upmarket RTR' niche was filled for many years by the Exley coaches, which were also made for 0 gauge. These used stamped brass shells formed to shape and beautifully finished in cellulose paints, with full lining and lettering hand-applied. Underframes, bogies and ends were rather crude plastic mouldings, but the overall effect was imposing; the thin metal of the shells made for good-looking flush glazing – real glass, on older models – while the excellent finish was highly attractive if a little 'bright and shiny'.

Exley made two ranges: Bespoke models, produced either as one-offs or in limited batches at premium prices and covering a wide variety of subjects both of 'grouped' or pre-Grouping origins, and a 'stock' mass-produced range of common types for the 'Big Four', sold at a more economical price – usually sans bogies, which came separately. These standard coaches – marketed as the Zephyr range – used a generic basic shell to represent coaches of all four groups, which meant that the cross-sections, roof and side profiles and certain characteristics were compromised. However, the stamping process did allow window variations to give a much wider choice of carriage types, even if in strict scale terms many of them were not accurate models. The restricted manufacturing method also excluded certain types from the standard issues; proper Gresley LNER bow-roofed stock was never offered, for instance; neither were Pullmans. Even the Zephyr coaches

Above: Besides the thinner sides, the other great advances in modern RTR coaching stock have been in the matter of correct ride heights, general accuracy to prototype, and the quality of detailing and finishing. This BR 57ft suburban brake from Bachmann is typical in its mix of virtues and drawbacks. The BR 8ft 6in bogies, for instance, are authentic, crisply moulded and exquisitely detailed but, frustratingly, they are a bit too 'tight' internally to accept EM or P4 wheels without modification. The tension-lock couplings are mounted on the bogies by screws, so are easily removed in favour of something less obtrusive.

The moulded sides are spot on dimensionally and fully detailed with commode handles, hinges, door stops and handles – but are still that tad too thick around the window openings. See p271 for a 'dodge' to alleviate this ... There is a basic interior with partitions and seats, wanting only a lick of paint and a passenger or two to finish it off. The buffers are the right pattern and to scale, and the end detail is excellent. Only the moulded-on shell vents on the roof fall short of ultimate refinement. The painting, lining and lettering, however, are above reproach.

weren't cheap, costing three or four times the price of a normal mass-produced RTR coach, even before you bought the bogies! Nowadays, an Exley coach is a collector's item, with a price-tag to match.

New-generation RTR

In recent years, mainstream 4mm scale RTR coaches have undergone a similar process of evolution and upgrading to their compadres from the motive power department, with the

result that there are now some truly excellent scale models to be had straight off the model shop shelf. Naturally, these focus on the more prevalent prototypes, with the ubiquitous BR Mk 1 being well to the fore. Just about everybody has had a go at these coaches, starting with Tri-ang (which has had several bites at the cherry over the years, eventually getting up to scale length, if never to flush glazing) and moving through Hornby Dublo SD6 (too short), Trix (who made them in their perverse 3.8mm/ft scale) and Lima (who made them scale length with reasonable glazing but sat them too tall on their bogies) to the Mainline/Replica/Bachmann models of the 1980s – scale length, a fair number of variants and the later cast-steel Commonwealth pattern of bogie – but with the glazing still regrettably recessed and of slightly suspect proportions.

Hornby's current Mk 1 coaches are very good models, true to scale in all respects and offering a good choice of vehicles including full brakes, buffets and sleeping cars. But that glazing – although nowhere near as over-recessed as of yore, is still not *quite* where it should be. The definitive RTR Mk 1 arrived with the current Bachmann offerings, beautiful models in every regard with correct configurations, full detailing including interiors and – at last – really good flush glazing. Although not every Mk 1 variant is available (that would be impossible as there are more than 70 of them!) the key vehicles needed for most formations are there in either the Hornby or Bachmann ranges; even the Mk 1 Pullmans and the distinctive flat-sided GUV luggage vans are now listed. Bachmann also offers the equally distinctive fully compartmented suburban coaches that

Above: One of the older BR Mk 1 models – this is a Replica Railways BCK in Southern Region green with Commonwealth bogies. Plus points are scale length and correct ride height, but the detail falls some way short of later productions and the sides – while not grossly thick – result in glazing that's far from flush. These coaches also formed part of Bachmann's range but have now been superseded by their new Mk 1s, which are some of the best 4mm scale model coaches around. The older models are a popular starting point for reworking with printed or etched brass overlay sides from Southern Pride, MJT or Comet; look out for them at swapmeets or on eBay.

Below: Correct ride height has long been a weakness of many RTR coaches, especially Lima and older Hornby. This is no trifling matter, as can readily be seen in this comparison between the lofty Hornby Pullman on the right and the authentic Bachmann Thompson on the left; more than 1mm of error! Correction calls for the lowering of the body on to the bogies – not always easy.

also formed part of the Mk 1 family. All this Mk 1 stock is available pre-finished in all of the major colour-schemes the type carried, from the original carmine and cream ('blood and custard') main line scheme through the plain maroon or red for secondary stock, the post-1957 'regional' liveries, and BR Corporate blue/grey to the Executive InterCity, Regional Railways, and Network SouthEast schemes that saw the last of the Mk 1s out of regular main line service in the mid-1980s.

For the same 'blue diesel' era, the later BR 65ft long Mk 2 stock – with welded monocoque bodywork and welded underframes with the B4 bogie design – is also available in depth from both Bachmann and Hornby, again in a huge variety of liveries. These later BR coaches were never built in that many variants; classes were standard or first, with the traditional compartment layout soon giving way to the modern open saloon. Ordinary (compartmented), open, buffet, restaurant and open brake coaches were about it. Mk 2 coaches were also bought by the Irish CIE in a 5ft 3in gauge version – which you can also get in model form, although still for 00 rather than the correct 21mm gauge track! The BR Mk 3 air-conditioned coaches are also available – although the variants are even fewer: open coaches in standard and first classes, a trailer guard's standard open, a sleeping car and a restaurant/buffet. All these Mk 3s form part of the Hornby range. The similar Mk 4 coaches are also in the range, as standard and first class opens and an eponymous 'catering vehicle'; BR-period modellers never had it so good!

'Grouping' stock

Steam-era stalwarts favouring the 'Grouping' period of the 'Big Four' (1923–1947) also fare pretty well. Bachmann have for several years offered some very nice ex-Mainline 60ft 1930s-vintage GW Collett stock, although this does suffer the old RTR bugbears of (slightly) over-recessed glazing and limited choice of types. But it's otherwise to scale length, sits on the correct 9ft 'fishbelly' bogies, has interior fittings, excellent and accurate roof detail and very good paintwork. Older GWR coaches are currently

represented by Hornby's bow-ended 57ft Collett 'excursion' coaches – models inaccurate in a few dimensions and some detailing but spot-on for profile, window proportions and general 'feel'; they even have the correct 7ft plate bogies. Hornby also offer some 57-foot clerestory stock, which lacks any relief panelling, has a very simplified lining scheme and (as with the older and celebrated Tri-ang 'Lord of the Isles' clerestories) doesn't follow the prototype *exactly*. It does, however, catch the character of these Dean carriages rather well.

To go with their GW 'Castle' and 14XX, Airfix introduced the first true-to-scale RTR GWR coaches, the 1935 main-line 'Centenary' stock and the diagram A28 auto-trailer. The auto-trailer is a staple piece of GWR rolling stock which, confusingly (and in common with a good number of other models at the time) appeared under both the Airfix and Mainline brands. Whatever it said on the box, the model was excellent, being to scale in all important respects and having glazing that, if not quite flush, was certainly not over-recessed. Again, this model is available in the current Hornby range.

The other seminal GWR coach type introduced by Airfix was the bow-ended B-set coach. These were six-compartment 57ft steel-sided brake-composite suburban vehicles on 7ft plate bogies. A 'set' consisted of a pair of coaches close-coupled together, to aid which some coaches had special short buffers on the inboard ends. Airfix put these stubby buffers on both ends, easy enough to correct, but the coaches were otherwise good and accurate models, if a little bare about the underpinnings. Airfix attempted true flush glazing on these coaches, but this resulted in moulded glazing strips of considerable thickness which have an odd 'pebble glass' look to them. The roof ventilators on all these Airfix coaches (and the Mainline Collett stock) were separately applied, a great advance on the moulded 'pips' so often expected to pass muster.

LMS 'Period I' panelled corridor coaches were produced by Palitoy as part of the Mainline range. These were basically good models, to correct scale length and having reasonable interiors and substantially correct underframes with riveted 9ft bogies. There was an all-first, a composite and a brake, plus a very nice matching 50ft full brake. Although not *quite* up the refinement of the latest RTR, with a bit of work (separate roof ventilators, a little added underframe detail, some paint and the odd passenger for the interiors, and better corridor connections) these older Palitoy (now Bachmann) coaches make very satisfactory models indeed.

A stately 68ft LMS 'Period II' 12-wheeled dining saloon was a splendid if isolated offering from Dapol, who otherwise left LMS coaches well alone. It was memorable not just as a good model of an uncommon prototype, but also as the first plastic RTR coach to breach the £20 price barrier – a sum that is now pretty much the benchmark cost of a coach from Hornby or Bachmann. The LMS 'diner' is now a Hornby model. Another isolated (but welcome) addition to the ranks of RTR LMS coaches came from Lima, who produced a rather good rendition of the 'Period III' short, flat-sided 42ft non-corridor luggage/parcels van. As with all Lima stock, it rode too high on BR 8ft 6in bogies fitted with horrible wheels having too small a diameter and a monstrous flange. However, lower it a tad in the pivot bosses and stick it on scale 9ft LMS bogies and you have a truly accurate model – see photo! Hornby was the late-comer to the LMS coaching stock game, but when they did wade in they did so in style, with an adequate selection of state-of-the-art LMS 'Period III' stock that has every refinement you could wish for including full interior detail, true flush glazing, sprung buffers and a superb finish. LMS adherents have little to complain about, then …

For a long time, none of the big RTR manufacturers made any LNER coaches at all.

Eventually, Triang-Hornby produced some rather approximate Thompson steel-sided stock to go with *Flying Scotsman*, and then belatedly, produced some Gresley panelled bow-roof stock. This was dimensionally inaccurate but caught the distinctive 'look' of these vehicles very well; rather better, in fact, than the current Hornby versions which, while being to scale and having a very advanced specification, somehow miss the mark in catching the true Gresley character. Hornby tried very hard with these coaches, and offer a good range of types, so most people will probably forgive them their slightly too-angular appearance. The all-steel Thompson coaches are now available in reasonable variety from Bachmann, models that are accurate in

Below left: Among the first of the 'new-generation' RTR coaches were the LMS 'Period I' panelled stock from Mainline, eventually assimilated into the Bachmann range. Although suffering the usual window recession – nowhere near as evident on a panelled coach anyway – these were excellent models, true to scale, accurate in detail and nicely finished. Only the lack of separately applied detail and a few compromises around the roof vents, buffers and underframes mark them out from current production standards.

Below: Reworking older or less-detailed RTR coaches is often well worth the trouble. This is a Lima LMS 42ft luggage van modified by John Chambers with new bogies and sprung buffers from MJT, wire handrails in place of the rather undernourished moulded-on originals, and a few telling details like the brake hand wheel which is a Crownline etching. Even the paintwork is original Lima – although not as clean as it once was!

outline and running gear but which, once again, suffer the perennial problem with steel-sided stock – glazing too deeply recessed. You may think all this harping on about sunken windows is a minor point, but flush glazing is *such* a predominant characteristic of steel-sided stock that it just can't be ignored.

The same comments hold true with the Bachmann models of the post-war Bulleid 63ft all-steel stock. Nice enough models as far as they go – which isn't far enough, with just four vehicles, a CK, SO, SK and BSO; the lack of variety is critical in that these coaches normally ran in fixed 'sets' – and you can't get the brake composite that featured in most of these! Neither can you get a matching restaurant car, let alone the extraordinary 'Tavern Car' – painted externally with faux brickwork and mock-Tudor beams!

No such criticism can be levelled at Hornby's excellent new Maunsell stock, which offers a good selection of types enabling all the usual 'set formations' to be represented with models that are fully up to the very best RTR standards for accuracy and detail, possessed of the finest flush glazing yet seen. The introduction of these vehicles plugs the largest hole in RTR coaching stock provision, at last giving all those 'King Arthurs', 'Nelsons' and 'Schools' some appropriate stock to haul.

Pre-Grouping coaches have never figured very large in the RTR ranges – the honourable exception being Tri-ang, who produced some appealing, fully panelled stock to go with their two 'vintage' single-driver engines. To accompany the GWR Dean 4-2-2 *Lord of the Isles* they produced two exquisite GWR clerestory coaches of typical Dean 1890s outline. Although not strictly correct to any prototype and riding on standard BR 8ft 6in wheelbase bogies, these coaches were very popular and the subject of endless reworkings and repaints. The 'Grampian corridor carriages' provided to go with the famous Caley No. 123 also had BR bogies rather than CR six-wheelers, but again, caught the character of these stately vehicles rather well – in spite of dimensional inaccuracies.

Model Pullman cars

Pullman cars have always been popular in RTR model form, starting with the magnificent Hornby 0 gauge tinplate versions of the 1930s – complete with opening doors, interior details and brass trimmings. Trix also made some rather fine tinplate Pullmans in 00, which could be fitted with working lights; they weren't scale models but certainly had the Pullman 'look' and a very good paint finish. The first model Pullman cars with any pretensions to scale accuracy were the Graham Farish 00 models of matchboard-sided stock already mentioned, which appeared in the 1950s. These were moulded in a bakelite type of plastic to scale length and had interior fittings – but unfortunately they were prone to warping badly, while as usual with older RTR coaches there were insufficient variants – only a parlour car and a brake – to replicate prototypical formations.

Hornby Dublo/Wrenn also produced some Pullman cars in their plastic Superdetail range. There were three types: a brake second (*Car No. 79*) and a parlour second (*Car No. 74*) patterned after 1928-built steel-sided prototypes originally constructed for the 'Queen of Scots' train on the LNER; and a kitchen first (*Airies*), which was based on a 1951-vintage all-steel vehicle with LNER-pattern Gresley 8ft 6ins bogies, allocated to the Southern Region. Dublo also fitted the Gresley bogie (wrongly) to the two 1928 cars; these should have had the Pullman 10ft WB type. These Dublo Pullmans were nice enough models but woefully short of scale length (58ft 6in rather than 63ft) and, unfortunately, the kitchen first and the two second class cars were types that never ran together. Wrenn later used these models as part of a charming but somewhat approximate 'Brighton Belle' set – the only electric multiple-unit made up of Pullman stock.

Someone at Margate likes Pullmans, as all those to appear in the Tri-ang, Triang-Hornby and modern Hornby ranges have been distinctly above-average models. The best of the older models was the all-steel Pullman that appeared during the later 1970s – completely

Above: Triang-Hornby's ace Pullman car, the 1928 steel stock which appeared in the 1970s. They were perched too high on their bogies, but were otherwise very convincing; even Pendon has one, suitably reworked by Mike Doherty. The current Hornby Pullmans are even better.

Above: In many ways 2mm scale is a good size for replicating coaches and there are some very good models about. To my eye, this Minitrix LNER Gresley brake composite does a far better job of capturing the distinctive outline and character of these vehicles than any of the 4mm versions.

bereft of any acknowledgement as to maker! Again, the two versions – first kitchen and second brake – were not enough for a train, but the first was useful in that it was a type of car often used singly in otherwise non-Pullman formations. These were cracking models, completely to scale with the correct 10ft bogies and glazing that was not too far out of place. The only real fault was that they rode about 1mm too high on the bogies.

Which brings us to the current Hornby Pullmans; some of the finest RTR 4mm scale model coaches yet produced. These form the first really comprehensive selection of matching Pullman cars ever offered, with matchboard-wood and steel-sided variants of the classic inter-war Pullman design, as used on most of the famous 'Pullman Limited' trains up to the end of steam and the arrival of the BR Mk 1 Pullmans in the 1960s. Enough different coaches are provided to enable many of the best-known Pullman trains of the inter-war and BR periods to be represented and when they come up with the 'Devon Belle' observation car I'll be at the head of the queue!

As for the BR Pullmans – well, Bachmann have all the main variants in their comprehensive 'Mk 1 range' in both proper

Pullman umber-and-cream and naff grey-and-blue liveries. So the 'Master Cutler' and the 'Manchester Pullman' are now both on the cards. Triang-Hornby also made a version of the charismatic 'Blue Pullman' diesel train sets, a model that looked the part even if its mechanics were a little unrefined; they produced the power cars and some (but not all) of the centre vehicles. The latter, especially, were never that plentiful and are now greatly sought-after. Another past gem ripe for a work-over and re-introduction, I fancy…

N scale RTR coaches

The story of RTR coaching stock in N is a bit like that of the locos; the more recent prototypes – mostly BR-era – are available from Bachmann/Farish, to a very good standard as regards scale dimensions, finish and general authenticity. As usual, the hands-down winner is the BR Mk 1 stock which is available in real depth, with not just the common corridor compartment and corridor open coaches and brakes, but restaurant, buffet and mini-buffet cars, full brakes, GUVs, Mk 1 Pullmans and the suburban compartment stock. A full gamut of appropriate liveries is available for all these coaches. Modellers of the contemporary

Above: With sides printed on clear sheet plastic, as with most current Farish N coaches, there's no problem in reproducing convincing flush glazing in the miniature scale. This is a production technique particularly well suited to modern all-steel stock, like this BR Mk 1 – and particularly to the very clean-sided contemporary Mk 4s. Lack of relief for handrails, handles and hinges is the main drawback to printed sides, but in N gauge these things are less evident.

Note the degree of close-coupling Steve Earl uses for his fixed rakes of N gauge coaches; even coupled this tight, they will still squeak round a 9in radius curve. The secret is to lop off one buffer on each coach end on the diagonal opposites and to replace the ordinary couplings with rigid drawbars linking adjacent bogies. Within the train, such a subterfuge is unapparent. End vehicles, of course, keep both buffers – see the tailpiece at the end of this chapter!

scene are also well-catered for, with 65ft Mk 2 coaches, Mk 3s with skirting and the Mk 4 trailer opens and catering cars. All these models use pad-printed sides on a clear shell, so are truly and effectively flush-glazed – and look all the better for it.

Grouping stock is now better represented in N than ever before. LMS Stanier Period II/III steel-sided stock is available from Farish – all-new models with state-of-the-art printed sides, flush glazing and the correct LMS 8ft 6in bogies. There's an adequate basic choice of vehicles in LMS and early BR liveries. For the GWR, Dapol have the classic 1930s Collett 57ft stock – to scale length, nicely detailed (especially the roof vents and buffers) and on

correct 'fishbelly' bogies. These coaches have traditional moulded bodies with inset glazing – not too badly recessed, but not as flush as Farish. For GWR branch lines in N, Dapol offer the two key vehicles: the 59ft auto-trailer, Diagram A 30, and the B-set brake composites. Also available from Dapol is Gresley LNER bow-roof stock; neatly moulded bodies with the beading not overdone and good glazing. The roofs are nice, too – important with Gresley coaches. There's only a basic selection so far – all-first, a second and a brake composite. This only leaves the Southern – the 'Sunshine Line – out in the cold, as usual. What has everybody got against Mr Maunsell's coaches? The only thing that even approximated to them was the old-style Farish coach, which was in fact neither one thing nor another.

In truth, most older N scale RTR coaches were not so good; Minitrix made a range of passable BR Mk 1s and Lima also had a crack; the usual glazing comments apply. Most of the non-BR Farish coaches were generic rather than being accurate models of any prototype; they were all-moulded plastic vehicles, complete with the usual giveaway of deeply recessed glazing, and having running gear that was based around the good-old BR 8ft 6in bogie. The best of these older Farish N scale coaches were – surprise, surprise – the Pullmans, a reprise of the handsome matchboarded-sided stock the company had originally produced in 00. As usual, there weren't enough variants for authenticity, but that doesn't stop a rake of them looking pretty impressive – especially when close-coupled. The main N scale bugbear is the couplings, which space the coaches with the corridor connections far enough apart to trouble an Olympic long-jumper! Close-coupling is as worthwhile as it is simple to achieve; see how in the 'Couplings' chapter that rounds off this tome.

RTR coach window improvements

Throughout these ramblings you will have noticed that I set great store by the look of the *glazing* on model coaches. More modern coaches, with their large, flat, flush-mounted expanses of glass, suffer the most; any shortcomings in this department can have a considerable impact on the whole 'look' of the model. Apart from glazing set the thick end of six scale inches back in coach sides that should only be three inches thick in total, notable failings are ill-fitting 'glass' leaving a gap between the face of the glazing and the coach side, or moulded glazing with edges that are vague and rounded rather than crisp and square. Some moulded glazing is far from flat-faced – especially the really thick stuff – while some model 'glass' isn't all that transparent, with an unconvincing dull finish.

Taking the trouble to improve glazing is time well spent. Wrinkled or dull/scratched clear plastic can be replaced with something flatter, thinner and sharper. Professional model coach builders often use real glass, in the form of microscope slide cover slips, available from scientific instrument suppliers; fix them in place with cyano. Failing real glass, the next best thing is an optical-quality clear acrylic sheet, such as Charvo – this isn't cheap, but a sheet goes a long way. Cobex is another clear plastic much favoured for model glazing, and you can buy this from materials suppliers like Eileen's or Squires. Even good-quality clear styrene sheet is better than a lot of moulded glazing; I find the Evergreen brand to be best.

This leaves the problem of flush-glazing that isn't flush. You can buy 'flush glazing kits' for many RTR coaches, but these are almost invariably vacuum-formed and suffer from the rounded-edge problem, which to my eye looks just as bad as the recess. There are two options; you can either cut and file individual 'panes' of clear glazing material to fit the

Above: Window improvements. On plastic-bodied RTR (or kit) coaches with over-thick sides, the excessive recession of the glazing can be simply disguised by painting the reveals – the edges of the window openings – a dark neutral shade as on this Bachmann Thompson coach.

window openings exactly so that they can be set in the right relationship to the coach side – a tedious and time-consuming task but one that many modellers have found worthwhile. The second is the simplest; you simply paint the reveals of the window openings (the thickness of the coach side seen in front of the glazing) a dark grey-brown shade rather than leaving it in livery colour. This ploy is surprisingly effective in disguising the fact that the windows are inset when they shouldn't be, especially in N scale. In the USA (where the same glazing problems apply to RTR steel-sided coaches), you can buy glazing inserts laser-cut exactly to size for many popular passenger vehicles; these only take moments to install and look superb. It would be nice if we could get something similar over here.

Kit-built coaches – 4mm scale

RTR coaches in 4mm scale are now at the point where they are more than good enough for all but the hyper-fastidious or the hair-shirt merchants. As already remarked, you're never going to get *every* vehicle you need 'off the peg', while there's the usual satisfaction to be had from building your own models and ending up with a collection that's just a little bit different. And then, there are those people who just *like* building coaching stock. These dedicated souls have elected to plough one of the harder furrows in the hobby, for coaching stock construction is far from being the easiest of disciplines. Consistency is very important, especially in a rake of matching vehicles, while there's a lot of repetitive work – fitting droplights, door ventilators, door-handles and hinges, partitions, commode handles, roof ventilators, steps and so – that must be done well and carefully if the result is not to be compromised.

Then, of course, there's the small matter of painting the finished thing, which is never easy; even a plain steel-sided vehicle in a single colour calls for care and a degree of skill with the airbrush or aerosol, for there's nothing like the flat expanses of a coach side for showing up orange-peel spraywork and other paintwork defects. Even that pales into insignificance when one comes to consider a fully lined panelled period coach in the full glory of Midland or LNWR paint. Strictly for the brave … Not without reason do professional painters like Ian Rathbone or Chris Wesson charge as much – or more – to paint a panelled coach as they do for a fully-lined loco.

I'll confess straight away that I'm not much of a coach builder and even less of a painter, and make as much use as I can of RTR vehicles as the basis of my passenger stock. However, when you have a predilection for modelling the lesser railways of East Anglia, what the big makers offer you doesn't go that far. Fortunately, the trains I need to model were noted for their eclectic mix of oddball and cast-off coaches culled from all over the former LNER system, so I have rarely been faced with building more than one or two vehicles of the same type. My experience has been that kit-built coaching stock is a lot less daunting when you're only faced with the odd specimen rather than a whole train's-worth. Taking this approach to round out an RTR-based fleet is very rewarding, with particularly happy hunting in the field of the non-passenger coaching stock – vehicles you can usually tack on to any train, of whatever provenance.

RTR reworking kits
With the advent of the 'new-generation' 4mm scale-length RTR coaches using the now-universal form of construction of separate plastic sides inserted into a common underframe/floor/ends moulding, it didn't take long for the more enterprising etchers to realise that they could produce alternative brass sides to replace or overlay the plastic RTR side, thus creating different vehicles. The model coaches that really kicked off this approach were the Mainline/Replica/Bachmann BR Mk 1s, an ideal subject in that there were a huge number of prototype vehicles to choose from, all using the same running gear, dimensions and basic outline. Firms like Comet and Southern Pride were soon offering alternative etched-brass overlay sides for all manner of Mk 1 variants, from the more obscure 'ordinary carriages' to specialised vehicles like sleeping cars, TPOs and Pullmans. The same technique has subsequently been applied to all manner of RTR coaches, such as Bachmann's Bulleid stock and even Hornby's GWR clerestories.

This reworking of RTR coaches is a modelling approach that has gained great favour, particularly with operators of larger layouts needing to create prototypical train formations quickly and easily. The use of replacement etched sides also solves the flush-glazing problem, making them a popular upgrade in the quest for better-looking steel-sided stock. However, you still have to paint, line and letter an etched side, although that can at least be done flat 'on the bench' before it is glued in place, which makes life a bit easier. Easier still is to use a pre-finished overlay side printed on clear plastic, an approach pioneered for 4mm RTR modification by Southern Pride. This printed overlay idea worked even better in N, especially when Graham Farish switched to *making* their coaches as clear plastic shells with printed overlay sides! Substituting alternative printed sides from the likes of Taylor Plastic Models gave you a result that was indistinguishable from the factory product. Etched overlay sides have also figured in N, although not as extensively as for 4mm. The Gresley panelled overlays from Fencehouses Models are exquisite, while Ultima Models has a large range.

As well as alternative sides, you could soon also buy all manner of other components

designed to upgrade or alter plastic RTR coaches in both 4mm scale and N. These range from simple detailing kits and more refined bogies and underframes cast to ends to transform ordinary Mk 1 coaches into EMU driving trailers, and the like. There is now a huge and bewildering choice of such kits and components, from big ranges like Comet, MJT and Southern Pride and a veritable gaggle of smaller concerns

Complete kits – stamped metal

Leaving aside early efforts using litho papers or milled wood, DIY complete coaches arrived in quantity and variety with the introduction of stamped-metal kits for steel-sided vehicles, usually produced in aluminium. There were two main ranges – Westdale and BSL. Westdale produced kits in both 4mm and 7mm scales and took the Exley approach, forming the sides and roof as one piece, with the windows punched out and the whole thing bent to shape. You simply added ends, a floor and an underframe – plus an interior if you were so minded – and you had a basic coach. Westdale kits are still going strong in 7mm, and a hard core of 4mm modellers still like them when they can lay hands on them, but the tooling was later acquired by Derek Lawrence, who only sold the coaches in pre-built form.

The extensive range of coaches originally produced by Hobbytime/BSL initially centred on Southern Bulleid and Maunsell stock, using separate jig-stamped aluminium sides with cast metal ends and a milled wooden roof. Some underframe parts and the (rather crude) bogies were plastic mouldings, with an aluminium floor and sheet-plastic interiors. The use of stamping enabled a very wide range

Above: Kit-built coaches are the way to acquire models of less common prototypes – like this EM LNER Dia. 226 Gresley kitchen car built by Louis Baycock from MJT parts. This lovely coach was spray-painted with an aerosol of car touch-up paint from Halfords – VW Gambia Red in this case.

of variants of each coaching stock 'family' to be produced, making these kits a very valuable resource to those who set store by prototypical train formations. The BSL range was soon expanded to cover other flush-sided Grouping prototypes and played a significant role in the development of the 4mm hobby. Now modified and upgraded, with metal roofs, sprung bogies and far more refined detailing, these kits are still very much around as the Phoenix range, produced for several years by Branchlines and currently under the wing of the Southern Railways Group, who became involved as the range is such a key resource for SR modellers.

While demanding quite a bit of work – you have to scribe your own door-openings and add all the coach side detail – aluminium-sided coaches are still popular, not least because their method of construction facilitates pre-finishing of the sides, as for the brass overlays for RTR coaches. The actual assembly of aluminium-side coaches usually uses an all-glued construction, which many modellers find a less daunting prospect than the soldering needed to put an all-etched brass coach together. The Phoenix kits also come with all the parts formed to shape, including the subtle curved profile of the sides – another bonus compared to the 'bend it yourself' approach usual with etched coaches.

Above: Pre-printed plastic sides on a PC Models LNWR compartment coach. To many modellers, painting and lining of this crispness and quality is worth the sacrifice of relief detail in the panelling and for door and grab handles.

Printed-side coaches

Pre-finished sides are the main virtue of a family of composite kits using printed overlays on a variety of supporting shells – an approach nowadays associated more with RTR overlay sides than complete kits. First in the printed-side complete kit field (if you discount the old Hamblings 'Litho papers') were PC models, who produced a fairly extensive range that first appeared in the late 1960s and, as Wheeltapper Coaches, is still around today. The range included several 'tricky' subjects and liveries, including LNWR compartment stock, teak-finished Gresleys, fully lined GWR 'Toplights' and gold-lined olive green SR Maunsell stock. These PC kits used sides screen-printed on clear plastic sheet, with fully lined liveries beautifully executed. Although the various panelled prototypes lacked relief detail, the full livery to a large extent disguised their 'too-flat' look. The sides were mounted on a composite shell made up of a real hodgepodge of materials – sheet and vacuum formed plastic, the odd bit of pressed aluminium, a few etched brass or turned parts (including very nice sprung buffers) and plenty of whitemetal castings. Again, an all-glued construction was used and the printed side, of course, greatly simplified painting. The downsides were lack of relief details on the sides (things like grab rails and

door handles are printed on 'flat'), and rather fiddly assembly.

Much easier to put together are the more recent printed-side coaches from Southern Pride Models, which are based on a variety of moulded-plastic RTR coach body shell components and are thus akin to the 'RTR overlay' approach already described. The Type 1 kits come with the fully-printed sides already in place on the shells which are simply finished off with RTR running gear (mostly Bachmann) as appropriate. The Type 2 kits ask you to fit the sides to RTR shell components (floors/ends and roofs), which will sometimes need some modification. Southern Pride's printed-side range is firmly based on relatively modern flush-sided steel stock, for which this technique is ideal. The BR Mk 1 coaches – including the Pullmans and things like Mk1 EMU stock and Royal Mail TPO vehicles – form the backbone of the range, but – as with BSL – the SR Bulleid stock was the original starting point, hence the name. Southern Pride also make composite brass and resin coach kits, of which more in a moment.

Plastic coach kits

The injection-moulded plastic coach kit first appeared in the late 1960s, when Ratio introduced their exquisite GWR 4-wheelers and Ian Kirk first dipped a toe in the Gresley waters. The Ratio GWR range of four vehicles became a lynch-pin of GWR branch line modelling, but, oddly, the range was never extended, at least not by Ratio. Shire Scenes later stepped in with etched brass alternative sides that used the Ratio underframe, ends and roof to produce all manner of GW 4-wheelers. Ratio themselves went on to develop a selection of delightful Midland Bain suburban bogie compartment stock, three clerestory and four arc-roofed vehicles, of characteristic square-panel design. Sufficient types are included for authentic train formations, with a few extra coming via alternative brass sides, by Branchlines in this instance. They then branched out into 1900-era 50ft LNWR corridor stock, a range of four exquisite vehicles and just about

adequate as a basis for an LNWR rake. There were no additions for a long time until there appeared a very high-quality kit for the SR 'Bogie B' utility van, which included some etched-brass components.

The Kirk range was produced on ingenious home-made tooling that resulted in kits which, while not as delicate and finely detailed as the Ratio offerings, were accurate to scale, robust and complete and came at a very reasonable price. Built 'straight from the box', a Kirk coach was comparable in quality to the best contemporary RTR offerings – but to scale dimensions and outline. More importantly, for a generation of LNER modellers bereft of any RTR stock, they offered an economical and easy-to-build alternative to the high-end etched coaches that were otherwise all that was on offer, with a good selection of prototypes that allowed prototypical train formations to be built up.

Initially, the Kirk range concentrated on 4mm Gresley LNER panelled stock, of which there eventually came to be a very comprehensive range of nearly 40 kits, covering not just the 61ft 6in main line coaches but also the shorter 51/52ft 6in 'cross country' stock in corridor and non-corridor versions, the articulated restaurant car sets and all the various 'ticulated suburban sets, including two – the GN-lines 'Quad Art' and the GE-section 'Quint-art' – in which your author travelled to school. Some of these LNER coaches also appeared in a small, 7mm Kirk range. SR modellers, particularly of the inter-war Grouping period, shared the lot of the LNER boys when it came to coaches. For these hapless souls, Ian Kirk went on

Above: Top of the tree in plastic kit coaches – a GWR 'Toplight' brake third from the Slater's range, built for 4mm scale/00 gauge by Andrew Duncan.

to produce a modest selection of Maunsell coaches – the only kitbuilt models of these distinctive vehicles to incorporate the outside window locating frames into the coach sides, a feat that has so far eluded the etchers!

The original Kirk range was sold, but a second range then grew under the Mailcoach label. Once again, the LNER was the star player, but this time in the glamorous form of the flush-sided part-articulated 'Coronation' stock, with the whole nine-car train eventually becoming available. The range also included a small selection of the steel-sided LNER 'Tourist stock' – which carried the unique green-and-cream livery – and a couple of Thompson steel vehicles. Oh yes, the GWR also got an uncharacteristic look-in, with a kit for the Dia P16 outside-framed 'Monster', a heavy bogie van for bulky loads.

The subsequent history of the Kirk range is somewhat convoluted. The original range was sold off to Colin Ashby, who eventually sold on the LNER kits but retained the SR range which, at the time of writing, seems moribund. The Kirk LNER kits, together with the entire Mailcoach range, were then acquired by Tony Brown, who merged them with the Cooper-Craft business he already owned. So now the Kirk coaches are stable mates to the excellent Cooper-Craft plastic kits for BR Mk 1 coaches which, until the advent of the latest Bachmann RTR models, were the best Mk 1s you could buy, very accurate in outline and detail and offering that sine qua non of steel sides, decent flush glazing. The range, however, is small – only five types covering some of the less-common diagrams. Providing your painting is up to the mark these are the only other 4mm scale plastic Mk 1s that can mix seamlessly with the Bachmanns. Cooper-Craft will sell you their super-accurate Mk 1 underframe separately, a valuable resource when taken alongside the various etched Mk 1 sides available from the likes of Comet.

This just leaves Slaters, purveyors of probably the most sophisticated plastic coach kits – although, as they include a host of etched brass, whitemetal and lost-wax cast components, might almost be classed as composite kits. The coach sides, ends and roofs are moulded, however, so they are certainly plastic-*bodied* coaches – albeit with fully detailed metal underframes and sprung bogies. They also boast cast brass handrails, working corridor connections and full interiors. From this you'll surmise that they are far from 'shake-the-box quickies' to build – but from which you should also deduce that the end result, paintwork permitting, is something just a bit

Below: A typical etched coach kit in the later stages of construction – just the interior and roof to do… This 4mm scale D&S Models NER matchboard-sided third class 'excursion coach' comes with a vacuum-formed plastic roof but is otherwise all-metal with etched, whitemetal-cast and turned brass parts. However, you don't get any seats and these have to be sourced separately; I opted for Ratio's plastic versions. The bogies are compensated and the underframe is fully detailed. Building and painting a model like this is no five-minute task!

special. Which it needs to be, as these kits rank on cost with the most sophisticated of etched offerings – but quality never does come cheap! The 4mm range includes GWR 'Toplight' and clerestory stock, while in 7mm Slaters offer SR Maunsell coaches and a selection of MR designs, plus 7mm versions of the same GWR 4-wheelers that Ratio make in 4mm scale.

Etched brass coaches

The etched brass coach kit bowed in early in the 1970s and was soon challenging the stamped-side technique as the way to go for metal-bodied coaches. The etchers had an ace up their sleeve, of course, for as well as piercing out windows, they could *half*-etch. This meant not only engraved door outlines on flush-sided stock, but full panelling and beading on wooden bodies – something that had to be laboriously applied to stamped aluminium sides. When it came to panelled stock, the etched kit was soon King of the Roost – which it still is, in spite of the best efforts of the plastic moulders. For the etched kit has another ace to play, in the form of a simple (although not so simple as some think it is!), origination process. This means that, providing you can draw the artwork required to an adequate standard, you can produce etched parts. However, there's a big difference between producing a selection of etched parts and producing a kit! Much depends on devising the best way to break the model down into manageable components and sub-assemblies, in providing adequate alignment and locating aids and in generally making the thing a pleasure to build rather than a spell in a brazen purgatory!

From which it might be inferred (correctly!) that etched coach kits are a very variable breed. They range from masterworks of chemically milled origami that practically throw themselves together and come complete with every fitting down to the antimacassars on the seats, to very bald affairs which give you a set of basic sides and ends, a bag of desultory castings and a single side of typescript by way of instructions. Both extremes can result in excellent models; it's just the journey between opening the box and admiring the finished result that varies somewhat! One weak area in many otherwise excellent etched coach kits concerns the roofs, all-too-often supplied as rather crude vacuum-formed plastic – tricky to trim to size and difficult to attach satisfactorily to the brass body. Formed brass (best!), milled-wood (close second) and extruded-aluminium roofs are to be preferred.

In terms of the modelling skills required, the etched kit is often seen as somewhat demanding. *How* demanding depends on your view of, and happiness with, the whole business of soldering, the basic assembly technique on which all etched brass models depend. There have been several attempts to design 'superglue-assembly' etched coach kits, but these have never really caught on – probably because soldering isn't half as difficult in reality as the myth would suggest. With a compact but powerful instrument soldering iron, Fry's Powerflow flux and a good free-flowing low-temperature modelmaker's solder like Carr's 145°, soldering etched brass is actually pretty straightforward – no harder than gluing, which is, in effect, what you're doing. Soldering aside, etched kits do call for a degree of delicacy if you're not to end up with distorted components and pockmarked sides. The 'panel' areas of etched sides are only 5–6thou. thick and often rather soft, so care is needed to keep them smooth and flat.

There are so many etched coach kits available that I couldn't possibly take you on a make-by-make tour. All I can usefully do is take a lightning look at the main ranges, throwing in the odd personal aside. So I'll start with the grand-daddy of them all, Blacksmith, which numbers among its ranks the pioneering George Allen and Mallard kits that started the whole business rolling. Unsurprisingly, in a range that has been around for so long and to which so many different people have contributed, the standard is a bit variable; the older kits are rather complex by modern standards, while some of the early hand-drawn artwork lacks the crispness of kits produced using computer-aided design. The range of subjects is huge, although with the GWR to the fore. The SECR is strongly represented and the range rambles around the LNWR, LYR and the Somerset & Dorset, among others. In terms of builder-friendliness, these kits fall in the 'moderately difficult' range. Another very catholic range is D&S, currently in a state of flux on the retirement of its originator, Danny Pinnock. These are excellent and fully detailed kits which go together very well, once you can decipher the rather 'dense' instructions; they are very complete with sophisticated equalised bogies and compensated six-wheel running gear; not easy, but not as difficult as they may at first appear. Subjects are very varied and mostly of pre-Grouping origin; the range is a prime resource for modellers of the old GER, GNR and NER, while it also covers the LYR, LNWR, GCR and odd bits of the GWR.

Of the other large ranges, three are very much governed by prototype allegiances. Roxey Mouldings (they started out making plastic coaches) are very much Southern-orientated, covering the vital Maunsell coaches in some depth and producing a selection of characteristic Southern EMUs, as well as providing LSWR modellers with a comprehensive selection of bogie and non-bogie stock. Roxey has also dabbled with SECR 'Birdcage' stock and diverse Chatham and Brighton pre-Grouping vehicles. This last is territory also occupied by Branchlines, which specialises in older stock, mostly four or six-wheeled and including some peachy veterans that have long been the delight of the light railway brigade. Branchlines – which has a link with Phoenix – have also made a specialty of Southern EMU stock. London Road Models, by contrast, are resolutely LNWR, with very few interlopers from elsewhere, but a bewildering selection of Crewe types on offer. In terms of standard and difficulty, these three ranges are very much on a par; they are good-quality, accurate kits, but assume some basic familiarity with the prototype and with etched kit assembly techniques and are probably somewhere between Mallard and D&S.

A small if somewhat esoteric range that deserves mention here is Roger Chivers' Finelines. Not only does this offer some truly tempting NPCS prototypes, but great effort has gone into the design of the kits to make them truly easy-to-build, with extensive use of well-thought-out fold-up assemblies and good locating systems. If you're looking for something simple in the etched-kit line to cut your teeth on, look no further. From a tiddler to a giant, Comet's huge range of more modern steel-sided stock – already noticed under the etched-side banner – is also builder-friendly and includes some smaller, simpler NPCS vehicles that make ideal first-step projects. The range covers all 'Big Four' 'Groups' as well as BR Mk 1s. Comet's running gear and detailing is straightforward and serviceable rather than pandering to finescale pedantry; an instance is roofs, where they make extensive use of a generic easy-to-fit extruded aluminium profile that is close to, but not-quite-right-for, the majority of the coaches they portray. For all but the most fastidious, these kits are an excellent bet.

Just time to notice a final quintet of makers who specialise in specific prototypes, with either full kits, partial kits designed for use with other maker's sides, bogies or running gear, or just basic sides/ends/roof/floor 'bare bodies'. These are MJT, which mostly marches to the beat of the Gresley drum, and who can provide you with anything from a bare pair of etched sides to a complete all-singing coach kit with compensated bogies, sassy corridor connections and more fine detail than you can shake a stick at. Not as hard to build as the advanced specification might lead you to suppose. Kemilway (another of the etched coach pioneers) plough the same LNER furrow, with more of a nod in Thompson's direction and a somewhat steeper price for the complete product.

Some commissioned GWR coaches apart, 5522 Models concerns itself primarily with the LMS, exploring the remoter reaches of that company's coaching stock diagram book as well as providing parts to enable Comet LMS sides to be made up into fully authentic vehicles to a rather more exacting standard than Comet themselves aspire to. The other 5522 speciality was the Highland Railway, although these kits have now passed to Lochgorm Models. Also produced by 5522 was a range of Caledonian vehicles sold under the Caley Kits label. Haye Developments has a modest selection of GWR coach bodies centred on the 70-foot stock in various forms – some of these kits being produced at the behest of Pendon Museum. Nowadays, Haye kits are under the Westdale umbrella. Lastly, David Geen has garnered together a selection of complete etched-brass kits for pre-Grouping Highland, LNWR and GW prototypes – models formerly produced by Alan Gibson and Micro-Rail.

Resin/composite kits

Very much the new kid on the block here in Britain, although well-established in the USA, resin kits offer great potential for limited run production at moderate cost combined with the ease-of-use and the ability to replicate curved and irregular shapes – previously the province of the plastic moulding or whitemetal casting. The technique is particularly suited to 0 scale, and ranges like Westdale make a lot of use of resin mouldings for things like ends and roofs. In 4mm scale, the main resin-coach players are Southern Pride, which uses a combination of etched brass sides with resin ends/roof domes and formed plastic roof sections to produce kits for the BR all-steel welded Mk 2 stock which, with their curved corners and roof ends, are not really a practicable proposition as all-etched kits. Using resin mouldings for the ends and underframes saved a lot of weight by comparison with whitemetal castings. Resin has great potential both for modelling today's 'curvy-swervy' streamlined rolling stock and as a useful weight saver where long trains are contemplated.

Close coupling and corridor connections

One last aspect to touch on before we leave the glamour of passenger stock for the grit of the goods department – the thorny question of inter-coach gaps. For many a year the convention has been that we need a yawning chasm half a cricket-pitch long between coaches in order to get them to run around our grossly under-scale curves – which in turn meant that our corridor connections – far from touching – rarely got closer than hearty hailing distance. Close-coupling and connected-up flexible gangways were deemed impossible, to the extent that no-one, it seems, even tried. So corridor connections were relentlessly rigid and dummy while couplings were arranged to maintain the coaches at their customary arms-length.

Then along came the NEM, with their clever coupler-mounting boxes that closed the coupling distance up on straight track and progressively opened it out on curves – which at least meant the train looked reasonably well-connected for at least *part* of the time. However, this is still only a partial answer – which begs two key questions: 'How close *can* you couple scale-length main line coaches and still get around typically tight curves?' and 'What happens if you use truly flexible corridor connections and make them touch?' To which – after considerable practical experiment – I can provide the following answers. First, using bogie-mounted couplers in 4mm scale, set to give a buffer-to-buffer distance of 2mm or a tad more (less than half the clearance RTR couplings typically provide), you can get scale 60ft coaches around a 2ft 6in radius curve in 00; in N scale, a buffer-to-buffer setting of 1.5mm will get you round 12in radius curves, while 1mm is adequate for 15in. In both cases, rigid bar-hook semi-permanent couplers were used – see Chapter 13.

As for the corridor connections, the answer proved to be even more satisfactory. Trying a variety of folded-paper and foam-rubber-cored systems along the lines of those illustrated, demonstrated that no problems arose, *providing* the connections were truly flexible and the meeting faces perfectly flat and smooth and free to slide over each other. Indeed, there was a further unexpected bonus, in that trains thus corridor-connected ran more smoothly and moved, like the prototype, 'all of a piece'. Gone were two common ills of model passenger trains – the coach that wobbles and shimmies to a rhythm all its own, and 'surging' due to

Above: Close coupling and corridor connections that touch are not necessarily the province of those with acres of space for sweeping curves; Andrew Duncan's 00 'Maiden Newtown' layout uses hidden curves down to 2ft 9in radius, yet he can still run his Slater's 'Toplights' with their exquisite folded-paper gangways firmly in contact and the coupling distance only a little over scale. Not only does this look much better, but the stock runs more steadily than when 'loose coupled'.

the slack between vehicles. The slight steadying pressure exerted by the corridor connections – especially the foam-cored ones – was apparently adequate to damp out these undesirables. Several birds slain with but a single pebble!

Below: The last word on coaching stock comes from Steve Earl, who never forgets the rear gangway closing panel and the all-important tail-light ...

Chapter 11

GOODS ROLLING STOCK

On the average model railway set any time between the 1840s and about 1970, 'common carrier' goods working is a bedrock of operation. It was also, for most of railway history, the key business of the prototype; ask a true traffic man about passenger trains and he'd tell you they were nothing but a nuisance, mere flighty trifles that got in the way of the real wage-earner of the railway: freight. Goods working, as we can represent it on our model railways, forms an important part of the next chapter, so here, we are concerned with one of the main elements in

this fascinating business: the humble goods wagon, in full-size and model form.

I'd better come clean and confess at this point that I'm something of a wagon freak, to the point where a lot of my layouts have been of freight-only subjects and the accumulation of a wide and realistic selection of goods rolling stock has formed a goodly part of my personal involvement in the hobby. So you'll have to excuse any excesses of wagonophilic zeal. The great thing about wagons as modelling subjects is the beguiling mix of basic simplicity with infinite variety. It's thus a field rich in

modelling challenges and possibilities, where RTR models – either in the form described on the box, or (more likely in my case) altered, improved, reworked and individualised in half a hundred ways – mix and interbreed with plastic kits and cohabit with more exotic kit-built or scratchbuilt specimens in etched brass, whitemetal or home-brewed Plastikard. More on this riot on the workbench later; as with the other aspects of realistic railway modelling, it's first necessary to make the acquaintance of the prototype in order to understand a little of the 'Why?' leading to a lot of the 'What?'

The wagon fleet

In reality, in the traditional steam/early diesel era the railways rostered maybe a half-dozen coaches for every passenger engine, but probably near on a hundred wagons for every goods loco. The small size and capacity of traditional British four-wheeled wagons – coupled with the 'common carrier' status of the railways and the inevitable fluctuations in demand – led to *vast* wagon fleets, hundreds of thousands of vehicles strong. Many types of wagon – such as the basic seven-plank 12-ton wooden coal wagon and its successor, the 16-ton all-steel mineral wagon – were *built* in batches of several thousand at one go. On any model railway setting out to replicate the balance of freight vehicles on the prototype, it is almost impossible to have too many of them!

The story of British wagonry is essentially a tale of endless variations on relatively few and familiar themes: the mineral wagon, the general-purpose open goods truck, the low-sided or flat wagon, the covered van, the tank wagon and a gaggle of 'special purpose' types. The size of these vehicles was restricted by the nature of the freight-handling infrastructure they had to use, with its cramped loading gauge, frequent use of wagon turntables, sharply curved sidings and weight-restricted structures. Many of these facilities dated back to the earliest days of the railways and had thus evolved around the dimensions of the rolling stock then in use – typically, vehicles about 12–15ft long on a wheelbase of 9ft or less and

Above: The sheer numbers of ordinary merchandise and mineral (coal) wagons in service well into the 1950s almost defies belief; the numbers were in the hundreds of thousands. This veritable sea of mixed wooden and steel mineral wagons was awaiting loading at Calverton Colliery in June, 1955. There were about the same number of loaded wagons awaiting despatch. It would take a little while to model this lot! Author's collection

Opposite: *The bedrock of railway operation: common-carrier goods. Here is the main means of conveyance that kept the lifeblood of British commerce circulating for well over a century – the traditional loose-coupled 'mixed goods', trundling along at a heady 25mph. This highly typical example is passing Bushey water troughs on the West Coast Main Line behind LMS 4F No. 4445; the single lamp over the right-side buffer indicates the lowest class of ordinary goods train.*

There are a couple of things to notice about this train. First, although No. 4445 is in well-worn post-1928 livery, the first two wagons are still in LNWR colours – at least a decade after the Grouping. More significantly, the distinctive Southern Railway ventilated van is the only *van in this 20-wagon train; leaving aside the LNWR one-plankers and the pair of tank wagons, every other vehicle is a sheeted five-plank open merchandise wagon – by far the predominant type of general-purpose freight vehicle. Strange, then, how hard it is to buy a model of one!* Author's collection carrying no more than 10 tons. A century later, these average dimensions had only grown to 17ft 6in long on a 10ft wheelbase, with a maximum load of 16 tons.

Wagon evolution

As well as not growing much in size, the British 4-wheeled goods wagon changed equally little in substance over some 120 years. A traditional wagon consisted of two main assemblies, the chassis or underframe and the body. Initially, from the dawn of railways until about 1925 or so, both were made substantially of wood, with a limited amount of ironwork in the running gear and to hold the body together. In the later 1880s, a few railways (notably the GWR) did experiment with all-metal wagons using riveted sheet-iron bodies on iron and steel underframes. These early iron wagons usually had a heavier unladen weight and hence smaller payload than equivalent wooden wagons while being only marginally more robust and somewhat less easy to repair. Nevertheless, the GWR persisted and by 1900 had many hundreds of 'Iron Mink' vans and Diagram 04 iron open wagons.

Below: A typical short-wheelbase, early private-owner mineral wagon of the later 1860s, with spring buffers at the near end and solid dumb buffers at the other. The brake operates on two wheels on one side, with a single lever only. Wheels are built-up split or open-spoke – notice the example leaning against the wall behind the wagon. Axleboxes are grease-lubricated and the load is 8 tons, for a wagon tare weight of 5 tons 14 cwt; not very efficient! Author's collection

The earliest wooden railway wagons were very crude indeed. They had a simple perimeter frame of timber baulks and rudimentary running gear suited only to modest loads and low speeds – cast-iron axleboxes using heavy grease (tallow) for lubrication, supported on simple leaf springs and located by 'W-irons' fabricated from wrought-iron strip by a blacksmith. Wheels had eight spokes and were built-up, usually using wrought-iron 'split' spokes riveted to iron hubs and rims, with a forged tyre shrunk on. Brakes were minimal – a single wooden block applied directly by a lengthy lever. This was soon found to be inadequate; all too often, the brake was on the 'wrong' side when needed, so the arrangement was simply doubled, with a block and lever on each side. Couplings, of course, were hook-and-chain or chain-and-shackle, while buffers started out as solid wooden baulks (dumb-buffers) – often just the ends of the solebars extended a few inches beyond the wagon ends. It wasn't long before that arrangement gave way to the familiar cast-iron device sprung by a leaf spring set horizontally between the frames; these were intended to cut down the 'shunting shocks' which had led to many early wagons being literally knocked to pieces. Even so, many older mineral wagons ran to sprung buffers at one end only, making do with dumb-buffers at t'other.

Not a lot changed in wagonry over the railway's first half-century. The vehicles got a bit bigger, sprung buffers became universal and there was more reinforcing ironwork incorporated in the body. Wheels used built-up split-spoke or one-piece cast iron 'open-spoke' centres with *steel* tyres and the brakes got better, a *lot* better (although still far from good!). From the early 'single wood block a side' the first move was to a pair of blocks or cast-iron shoes on one side only, but now applied by shorter levers acting through cranks and push-rods that magnified the braking force (single side brakes). The next step was either to add a second actuating lever on the non-braked side – to give a twin-shoe 'either side' brake – or to simply double

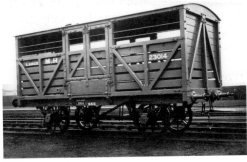

Above: A private owner coal wagon to the first RCH design, built by one of the largest of the independent constructors, the Gloucester Railway Carriage & Wagon Company. In 1893, this was the state of the PO coal wagon art: 16ft long 10-ton on a 9ft wheelbase underframe, all-steel in this case, with sprung buffers all round, but brakes and lever on one side only. Wheels are still of the split-spoke pattern and the axleboxes remain of the grease type. Author's collection

Above: Typical of traditional wagon construction towards the end of the pre-Grouping era is this Midland Railway large cattle van. The design dated back as far as 1875, and even by 1914, when this example was built, it was still basically an all-wooden vehicle, albeit a big one – with a wheelbase of 11ft, oil axleboxes, eight-spoke cast-steel wheels, long-travel buffers and screw couplings. Brakes are still single-sided though. Wagons like this lasted in service until the early BR era. Author's collection

the single-side arrangement, resulting in four-shoe independent brakes. Both these systems meant that leaning on a lever only got you two brake shoes acting, so the final development was to link the independent brakes by a cross-shaft and cam system (Morton Cam brakes) which would apply all four shoes no matter which lever was used.

With the increasing facility in rolling and fabricating steel sections that had evolved by the early 1890s, wooden wagon underframing gradually began to give way to steel, which became quite widespread on all classes of wagon by World War I. Over the same period, a fundamental change in the running gear of wagons saw the old grease-lubricated axlebox replaced by the far more free-running oil-box, with much more accurate bearings supporting turned steel axles. These carried steel-tyred wheels with cast-iron solid-spoked centres; for heavier duties, the spoke count went up from eight to ten or even twelve. The minimum brake requirement was also upgraded, to twin-shoe 'either side' for mineral wagons and to four-shoe Morton for most new common-user stock.

The combination of steel underframe, oil boxes, cast-centred and steel-tyred wheels and Morton brakes resulted in far more robust wagons capable of carrying heavier loads at higher speeds. Bodies, while still basically built of wood, now incorporated a great deal more ironwork for greater strength and easier repair. The strength of the steel wagon underframe encouraged some railways, such as the L&Y, to develop larger, high-capacity wagons, but these inevitably fell foul of the limited capacity of existing handling facilities and consequently were always somewhat restricted in use; they never became common-user types. Also during this period, the first 'express' goods stock (as opposed to NPCS) was developed, with vacuum brakes and screw couplings being fitted to steel-underframe stock rated to run at a dizzy 40mph or so.

The Grouping era

Post-Grouping wagon development saw the steel chassis widely, but not universally, adopted; some private owner (PO) wagon builders, along with the LMS and LNER, stuck

Above: This is a 4mm scale model of one of the LNER's traditional all-wooden ventilated 12-ton vans, which were being built up to the late 1920s. The model – which is itself at least 25 years old – is from an early Ian Kirk plastic kit and is a little battered! The felt-covered roof was modelled using a single layer of toilet tissue stuck to the plastic moulding.

Below: A pair of LMS ventilated vans modelled in 4mm scale, showing the transition from wooden to steel-frame construction that took place after 1929. The nearest van is to the design that was widely adopted on the LMS, LNER and BR, with corrugated steel ends incorporating integral corner plates and wooden sides braced with steel-channel stanchions. This one, built from a Ratio plastic kit, has a 10ft wheelbase steel underframe with either-side brakes and three-hole disc wheels – but I could fill a page with pictures of variants of this van!

The other van is to an earlier all-wood design, with a 9ft wheelbase and single-side brakes; the model was scratchbuilt from Plastikard.

with wooden underframes for some basic wagon types until the 1930s. More and more steel was, however, being incorporated into body structures, with steel corner plates and strappings replacing iron, increasing use being made of rolled-steel channel and T-sections for reinforcing the woodwork and, ultimately, complete van ends of corrugated pressed-steel, introduced by the LMS in 1926. The result was vehicles that essentially had bodies entirely *framed* in steel, the woodwork being confined to floors, roofs and cladding. Here, too, there was change, with sheet plywood being introduced as a material in place of individual planks. The LMS also experimented with some all-steel ventilated vans in 1929–30, but these were apparently somewhat prone to internal condensation, which often did their payload no good at all!

The traditional eight-spoked wagon wheel was joined in the 1920s by disc wheels with cast steel centres, initially solid but soon in the familiar 'three-hole' form. The holes allowed the wheelsets to be craned on hooks or slings and also permitted 'spragging' – passing a special hook and chain through the wheelset and securing it to render a wagon completely immobile. At the same time as these new disc wheels appeared, better vacuum braking systems for wagons were being introduced. The original installations had simply added a brake cylinder and crank to the cross-shaft of ordinary hand-operated Morton gear, which resulted in a lot of brake force going through two pairs of opposed brake shoes. The result was a high rate of shoe wear, while the unbalanced action tended to try to spread the wagon wheelbase, calling for tiebars between the axleboxes. The new 'balanced' gears had eight shoes, two per wheel, arranged on the clasp principle so that the forces were balanced about each axle, hence avoiding any undue strain on the wagon structure.

The age of steel

The composite and all-steel vans were followed, in the early-1930s, by mass-produced all-steel mineral wagons. These were initially produced as a long wheelbase large-capacity

(20 ton) PO design by the Butterley Iron Company – vehicles not dissimilar to the fabricated sheet-iron bodied vehicles the GWR had been using for its own loco coal traffic since about 1905. The Butterley design, however, was produced using steel pressings – lighter, stronger and cheaper than fabricating from sheet and angle-iron. Butterley and the Metropolitan Carriage & Wagon Co. went on to develop a production all-steel mineral wagon conforming to standard RCH (Railway Clearing House) dimensions – at which point the LNER and LMS sat up and took notice; these new steel wagons had a 30 per cent greater payload (16 tons) than the traditional wooden equivalents in a vehicle no bigger and no heavier in tare weight – but considerably more robust and cheaper to maintain. Both these railways soon produced their own all-steel mineral wagon designs using either riveted or welded construction, and the LNER went on, post-war, to develop an all-steel general-purpose open wagon.

The MoD adopted the steel mineral wagon as a standard type during the Second World War – a period which also saw great advances in mass-production welding techniques. No surprise, then, that when BR embarked on a massive post-war wagon-building programme to replace worn-out pre-Grouping and ex-PO vehicles, a version of the LMS/MoD all-welded 16-ton design found favour as the new standard mineral wagon. These were built by the tens of thousands, mostly unfitted and on a traditionally short (9ft) wheelbase, with or without bottom doors.

Alongside the conventional mineral wagons – which normally had side and end doors but only sometimes bottom 'drop' doors – there had evolved an alternative, larger capacity vehicle that had its origins in the North Eastern Railway's policy of carrying coal traffic in its own wagons rather than relying on private owners. This standard NER coal wagon was a massively built wooden *hopper* – that is, a vehicle having solid sides and ends and discharging through bottom doors *only*; these were derived from the slope-sided chauldron wagons found on the early waggon-

Above: The 'P' prefix to the number gives this one away; it is one of the 1930s-era private-owner (PO) large-capacity, riveted-construction steel mineral wagons built by Butterley Iron or Metropolitan Carriage & Wagon Co. and based on the GWR loco coal wagon design; 21 tons of payload for a tare of 9 tons 4cwt is a bit more like it. Author's collection

ways of the North East, which used the same principle. Such a system requires elevated coal drops or staithes for unloading, both features of the NER infrastructure from the outset. 'Hops with drops' was a very efficient method of handling coal in bulk but only a few other railways adopted it, most notably the LYR. However, it did form the basis of the large-scale coal export facilities built by the LNER at Immingham docks.

In spite of this investment the LNER – always rather conservative in wagon matters – was slow to realise that by using an all-steel construction the massive NER design of wooden hopper could be made cheaper, lighter and stronger. The GWR had produced iron hopper wagons for loco coal use as long ago as 1893, while the LMS had adopted all-steel construction for some high-capacity coke hoppers built in 1930; but it was not until 1936 that there appeared the first LNER 20-ton capacity all-steel hopper coal wagon. However, the result was a very successful design, perpetuated almost unaltered by BR in 21- and 24-ton versions and built to the tune of many thousands of vehicles, which proved compatible with a whole range of mechanical bulk coal handling facilities introduced after

Above: The most basic wagon type in the fleet was the no-frills version of the common open merchandise wagon. This is a late GWR-built 13 ton 5½ -plank vehicle on a 9ft wheelbase underframe with single-side brakes, although with two levers for either-side operation and is almost certainly a Second World War vehicle to 'utility' specification. The replacement of the two lower planks on each end by steel channel pressings are the only signs of modernisation. Rather a primitive vehicle to find still running in 1962, when this official BR photograph was taken! Author's collection

Below: The new era in wagonry on Britain's railways: 45-ton payload air-braked roller-bearing bogie palet vans, owned by a leasing company and in dedicated service for one traffic: artificial fertiliser. The whole side of the wagon opens up as four sets of wide doors to permit rapid and easy loading by forklift and the massive braced ends ensure the load doesn't shift. Screw couplings and Oleo hydraulically-damped buffers ensure smooth operation at a line speed of 75mph. Author's collection

the war. While sticking to conventional mineral wagons for coal traffic, the LMS did go on to build all-steel iron ore, lime, ballast and covered grain hoppers. The GWR also had a steel-covered grain hopper, the V25 'Grano' introduced in 1935, and various designs of stone and ballast hoppers. The BR 21-ton steel hoppers were adapted for stone, ore and grain traffics, and remained in service until replaced by the new, all-welded air-braked BR 'HAA' hopper design in 1964. Thus, the type effectively saw out bulk and common-carrier mineral working on Britain's railways.

Most other BR 'standard' wagon types similarly perpetuated or slightly developed existing Grouping designs. The Western Region carried on building GWR wagons, including the characteristic (some would say anachronistic) single-ended 'Toad' brake vans. Although the LNER 20-ton long-wheelbase/short body double-veranda brake van was officially adopted as the new BR standard design, such large numbers of the GW type and the LMS-design 'long-body' 20-ton Stanier van were built as to call into question the notion of any 'standard' design! Ashford works ignored all these options and just quietly went on building their own Southern 25-ton variation on the short-body/long-chassis theme. BR 'standardisation' was a bit like that! Other Grouping wagon designs perpetuated in quantity included the LMS and LNER vans, the LNER all-steel opens and the highly characteristic elliptical-roof SR van, a design that actually originated on the SECR. However, under BR most of these vans came with all-steel ends, ply siding and, of course, a much higher proportion had the vacuum brake, usually one of several variants of the balanced eight-shoe clasp gear.

Modern goods stock

With the post-Beeching rationalisation of the railways and the rapid growth of heavy road haulage in the later 1960s, the need for freight rolling stock declined dramatically. With the abolition of the railway's common carrier obligations in the early 1970s, the justification for the existence of a large part of the wagon fleet vanished practically overnight. The remaining freight emphasis shifted to high-speed scheduled services and bulk capacity, with block loads carried in new bogie or long-wheelbase, air-braked stock. There ensued a terrible cull of the traditional SWB 4-wheelers, ruthlessly scrapped in their thousands in very short order – a process hastened by the discovery that the new and far more rigid continuous-welded track then coming into use did not suit them at all; some wagons could oscillate to the point of derailment at quite modest speeds!

By the early 1980s, the traditional British 'short' wagon was all but extinct, as was the brake van that had until then brought up the rear of every goods train. Such general merchandise traffic as remained was carried in a modest fleet of new air-braked vehicles, first introduced in 1970 and consisting of just three basic types: 'OAA' et seq. open merchandise wagons, 'SAA' steel-carrying (flat) wagons and 'VAA' all-steel vans. All were designed for 75mph running, while the brake van gave way to a 'FRED' (flashing rear end device). There are many minor variations on these basic wagon types, denoted by the second and third letters of the TOPS code – often denoting differing door arrangements, loading or cargo-securing systems. These wagons are all built on a long-wheelbase air-braked underframe based on a design first introduced for ferry-born Continental traffic in 1959 and thus conforming to the Europe-wide UIC regulations. These underframes are of welded-steel construction on a wheelbase of 6.325m (20ft 9in) with an overall length of 11.25m (36ft 11in) over the buffers, which are of the Oleo shock-absorbing hydraulic variety. Other refinements on these new-generation underframes include two-stage damped suspension, disc brakes and roller bearings. Couplings, however, are still traditional screw-link.

Surviving coal traffic – mostly for power stations or heavy industry – is carried in the welded-steel mineral hoppers already mentioned. These were first introduced in 1964, most of them being the variant fitted for use with 'Merry Go Round' automatic continuous discharge systems and classified

Above: The modern mineral wagon: a block MGR coal train made up of TOPS code HAA self-discharging 30-ton hoppers loaded with pulverised fuel for power stations. The Class 58 diesel is fitted with a special 'creep' control to allow it to run steadily through the unloading facility at the discharge speed of a quarter of a mile per hour. It's going a bit faster than that here! A. O. Wynn

'HEA'. There is also a non-MGR version, 'HBA', and a 'covhop' roofed version for non-coal traffics like grains or pelletised materials – the 'CBA'. All of these hopper wagons use a welded underframe with a wheelbase of 18ft 6in (5.66m) and are 30ft (8.6m) long over the buffers. Running gear is as for the other air-braked vehicles.

Other mineral traffics – iron ore, lime, chemicals, china-clay, fly-ash and stone for the construction industry – are carried in a variety of specialised wagon types that are very much 'restricted use', being purpose-designed, privately owned or leased and dedicated to specific workings. The same regime of 'private trains' made up of specialised and dedicated vehicles now applies to most other regular rail-born freight – oil, gas and liquid chemicals in bulk, palletised goods, steel coil, motor vehicle parts in stillages and finished motor vehicles. Many of these vehicles run as permanently coupled block trains, with normal link-and-hook couplers on the outer wagons of the blocks only; internally, they are coupled by permanent drawbars or by a variety of auto couplers.

The actual ownership and working of these wagons on the modern railway is a business of labyrinthine complexity, with a maze of leasing arrangements, operating companies, forwarding companies, contractors and sub-contractors. The haulage arrangements are equally baffling, with various rail-freight operators providing motive power decked out in a range of liveries. These essentially-financial arrangements constitute a topic too involved (and probably just a tad too dry) for inclusion in these pages. The fact that I find the whole business totally baffling and monumentally boring has only a minor bearing on the omission!

The only other widespread 'general traffic' vehicles on the modern railway are the various types of container wagon, usually run as fast (75mph schedules) fixed-formation 'liner trains' strictly dedicated to carrying merchandise packed in standard ISO shipping containers. These specialised wagons are low-loading, air-braked and mostly bogie vehicles, designed to run in permanently coupled blocks between the major ports and 'intermodal' yards having the necessary container-handling equipment. Although very much a general traffic vehicle in

Below: Despite appearances, this isn't a PO wagon; rather, it's a restricted-use GWR wagon in dedicated service for Foster Yeoman's Mendip stone traffic – a common arrangement today. The wagon is pure 'modern' GWR, having an all-steel underframe with 'OK' oil boxes, Dean-Churchward brake gear with blocks on all wheels (and an axlebox tie-rod for good measure), 'Instanter' tight-link couplings, and GWR heavy-duty self-contained buffers. It is preserved by the GWS at Didcot.

terms of lading (there being an ISO container for just about every commodity imaginable), in terms of working these are very much 'restricted use' wagons, never straying from their proscribed routes.

Wagons – common-user or restricted?

Distinction is drawn above between general traffic wagons and those in restricted use, but what do these terms actually mean? Well, in 1845 the 'principal railway companies' of the day established the Railway Clearing House (RCH), an organisation set up to deal with matters of revenue apportionment and to institute common working arrangements between them. Once the RCH was in place to look after the administration, the bulk of the wagons in the general traffic fleets of the various main line railways – the open merchandise wagons, ordinary covered vans, low-sided, bolster and flat wagons – were placed in 'common' use. That is, they could run over any railway in the entire national network and would be worked through laden to their final destination, wherever that might be. (The exception being, of course, where there was a 'break of gauge' between Brunel's GWR and everybody else – the ultimate Achilles' heel of the broad gauge).

Having arrived at a destination and been unloaded, a common use wagon could then promptly be reloaded and sent to any other destination on any other railway as the needs of the traffic dictated. So, such a wagon might run for months without ever turning a wheel on the metals of the company that actually owned it; only if it developed a defect was it likely to get sent home sharpish! This meant that a common-user wagon belonging to any pre-Grouping company could be seen anywhere in the country. A 1923 photograph of the goods yard at Horrabridge in Devon, on the GWR Plymouth–Tavistock line, shows wagons of the Furness and Great North of Scotland railways, while the well-known H. C. Casserley pictures of Inverness taken at much the same date reveal the Highland capital as host to stock from the LBSCR, SECR, GER, GWR and even PD&SWJR!

This feckless mélange rather calls into question a classic model railway cliché: all those many model GWR layouts populated exclusively by dark grey wagons with 'GW' writ large upon their planking. Adherents of other lines seem a little less inclined to restrict themselves in this way – possibly because there isn't as good a selection of RTR and kit wagons for their chosen railway! This lack is a blessing, for to reflect the real situation probably no more than 50 per cent of the wagons at any given location on *any* railway should be 'home road', and quite a lot of those will be 'non-common-user' stock, of which the GWR – as it happens – was particularly fond. Non-common-use wagons were distinguished by an 'N' marking at the lower corners of each side – which meant that while they could still work through to destinations on other railways, once unloaded they had to be returned empty to the owning railway at the first opportunity, and to the nearest point of junction. This operating inconvenience meant that 'N' wagons spent most of the time on their home metals, as was the intention; it was basically a device to prevent other railways from playing fast-and-loose with your best rolling stock.

As well as 'non-common' stock, there were also a goodly number of vehicles that were dedicated to a particular traffic as 'restricted user' wagons. Examples would be the specially cleaned open wagons used for sand traffic to glassworks, wagons used to convey only a particular mineral such as china-clay, soda ash or limestone, and such dedicated vehicles as milk tankers or beer vans. 'RU' wagons carried special branding delineating the traffic and services for which they were reserved and would not be found away from their proscribed orbit. An exclusive sub-class within the restricted user category were special traffic types – vehicles designed and reserved for a very specific lading or mode of operation. A classic contemporary example of such a vehicle would be a nuclear flask wagon – very highly specialised, requiring dedicated handling facilities and totally unsuited to anything other than its designed purpose. Unsurprisingly, you're highly unlikely to find one of these babies parked casually in the goods yard at Nether-Wallop-in-the-Wolds! The same is true of such exotic one-offs as giant multi-axle transformer trollies or crucible wagons built to carry molten steel.

Internal use wagons

This 'never seen here' caveat is fortunately not applicable to many of the oddball wagon types found in a last, large and very mixed group of 'restricted' stock – the vehicles used by the railways for their own internal engineering or operational purposes. This eclectic assemblage included the large fleet of the Permanent Way Department, which embraced spoil and ballast wagons, ballast hoppers, sleeper wagons, rail wagons, diverse crane trucks, tool vans, mess vans, ballast plough brake vans, and – more

Below: Very much a restricted-use vehicle for abnormally massive loads, this Midland Railway heavy well-wagon is a type that was very rarely seen out and about. The same was true of virtually all 'special traffic' vehicles, much to the chagrin of modellers with a taste for the offbeat! Author's collection

recently – the various powered gadgets upon which PW maintenance has increasingly come to depend. Alongside and often mixed in with the PW fleet were the various flat and open wagons, supply and tool vans and cranes used by the building maintenance, engineering or signal-and-telegraph departments.

The steam-era motive power department also needed wagons – loco coal wagons, special wagons for the conveyance of dry loco sand, lubricating oil and stores of all kinds from cotton waste to complete locomotive boilers. There were also chemical wagons and sludge tenders run in connection with the operation of water softening plant. Even the breakdown train and things like snowploughs and mess vans were technically 'internal user freight stock'. The general operating department of yore also had its own requirements: pressurised gas tank wagons to supply gas for carriage lighting, tank wagons or old tenders for the conveyance of fresh water to places without a suitable supply, fodder wagons to keep the shunting and dray horses

Below: An example of the last common type of RCH 16ft 6in wooden mineral wagon with 9ft wheelbase, the 12-ton seven-plank design that appeared in the early years of the 20th century. This scrofulous specimen represents the dilapidated state most ex-PO wagons ran in after Nationalisation, when they were being phased out rapidly in favour of the new 16-ton steel mineral wagons. This 4mm scale model is a much-abused pre-painted-side Cambrian plastic kit.

fed, supply vans to keep stations and goods depots stocked with all manner of supplies and sundries (including, of course, tickets, waybills, a multitude of forms and a panoply of other stationery), fire engine trucks, weed-killing vehicles, and scale test vans.

Private owner wagons

These are vehicles owned by those whose traffic they carried rather than by the railway doing the carrying. They can be conveniently divided into several classes, dependent on purpose, with a clear distinction drawn between the numberless hoards of coal wagons and the much thinner ranks of those intended for other traffics. It was the coal wagons that set the trend as, from very early on in the evolution of railways, it became apparent that it was never going to be possible for the railway companies themselves to roster enough wagons to carry all the mineral traffic offering. It wasn't long before the coalmasters, in particular, became exasperated with waiting for the railways to provide the wagons needed for their trade, and resolved to do so themselves. Thus, in the later 1840s, the first private owner wagons came into use. The principle is very much alive today, where the vast majority of freight stock is non-railway owned.

All PO wagons, although owned by non-railway enterprises – soon ranging from the largest collieries and mineral extractors to industries of all kinds, small coal merchants and even private individuals – had to be registered with a 'host' railway which, of course, charged for the privilege. These registration details were carried on a cast-iron plate fixed to the wagon underframe, rather like the tax disc on a car. Full details of ownership were required to be included in the signwriting of the wagon, as were instructions as to where and by whom the wagon was to be repaired. The registration, regulation and administration of the PO wagon fleet was entrusted to the Railway Clearing House – also the obvious body to look after the business of charging the new private owners for the services of the various railway companies involved in moving their wagons.

The advent of the PO wagon gave new impetus to that branch of the railway industry specialising in rolling stock construction. Firms like Birmingham Railway Carriage & Wagon, which was already contracting with the main railway companies, embraced the private owner wagon business with open arms, while the new trade gave rise to a host of enterprises that soon came to range from giants like Gloucester, Hurst Nelson, R. Y. Pickering and Charles Roberts – firms turning out many thousands of vehicles a year – through substantial outfits like Midland Carriage & Wagon, Lincoln Wagon & Engine, Proctors, Derby Carriage & Wagon and The Butterley Co. building wagons by the several hundred, to small local enterprises constructing a mere handful of wagons in a twelvemonth and existing largely on repair work.

Before long, these non-railway-owned fleets had proliferated to the point where most of the nation's mineral traffic moved in such vehicles. Many of the pre-Grouping railways didn't even number many (if any) common-user mineral wagons in their inventories, the main exceptions being the CR and NBR in Scotland, the NER – which built a vast fleet of hopper coal wagons geared to its Tyneside staithe system – and the L&Y, which moved much coal in large-capacity double-end-door wagons for export via end-tipplers at Goole Docks in England. The private-owner wooden open mineral wagon soon became the most widespread and numerous type of vehicle seen on our railways prior to nationalisation.

The RCH wagon

Originally, most PO coal wagons followed the prevailing practice of the wagons used internally in the collieries. They thus differed considerably in size, loading and discharge arrangements, method of construction, robustness, bearings, braking and buffer arrangements. Many of these early PO wagons were very small, running on wheelbases of 6ft or less, and had the crude 'blacksmith's'

running-gear already described. Coal trains could thus only be run at a speed suited to these somewhat homespun vehicles – that is, very slowly indeed!

Unsurprisingly, the railway companies soon began to insist on a far better standard for privately owned wagons, so that they could at least be run at the same speed as the 'ordinary' goods traffic rather than providing mobile bottlenecks. These requirements were soon being enforced through the RCH, which eventually reached the stage of issuing a set of standard wagon sizes, payloads and specifications and developing a range of standard components – most notably axleboxes, brakes and buffers, which became more-or-less a required fit. In fact, many of these RCH designs and components – which were updated periodically and thus represented the 'best practice' of the time – were so successful that they were adopted not just by the various PO wagon builders, but also by the main line railways for their own stock. An RCH PO wagon – the vast majority after about 1890 – was thus one conforming to RCH specifications.

Below: A typical turn-of-the-century private-owner coal wagon. This is to the Railway Clearing House design, a 16ft 6in wagon on a 9ft wheelbase to carry 10 tons. This example has wooden solebars, grease axleboxes, eight-spoke wheels and either-side brakes. The 4mm scale/00 model was built by Andrew Duncan from a Slater's pre-painted-and-lettered plastic kit.

Above: Long a favourite among modellers, the charismatic six-wheel milk tankers operated from the mid-1930s onwards by the big dairy combines were something of an oddity, in that the two major components of the vehicle often had different owners! The dairies owned the special tanks – stainless steel (as here) or glass-lined – but the underframes were provided by the railway companies and numbered in their wagon fleets. This one is a Southern Railway example, now preserved at Didcot. Gorgeous!

Non-mineral PO wagons

Leaving aside the mineral wagons, most other types of private-owner wagon were intended for specific traffic and were often highly specialised vehicles in their own right. In many instances the railway companies themselves did not number suitable vehicles for the traffic in their own stock. Examples of specialised PO types include roofed-in open wagons for minerals – like unslaked lime, some ores, foundry sand and salt – that must be kept dry; small-but-strong wagons for extra-dense traffics like lead ore or pig iron; large-volume wagons for high-bulk, low-density traffics such as empty casks, loose fodder or loose-baled wool; special hopper vans for malting barley, and insulated or refrigerated vehicles for passenger-rated perishables traffics. There were also special PO wagons for the conveyancing of 'awkward' commodities such as rolls of linoleum, acid in carboys and gas tar.

The entire British railway tank-wagon fleet has always been privately owned, for obvious reasons. Tank wagons are almost invariably devoted to the carriage of a particular product and cannot be used for any other; petrol and milk would hardly be considered happy bedfellows, while the consequences of mixing the wrong chemicals within the confines of a wagon tank could easily be on the exciting side of imprudent! Tank wagons were anyway very variable beasts – steam-heated for heavy oils, glass-lined for milk or corrosive-liquid traffic, insulated or jacketed for temperature-sensitive cargos, fitted with differing loading systems and varying in volume with the density of the liquid being conveyed.

Other PO vehicles were those belonging to contractors working for the railway. The various civil engineering concerns engaged on railway construction (who would often also undertake comparable non-railway contracts like dam construction) had their own extensive wagon fleets, which were worked as needed on the normal rail network. The same was certainly true of the special weed-killing trains of the Chipman Chemical Co., used to spray the trackbed with a noxious brew that would probably have felled a rain forest.

A last type of highly specialised PO vehicle which could turn up literally anywhere was a weighing-machine regulating van of Pooley & Co., Birmingham; these were worked around the entire network at regular intervals, visiting any and every railway installation having any weighing machines – from a parcels scale to a track weighbridge – which determined the levy of carriage charges. Such scales and balances had to be periodically checked and certificated under the Weights and Measures Act by an approved contractor; Pooley's had most of the railway contracts for this work.

Private owner wagon working

The working of PO wagons over the railway network was both an important part of the railway's business and a very involved operation. As far as the railways were concerned, PO wagons were very much 'non common user' and many worked substantial mileages unloaded; pit-props aside, there wasn't much in the way of return traffic to the collieries. To save this uneconomic empty-wagon mileage, virtually the entire fleet of colliery-owned mineral wagons was 'pooled' during the First World War, which meant that any wagon could turn up pretty much anywhere, no matter who owned it or where it was nominally registered. The usual exceptions to this common-user arrangement were wagons belonging to retail coal merchants, to industries operating their own coal supply arrangements, and even to private individuals. These wagons bore the markings 'non pool' to indicate their status.

To take the working of PO coal trucks first, these formed the single most numerous class of railway wagon on the British railway network – and that by a handsome margin. They were owned by three different types of enterprise: collieries, coal factors and merchants, and individual industries. The wagons were of the same type – it was the way they were used (and hence the way they appeared in trains) that was different. Colliery-owned wagons dominated the fleet and were employed by their owners to supply ex-pithead coal direct to customers or for export. Coal factors (wholesale dealers), on the other hand, used their wagons both to receive coal stock from their preferred collieries and to deliver to their customers, while retail coal merchants would send their own wagons for loading at collieries with which they had struck a bargain – often a different colliery every week, dependent on market fluctuations. The wagons would be returned, loaded, to the merchant's own depot. Some major coal users – larger industries and, in particular – gasworks – also ran wagon fleets to transport coal purchased at the pithead to their own point of consumption.

In terms of how these PO wagons were marshalled into trains, the real distinction lay between dedicated coal trains and general goods trains conveying coal traffic. A dedicated coal train ran from the pithead to either a single delivery destination – usually a coal port loading ships with coal for export or a bulk user like a steelworks – or to a major marshalling yard, such as Ferme Park on the GNR/LNER main line just north of London.

Above: A prototypical working using PO coal wagons features on Andrew Duncan's 00 gauge layout, which is firmly based on the GWR line from Yeovil to Weymouth. Here is the weekly 'Steamer Coal Train' rumbling past Maiden Newtown signalbox on its way to replenish the coal bunkers of the Channel Islands steam packet boats. This train was made up of around 40 'pooled' colliery-owned wagons behind a 28XX 2-8-0.

On the model, the 'Parkend' wagon, which is first in the rake behind an anonymous 28XX class loco (Hornby body, Comet chassis), is a Bachmann Branchline RTR vehicle, but most of the 30-odd vehicles in this train are built from plastic kits.

These coal trains were often long – 40–100 wagons – and made up of colliery-owned wagons in 'pool' service. Thus, such a coal train would often consist of long 'cuts' of wagons bearing the name of the same colliery; some of the colliery fleets were many thousands strong, and big names like 'Ocean', 'Denaby', 'Alloa' , 'Manvers Main' and 'Vauxhall' would figure in just about every coal train, often in blocks or cuts of several wagons. Occasionally, one comes across entire trains made up of wagons from a single owner, but these were rare and often specially-arranged for publicity purposes. The advent of pooling made for far more mixed train formations.

When the big coal trains had toiled into yards like Ferme Park, they were split up into individual vehicles or cuts of wagons bound for a single destination – railway motive power depots, coal distribution or stockholding yards, retail coal yards, gasworks or power plants, steam pumping stations, industries, bunkering depots for coal-fired steamships, or coal stockpiles. These wagons would usually be delivered to their final destinations by that railway maid-of-all-work, the pick-up goods train.

A model wagon fleet

As I hope has been gleaned from the foregoing, it is difficult to have too many wagons on a model railway, as endless variety and a constant change in the vehicles at hand was a principal characteristic of goods working. Indeed, when it came to common use types, the chance of the same wagon reappearing regularly at any given destination was almost nil. Here today,

Below: Even a very small layout like 'Cade's Green', which has siding capacity for just 24 wagons, can call for a surprisingly large fleet to give adequate variety and to cover every traffic eventuality. I have over 60 vehicles which see regular use in working the branch goods traffic, of which a random selection can be seen here. All these models are either adapted RTR or plastic kit models, but whitemetal, etched-brass and resin kits also feature, as do a handful of scratchbuilt vehicles.

somewhere utterly else tomorrow, was more the theme. A bit of a problem on our model railways, where the available selection of wagons is inevitably far too modest and thus somewhat at odds with this requirement for constant turnover. Fortunately, with the more general wagon types, individual vehicles are not that readily identified unless you're into number-noting; so long as there's a reasonable stock from which to ring the changes, you can produce the right effect. Giving wagons different identities on each side can double the possibilities at no extra cost, always a sound wheeze! Another popular ploy is for groups of modellers to rotate their wagon fleets around each others' layouts, swapping batches of wagons on a regular basis – a sociable way of replicating the constant wanderings of the common-user wagon.

The only goods vehicles that can put in authentic reappearances at a fixed location are those not in common use or dedicated to a traffic or service originating and terminating on the actual layout. Leaving aside brake vans on branch lines, which were often permanently assigned on a restricted use base, the most common example of a wagon that would always come home to roost was a non-pool PO coal wagon owned by a local coal merchant, which would naturally return, pigeon-like, to

his premises. The other common scenario in which groups of wagons would either not stray or would keep returning to a given point centres around special traffic vehicles. Thus, the china clay wagons on my own 'Trerice' layout can realistically return regularly as the layout represents the point of origin of the special traffic and the wagons are dedicated types. Even so, in the context of even such a small layout I have over 40 such wagons to choose from!

So – what should an authentic steam-era model wagon fleet consist of? That may seem like a 'how long is a piece of string?' question – but actually, it can be answered quite concisely. Leaving aside coal wagons and any special traffic for a moment and just considering the goods working of a typically modest wayside or terminal station – the most popular modelling subjects – the answer runs along the lines of: more ordinary open merchandise wagons than you can shake a stick at, nowhere near as many covered vans as you would think, a mere smattering of livestock wagons, flats, tank wagons, double-bolsters and the like – and very few, if any, 'glamour' specials. To which, of course, must be added such mineral wagons as might be called for by the individual situation portrayed on the layout: a coal or lime wagon or two for a country goods yard, but a plentiful selection if you're modelling a colliery district or a branch serving a limeworks!

It is the predominance of that humble open merchandise wagon – even late on in railway history – that comes as the biggest surprise, but totting up the numbers suggests that throughout the heyday of the traditional railway there was a ratio of around four or five such opens for every van, while for every other, more specialised type the proportion was somewhere between 10 and 20 to 1. There were a *lot* of opens, second only to the basic mineral wagons in numbers and probably more omnipresent in the general railway scene. So, as realistic modellers, we need a good stock of such vehicles. But not, please, in identikit serried ranks, alike as peas in a pod; the joy of the common open is that

Above: The wagon type we all need plenty of – the common open merchandise wagon, workhorse of the railways from the 1830 to the 1980s. This is a relatively late example of the breed, an LNER all-steel vehicle of the late 1940s – quite a common sight on BR, as the nationalised railway adopted the design. The round dimples on the side puzzle many folk; they house lashing points on the inside of the wagon body. The (elderly) model uses a Hornby-Dublo SD6 body moulding on a home-made underframe; nowadays, you can get a kit from Parkside-Dundas.

it exhibits such infinite variety. Not only are there a goodly gaggle of different designs – especially amid the ranks of the pre-Grouping wagons, but the adaptability and utility of the type gave rise to all sorts of lading.

By the onset of the Second World war, many of the smaller pre-Grouping open wagons, with their 8- or 10-ton payloads, short wheelbases, low, 2ft 6in/four-plank sides and basic running gear, had been replaced by new 12-ton vehicles with a 9ft or 10ft wheelbase, oil axleboxes and four-shoe Morton brake gear. These had bodies 17ft 6in long by 8ft wide, with sides 3ft 3in high made up of five or six planks; they were referred to as 'high sided' opens, to distinguish them from older low-sided types. (But, of course, they weren't as 'high-sided' as a seven-plank mineral wagon, with which some folk – misled by the description – are apt to confuse them!) By the late 1930s, the design of these high-sided opens had settled down to the extent that the GWR, LMS and LNER were building all-but-identical vehicles, on 9ft or 10ft WB steel underframes with four-shoe Morton or, increasingly, vacuum brake gear. The bodies

Above: The essential Grouping five-planker, commonest of all non-mineral wagon types and built in huge numbers to this basic RCH/ GW design by the GWR, LMS, LNER and BR. This truly excellent 4mm scale RTR model was an early introduction from Airfix, perpetuated (as here) by Dapol, but – so far as I can discover – unaccountably absent from any current list. Bring it back – we need it!

Fortunately, Ratio offers a good plastic kit for the GWR variant and Parkside do the RCH five-plank mineral wagon which is essentially the same animal in slightly beefier form.

were steel-framed with five-plank sides and had a distinctive door design with the bottom plank angled outwards to offset the hinges, so that the door dropped to the vertical well clear of the wagon running gear. BR continued to build wagons to this same basic design in huge numbers well into the 1950s, so for any layout set in the post-1930 era they are an absolute 'must have' – the 'essential five-planker'.

After opens, vans are the next widest field for modelling endeavour. Again, there's plenty of variety both in basic design and in detailing, with a lot of the more modern vehicles being vacuum-fitted. Vans come in a lot of sub-categories or in variants adapted for particular classes of traffic: basic unventilated vehicles for non-perishables, or ventilated in various manners and degrees for carrying foodstuffs, possibly also insulated or ice-block refrigerated. Van bodies can be timber or steel framed, with vertically or horizontally planked or sheet-ply sides; they can sport plain old 'cupboard' doors, sliding doors, ramped doors, end doors or roof doors. Variations on the same basic

Above: Here's another Dapol five-planker, loaded and sheeted and ready to roll. Note the method of roping the sheet. This one has been converted to the fitted version with Morton AVB with a tiebar between the axleboxes.

design might be dedicated to the carriage of beer, gunpowder or motor-cars, fitted out for the carriage of bananas (steam-heated), fitted with reinforced bodies or shock-absorbing underframes. A few might sport private-owner liveries for contract delivery services, while some of the more specialised variants might be dedicated to a particular traffic or service: vehicles used for fish, for instance, were rarely common-user! But the vast majority of vans were in general traffic and thus widely travelled.

Below: The bread-and-butter 12T ventilated van, another numerous and basic wagon type. These two – LMS to the left, SR on the right – are in N, basically Peco RTR vehicles but with a few touches from Steve Earl. The tarpaulin covering a leaky roof was a not-uncommon sight, while the SR van has replacement metal buffers. Both are on 10ft wheelbase steel underframes. Lack of underframe variety creates a bit of a challenge to wagon modellers in N.

Although van design never converged quite to the point that the five-plank open did, the exigencies of World War II led to certain types being selected for propagation in very large numbers, most notably the LMS steel-ended vans and the distinctive SR elliptical-roof design. These wartime vans spawned all sorts of odd variants, from utility underframes with twin-shoe either-side brakes and a 9ft WB to ply sides or even vans using odd-sized or unpainted planks. BR continued to build the basic van designs of the 'Big Four', but again with endless minor variations – so there's lots of scope for rewarding reworking of the various van types available in RTR and kit form. This is particularly true of the underframes, where the same basic body design might be found sitting on anything from a SWB utility chassis with spoked wheels, three-link couplings and leaf-sprung buffers, and boasting nothing grander by way of braking than the minimal twin-shoe either-side set-up, to the latest LWB 'express goods' job fitted with plate axleguards, link-suspended extra-long multi-leaf springs, roller bearings, hydraulic Oleo buffers, screw couplings, through piping for steam heat and state-of-the-art BR twin-cylinder eight-shoe balanced vacuum brakes.

Cattle wagons (also used for the transport of other farm stock like sheep or pigs but rarely for horses) are a very separate sub-class of van, often larger and longer than ordinary goods vans and, of course, built with well-ventilated sides and well-drained floors and fitted out with ramped doors and movable partitions. As cattle were regarded as a 'perishable' traffic, many of these vans were vacuum-fitted for running in the faster goods trains. Most of the main railway companies had their own often-distinctive designs of cattle wagon, and in some locations (Irish Sea ports, for instance) they accumulated in quite considerable numbers. Cattle wagons in pre-BR days were generally 'non common user', so were worked back empty. Loaded cattle wagons were always marshalled at the front of a mixed goods train, to ease the task of 'watering' the beasts en route. In times of need, cattle vans (suitably disinfected!) could

Above: A contrast in 4mm scale plastic kit-built cattle wagons. The last word on the left is a 1950s vintage BR 8-ton vehicle, with a 10ft wheelbase vacuum-braked steel underframe, screw couplings and all mod cons. On the right is a 1920s-era LNER van – all wooden construction on a 9ft wheelbase (with a considerable overhang each end) and single-sided brakes, albeit with either-side levers. The BR wagon is the famous Airfix 'two-bob kit' version; the LNER van is from Parkside-Dundas.

be pressed into use for 'ventilated van' traffics such as farm produce or beer in kegs.

Low-sided and flat wagons were the other sizeable group and, like the vans, came in many variants according to use and origin. Low sided wagons were from one to three planks high and were often arranged so that the whole side (and sometimes the ends as well) dropped on hinges to facilitate easy loading. Typical ladings included dense materials like pig-iron or some heavy ores, castings, items of machinery, large crates and packing-cases, vehicles and implements and – from the late 1920s on – containers of various sorts. Flat wagons have no sides per se (although usually a perimeter framing of some sort), but may have provision for upright iron 'side stakes' to restrain loads like loose unsawn timber. The air-braked BR steel-carrying flat wagons were adapted in this way to carry pulpwood for the paper industry. A very numerous form of flat wagon was the express container flat, designed for use with the railway's own containers. These consist of little more than a vacuum-fitted steel underframe having a flat steel deck incorporating securing points for the container anchors – special chains with screw-tensioners, carried in an under-floor well at each side of the wagon when not in use.

Most common of the traditional flat wagons were those fitted with 'bolsters' – swivelling timber support beams, usually fitted with upright steel stakes at each end to restrain the load and mounted on the deck of the flat wagon, which then becomes a 'bolster wagon'. These came in different sizes, with the most common being the SWB single-bolster, always used in pairs – sometimes separated by a completely-flat 'runner' wagon, but often permanently coupled as a 'twin bolster set'. This wasn't to be confused with a double-bolster wagon – a longer wheelbase (14ft 6in or so) flat wagon with a bolster over each axle; larger still were bogie bolsters – vehicles some 40ft long carried on pairs of SWB plate or diamond-frame freight bogies and normally fitted with four bolsters; these were by far the most common form of bogie wagon seen on British railways. Normal loads for bolster wagons included timber as logs or baulks, steelwork or ironwork, large

Below: Not the most common of tank wagons, maybe, but certainly one of the nicest! Here is the six-wheeled milk tank in 4mm scale model form, courtesy of Lima – who made this very nice RTR version. Like all Lima models, it sat a tad high and had horrid wheels, so I've fitted scale (P4 in this instance) wheels and lowered the ride height. The only other modifications of note are the fine round-section tiebars in place of chunky plastic originals, and some new large-diameter heads (MJT turnings) for the original buffers.

pipes and a variety of fabricated items such as lattice girders. As unsawn timber – in the form of whole tree-trunks – was a common traffic at many rural stations, bolster wagons in any of their forms are quite at home on a country branch line.

By contrast with these common-use types, the rest of the traditional wagon stock came (relatively) in penny numbers. Implement wagons – most notable 'Lowmac' all-steel well wagons – have long been favourites with modellers, not just because the vehicles themselves are interesting and different, but also because of the nature of the loads they traditionally carried: traction engines and steamrollers, colourful horse-drawn pantechnicons, farm machines like threshing-boxes and reaper-binders, circus and fairground wagons, excavators, large items of fixed machinery as well as all manner of military vehicles and equipment. The other advantage of the implement wagon is that it's another specialised type that can realistically turn up almost anywhere – they were a regular feature of country goods yards, almost all of which offered the 'end-loading' dock or ramp needed to handle them.

Tank wagons, while quite numerous, were sociable beasts, tending to stick together in complete trains or at least as blocks of wagons in general freights, although individual vehicles, usually carrying paraffin, could figure in pick-up goods trains *en route* to a local oil dealer. Milk tanks also often ran singly or as small cuts, and were usually worked as 'tail traffic' on passenger trains rather than in ordinary freight trains. One other tank type that did turn up in the pick-up goods was the oil-gas tank wagon, examples of which were stationed at many branch line termini to refill the reservoirs of gas-lit coaching stock where this was still in use – another example of a 'special' that can pop up more-or-less anywhere. There was considerable variety in tank wagon design, not just as regards the tanks themselves but also with respect to the underframes, many of which were of wooden construction until surprisingly late; not being subject to the hurly-burly of general freight working and common use, tank wagons were often surprisingly long-lived. They are also colourful and characteristic additions to the wagon fleet that often offer a considerable modelling challenge.

While a lot of agricultural produce travelled in ordinary merchandise wagons of one sort or another, one commodity – grain – did give rise to a fleet of specialised wagons. While a certain amount of grain was shifted by the sackload in vans or sheeted opens, moving any quantity of the stuff called for a different approach, resulting in a variety of hopper-based designs. Initially, these were built in van form with either bottom or side discharge doors. The GWR and LNER started out sharing a common LWB side-door design, but while the LNER stuck with wooden hopper vans, moving to a bottom-discharge design, the GWR and the LMS switched to all-steel bottom-discharge hoppers with hatched roofs, a type perpetuated by BR as the 'covhop'.

The only other general class of vehicle that might reasonably figure in the average model railway inventory are 'well' and 'trolley' wagons. 'Weltrols' – all-steel wagons consisting of a pair of low-loading girders with an open well between them slung between bogies – have always been popular with model train-makers; Trix, Dublo and Tri-ang all offered the type, for all that it was far from common in reality. The same goes for such other large-but-scarce beasts as 'Flatrols' (similar to a 'Weltrol' but with a deck on the girders rather than an open well), 'Trestrols' (Flatrols with an inclined trestle to support loads like extra-large sheets of steel or glass within the loading gauge), 'Boplates' (bogie flat wagons with a trestle for carrying steel hull plates for ships) and various types of low-loading boiler wagons. Such offbeat types often make appealing models – but in reality these are vehicles that would only be seen on a main line goods while in transit or in an area of heavy industry.

Once you get into the area of the truly specialised vehicles, the numbers drop off the bottom of the scale and the chances of the likes of an LNER 'Protrol F' (ship's propeller wagon) or a 120-ton payload 'Flatrol AA' turning up in the sort of situation most of us can hope to model are just about nil, even if we had the space to run something that big! The same goes for smaller and less extreme 'specials' like the GW 'Coral A' plate-glass wagon – which for many a year seemed to figure on every 4mm scale GW branch line layout, simply because K's made an attractive kit for it! But in truth such things were rarer than a Heath Fritillary butterfly; the GWR only had 15 of them and they were normally kept tucked away at Swindon. As branch line goods-yard fare, it was well on the far side of 'extremely unlikely'. But then, the odd item of exotica forms an interesting diversion, while even on the most rigorously realistic of layouts Homer can nod occasionally …

Building a model wagon fleet

It has long been an oddity of the British model railway scene that the most common, and therefore most necessary (from the authenticity/operational viewpoints) items of freight rolling stock have either been completely ignored by the big RTR makers, or served by poor or inaccurate models. You wouldn't think it possible to go too far wrong in creating a 4mm scale model of something as basic as the ordinary British open mineral wagon, about as near to a box on wheels as railway rolling stock ever gets. However, it is only comparatively recently – since the introduction of Bachmann's Blue Riband range – that we've actually been able to buy an accurate 4mm-scale RTR version of either the 16-ton BR steel mineral or the 12-ton seven or eight-plank wooden wagon that preceded it. There have been plenty of bad eggs to choose from, mind – but nothing that wasn't either too long, too narrow, the wrong height, sporting an incorrect arrangement of doors and ironwork, sitting on an underframe of the wrong wheelbase or possessed of totally inappropriate running gear.

The story's as bad for that other workhorse of the steam-era railway, the common old open merchandise wagon. Never mind that there were half a million of the things rumbling around and that they would form the commonest type in any general goods train or at any goods depot – they have been universally ignored by the RTR makers. Even today, there's no authentic RTR model of even the most common design; the type is represented by a solitary lacklustre example, a very basic five-plank open with its origins in a Hornby Dublo model introduced in 1958! Vans are rather better served, but once you get down among the humble low-sided and flat wagons, the RTR picture's very sparse. Nobody, for instance, makes a single-bolster wagon – a fundamental type with 1,001 uses – although the far-less-common bogie-bolster has always featured. The only flat wagons truly well-served in all the scales are container wagons – although once you include the container these are more akin to vans! RTR tank wagons are equally scarce, the two cattle vans offered in 4mm scale are both inaccurate and dated models, the only steam-era grain wagon ditto, while the fecund family of implement wagons are represented by but a single type – the BR 'Lowmac'. Among the more specialised wagon types, however, there are some surprising *inclusions*. Bogie well wagons – 'Weltrols' – have always featured, and peak-roofed salt vans have an irresistible appeal – having featured in all ranges and scales from Hornby clockwork onwards! And what is it about bulk chlorine tankers and cement silo wagons that so excites RTR train-makers?

The only area of prototype wagonry which is universally well represented in the current RTR ranges is the post-1970 air-braked stock that dominates the current rail freight scene. Between them, Bachmann and Hornby in 4mm scale and Dapol, Graham Farish (Bachmann) and Peco in N can sell you just about everything you need to create the very model of a modern model railway. This is, I suppose, only to be expected, as it represents the sort of equipment that today's generation of railway enthusiasts (a breed far from dead and by no means all buried in nostalgia) will be familiar with. I suspect that the 'what gets seen is what gets sold' syndrome accounts for the

dearth of RTR steam-era freight stock; there's a whole generation out there who have never even clapped eyes on a traditional steam-era goods train. Most of today's enthusiasts have become familiar with steam *passenger* trains through main line steam runs and workings on 'heritage' railways – but only recently have these lines begun to make use of their very limited collections of freight stock to run 'demonstration' goods trains. By their nature – they can only use the wagons available, an unrepresentative handful – these are often far from authentic.

Wagon kits – the vital resource

Fortunately for us modellers of the traditional railway scene, we don't have to rely on the products of the big RTR makers to populate our layouts with an authentic selection of wagons, whatever our choice of scale or era. RTR is not anyway an option in 0 scale, but in both this and 4mm scales there is a tremendous choice of wagon kits available, many of them in easy-to-build plastic. In N, the prospect isn't quite so rosy, although in this small size the minor detail differences between basically similar vehicles are not so apparent, which means that with a bit of adaptation the (now pretty reasonable) choice of RTR can be made to go a lot further. Many of the wagons offered by Peco and Graham Farish are anyway of generic design rather than following specific prototypes exactly. Peco also offer many of their N scale wagons in kit form at a bargain price, great news for wagon-bodgers in the small scale. Makers like Parkside-Dundas have also now turned their attention to 2mm scale, with some stunning results in terms of refinement and detail.

Wagons are such a vast and convoluted breed that I can do no more than skim the surface of the pond in suggesting the best way of modelling the many different types. It may sound like a bit of a cop-out, but so vast is the choice of wagon kits on offer that it would probably be easier to look at what *isn't* available! Trying to present an overview of the possibilities and give a meaningful assessment of the quality of what's available across three scales and a huge range of prototypes would involve a task of more than Herculean proportions, something quite beyond the scope of a modest wee tome like this. Once you do dip a toe in the kit waters, however, the world becomes your oyster as almost any wagon you could think of – right down to the oldest, oddest and most obscure – will be on somebody's kit-list, somewhere, probably in both 4mm and 7mm scales. All of which means that if you need to build *anything* in the pursuit of a realistic model railway, it'll probably be a wagon kit. So it seems only fitting to take a look at what the various types of kit consist of and to consider briefly the 'how' of wagon kit building.

The wagon kit comes of age

In the very beginning were flat-printed colour litho papers, common to both 0 gauge and the emerging 00. These were designed to be simply stuck to solid wood or card body shells and were thus totally devoid of any relief detail – thus putting them on a par with tin-printed Hornby or Hornby-Dublo, the RTR benchmarks of the time. Much more authentic were ERG's 'card parts' – accurate drawings of wagon components printed on high-quality card of appropriate thickness, which you cut out with a razor blade and soaked in evil-smelling Shellac varnish to make sure that the finished models wouldn't wilt on wet days. I cut my teeth (and frequently my fingers) on those! For either of these alternatives, you had to concoct your own running gear, usually cobbled together from stripwood and crude type-metal cast parts obtained from firms like Bonds, LMC, W&H Models, ERG or Hamblings.

The first complete wagon kits in 4mm scale were the milled-wood and die-cut card offerings of Ratio and CCW (who also made them in 0), which had cast and stamped-brass fittings and made up into pretty presentable models, given a modicum of care and proficient use of the paintbrush. The 00 plastic wagon kit also has a surprisingly long history, first appearing as the Rex Masterpiece range in the early 1950s – simple, flat-moulded

Above: If you want an ordinary Stanier LMS 20-ton brake van in 4mm scale – no problem, just pop in to your Dapol dealer. If, however, like me, you lust after the much rarer 'reversed veranda' version, then you'll need to look a bit harder; in this case, for a Finelines kit in etched brass by Roger Chivers. This is just one example of the depth and variety available in the wonderful world of wagon kits; someone, somewhere, makes the wagon you want…

sides and ends for generic wagon types, all of which sat on the same crude Mazak underframe. This was devoid of any brake gear – and anything else resembling detail, if it came to it, but that was typical of most of the castings of the time, made in metal dies which made it difficult to incorporate much fine relief. Whitemetal casting changed all that in the later 1950s; its simple origination process using vulcanised rubber moulds gave it the ability to take very fine detail indeed, soon resulting in the exquisite fittings such as those found in Kenline's new 4mm scale authentic-to-prototype wood-and-printed-card wagon kits. It wasn't long before the world saw the first all-cast whitemetal wagon kit in 4mm, made by Bob Wills in the back room of his model shop at the bespoke end of Croydon. Soon, you could buy a wide range of cast wagon fittings for 4mm from both Wills and K's, as well as a surprisingly eclectic choice of complete kits: Highland Railway twin-bolster wagons or an LT&SR bullion van, anyone?

In 1959, Peco introduced their 00 Wonderful Wagon kits which – by the

Above: The Peco Wonderful Wagon of 1959. The body – embossed pre-printed paper overlays on a cast-Mazak shell – combined the virtues of the litho side with relief detail; hardly cutting-edge, but the underframe! An accurate RCH 10ft wheelbase wagon chassis, moulded in flexible plastic, it was fully detailed and true to scale, featuring metal W-irons, with sprung axleboxes and sprung buffers with metal heads. Now that was wonderful. Still is, being considerably better than many more recent offerings!

standards of the day – *were* pretty wonderful. Full of typical Peco ingenuity, they had moulded flexible-plastic underframes that were not only accurate models of the late-type RCH design, but which came with separate metal W-irons and turned buffer heads to allow both the axleboxes and buffers to be sprung – the springing medium being that flexing plastic. Refinement indeed! Not only that, these underframes had wheels to BRMSB scale dimensions moulded in hard nylon with integral pinpoint axles running in brass bearing cups, which gave very free running at a time when most model wagons had wheels that barely turned. The bodies were based on a plain cast Mazak shell, intended to impart a reasonable amount of mass to the finished model. The Mazak was overlaid with fully printed and embossed card sides which gave pretty good relief detail as well as avoiding the task of painting and lettering. These classic kits are still around and, while the relief detail lacks crispness in comparison with modern moulded plastic the overall effect and scale proportions make for a satisfying model.

The modern all-plastic wagon kit emerged in 1959, in the shape of Ratio's original 4mm scale GW 'Iron Mink' and SWB iron ore hopper, shortly followed by the coke wagon. Just a year later, the nation's leading plastic-kit maker, Airfix, introduced its own range of state-of-the-art 00 plastic wagon kits, starting with the (then new) LWB Esso tank wagon and the BR 8-ton cattle van, followed up with the standard BR 20-ton brake van and finally the immortal 16-ton mineral wagon. These were stunningly accurate models, deviating from strict scale only in the use of rather chunky hinges to the doors – but that was because they were made to open! At just 2s (10p) a pop, these kits were the bargain of the age and they can still hold their own, 45 years on; yup, you can still buy them (from Dapol), although they do cost a *tad* more these days! It's worth noting that the cattle wagon and the 20-ton brake van are the only *accurate* models of these two types ever mass-produced, which (especially in the case of the brake van) I find incredible! The only alternative to the Airfix old-stager if you want an authentic BR brake van is an etched kit (from Connoisseur/Pocket Money, good, but basic) or a heavy reworking of an old Lima RTR model.

Etched brass as a kit medium arrived in the early 1970s, but has never become as widespread for modelling goods stock as it has for coaches and locos. The main reason for this is the amount of relief detail commonly found on goods wagons – strappings, timber framing, end posts, corner plates, door bangs and so on. Such detail can readily be incorporated into a cast-whitemetal or moulded plastic bodyside or end, but has to built up in etched brass by applying overlays, often several layers of them. Etching thus only really makes sense for wagon types having little such relief detail – flush-sided or slatted vans, brake vans, some flat-sided opens and, of course, all-steel vehicles like hopper wagons and 'Lowmacs', container flat wagons and the like. Various people have *tried* to produce brass kits for more traditional wooden wagons, mind, but the results have usually been very fiddly to build, or lacking in sufficient depth of relief to look right.

The new kid on the block in the world of wagon kits is the use of vacuum-assisted resin mouldings, often in the form of a one-piece body with solebars and bufferbeams to which running gear is added using cast and etched components. The resin moulding process uses cold-cure silicon rubber moulds that not only provide for very fine detail indeed, but also permit undercuts that would simply not be possible in plastic or whitemetal. The 'cold mould' process also permits the use of original patterns fabricated in ordinary modelling plastics, thus making the process ideal for limited-run production of more specialised prototypes. Resin moulding is a production method that is very well established in the USA and Europe, but which is only just gaining ground here. It offers tremendous potential for wagon kits combining stunning detail with extreme ease of construction. The pre-painted and lettered cast-resin PO wagon body has already appeared.

Wagon kit construction

One of the reasons why I have far more wagons than I can possibly fit on my (admittedly modest) layouts is because I can't resist building the things. There's nothing like a newly opened wagon kit to bring a smile to the gnarled and bewhiskered features, be it plastic, whitemetal, etched, resin, composite or even card; yes, I do still hanker for those old ERG parts... One reason for this unfettered joy is that there are very few truly *bad* wagon kits, at least in 4mm scale. Even the most lackadaisical of them poses little more than a modestly-stimulating challenge in the building, while the best kits are now so good you can almost assemble them in your sleep. When faced with something like a Slaters or Parkside Dundas 0 gauge offering, it is very hard indeed to find fault – one sallies forth safe in the knowledge that construction will be an all-but elysian interlude of calm amid the toil and tussle of everyday life.

Below: Kits are a vital resource for the railway modeller bent on building up an authentic wagon fleet. They come in all sorts, sizes and sophistications, but the straightforward, economical and easy-to-assemble plastic kit predominates. I have always made extensive use of kit-built plastic wagons for all my layouts; here's one – a GW open merchandise wagon with sheet rail – well under way. This is a Cooper-Craft kit; a few other makes are in evidence, as are the tools of the trade.

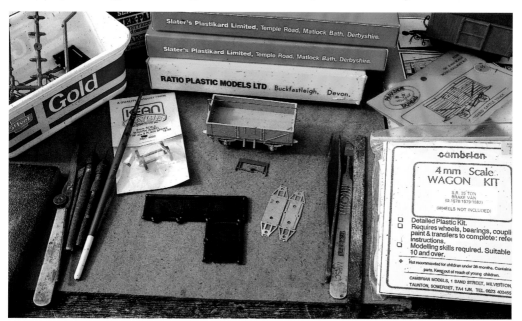

To build a plastic wagon kit, all you need is a bottle of solvent cement and a fine brush to apply it with, a flat surface to work on, a craft knife to part the mouldings from the sprues and a small fine file or some abrasive paper to smooth away mould part-lines or attachment pips. A pair of fine tweezers are also useful for locating the finer components, and I find it no bad idea to have a small engineer's square at hand to check that my corners are truly right-angled. The other great aid to wagon kit construction – whatever the material involved – is Blu-Tack, a pack of which will often save the day when you run out of hands. Otherwise, the pictures should give an idea of the actual work involved; although the kits do vary in detail, the basic layout and mode of assembly is pretty consistent. Most modern plastic kits are so simple and straightforward and fit together so well that they can be built quite satisfactorily in basic 'out of the box' form in only a few minutes. But such haste is to miss the point – and the opportunity for a few of the improvements detailed in a paragraph or two for – as some sage remarked – 'there is no thing made that cannot be made better …'

Below: A cast-whitemetal wagon kit for an SR 12T van, in this case. Unusually, this is an H0 scale model by Firedrake Productions. British H0 has a small but dedicated following, so the suitability of the whitemetal casting process for small-scale production is a boon to such special-interest groups. The main drawbacks to whitemetal wagons are the weight of the finished vehicle and the fragility of fine cast details.

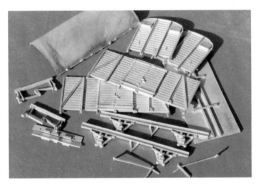

Whitemetal kits are both a bit more variable and somewhat more demanding to build. The very best of them fit together as well as the plastic variety, but the nature of the manufacturing process means that a little more preparation will almost always be needed, while slight shrinkage and mild distortion of the castings is not unusual and often unavoidable. So a little more care is needed to get everything fitting accurately and sitting level and square. This is particularly important with those kits that incorporate the wagon-side and the underframe as a single casting, as any mis-matching here will result in a vehicle which is not only out-of-square but also has axles skewed in relation to each other and to the track centreline – a recipe for persistent derailment. For this reason, many kits now come with the running gear as separate items, either based on etched-brass fold-up W-irons or having the complete axleguard (Wiron+axlebox+spring) as a separate casting mounted to the solebar. Either of these approaches make it simple to get accurate axle alignment even if the actual body is slightly out of kilter (which it often was on the real thing!).

Other than the need for a little care in the preparatory stages, there's nothing daunting about a building a whitemetal wagon. You *can* take a brave pill and solder them together with 70° low-melt eutectic alloy solder, but that's not necessary or – often – desirable. Using a modern five-minute epoxy resin adhesive for basic assembly gives you plenty of time for that all-important adjustment and forms a perfectly adequate structural bond, while cyano-acrylate 'super glue' is just the job for adding detail neatly and quickly. The same level building surface is still essential to get the wagon sitting 'true' with all wheels firmly on deck, while the files and abrasive papers will tackle the preparatory work on the castings. For working on whitemetal, cheap, Chinese-made needle files are fine; the soft metal is surprisingly unkind to files (it clogs and blunts them) and nothing is gained by ruining expensive tools.

Worthwhile wagon-kit mods

The things that I do to wagon kits are many and varied and would (indeed, have) filled a book. This is not the place to delve into the more esoteric or ambitious of these modifications, but some basic ones make such a difference to, particularly, the running of the finished models that they are almost mandatory. The number one rule in Rice's book is *no naff plastic-rim wheels*. A lot of 4mm scale 00 kits come supplied with these, mainly so the manufacturer can put the magic words 'complete kit' on the box, but they are universally awful. Bin them and buy some decent steel-tyred wheels by Maygib or Gibson, or the all-metal variety from Markits/ Romford. The steel-tyred types can be had for 00 fine scale, EM and P4 standards and for spit-spoke, solid spoke, 10-spoke heavy-duty, solid disc and three-hole disc variants.

The Romfords come for 00 and EM only in plain eight-spoke or three-hole disc formats, and also in a disc-braked version for modern air-braked wagons. All of these wheelsets come on 26mm long x 2mm diameter pinpoint axles and are usually supplied with turned brass bearings designed to be inserted into the axle-holes in the moulded underframes. You may need to open these out to 2mm diameter or deepen them slightly to suit the bearings, so a 2mm drill and a suitable pin-vice must join the tool list. 0 gauge wagons all come either without any wheels at all, or with Peco or Slater's steel-tyred plastic centre wheels, both of which are excellent. In N scale, standard wheels are Peco's moulded nylon affairs – much better than most plastic wheels, but Gibson does a steel-tyred wheel which is better still and comes in Parkside Dundas N scale wagon kits.

The other similar mod concerns the buffers, particularly of 4mm plastic kits. Many of the newer examples are supplied with either completely separate all-metal sprung buffers or turned-metal buffer-heads designed to fit into the moulded plastic buffer housings. Either of these options is fine (although I go for springs if I'm given the option) but what is definitely *not* fine is a flimsy, undernourished all-plastic buffer of the sort that figures in many older kits by

Above: The improvements and refinements that can be made to model wagons in 4mm and 7mm scales are legion, aided by a veritable cornucopia of detailing parts, improved running gear components, materials and transfers. There's also plenty of published information to guide you through the maze of possibilities for upgrades or alternative versions. Here are a bevy of kits undergoing various degrees of refinement and modification chez Rice.

The Parkside Dundas BR mineral wagons have been mildly modified with Plastikard Microstrip to replicate a slightly different version (reinforced corners); one of them is just receiving underframe detail made up from ABS and MJT castings with some etched parts from Mainly Trains. The LNER cattle van (also Parkside) has had the original underframe detail totally replaced to model a fitted variant; once again, the etchings are Mainly Trains. All the wagons seen have been fitted with metal buffers – castings from FourMost or MJT. The Ratio GW 'Iron Mink' van – sans roof – has received an internal lead weight to bring its weight up to the standard used on 'Hepton Wharf' – 30 grams an axle.

Airfix, Ratio, Kirk, Cooper-Craft, Cambrian and Parkside Dundas. These come in two forms: either complete moulded buffers designed to be stuck into holes in the bufferbeams (Airfix, Ratio, Cambrian, Cooper-Craft, Kirk) or plastic buffer heads intended to be cemented into buffer-housings moulded integral with the bufferbeams (Parkside Dundas). In the first case, total substitution is the only answer from the point of view of both appearance and function; I go for complete Gibson or MJT sprung buffers or the MJT cast variety that incorporate a turned steel head. In the second case, I substitute either the simple turned brass or steel bufferheads from Ratio or Slaters, or convert the buffers to sprung using the turned heads and springs supplied by Gibson or MJT. Many older RTR wagons also have unrealistic or flimsy plastic buffers that cry out for improvement – for which the ploys outlined above are equally effective.

Whitemetal kits, thankfully, *come* with metal buffers – usually all-cast, which can be fine so long as they're reasonably robust and the actual faces of the buffers are nice and smooth (carefully remove any part-lines or other irregularities), and properly round. Where the heads are suspect or of an odd shape (usually a lopsided oval) then I either lop them off, drill out the housings and replace them with turned heads à la Slaters as for the plastic kits, or substitute better complete cast, turned or sprung buffers. Why do I take all this buffering trouble? Well, not only do decent buffers *look* a whole lot better, but if you're going to have *any* hope of shunting reliably using the bufferheads to fulfil their proper function – as called for by virtually all of the more realistic coupling systems – then smooth-faced, accurately aligned and robust buffers are an absolute necessity.

Avoiding troublesome trucks

A typical all-plastic kit-built open wagon in 4mm scale weighs about 20 grams, a flat or bolster as little as 15 grams. A cast-whitemetal van, on the other hand, can easily turn the scales on the high side of 80 grams. An average RTR wagon hits the middle of this range at around 40–50 grams. Such substantial disparities in wagon weight form a sure-fire recipe for Trouble with the upper-case T, causing bother both when pulling (especially around tight curves) and in pushing. The trouble comes, of course, when the flea-weight plastic jobs are marshalled in front of the leaden behemoth, when the effect of too much mass at the back end of an otherwise lightweight train can easily result in derailment of the lighter wagons – either by being 'straightlined' on the

curve under traction or by being 'bunched' when setting back. The problem is often exacerbated by differing degrees of freedom in the running of the wagons; the combination of 'heavy' with 'stiff' is truly Bad News.

Both of the 4mm 'Scale' societies have a recommended standard 'weight per axle' of 25 grams, or 1oz in old units. It is rarely a problem to bring a lightweight plastic wagon up to this minimal ballpark using either lead sheet (3mm roof flashing from your local builder's merchants) or fine shot 'liquid lead', which can be poured into all sorts of crevices – if not always the ones you *want* it to fill! If you've got a fair number of whitemetal wagons in your fleet, I find it's worth bringing the plastic ones up a bit above the minimal 25 gram-an-axle, to 30 or even 35 grams. I use an old pair of letter scales to determine my wagon weights – they're fairly accurate and big enough to stand even a bogie wagon on.

The other consistency factor that affects wagons a lot is freedom of running. It only takes one sticky wagon to result in jerks, 'bunching' and – all too often – everything landing in the ballast, so ensuring that they are all rolling freely is worth the trouble. The usual way of assessing this is to use a fixed gradient – mine is a four-foot plank with track on it, raised an inch at one end to give a gradient of 1 in 48; this links (temporarily, for wagon-testing sessions), to a couple of yards of plain track laid on the flat. The requirement is that all wagons shall start running when placed at the head of the grade, and shall build up enough 'oomph' while running down it to go at least a yard on the flat. The usual cause of stickiness is ill-adjusted bearings (too sloppy or too tight on the pinpoints), something rubbing (check the brake gear and clearances inside the solebars and under the floor) or skewed axles. (Oh dear! Back to the bench for a rebuild...) I *never* use oil to lubricate wagons, but a soft (3B) pencil rubbed in the cups of the pin-point bearings can often work wonders. I test my wagons on building/putting into service and as part of a maintenance regime that also encompasses wheel-cleaning, coupling adjustment and a check on those all-important buffers. Well worth the effort.

Chapter 12

OPERATION

There are a lot of people who build working model railways but rarely, if ever, actually run trains on them – for which odd state of affairs I have discerned three main reasons. Firstly, for a surprising number of modellers it is the *building* of the layout that is the hobby, not the running; that's something you do to test that what you have done works, before you scrap it or sell it to make way for the next project. Then there are those who never actually progress things to the point where they *can* run trains, often because they either lose interest, discover a fatal flaw in the design, hit an immutable technical problem, or just grow dissatisfied with what they've done and decide to start again. And again, and again ... Finally, there are those who get everything working but then aren't sure what they should be doing with it all once they *have*. All of which is in stark contrast to the opposite persuasion, the dedicated operators – who traditionally don't care what the layout *looks* like so long as it *goes*. These are the folk whom Cyril Freezer once memorably described as 'quite happy to run a string of clockwork tennis balls so long as they observe the signals, run to timetable and obey the Rule Book'.

In my book, the folk who never get to run their railways are missing out on a good slice of what railway modelling is all about. Apart from the social aspect of operating – which, at its best, is a team sport – there's a deal of satisfaction to be had from understanding how the real thing was worked and in getting as close as possible to this in miniature. Which

– even on the most carefully-researched and painstakingly constructed of fine scale layouts – isn't as close as all that; there are all-too-many full-size traditional railway operating practices we just can't replicate – at least not with the current state of the miniature animatronic art. For on the pre-computerised/mechanised traditional railway many of us are seeking to model, almost everything depended on *people* on the ground interacting with the physical plant of the railway.

Consider for a moment the sheer *animation* involved in much traditional railway working: signalmen waving flag signals from their cabin windows or tripping down to the track to exchange tokens, lordly guards who stepped from their vans to give the right-away or oversee shunting moves executed by shunters who jogged alongside wagons leaning on brake leavers and wielding shunting poles with deceptive ease; crossing-keepers who emerged from their lineside dwellings to open and close level crossing gates manually, goods porters and coal merchants busy loading or unloading wagons, weighing and bagging coal, loading drays – all done by sweat and toil. Then there were firemen walking to the box to sign the register under Rule 55, PW gangs constantly busy about the track, station staff handling perishables, parcels, newspapers, luggage, baskets of homing pigeons or day-old chicks and the all-important 'Ticket returns to Audit Office'. Then, there were the horses – shunting motive power well into the BR-era and prime movers of much railway road haulage.

Above: *In the days of steam, real railway working involved a lot of people on the ground. Here's an old Beattie 0330 class 0-6-0ST shunting at Barnstaple in the 1890s – with guard, shunter, driver, fireman and goods agent all in attendance.* Author's collection

The railway of yore was positively heaving with animated activity – all scuppered on our models by that ever-irksome 'pillar of salt' syndrome.

Also, there's the matter of inertia, something real trains have in abundance but models hardly at all, at least below 0 gauge. Inertia and it's inverse counterpart, momentum, were the railwayman's biggest bugbear and yet his greatest ally. Getting a train started and dragging it up adverse gradients – that is, overcoming inertia – was the most back-breaking part of the job. Yet, once the train was on the roll, due to the very low friction inherent in the steel-on-steel railway, it would carry right on rolling – often for miles – and so needed minimal effort to keep it moving. This tremendous momentum was what made

railways such an efficient way of shifting heavy goods and lots of people with comparatively little power. Momentum was also the chief tool in the shunter's armoury; even if detached – by a seemingly-casual flick of the shunting pole – from a train moving at no more than walking pace, a fully loaded wagon (all twenty-odd tons of it) would rumble off quite happily for a surprising distance – usually until the shunter leaned on the brake lever, it came up on standing stock or – if calculations went a little awry – smote the buffer stops. Detach a model wagon from a train moving at scale walking pace (more on 'scale' speed in a minute) and chances are it'll stop dead. It certainly won't glide off into the distance under its own stately momentum because – for all practical purposes – it hasn't got any! As with many aspects of the prototype, physical properties don't conveniently scale down in the same ratio as size when we build our models. The model may be 4mm scale, but frictional resistance and Newton's First Law are still very firmly at 12in = 1ft!

Operational possibilities

Given all these limitations, what can we do to make our railways operate in any sort of realistic fashion? Well, for a start, as in almost all other aspects of railway modelling, we need to invoke the art of compromise and to exercise a little imagination. The first thing to do though is to take a close look at those aspects of operation we *can* represent realistically, and to place those at the core of our proposed modus operandi. Playing to our strengths, in other words. So – at the basic level we can make our trains move smoothly and realistically – hopefully smoothly enough to at least convey the *illusion* of momentum. We can run at realistic speeds, with steady and suitable rates of acceleration and braking. We can assemble realistic train formations made up of models that are authentic as to outline and purpose, maintaining appropriate relationships between train weight modelled and the motive power provided.

We can also carry out a very large percentage of the basic manoeuvres seen in reality. Our passenger trains can stop at stations, detach or change locomotives, add and remove odd vehicles like luggage vans, catering vehicles or 'specials' – or, indeed, break up and remarshall the entire train formation. At terminals, we can uncouple and run round, have stock removed by a station pilot and sent to sidings, or put a fresh engine on the other end. In truth, there's not much else you can do with a passenger train except run from A to B; even 'slipping' carriages from the tail of a non-stop train and bringing them to a halt at the platform is not impossible, especially with the aid of DCC.

Goods trains can also trundle from A to B, very often stopping for a spot of shunting at C and D on the way, or retreating to lie-byes, loops or convenient goods yards to get out of the way of hurrying passenger or perishables workings. We can do most of that – with the exception of certain shunting moves, of which more in a moment. Furthermore, we can determine the make-up of our goods trains by considering the nature of the traffic and the industries served by the lines we're modelling (or those it connects with), giving something other than random form to our train make-up. We can make sure that the appropriate wagons finish up at the appropriate places on our layouts, or that empty wagons are provided for the forwarding of the traffic that might be expected. We can also, by various ploys, simulate the loading and unloading of freight.

When it comes to locomotives, it behoves

*Below: **The easy bit. A train passing at speed on open line (even if going in circles) is just about the simplest aspect of prototype running to replicate on a model – provided you have the space. In model railway operational terms, this is what the 'lineside' operating stance is all about. Ex-LMS 5XP 4-6-0 No. 5681 Aboukir hurries south with an express from Liverpool, Lime Street in 1949; note the BR regional 'M' prefix to the LMS number.** Author's collection*

Above: Many of the well-known large scenic layouts built in the 1950s were designed for 'lineside' operation and usually presented plenty to look at. The whole point of this type of model was to provide a setting for the trains, the 'stars of the show', so convoluted track plans and plenty of running line were the order of the day. This is Axeford Junction, on the original 'North Devonshire Railway' – for many years, the doyen of this genre. In its final incarnation, the NDR had an extensive network of hidden loops that could hold some twenty different trains 'offstage'. Ken Northwood

Above: The opposite extreme to the NDR is the modern 'shunting plank' – typified by my own 'Trerice'. Such layouts are popular not just because their small size and ready portability makes them easy to house and to transport to exhibitions, but also because they offer challenging operation. Far more so, in fact, than merely circulating trains on a 'lineside display' layout. Essentially, they depend for their interest on the minutiae of goods working and shunting, very much an 'inside' aspect of railway operation when done properly. Matt Doe

us to take account of their prototypical needs and limitations. Apart from using the right loco for the job, we can take account of the operational requirements needed to keep it in traffic; at due intervals, we can position it for servicing, refuelling or replenishment, turn it on a working turntable, or send it on-shed for heavier maintenance. On a less-prosaic note, we can certainly recreate the strictures under which real running superintendents traditionally operated – the notoriously poor availability of steam engines, the constant battle to have enough serviceable locomotives to work the traffic offering, the need to schedule time-consuming operations like boiler wash-outs and the necessity to be able to cover breakdowns or other untoward happenings.

Operating stance: inside or out?

All of the above aspects of railway operation can be approached from two viewpoints – depending on the 'operational stance' chosen for a layout. Operating stance is an American concept little heard of in this country. All it really means is the underlying philosophy adopted in designing and operating the model, usually categorised by reference to the lineside fence. 'Outside the fence' operation is concerned with recreating the lineside experience familiar to the train watcher – a parade of trains passing by, hopefully accurate as to type, formation and timetable sequence, but otherwise regarded as objects to be viewed passively. The stuff, in other words, of many a successful exhibition layout.

The 'inside' style of operation seeks to

take things a great deal further, by looking at the whole business of railway working from the professional's point of view – thus taking into consideration a multitude of factors that need not concern the fence-leaner. Inside operation sets great store in doing things 'by the book', in following as closely as possible full-size operating practice in all its minutiae. Signalling will fulfil the same critical function as it does in reality, so an 'insider' layout will certainly call for correctly-placed, fully working signals. Operationally, it will firmly separate the signalling and train-driving functions. For ultimate authenticity, such a layout will also employ authentic documentation to enable it to function: a Rule Book, a Working Timetable, Traffic Notices and often, individual Wagon Waybills. This documentation gives structure and purpose to the railway operation.

Doing it 'by the book'

On the true insider layout, every prospective operator will first need to be thoroughly familiar with the Rule Book – a copy of which every real railwayman carried with him at all times when on duty and which set out the correct procedures to be followed in every eventuality. Many model railways use prototype Rule Books to ensure authenticity in working practice. All the trains appearing on the layout will run in accordance with the Working Timetable (WTT) – the document setting out every scheduled movement, loaded or empty, passenger, freight or light engine – on a given stretch of railway, together with any conditions and special instructions applying and the arrangements for handling non-scheduled workings such as engineers or PW trains, extra or relief trains and special traffic workings. The Rule Book, in conjunction with the WTT, is the authority to which all grades of staff refer and under the provisions of which the railway works its traffic.

Traffic (or Working) Notices are supplements to the WTT covering specific periods, and contain extra information in relating to the stretch of line concerned: additions or amendments to the timetable, scheduled PW works and details of accompanying speed

restrictions, arrangements for special or seasonal traffic movements, restrictions applying to new locomotive types or rolling stock, changes to the duty rosters. Waybills are the dockets and labels issued by the traffic department to authorise the movement of goods wagons; the docket would go to the Traffic Office to enable the carriage to be charged as due, while the labels were attached to the clips provided for the purpose on the wagon (one each side) and were the documentation to which the train crew – under authority of the guard – would refer to get the wagon routed through to its proper destination.

All these documents can be replicated for a model railway and used to direct operations in a very prototypical manner. In Britain, this

Below: Going by the book. For really prototypical operation, it is necessary to determine exactly what each train is doing and why. The published timetable is one source of such information, along with Working Time Tables and their associated notices (much harder to find!) and the railway's Rule Book.

Above: 'Random element' operating cards, used in conjunction with a timetable or sequence to generate a lifelike framework for operation. Very much akin to the 'chance' and 'community chest' cards in Monopoly, from which I stole the idea. 'Signal Passed at Danger; crew suspended' is the equivalent of 'Go to Jail', while 'Bonus turn – finish early' would probably equate to 'Advance to Go; collect £200'.

approach is normally referred to as 'Timetable Operation' and forms an absorbing, satisfying and very educative way to run a model railway; it gives a real 'feel' for the complexity and methodology of full-size railway working, as well as being a considerable challenge to execute properly. At least, if the worst comes to the worst on a model, it only results in a red face and some spilt plastic coal!

The random element

The whole elaborate structure of prototype railway operation existed for but a single purpose: to work the traffic offering, be it freight or passenger. This traffic came to the railway in two forms: pre-booked or regular traffic, of which the operating staff had prior notice, and sporadic traffic – that which could turn up at any station or freight depot,

all unannounced, and demand carriage forthwith. This, of course, the railways – being common carriers – *had* to provide. There was thus a certain 'random surprise' element to the traffic working. The fixed, regular, day-in, day-out stuff was planned in to the WTT as the scheduled passenger and freight workings which, by their nature, usually had a degree of spare capacity. To meet unforeseen demand, the WTT also made provision for the extraordinary, such as adding an extra coach if a large party wished to travel by a particular passenger service, or providing the stationmaster at some sleepy country station with the necessary wagons to handle an unheralded consignment of turnips.

The other random element in any operation is, of course, the things that go awry – which, on something as involved and complex as a railway, are many and various. We're all familiar with the modern classics: point or signal failures, derailments, train breakdowns, overhead line faults, staff and equipment shortages, leaves on the line, the wrong sort of snow...to which, in the days of steam you could add delays due to bad coal, damp sand, fog, brakes leaking on, additional water stops, broken couplings, hot boxes, line overcrowding, PW slacks, lots of conflicting routes through junctions, bad weather, cows on the line...The list, in fact, is almost endless.

To introduce these random factors into model railway operation and thus keep the operators 'on their toes', use can be made of either card-based or computerised systems to throw a variety of spanners into the works. The simplest method is very much akin to the 'Chance' and 'Community Chest' cards in the Monopoly board game – except in this context they are usually classified as 'Hazard' and 'Traffic'. 'Hazard' cards either give an 'all clear' indication – no untoward event affecting railway working – or detail some problem that the operating staff will need to address: loco No. 1234 has a hot box and is unable to remain in traffic; a temporary speed restriction has been imposed at point 'Y'; no locomotive water is available at Station 'X'; fog on the line; certain rolling stock not available due to a late-running service – and so on. 'Traffic' cards represent the unannounced goods consignment or the Church Outing, usually calling for extra provision of rolling stock or perhaps an extra train working altogether. These random cards are usually drawn at specific points in the timetable or operating sequence and ginger things up no end.

Journeys to nowhere

A real train departing from a station or yard is starting on a journey which might take it a few miles or many hundreds, over the course of a trip lasting anything from a few minutes to many hours; days, even, if the train be trans-continental. By contrast, even on the largest of model railways, a departing train will be lucky to run for more than a few tens of feet before it either repeats itself by going in circles or comes to an ignominious halt, having run out of track. At best, this process will take only a few minutes, unless the train is left lapping a continuous run. On the relatively small layouts that predominate in this country, a little such lappery is the best that can usually be achieved by way of 'long distance' running; not very realistic, surely?

Here, we need to distinguish between a realistic illusion and reality. A train lapping a continuous run is, in reality, going absolutely nowhere; but it is still covering distance, so gives the *illusion* of progress. This use of continuous runs to simulate distance is a very old-established operational device in British model railway operation where – a few garden railways excepted – larger, main-line layouts are very rarely linear. This is in fundamental contrast to the way they do things in the USA, where the aim of the big basement-busting empires is almost always to create a main line of sufficient length to give a train scope to cover a real journey – or at least a reasonable simulation of *part* of a journey.

On our more restricted sites, the only way most of us can hope to provide any real length of run – actual or illusory, is either by the use of imagination and hidden trackage or by allowing our trains to perform a number of circuits of a continuous run. Quite a common and workable means of getting a decent length of run is to build a layout that has a station of origin and a destination station both connected to an oval of some sort, so that the train can complete an appropriate number of laps en route from one place to another. The famous 0 gauge 'Gainsborough' model railway uses this device, with trains leaving King's Cross to lap a large oval several times before arriving at Grantham, then lapping a second oval between there and Doncaster.

However, even this compromise requires a lot more space than most of us have available – so we are perforce reduced to simulating the start or finish of a journey only, with the train in reality departing offstage into a fiddleyard or other form of hidden staging where imagination sends it the rest of the way. In the cause of realistic operation, however, that train is now 'lost' to the layout until a sufficient period of 'timetable time' (which is usually a lot quicker than real time – see below) has elapsed for it to have reached its supposed destination, been serviced as required, and made the return run. This 'staging time' device can be used even where both ends of the journey are modelled; the train can leave station A and simply sit in the offstage holding track, out of sight and mind, until it is due – by timetable – to arrive at station B.

Fiddleyards and staging tracks

Real railways have no need of fiddleyards or staging tracks. Neither do traditional continuous-run ovals or fully modelled point-to-point layouts. The fiddleyard is really a child of the British preoccupation with modelling branch line termini, whereas the staging track is an American concept tied up with timetable operation; both are 'offstage' locations to which trains may be banished once they have performed their allotted roles in the working of the modelled part of the layout. The difference is that a fiddleyard is designed to allow the hidden trains to be stored, manipulated, remarshalled, removed or assembled, whereas a staging track is simply a parking slot in which a train can be 'lost' until it is next required by the exigencies of the timetable, as described above.

Above: Fiddleyards don't come a lot simpler than the rather ramshackle affair that serves 'Trerice'. (Purely temporary, of course – as it has been for the last eight years...) This consists of a simple two-road sector plate, located and powered by a sliding bolt. It does the job – at least until the projected 'cassette' yard gets built – but the wiring is far from elegant. Each road will hold a loco, six wagons and a brake van and has a dead section at the end to prevent over-runs.

Above: One advantage of modelling a small subject in a small scale is that you don't need to waste a lot of space on fiddleyards. Martin Allen's 'Haverhill South' in 2mm fine scale gets along very nicely with this neat train turntable – a form of sector table – that will hold three complete trains and permits them to be turned. This is equivalent in capacity to my set-up on 'Trerice', but avoiding much of the handling my stock gets.

Thus, a fiddleyard needs to be easily accessible and laid out to handle several trains and additional items of motive power or rolling stock. It may employ any one of a number of different methods to feed the trains on to the layout tracks and use a variety of mechanical devices to allow it to function, many of them quite sophisticated. A staging track, by contrast, is simply a length of concealed track tucked away under the scenery, hidden behind buildings, or even banished to a different room. Several staging tracks may be gathered together, in which case you have a staging yard; very common on classic American basement layouts, but rare here. Fiddleyards, on the other hand, are our forte.

Fiddleyard formats

The particular type of fiddleyard chosen for use with a given layout will depend on a number of factors: space available (as always!); required capacity in terms of number of trains to be accommodated; style of operation envisaged; amount of stock to be handled;

need to turn engines; need to break up and assemble trains; the coupling system in use; and the need to carry out maintenance tasks – such as wheel-cleaning – during running sessions. (Very relevant to exhibition layouts, that.) All too often, fiddleyards are something of an afterthought – whereas in fact they are often the key to a successful layout.

There's an inverse ratio built into fiddleyard design, something along the lines of the simpler the yard, the more the locomotives and stock will need to be handled. At its simplest, a fiddleyard can simply be a plain piece of track, but every train that arrives in such a yard will need to be removed, replaced or remarshalled by picking up each item of the stock individually – a tedious business, and one apt to be detrimental to the models. Reducing the handling of delicate models is obviously a good idea, so fiddleyards are generally designed to cut this down by providing enough tracks and 'parking places' to allow the trains to remain largely on the rails. So, unless you are modelling something very simple indeed your fiddleyard will need at least two tracks, while even a modest branch line terminal can easily call for five or six roads (or equivalent) in the fiddleyard to give sufficient operational flexibility. The trouble is, all this takes space, and if you're not careful, the fiddleyard can end up by being as big as – or even bigger than – the layout itself. So a lot of effort has gone into devising fiddleyard systems that offer the maximum operation capability in the smallest possible area.

The simplest – but least space-efficient – way of laying out a multi-track fiddle or staging yard is to use normal track and pointwork, as a 'fan' (dead end) or 'ladder' (double-ended) yard. This is an approach more suited to staging than 'fiddling', for unless the tracks are widely separated (thus calling for even more space) it does not make for good access for stock handling. Doing away with space-consuming pointwork by using either a swinging sector plate (pivoted at one end) or sector table (centrally pivoted) can achieve the same result, in stock-handling terms – but at the expense of more 'fiddling'; pointwork can easily be set up for remote operation, but manipulating sector plates is a hands-on operation. On a small

Above: Double-ended 'ladder' staging tracks and the control panel on the Launceston MRC's 'Lydtor' continuous-run N gauge exhibition layout; the schematic track diagram on the panel shows the layout of the staging.

Below: The train stacker is effectively a vertical traverser and works on the same principle as a sash window. It can store a lot of trains in a very small area.

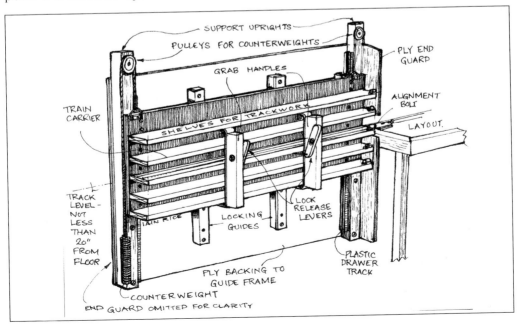

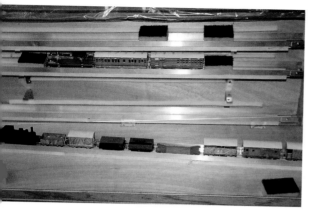

Above: A cassette fiddleyard – in this case, for 4mm scale/P4 on Vincent de Bode's 'Flintfield'. This is the most basic form of the system, with each cassette being long enough to hold a complete train. The alternative is to use a series of shorter units plugged 'end to end', with items that need to be handled – locos, brake vans, individual vehicles or short 'cuts' of stock – each having their own dedicated cassettes which can be exchanged or re-ordered at will. Which variant is best depends on how the fiddleyard is intended to be used.

The foam rubber pan scourers seen here are wedged into the cassettes to act as 'buffers' which prevent stock moving while the cassette is handled. Spare cassettes and trains sit on brackets in the box at the rear, which is used to transport them to and from exhibitions. The lid of the box forms the 'fiddling table' on which cassettes sit when in use. Vincent de Bode

Right: To avoid damage to locomotives or other delicate models being manipulated in fiddleyards – of whatever format – a 'handling cradle' can be used. Peco sell one for 00, but such a device isn't hard to make. Vincent de Bode knocked this one up for 'Flintfield' from PCB sheet and brass; it fits into his cassettes and you can drive a loco right into it as the sheet brass of the base conducts the power from the cassette. All the loco has to negotiate is a 10thou 'step' in the railhead – no worse than a slightly dodgy rail-joint. Vincent de Bode

home layout, this is not much of a problem, but is not always ideal for exhibition work.

More sophisticated are fiddleyards employing a sliding traverser or its vertically moving relative, a train stacker. The latter – which has much in common with a traditional sash window and is capable of handling a lot of trains in a very modest 'footprint' – is only just beginning to catch on here. It is really better suited to permanent home layouts – where it can be fixed to the wall – rather than as a free-standing component of a portable exhibition layout. Here, the traverser often finds favour, making use of sophisticated drawer guide systems or sliding door track to produce a really precise, smooth action.

The other favoured system, first described by Chris Pendlenton in the *Model Railway Journal*, is based on the use of cassettes. These take the form of long, shallow-sided boxes made of wood and aluminium angle and arranged on a flat deck, into which the trains run direct from the end of the fiddleyard lead-in track. The inner edge of the aluminium angle forms the 'rails' on which the wheels run, and the cassettes are either made long enough to take a complete train, or arranged as a series of shorter cassettes joined end-to-end to give an adequate total length. The advantage of this multiple cassette approach – used in conjunction with a suitable coupling – is that it allows the train to be broken up and remarshalled without the need to handle the stock. Either way, it is usual to provide short dedicated cassettes to take the locos, which can then be readily exchanged, turned or simply shifted to the other end of the train. The cassettes are usually aligned by pushing them up against a 'reference edge' and joined together electrically by spring clips; I use ordinary office-type Bulldog clips. There

are many variations on this simple basic device The only real caveat is not to make the cassettes too narrow; at least inch-wide angle is needed to get adequate side clearance to allow stock to be handled if needed, and to clear the aligning clips. Inch-by-inch angle also makes for structurally strong units.

Scaling time and speed

Not even Professor Stephen Hawking could quote you a figure for '4mm scale time'. Like friction, inertia, flexibility and other direct physical properties, you can't 'scale' time. Unless you have a Black Hole in your immediate neighbourhood (in which case you'll probably have other things to worry about), time is absolute. That doesn't stop railway modellers having a go at it, mind: 'Scale time' and its relative 'Scale speed' have been the subject of endless debate in model railway circles, with reams of dubious mathematics being produced in support of this 'patent formula' or that 'scientific approach'. All poppycock, as any physicist will tell you.

The thing we *can* scale is distance, so a scale mile is certainly a real enough concept; in 4mm scale, for instance, it is 5,280ft (the real mile) divided by the linear scale ratio of 1:76.2 , giving a figure of 69.29ft – say, 70ft for easy reckoning. This serves to remind us that even the largest of the US linear basement layouts – those with main line runs of 350ft or more – are actually only a scant five scale miles long! As distance is one component of speed, then a lot of people have seized on the 'scale mile' as a basis for arriving at a 'scale speed'. The problem is what you do with the other component. Simply dividing it by the scale ratio – as oft-times advocated – is nonsensical; an hour would be gone in less than a minute, so to try to accomplish anything meaningful in your 'scale hour' you'd be busier than Bugs Bunny on fast forward!

Taking a 'correct' approach and leaving the time 'real', then a train travelling at a 'scale' 60mph will need to cover our 70ft scale mile in a minute; quite a reasonable-sounding figure, for those of us lucky enough to have a minute's-worth of track! A 20 x 10ft oval (which most British modellers would regard as a pretty good-sized run) approximates to about 52ft, to give an idea of what we're talking about in real terms. A few experiments running express trains on the 15 x 6ft continuous run of Andrew Duncan's 00 gauge 'Maiden Newtown' layout (a shade over 35ft) at 30 seconds a lap suggested that such a rate of progress looked pretty reasonable; if anything, a tad slow. Interestingly, just setting the trains going at what – subjectively – felt to be 'about right' for typical 60-ish express speed then applying the stopwatch gave a rate of progress about 10 per cent faster than the true 'scale' value.

If speed is a knotty enough problem, what then of acceleration? In this age of hare-brained hot hatchbacks that can go from nothing to the legal limit before you can blink, we tend to overlook the truly ponderous (or should one say stately?) manner in which a heavy main-line train gathered way. When James Holden built the famous GER 'Decapod' to prove that steam traction could equal the accelerative powers of the new-fangled electric trains, the target was to reach 30mph in 30 seconds from rest. Well, even the ex-Belgian Post Office Citroën 2CV I drove while a student would do better than that – and most steam trains (even the grandest expresses) were nowhere near as quick away from rest! The problem for we modellers is that we're often representing the very start of this process – when acceleration was at its most leisurely. Which means that most of what we're representing takes place at 10mph or less! Yet another reason why the slow-speed performance of even our fastest express locomotive is of significance, and why the best DCC systems have need of 128 steps in their speed control map.

Oddly, the fastest accelerations on the real railway – leaving aside modern electric multiple-units operating high-density rapid-transit services – were to be found in the goods shunting yards and on country branch lines. Shunting was, in many ways, the apogee of practical railway operation, often carried out with a slick deftness and at surprising speed – far faster than many modellers seem to imagine. The ex-GER 'Buckjumpers' that worked Temple Mills and Ipswich Upper yards in the days of my youth were capable of very spirited sprinting indeed – full gear and a wide-open regulator saw to that. They could stop pretty smartly too – a powerful steam brake and straight lever reverse could do wonders on a dry rail! (On wet days, it was not unknown for the wheels to be going backwards while the loco was still going forwards!)

Suburban trains on lines with close-spaced stations have always demanded brisk acceleration, but branch line passenger workings – often very lightly loaded and thus enjoying a pretty useful excess of locomotive power – could often step away to even better purpose. Up to about 30mph or so, the classic GW combination of the 14XX auto-tank and trailer car was pretty much the fastest thing on rails. Again, this is an instance in which many modellers take things a tad too cautiously; study of archive film footage will soon suggest that the only 'slow' aspect of the country branch was the station working and the slothful nature of the timetable. True, maximum speed was rarely that exciting – 40mph or so being about the most you'd

Below: The case for sequence operation is particularly strong for branch line layouts. Here's the Looe branch train laying over at the terminus in April, 1965. The winter timetable on the branch was far from frenetic (unlike summer!) and such layovers could last an hour or more – hardly the stuff of riveting operation on a model! Author's collection

encounter – but the train generally got up to this heady velocity in pretty short order.

The conclusion I've reached in my own modelling over the years is that the most realistic speeds and accelerations are those which give the right *impression*, that just 'look right'. To arrive at suitable values, a study of a good selection of railway videos showing the sort of train operations we're setting out to represent is far more useful than any amount of clever theorising or wizardry with calculator and stopwatch. As with so much in successful railway modelling, it's coming up with the best blend of what is practicable with what appears convincing that produces the most satisfying result. This comes, in turn, from developing a 'feel' for how the real thing ran. Thus endeth the lesson…

'Fast time' or sequence operation?

Having, with lordly disdain, dismissed any notion of 'scale time', how does one then apply the strictures of timekeeping to a model – where distances bear no relation to reality and speed is an inspired guess? Given that we can perform most prototype evolutions – stopping/starting/changing direction, coupling/uncoupling, accelerating and covering the (largely non-existent) route mileage – far quicker than the prototype ever could, how can there be any meaningful relationship between what we're doing and the clock? Even if we could operate our railways strictly in 'real time', does that in itself not lead to problems? For instance, with many of the sort of stations we tend to model the timetable would dictate that for most of the time we wouldn't actually be doing anything at all! On a traditional country branch line with a half-dozen workings a day, there was usually time to kill – hence the lineside allotments, immaculate station gardens and the wonderful standard of maintenance so often apparent in those old photographs.

There are two traditional ways of resolving this 'time/operations' dilemma. One is to use a clock with its rate of working adjusted to give a suitable pace to operations when carried out 'to timetable'. Hours and minutes still pass –

but they are no longer related to the antics of the planet; rather, they are derived from how long operations actually take when carried out at a comfortable pace, related to the number of minutes they *should* take in reality. A popular ratio for such a 'fast clock' is 5 or 6 to 1, when one minute of real time is shown as 5 or 6 minutes 'by the clock'. A 'fast hour' lasts 10 or 12 minutes, which means that to work through a typical full day's timetable on an average branch line – stretching, say, from a 'first train' at 5.30am to a 'last working' at 10pm – would take between three and three-and-a-half real hours. The use of 'fast clocks' has long been popular in the USA, where you can now buy such things, adjustable over a range of ratios, over the counter. This is a lot easier than modifying the mechanism or recalibrating the dial of a conventional clock.

The other way around the time dilemma is not to go by a clock at all, but simply to do things at a reasonable pace and *in the right order*. Under this 'operating sequence' system, when the 2.15 train is good and ready to leave, it is deemed to be 2.15! Until the 2.15 is well on its way, the branch goods due to arrive at 3.10 cannot put in an appearance. If the goods is allowed, say, an hour to shunt and is timetabled to return to the junction after the 4.5 departure, but before the 6.10 is due to come t'other way, it will do just that. This way of going about things suits the traditional British country branch line style of layout very well, as it enables one to cut out all those lengthy periods when nothing at all should happen; you keep the interesting bits without the any (doubtless prototypical, but still boring) gaps in the action. This is not to say that one abandons all attempts at temporal realism while working is taking place; due time can still be allowed for such functions as taking water, coupling up after running-around or blowing-off the brakes, while speeds and accelerations still obey the 'looks about right' rule. The WTT in this case is still relevant, in so far as it determines the *order* in which things need to happen; it is just the attempt to relate events to a clock which is done away with.

The shunting dilemma

The working of the pick-up goods train, the basic building block of the traditional railway's freight service, forms the operational heart of many a model railway. Why? Well, apart from the wide possibilities in terms of the rolling stock involved, running a traditional pick-up goods offers plenty of scope for shunting – the most complex (but ultimately satisfying) form of hands-on model railway working. It's also, however, the most demanding – both in terms of the skill, knowledge and concentration needed to carry it out properly and in the functional quality of the equipment. It's no fun at all trying to shunt over poor trackwork with a locomotive that won't answer the controller accurately and consistently, start reliably or run steadily, moving stock that is constantly derailing or buffer-locking or using couplings that refuse to co-operate when asked to perform. In my book, the layout on which complex shunting can be carried out realistically and reliably represents the pinnacle of model railway technology.

But no matter how good the technology, we still can't do everything the prototype did. Shunting on the steam-era railway was a highly-developed and skilled business that was executed with minimal use of locomotives; much of it was carried out by horses, a

Below: In the heyday of the railways, this was the most prevalent form of motive power used for shunting. John Dale has made a superb job of modelling this stalwart shunting horse for his 7mm scale 'Alexandra Yard', but only, alas, in inanimate form.

surprising amount by manpower – the toiling goods porter and his trusty pinchbar accounted for many wagon movements within yards. Confined urban goods depots used rope-and-capstan haulage, turntables and wagon lifts to get wagons to their correct unloading points, many of which were so sited as to be completely inaccessible to locomotives. Also, most of the large marshalling yards did their shunting by gravity, releasing wagons down the slope from a 'hump' to run into the correct road, their speed checked by track-mounted retarders, with yet more toiling shunters on the ground to apply the brakes to bring wagons to a stand, and couple them up to others already standing.

Uncoupled shunting

Even where shunting *was* in the hands of locomotives, much depended on clever use of momentum and uncoupling 'on the

Below: There were many aspects of traditional steam-era prototype operation that are all-but-unmodelable – no more so than in shunting, much of which was carried out by means other than locomotives. This is the goods depot at King's Cross in London, with a wagon being manually manoeuvred over a turntable by rope and capstan. Not even DCC is this clever!

move' to get the wagons to their final resting places. The two methods of using momentum to get wagons where they needed to be without the locomotive having to venture far were 'fly' and 'loose' shunting. Fly shunting was carried out with the engine moving in the direction of the shunt and the wagons *behind* it. Once the vehicles were nicely 'on the roll' the shunter would uncouple the wagons, whereupon the driver would 'open up' and the engine would sprint ahead of its train. The aim was to put enough distance between engine and wagons so that the former could clear the 'shunt' turnout before the latter arrived, giving the shunter time to change the points and so divert the wagons into the sidings before setting off in pursuit to (hopefully!) bring them to a stand at the appropriate place. This was a fairly dodgy procedure and was almost universally frowned on by officialdom. Often, however, it saved a run-around move – so was popular with train crews, particularly on 'bonus' workings, where time saved was money in the crew's pockets.

Loose shunting was a little less fraught with hazard, although still demanding of skill and good judgement. A loose shunt is carried out with the engine pushing the wagons being shunted – the more conventional

starting point. Once again, the vehicles are got rolling nicely at about 3–4mph, when the shunter will uncouple the wagons to be shunted. The rest of the train is braked smartly to a stand, leaving the detached wagons rolling on inexorably towards their destination under the control of the shunter, who uses his pole to apply the brakes as needed. (A shunter's pole was used as much for braking wagons – by inserting it 'twixt solebar and lever and applying downward pressure – as it was for coupling or uncoupling).

With both forms of 'uncoupled' shunting, much depended on the skill of the shunter; so long as he was up to snuff, all went well. However, he faced many potential mishaps; he had only to trip, drop his pole, pick a wagon with duff brakes to try to control things, or simply misjudge speed or distance – and the whole business could go spectacularly pear-shaped very quickly. Imagine the hapless fellow, stretched full-length in the ballast, watching in dismay as a couple of well-laden coal wagons trundled smartly into the distance, headed towards a standing wagon laden with something expensive and breakable or, worse still, the stop-block abutting the stationmaster's outhouse ...

Officialdom didn't think a lot of loose shunting either, although it was never specifically banned. In larger sorting or marshalling yards, where plenty of shunters were on hand to keep everything under control and there was space to do the work unhindered by the clutter of a country goods depot, then it was a useful aid to efficiency, being quicker and less demanding of locomotive movements than 'conventional' coupled-up shunting. It was the ad-hoc use of the technique in wayside goods yards that usually caused the problems. It was also a complete no-no where shunting had to be carried out on gradients or on main running lines. These restrictions were writ large in the rule book, and all references to the practice were usually hedged about with caveats of the 'due care' variety. One shudders to think what today's Health and Safety boys would have had to say about it! These restrictions

Above: This is the form of prototype operation we can replicate convincingly; 'coupled' shunting, often the normal practice at the sort of minor country stations beloved of modellers. Here, ex-GWR Collett Goods 0-6-0 No. 2209 is busy at Minffordd, on the Cambrian Coast line in July 1956. With sidings facing both ways and several different levels connected by steep gradients, this was a very difficult yard to shunt; there was a run-round off to the left, which the train is apparently just leaving after setting out. Note the steep falling gradient on the running line – the reason the complete train was shunted in the yard, most of which was at least relatively level! Author's collection

are actually Good News for railway modellers, as – given that we're usually modelling smaller general goods yards rather than large marshalling yards – then loose shunting would have been less likely, especially under the eye of a strict stationmaster. This meant that conventional locomotive shunting – the sort we *can* represent convincingly – would have been more likely.

Shunting in miniature

With all the no-nos listed out like this, it would seem as if realistic shunting is yet another aspect of the real railway that we can't properly replicate on our models. Well, there are certainly some things that are always going to be a challenge; miniature animatronics has a long way to go before we can buy a working shunting horse! Not to mention a shunter who can ply his pole to apply the brakes or couple up links… On the other hand, we *can* devise and fit remotely operated automatic couplers (something the real railways never managed to do, in spite of several attempts) and there's no doubt that such a fitment does permit many shunting moves to be conducted in a surprisingly convincing manner; more on couplings in the next chapter.

The lack of inertia inherent in small scale model wagons can be overcome with the artful aid of DCC and a useful device that has recently appeared in 4mm scale – the discretely motorised wagon. High Level were first in the field with these, using a variant of their super-smooth transmission in conjunction with one of the new breed of very small but powerful motors. With the independent control offered by DCC, one of these self-propelled wagons

Below: There was a time – not so long ago – when you wouldn't have put the words 'shunting' and 'N gauge' in the same sentence. Nowadays, with the vastly improved quality of mechanisms in N, realistic shunting in the small scale is perfectly possible, as here at 'Lydtor'. 'Jinty' No. 47643 is a mildly reworked Graham Farish RTR model.

can go a long way towards convincingly replicating the classic loose shunt, although unless you're a concert pianist it really needs two operators (one driving the loco and one the wagon) to bring it off successfully. That said, I wouldn't think a little bit of computer software or some natty electronic module capable of controlling such a function beyond the bounds of possibility and feel sure this is a line of development that will bear fruit sometime soon.

Carrying out ordinary 'coupled' shunting calls for no such trickery – just equipment that performs well. One of the keys to success is a smooth-running, reliable and responsive locomotive that can sidle along really slowly when required. Yes, shunting could be brisk, usually was – but some jobs still require care and a softly-softly touch: buffering-up to standing stock, positioning a wagon 'just so' for unloading, 'slacking back' to allow a coupling link to be lifted, and – especially important in model terms – getting an auto-coupler precisely spotted over the actuating magnet – all are tasks calling for precision and delicacy rather than speed and gung-ho.

It's not just the performance of the locomotive that determines the success with which shunting can be carried out. In the previous chapter, I mentioned the importance of even weighting, correctly gauged wheelsets

and true free-running on wagon performance generally. Well, when it comes to shunting, these are attributes that, along with accurately located and smooth-faced buffers and properly adjusted couplings, make all the difference between the frustration of jerky, uneven running, frequent derailment and constant coupler malfunction, and the sort of satisfying, slick operation that characterised the prototype at its best. To this end, time spent checking and maintaining freight stock is never wasted. Even something as straightforward as cleaning the wheels can make all the difference.

Not that all full-sized shunting was faultless; far from it! Derailments were frequent, if usually of a very minor nature. To meet this eventuality, many yards sported a cast-iron 'rerailing frog' on their inventory (this was a form of ramp that could be laid over the rail adjacent to a derailed wheelset, allowing it to be pushed or pulled back into place); similar devices were also often carried in brake vans. Even where such aids were not available, it was usually possible to get the odd errant wheelset back on the rails with nothing more than a pinchbar, half-a-dozen strong pairs of arms and a few stout pieces of timber. Things had to go fairly well astray before you were forced to call out the breakdown gang! So there's no need to feel too bad when the odd wagon fetches up in the ballast; strictly speaking, it would be unprototypical if it didn't! At least we don't suffer from many of the other shunting defects the prototype encountered: broken couplings, displaced loads, 'hot' axleboxes, broken axlebox springs, defective ironwork, broken buffer or drawbar springs, cracked wheel tyres, missing bolts or fixings and rotten woodwork, to name just the more obvious. (All are possibilities for the 'Hazard' cards in the operating lottery.)

Shunting direction and sequences

Of all the various manoeuvres involved in traditional shunting, running round – getting the locomotive from one end of its train to the other – was the most time-consuming and

Above: Shunting is often far from simple. Working a yard with sidings facing in opposite directions, for instance, can result in some pretty convoluted moves, as at 'Cade's Green', where 'Buckjumper' No. 68499 is propelling wagons destined for the goods shed while drawing cattle vans out of the dock, which faces the other way. The awkwardness of this yard was a deliberate feature of the layout design, to make for more interesting operation.

labour-intensive. It also required the availability of a suitable run-round loop, so could not be undertaken at (the very many) places where there wasn't one. Unsurprisingly, therefore, the prototype sought to avoid the need or running round wherever possible. However, this could be problematic, at least in the case of the classic pick-up goods train required to shunt the various station yards, private sidings and exchange points along the course of its allotted route The problem was that relatively few such minor goods facilities were laid out for 'either end' working. Normally, the various sidings were arranged with access from one direction only.

The normal practice was, wherever possible, to shunt 'trailing'; that is, with the access to the goods yard in the direction behind the travel of the train. In which case, no running-around is needed and providing the wagons in the train were marshalled in the correct order (and they were – or heads rolled!), all the shunting could be carried out using only two simple moves: 'draw ahead' and 'set back'. Thus, for a simple a trailing shunt of a typical wayside goods yard, the sequence was:

1) Train brought to a stand on the running line behind the goods yard entry turnout, under the protection of the signals and/or single-line working arrangements.

2) If the shunt was merely a 'set out' (that is, there were no outbound loads or empties to be collected from that particular yard, only inbound deliveries), then the relevant wagons destined for that location – the first group (cut) of wagons in the train behind the loco – were detached, and drawn forward by the loco clear of the entry turnout. This turnout was then reversed, and the wagons were set back into the yard and 'spotted' at the precise locations needed for unloading. This latter operation might require a series of draw ahead/set back moves and the changing of any necessary points within the yard. It was also the part of the process most likely to involve loose shunting, as described above.

3) Where there was outbound traffic, this was normally worked first to clear the way for inbound loads. In this case, the loco was uncoupled from the train and drew ahead over the turnout. With the turnout reversed, the loco set back into the yard, making the necessary moves to assemble the various outbound vehicles into a cut. This was then drawn out on to the running line, the point reversed, and the cut set back on to the train.

4) The cut of outbound wagons was then coupled to the inbounds for that yard, i.e. the leading group of wagons, which were detached from the rest of the train. The loco then drew both cuts of wagons – inbound and outbound – past the entry point, which was reversed to enable the inbounds to be spotted as in 2) above.

5) The outbound cut was then drawn ahead out of the yard, the entry turnout reversed, and the cut set back on to the train and coupled up. Hopefully, the train would then

be ready to proceed to the next station or yard down the line – but see 6) below! It can thus be seen that as the pick-up goods proceeds down its route, the inbounds are, confined progressively to the rear of the train and the outbounds accumulated at the front.

6) The Rule Book sets out the correct marshalling order for different classes of wagons or ladings within a freight train, and these rules take precedence over all other marshalling considerations. Thus, for instance, livestock wagons should *always* be marshalled at the front of the train, whereas tank wagons containing flammable loads, gunpowder vans and various other hazardous consignments must *never* be coupled next to a locomotive! Then there's the braking question; where the loco is fitted with the vacuum brake and the train contains fitted vehicles, then these should be marshalled ahead of unfitted vehicles such that the vacuum-braked stock can be connected up to the locomotive. All of this can call for a further series of draw ahead/set back moves using the goods yard lead to get the wagons in the right order 'by the book'.

7) Very often, as well as inbound/outbound wagons for the yard, there might well be other vehicles – awaiting or in the process of loading or unloading – standing in the yard in positions that block in or obstruct wagons or unloading spots needed by either the outbound collection or inbound delivery. Such wagons were assembled into a further cut which was attached behind the outbounds, but in front of inbounds, such that they could be re-spotted as required once the inbounds had been dealt with.

All that is merely a description of the most simple and basic form of shunt!

By now, you may be wondering what happened if the requirements of traffic called for a pick-up goods to work wagons into a siding or yard facing the 'wrong way'

– a 'facing' or 'opposing' shunt. The normal practice was, as far as practicable, to avoid the need by routing the traffic in such a way that wagons intended for a given yard always arrived from the right direction to enable a simple trailing shunt to be carried out – even if, in the first instance, this entailed working them *past* their eventual destination to some point further up the line where they could be marshalled into a working heading the 'right way'.

Where this wasn't possible for some reason, then three courses of action were open. If conditions permitted, the wrong-way siding could be fly shunted, as already described, or, assuming that a suitable loop was available at the *locus in quo* – then a run-around move would have to be made. However, more often than not there wasn't a loop handy, in which case the run-around would have to take place at the closest station or yard possessing the necessary trackage. Here, the wagons for the facing shunt would be cut out, run round, and placed *ahead* of the locomotive before being pushed to the location of the facing shunt ahead of the train. This method of working was standard practice in some instances – the Coniston branch springs to mind and, certainly in pre-Grouping days, it wasn't unknown to encounter a pick-up goods with the engine somewhere near the middle of the train! The practice largely died out during the Grouping period, but there were some locations – on freight branches lacking run-round facilities, such as Snape in Suffolk – where the whole train was pushed down the branch in order to work the yard 'right way'.

A distinction needs to be drawn here between the working of pick-up goods trains running between two points on a through route, and those serving terminal branch lines. Pick-up goods on through routes were either 'turn' or 'pair' workings. A turn train set out from A, ran to B, ran-around, and returned to A. The various yards and sidings between A and B were worked on whichever leg of the trip best suited the track layout and the traffic. A pair working only went up from A to B; a similar down train running from B to

A formed the other half of the pair. Again, the various yards were shunted by whichever train could access them right way – which meant that traffic from A destined for a station that was only served by the down goods would be worked through to B and left for the next down working. However, that said, on the more important lines, stations were usually laid out for either-way shunting to avoid excessive line occupation by slothful pick-up goods trains.

In the case of branch line freights, it is obvious that any station or yard facing the 'wrong' way on the outward trip would be 'right way about' on the way home; the train was marshalled accordingly, so that traffic requiring to be shunted on the return trip was placed at the rear of that intended to be shunted on the way out. Obviously, there was also scope to remarshall the train into an appropriate order while the terminus yard was being shunted. Shunting terminal yards is one occasion on which a run-round move would always be made. Normally, given that most termini are laid out with the goods yard entered from the approach end, the run-round move would be made before shunting commenced, to get the engine on the right end for a trailing shunt.

Wagon card systems

Real shunting – like all other prototype operations – was undertaken for the sole purpose of working traffic and hence earning revenue. All too often, however, shunting on model railways is a pretty random affair, done rather for its own sake rather than with any sense of meeting a traffic need. Such random shunting is really a form of cheating, in that as there's no structure or purpose to the operation you can hardly get it wrong! Whereas shunting in a prototypical fashion, to get the right wagon to the right place at the right time as efficiently as possible, is an altogether more demanding business.

I've described the actual mechanics of shunting in some detail, but what I haven't dealt with is the routeing of wagons – what determined where they went, and when. The key to all this is

Above: *Wagon labels – 5 x 4-inch rectangles of heavy paper held in a clip on the wagon side or solebar – were of a basic design which remained unchanged for all but a century and the basis of the routeing system used by the railways in pre-TOPS days. There are many variations in the exact design of such labels, but all contained the same basic information: wagon number, class of traffic, origin, destination, charging details, whether sheets have been provided, and any special instructions. The upper pair of labels, dating from the 1960s, are for stone traffic from Meldon Quarry on the Southern Region, while the lower two, of late 1940s vintage, are for agricultural traffic in East Anglia.*

the wagon waybill or label, a small square of stout paper bearing details of the destination of the wagon, what it was carrying, and to whom the load was to be charged. A few typical examples are illustrated hereabouts. These labels were attached to clips on the wagon solebars – one a side – and were the information used by guards, shunters and stationmasters when marshalling trains or organising the forwarding of traffic. This is an aspect of prototype operation we can very easily replicate on our models, by a variety of means.

Above: *Wagon operating cards serve much the same purpose on a model railway as wagon labels did on the real thing. Here are some examples from my own operating system; these actually cover two layouts – 'Cade's Green', the small branch line terminus which pops up in these pages, and the much bigger 'Blythburgh', which is as yet embryonic. Ipswich (Lower Yard) is the up direction fiddleyard in both cases. 'Blythburgh' – a 'through' design – also possesses a down direction, to Lowestoft. The paper clips indicate the next on-layout destination exactly.*

Below: *Just for the record… here is the obverse of one of the wagon operating cards shown above, which acts as an aide-memoir as to build date and ingredients of the model, and a repair record.*

Some modellers opt to actually place a 'label' – usually a tiny colour-coded token of some sort indicating a destination – on the model wagon. Alternatively, you can now programme your computer to generate wagon waybills and routings and produce all the necessary information on screen. That always seems to me a bit too high-tech and out of keeping with my steam-era layouts – so I prefer to use a paper-based system, of which there are several. There's not space to describe all the options here, so I'll content myself with a brief account of the well-established 'wagon card' method. Under this arrangement, each model wagon on the layout has a corresponding operating/record card, which I produce on the trusty Apple Mac and print on thin card. On the face of this card are recorded the salient (to traffic) wagon details – type, number, traffic dedication or restrictions. Details of the source of the model, build date, weight, modifications or repairs and so on are recorded on the obverse. Also on the face of the card is some facility for indicating a destination: a pocket or clip that will hold a separate label or – my own preference – a series of possible destinations inscribed up one end of the card, the relevant one being identified by means of a common-or-garden paper clip slipped over the card-end. These destinations are very precise: not just 'Bogsville North', but 'Bogsville North No. 2 down coal siding, staithe for G. Pugh & Son'.

When a goods is made up (on the layout or in the fiddleyard) the relevant cards are for the wagons in the train are brought together, and the destination clips adjusted to show where on (or off) the layout each wagon has to finish up. The cards are passed to the train operator who can then – wearing his 'shunter' hat – use them in the same way his full-sized counterpart would have used the wagon label in its clip: to tell him exactly where each individual wagon needs to go. In fact, such cards often include more information than the prototype shunter had as many of the details of his final shunt were decided by that awful autocrat, the station master, who would direct operations in his own yard.

At each goods yard or other shunting location, a box is attached to the layout fascia to hold the cards relating to wagons standing at that location. When wagons are shunted in or out of the yard, the cards are added to or removed from the box, as appropriate. Between operating sessions, or at some suitable juncture during operations – when the various wagons have been deemed to have been unloaded and reloaded, the 'destination' clip is adjusted and – in my variant of the basic system – the cards of those wagons awaiting collection as 'outbounds' are stood on end in the box to indicate to the crew of the next pick-up goods that they need forwarding.

Operational summary

The various aspects of model railway operation discussed here by no means present a complete picture; there are many relevant topics glossed over or ignored, and there is – I fear – something of a bias in the direction of goods working. I'll confess I belong to that school of operators who cling to the notion that passenger trains are the froth that obscures the serious business of running a railway – moving freight! (There are many who subscribe, of course, to the opposite persuasion: passengers are all and goods trains just get in the way …) Be that as it may, I hope I've suggested that *operating* a model railway realistically offers just as much scope and challenge as *building* the thing in the first place. Bring these two aspects of railway modelling together and you've got an absorbing hobby that'll last a lifetime.

Chapter 13

COUPLINGS

Couplings on the British, and indeed, European, prototype never strayed very far from the hook-and-chain principle that dated back to the simple coal-carts of the first tramways. The refinements came in the accompanying buffers, which developed from solid timber baulks through sprung steel heads in cast-iron housings to progressive-rate hydraulic shock-absorbers. To actually take the strain and unite the train however, you still had only a hook, spring-mounted to the locos and rolling stock and carrying either three forged oval links (a three-link coupling), or two shackles connected by a screw (screw-links).

The use of three-link couplings resulted in

Below: The real thing; a screw coupling on a BR 'Lowmac' wagon; not all that far removed from the primitive chain-and-hook or chain-and-shackle of the earliest wagons. (See the picture of the 1860s PO wagon on p282.)

considerable slack between vehicles, reflected in the description 'loose-coupled' applied to trains made up in this way – normally slow goods and mineral workings limited to a lowly maximum speed of 25mph. Screw-links enabled the couplings to be tightened once they had been hooked-up, bringing the buffer heads in contact to eliminate 'surging' and to reduce jolting and banging due to slack. Screw-link couplings were universal on passenger trains from about 1850 onwards and were progressively applied to some classes of freight stock from about 1900. Normally, they were limited to wagons fitted with vacuum brakes, which allowed far higher speeds: 45–60mph for 'express' freight and full express speeds for NPCS vehicles that could be coupled to passenger trains.

British couplings thus remained resolutely manual to the last, requiring someone to physically get down on the tracks and heave the links on and off the hooks. Various attempts were made to design 'universal' automatic coupling systems, but all foundered on considerations of cost and complication. The problem was always in evolving something to work with the traditional side buffers. In the USA – where buffers are unknown – the semi-automatic centre knuckle coupling had long been the standard, while many narrow gauge railways got along quite happily with the centre-buffer 'Norwegian chopper' that would also couple automatically. Both these types incorporated the 'buffing' function in the design of the coupling.

However, it became apparent that something had to be done about corridor coaching stock, where connecting-up and tightening screw-links became a real problem as the corridor connections became larger. This led to the introduction of semi-automatic couplers of the American knuckle type, pioneered by J. G. Robinson on the Great Central Railway. Fitment of such knuckles – in a clever arrangement that combined 'retractable' or hinged, swing-aside buffers with a drop-down mounting system that permitted the retention of a conventional hook to allow coupling to non-knuckle fitted vehicles – was adopted by Gresley for all corridor stock on the LNER and by Bulleid on the SR. It also became a universal fitment under BR. In Britain, such couplers are known as 'Buckeyes', after the Buckeye Steel Company in North America, who made the things. This type of coupling was, however, never fitted to freight stock.

Only in recent times, with the introduction of some types of short-buffer or bufferless multiple-unit passenger trains, have true automatic couplings appeared on British railways. There are various designs, depending on the stock and type of working, but there is not, as yet, a universal auto-coupler system. Automatic centre couplings without side buffers now also feature on some classes of heavy freight stock – most notably on the high-speed 100-ton stone hoppers used for the Mendip quarry traffic. It is perhaps salutary that when the experimental 12,000-ton 'super train' was tried for this traffic, it was the breaking of traditional screw-link couplings that caused its failure.

Model couplings

The modeller, faced with the prototype situation outlined above, can adopt one of two basic options: he can don a hair-shirt, give up drink and loose company, buy some strong eye-glasses and opt to use manually worked scale link couplings; or, he can turn a blind eye to the unprototypical appearance and opt for an auto-coupler of some sort. Most people, sooner or later, end up with option two – at least, they do in scales below 7mm: 1ft. There are a hard core of dedicated souls who

Below left and right: Prototypical link couplings at 4mm scale; pretty tiny! It is possible to manipulate scale couplings like this with a bent-wire coupling pole – I did it for years when I was young and foolish – but it's a real fiddle. You need a very steady hand and good eyesight, while access to the wagons needs to be close, unobstructed and well lit; trying to drop scale links over a scale hook at a range of a couple of feet when you can't see what you're doing is a long way from fun in my book.

Using overscale links and hooks makes life a bit easier, while strapping your shunter's pole to a small torch can be a big help, but the job requires concentration and patience – and it's horribly easy to derail stock in the process. All-in-all, I find I'd rather leave scale link couplers to the 7mm scale crowd.

persevere with scale three-links in 4mm scale and, I hear, even one or two in 3mm. They probably also go in for cold baths, listening to avante-garde classical music and rising before dawn in February. I never heard of anyone daft enough to try manually manipulated link couplings in 2mm:1ft scale, but I expect that there's someone, somewhere…

It is not just the difficulties of manipulation that mitigate against the scale links, but also the buffing question. Link couplings – unlike centre-knuckle types – take no part in the propelling of vehicles; they function only in tension. This means that when a train is reversed (the infamous and essential set-back move already described *ad nauseum*), the buffers on the model must work in exactly the same way as they do on the prototype. This is not the easiest trick in the book to accomplish reliably in the smaller scales (it is usually not too problematic in 7mm/ft). Many factors can intrude to upset this

rather delicate applecart, including the effects of over-tight curves, inaccurate buffer alignment, bumps and dips in the track, uneven weighting of stock, imperfections in the buffer faces and – worst of all in 'compromise' standards like 00 and N – lateral displacement.

This is when, owing to the generous running clearance inherent in these standards, adjacent vehicles crab or slew in relation to the track, displacing the buffers sideways from their true on-centre location; if two adjoining vehicles 'crab' in opposite directions, it's highly likely the buffer heads – rather than meeting face-to-face – will nip past each other then jam. This is a condition known as buffer lock and is a recipe for instant derailment and endless frustration. For this reason, the use of functioning buffers is usually faciliated by standards – such as EM, P4 or 3mm finescale – that have much tighter running clearances which help maintain the necessary accurate centring of vehicles on track and hence the vital buffer alignment. These standards also tend to use wider radius curves, cutting down one of the other chief causes of non-alignment.

Automatic options in 4mm

This leaves most of us to consider the various automatic options. In the popular scale, these come under one of three categories: RTR or aftermarket commercial couplers of either the knuckle or hook-and-bar 'tension lock'

Below: Probably the best-known of the true DIY auto-couplers, the AJ invented by the late Alex Jackson of the Manchester MRS. This truly clever 'hermaphrodite book' design can be used in 7mm, 4mm and 3mm scales. It permits 'delayed' uncoupling and operates with the lightest touch, but does require very careful making and setting up and won't tolerate bumpy track, excess side-slop or sharp curves. Take the trouble to get it right though, and the thing performs beautifully while being – as can be seen here – very unobtrusive. There is an extensive literature on this coupling, and it is often demonstrated at shows with a fine-scale bent.

Below: You can't buy AJs ready made, but you can buy a set of jigs and suitable wire (guitar string) to help you make your own.

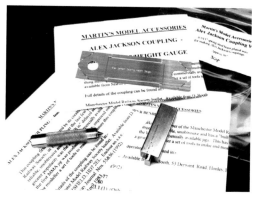

variety; 'scale' hook-and-bar designs, more sophisticated and less obtrusive but essentially a DIY job from bought components; or totally hand-made filigree-wire designs such as the Alex Jackson. The latter are something of a species (some might say a religion!) in their own right and – like the link couplings – do not incorporate a 'propelling' function. They thus rely on the side buffers to accomplish this and are consequently prone to all the buffing caveats outlined above! As with links – and for much the same reasons – the use of this type of coupling is very much associated with finer scale standards. They demand great care in the making and hair-trigger accuracy in the setting up, although jigs can be had to facilitate these operations; in other words, they are still more hair-shirt than easy-iron.

The DIY hook-and-bar designs are covered in detail later in this chapter, which leaves us to consider the more mainstream commercial offerings. In the days of the great proprietary systems, the auto-couplings employed were one of the key selling-points – as well as marking a fundamental point of difference between the Hornby Dublo and Tri-ang camps. Hornby (with Trix) championed the knuckle while Triang raised the standard for the hook-and-bar. Both Dublo and Trix adopted the ingenious stamped-steel Peco coupling designed and patented by Sydney Pritchard, while Tri-ang set out with a fairly crude hook-and-bar design that soon developed into the well-known tension lock. Both designs are still around today, although the Peco has had its day as a factory-fit on RTR models.

Knuckle couplings

Under this heading, we have two families of couplers to consider: Mr Pritchard's fixed-jaw Peco and the far more sophisticated hinged-jaw Kadee from America. Both originally date from the 1940s, but differ in intent; the Peco device was simple, cheap and ingenious and aimed at the mainstream and RTR market in which it excelled. The Kadee was always an aftermarket design aimed at the scale enthusiast – which meant that it could afford to be more delicate and costly than the Peco.

Above: The rivals: Peco/Hornby-Dublo bare their knuckle on the left, while Tri-ang respond by applying a tension-lock. Both had virtues and drawbacks – chief among which were their total incompatibility with one another!

It also underwent a far greater degree of development, to produce a very sophisticated device with magnetic actuation, delayed uncoupling and good prototype fidelity. The current generation of US knuckle couplers – both from Kadee and the other makers who stepped in once the original patent expired – come in a huge range of variants/special

Below: A cruel close-up of a Peco coupler fitted as an 'aftermarket choice' to the tender of a Kitmaster Bulleid Pacific. This shows one of the enemies of the Peco type: rust; which could pit the mating surfaces of the knuckles and stop them sliding over one another. However, it is a neat and clever device for all that, and less obtrusive than the tension lock.

applications and now include versions having knuckles of true scale size.

In the context of the contemporary modelling scene, the Peco is no longer a popular choice of coupling, being neither provided for nor supplied by any of the mainstream RTR makers. That doesn't mean it's extinct, but it does make it a somewhat eclectic choice as an aftermarket device – even in the Magni-Simplex variant that uses elements of Kadee's technology to achieve magnetic actuation and delayed uncoupling. The biggest problem for Peco-users today is that it isn't readily compatible with the coupler mounting systems now in use. There's no plug-in Peco variant for use with the standard NEM box of modern RTR, and even on older RTR stock with screw-mounted tension-lock couplings, fitting the Peco as a substitute demands a fair bit of improvisation. My own feeling is that the Peco is really most relevant to those who are already committed to it for historical reasons – it was, after all, the coupling of choice for 'scale' use not so very long ago.

The Kadee, by contrast, was for many years regarded as a fabulous and exotic beast on these shores. It was relatively expensive and not all that easy to obtain. In a British context, it needed a little adaptation to work in conjunction with side buffers and 4mm scale (as opposed to H0) mounting heights. However, the refined operating characteristics won many over – particularly those with a penchant for close-coupled corridor coaches, where many coupling designs are problematic if not just plain impossible. This was a natural application for the Kadee – particularly given that many prototype corridor coaches had knuckle couplings anyway; no apologies needed! On typical British freight stock, however, there's no getting away from the fact that the Kadee looks rather odd and obtrusive – although whether it is any more of an anomaly than a Peco or a tension-lock is certainly debatable.

The big difference between the Kadee and Peco designs is that the Kadee has a moving jaw, independently pivoted and sprung within the actual knuckle; it thus operates without requiring the whole coupler to move and consequently calls for a much smaller degree of displacement to function. The jaw is a force-fit on the pivot pin-cum-actuating arm, which can move freely in the main coupler shank/knuckle casting. This pivot-cum-actuator – the 'trip pin' in Kadee-speak – protrudes through the bottom of the shank casting as a curved arm describing a quarter-circle, so that the tip of the pin lies a little way above rail height and more-or-less parallel to the rails. It is the tip of the trip pin that is attracted by the actuating magnet, which pulls it sideways, thus opening the coupler jaw which is normally held in the closed position by a tiny coil spring. This is a vital part, so lose one of these – and ping! – your coupler will no longer function. Spares are available, but fitting them is a trial for saintly patience. Goodness knows how they do it on the production line! To overcome the spring, the magnets used for uncoupling are very powerful – which can cause problems with rolling stock fitted with steel axles or wheel tyres; more on that in a moment.

In the uncoupling mode, the Kadee incorporates a 'delay' position that prevents the knuckles re-closing once the vehicles are pushed clear of the uncoupling magnet, so that a single magnet can serve a whole fan of sidings. The magnets themselves are available in three basic formats: a permanent between-the-rails strip magnet, a powerful under-track electromagnet and a hand-held magnetic pick. This last is a device shaped like an upside-down tuning fork, with a powerful permanent magnet attached to each tip of the fork, which is inserted into the 'coupling gap' between vehicles to open the jaws and allow uncoupling anywhere on the layout where no track magnet is fitted. There are also various non-magnetic designs of 'coupler pick' which will open the jaws of Kadees by mechanical means. More prosaically, like the Peco, the Kadee can be parted simply by lifting one coupler vertically to free the jaws from the embrace of its neighbour, although you can't just lift a vehicle straight up out of the middle of a train – the trip pins catch on the bottom of the jaws if you try that useful fiddleyard trick. It is necessary to part the couplers, then move the vehicles apart slightly to achieve this.

Kadees in a British context

Apart from non-prototypical appearance, the chief drawback with Kadees used on British model railways is that 'unwanted magnetic attraction' nuisance associated with those permanent track magnets. These are powerful enough to cause problems with steel axles and wheel tyres, as commonly used on a lot of RTR and scale rolling stock in Britain. Steel-tyred vehicles experience a powerful 'braking effect' as they pass the magnets, which at best produces an unrealistic jerk and at worst can cause derailments, while the attraction of the magnets is such that even vehicles with plastic wheels (but steel axles) will be irresistibly drawn to the magnet positions from surprisingly far away; the problem is even greater with nicely free-running stock. Very trying when you would rather your trains stayed where you put them! This unwanted attraction is the reason that model rolling stock sold in the US comes with non-magnetic wheelsets – plastic, nickel-silver or zinc alloy wheels on plastic or brass axles. For we Brits, stuck with steel, the usual approach is either to use electro-magnets – which only exert magnetic force when energised – or to install the permanent magnets on a cam system so that they can drop down out of harm's way when not needed,

Other practical problems with the Kadee in a British context have to do with mounting height and 'reach'. The underside of the bufferbeam of an item of British stock in 4mm scale is a fair bit further from the rails than the bottom of the end cill on a typical US freight car in H0. As the height of the actuating 'trip pin' above the rails is a critical factor in the reliable functioning of Kadees, you can't simply stick the thing on to the bottom of a 4mm scale underframe without modification. It is either necessary to insert some packing – up to 1mm thick – to get the trip pin in the right place, or to re-bend the pin to suit the greater mounting height. Kadee supply a

Above: An American H0 Kadee knuckle coupling fitted to a 00 British wagon (a Ratio LNWR single-planker). Note how the coupling mount box has to be set out a little way from the face of the buffer-beam to give the coupling sufficient reach to work with side buffers. This is the standard Kadee No. 5 coupling in its dedicated mounting box.

Below: Here, 00 wagons fitted with Kadee No. 5 couplers are coupled up, showing the sort of buffer-head separation given. This could be adjusted by altering the amount by which the couplers are set out from the bufferbeams. In this configuration, the buffer heads will not touch when stock is propelled.

Above: The Kadee coupler setting gauge, which determines ideal mounting height and trip pin clearances. The gauge is made for American H0 use; British modellers often set their Kadees a little higher and bend the trip pins down a tad to compensate.

track-mounted gauge to enable you to check these factors. The reach problem is due, of course, to our fine British buffers. Kadees are designed to give a coupling distance suited to US all-bogie stock with no buffers, so we need to 'set them out' from the bufferbeams far enough to ensure that the couplings operate before the buffer faces meet – and also to maintain enough clearance between the latter for the train to negotiate the curves in use. Trial and error is, I fear, the only way to establish this.

Fortunately, the mounting systems used by Kadee makes it relatively easy to achieve the necessary settings. Kadees (and their clones) are available in a huge range of different configurations to suit a variety of mounting situations – now including plug-in versions for the standard NEM 362 swivelling box found on most recent RTR productions. The most relevant variants for British use are the universal-fit No. 5 (or its scale-size equivalent, the No. 58), the 'European equipment' No. 16 and the various NEM plug-ins. The No. 5 comes with its own self-contained moulded

plastic coupler mounting box, which enables the complete coupler assembly to be simply glued or screwed in place on almost any type of vehicle. Fitted with the front of the mounting box flush with the bufferbeam face, the shank length (pivot to coupling face) of the No. 5 is 9/32in/7mm – so given that most wagon buffers are 5–6mm long it is usually necessary to set them out by at least 1mm. The No. 5 is widely available, can be bought in bulk packs (10 or 20 pairs, with or without mounting boxes) and are by some margin the cheapest way to 'go Kadee'. The No. 16 is specifically intended for use with side buffers and has a longer-shank coupler – 10.3mm – sitting in a compact mounting box, but it is more costly and harder to obtain.

The NEM-mount couplers come in four shank lengths to suit almost any application: the 'short' (7mm) No. 17, the 'medium' (8.6mm) No. 18, the 'long' (10.75mm) No. 19, and the 'extra long' (11.7mm) No. 20. The NEM Kadees are set with the knuckle at the right height when installed in the standard box. For 'tricky' applications where the classic No. 5 doesn't suit, then a good place to look for an alternative is among the plastic-shank '30 series'. These have compact mounting boxes and come with three shank lengths each with knuckle offsets (upwards, or 'underset shank', or downwards/'overset shank'); No. 32 'medium, overset shank' is probably the most useful in a British context , with the No. 39 'long overset' variant for vehicles with longer buffers. They are only slightly more costly than the economical No. 5.

Hook-and-bar couplers

The hook-and-bar design of coupler was around well before Peco and Kadee bared their knuckles. In its most basic single-ended form – a bar across the buffers at one end of each vehicle and a hook at t'other – it dates back to the dawn of small-scale 'scale' model railways in the early 1930s and the writings of the Rev. E. Beal. In the USA, a self-contained 'either end' hook-and-loop coupling was described by my namesake, Allan Rice, writing in the *Model Railroader* in 1937. Allan wrote under the anagramic pen-name of 'Eric LaNal' – and his coupler design was accordingly christened the 'LaNal'. It was adapted and patented by Mantua in 1941 and enjoyed a brief vogue here in the immediate post-war period, when Mantua items imported from the USA were among the very few model railway products available.

Contemporary with the Mantua – but different enough from it to avoid the Patent – was a device called the Kup-eze (yes, really!) and this would seem to be the inspiration for the Farish/Tri-ang hook-and-bar coupler that first appeared from Farish in 1949 and from Rovex in 1950. Tri-ang used if from the outset, describing it as the Mk 2a coupling; no one seems too sure what became of the Mk 1... The basic principle of the design was a stamped-steel 'chopper' type hook pivoted in the vertical plane, which engaged with a flat steel bar. The hooks had their lower front edge angled up so that they would ride up over the bar when the couplings were brought together; gravity then causing the hook to drop down with the pulling face safely behind the bar. To uncouple, a 'drop arm' stamped integrally with the hook was raised by a ramp between the rails, lifting the business end of the hook clear of the bar. Well, that was the theory, although the light weight of the hook combined with a frisson of friction in the pivot meant that gravity didn't always oblige in the matter of coupling. This defect was addressed in the Mk 2b design that soon appeared, adding more weight to the hook by appending a hefty semi-circular 'skid' to the bottom of the drop-arm.

This basic Tri-ang design was a very reliable and unfussy coupler that would still function even when considerably bent out of shape by the rigours of enthusiastic operation. However, it was not without drawbacks. For a start, it wasn't self-contained; the mounting block which included the pivot eyelet for the hook was cast as an integral part of the underframe of the wagon or the bogie of a coach. This meant you couldn't fit a Tri-ang coupling to a vehicle of a different make. Functionally, apart from the odd instance of reluctant gravity, bad bumps in the track and

Above: The commercial hook-and-loop coupler. I've already illustrated the original Tri-ang tension-lock, so here are two variations on the theme; the modern plastic tension-lock eyesore (from Dapol, in this instance) at the left, and the neat non-locking design introduced by Airfix in 1979. This was relatively unobtrusive and greatly sought-after by 7mm scale narrow-gauge enthusiasts seeking a simple and robust 'chopper' coupling! Many recent Bachmann models have sported a tension-lock version of this compact design, probably the best option among the RTR designs.

jerky running in general could cause unwanted parting of couplers. On the other hand, they were far more difficult to uncouple manually when you wanted to. If an uncoupling ramp wasn't handy, it was all-too easy to derail half the train merely when trying to separate a single wagon – something that caused the youthful Rice endless frustration!

This characteristic became even more pronounced when Tri-ang introduced their Mk 3 coupling, otherwise known as the 'tension-lock' – which always sounded to me like something painful to do with wrestling. This version of the basic design sought to overcome two of the drawbacks listed above; it was self-contained, mounted by a single small, self-tapping screw to the underside of the bufferbeam on a wagon or the frame of a

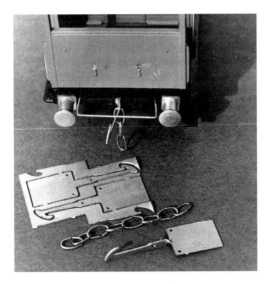

Above and below: The Sprat & Winkle laid bare. Here we have a finished coupling on an Airfix LMS brake van using the variant with the bar as a loop between the buffers, which are sprung in this case. Those suffering buffer-locking troubles are wont to simply solder this bar right across the buffer faces (provided, of course, the buffers are metal!).

The basic hook etch can be seen adjacent, with a bent-up hook to the right. The 'dropper' takes the form of coupling links from iron or steel wire; those shown here being EM Gauge Society (EMGS) steel coupling chain. The detail of the coupler can be seen in the drawing.

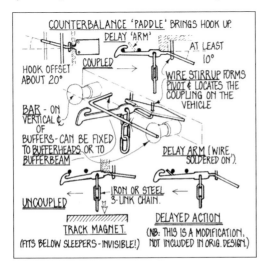

COUNTERBALANCE 'PADDLE' BRINGS HOOK UP.
DELAY 'ARM'
AT LEAST 10°
HOOK OFFSET ABOUT 20°   COUPLED
WIRE STIRRUP FORMS PIVOT & LOCATES THE COUPLING ON THE VEHICLE
BAR - ON VERTICAL ℄ OF BUFFERS- CAN BE FIXED TO BUFFERHEADS OR TO BUFFERBEAM
DELAY ARM (WIRE SOLDERED ON).
UNCOUPLED   IRON OR STEEL 3-LINK CHAIN.
DELAYED ACTION
TRACK MAGNET.
(FITS BELOW SLEEPERS - INVISIBLE!)
(NB: THIS IS A MODIFICATION, NOT INCLUDED IN ORIG. DESIGN.)

bogie on a coach, and the addition of a 'claw' to the coupling hook that nestled beneath the bottom edge of the bar prevented the hook from disengaging so long as the coupling was under tension – hence the name. Uncoupling was still by means of a ramp between the rails, but for the hooks to be lifted the train had to be set back to take the tension off the couplings and disengage that claw.

Without a ramp, uncoupling was next to impossible with the train still on the track. It was necessary to lift and twist adjacent vehicles, which often meant that by the time you'd persuaded the couplers to part you had derailed most of the train. One suspects that this feature of the design, incompatible as it was with the concept of the fiddleyard then coming into vogue, led to the Peco becoming the *de facto* choice of coupler for the 'scale' enthusiast. Nevertheless, the basic tension-lock design is still the standard fitment on British RTR equipment, although thankfully in the smaller and less-obtrusive version originally introduced by Airfix when they entered the RTR market in the late 1970s. This is a little easier to uncouple manually, but is still a fairly basic auto-coupling without a delay feature and suited only to mechanical actuation.

The Sprat & Winkle coupling

This rather more refined variant of the hook-and-bar concept derives from the H&N coupling devised by Mr Hope and Mr Nixon of Liverpool just after World War II. It was further developed and 'productionised' by Derek Munday for his EM model of the LSWR's Meon Valley branch – otherwise known by its colourful nickname of the 'Sprat & Winkle Line', hence the name of the coupling. Like the tension-lock, the S&W uses a hook with a claw to ensure positive coupling, engaging with a bar of fine wire. Unlike the tension-lock, however, the hook is inverted and thus moves down, rather than lifting, to disengage – a mode of operation readily achieved by magnetic means. The hook – which is supplied as a brass etching – is pivoted behind the bufferbeam and is held in the up, or coupled position, by a counterweight – simply a flat brass 'paddle' made as part of the hook. The hook is pulled downwards by a 'dropper' in the form of coupling chain links made of iron or steel wire.

The hook engages with either a wire fitted across the centres of the buffer faces – thus effectively preventing any possibility of buffer locking when propelling – or with a wire loop set between the buffers – less obtrusive where buffer locking is not a problem. Later versions of the design incorporate a delay latch which permits true delayed-action operation, as with the Kadee and the filigree Alex Jackson design. Either permanent or electro-magnets can be used for actuation, the only proviso being that the magnet is long enough to ensure that the droppers of both hooks in a pair of couplings are attracted. So long as the couplings are kept under tension the hooks will remain engaged, which means that permanent magnets are

Below: This is the 'Imprecise' coupler – my own miniaturised home-made wire variant of the basic Sprat & Winkle design. The hook is sprung up rather than counterbalanced, the loop is kept as small as possible and the dropper on this particular wagon is iron wire; most use the EMGS steel chain. It works in exactly the same way as the regular S&W using the same magnets; it's just a bit more discreet and, as its name implies, very forgiving of a range of inaccuracies.

usually adequate. S&W magnets are much smaller than the Kadee type but are still potent enough to affect steel axles or wheel-tyres, although not to anything like the same extent as the Kadee; the drag and attraction are less and vehicles can be left quite close to the magnets without galloping off unbidden.

The S&W hook is available in two sizes, sold as 4mm and 3mm scale versions, although many 4mm scale modellers use the smaller hook where curves permit, in the interests of a less-obtrusive installation. In the fiddleyard situation, the S&W lies somewhere between the knuckle and the tension-lock in user friendliness. It is a simple matter to use a small screwdriver or similar implement to push the hooks down out of engagement, but stock must be pushed apart slightly before individual vehicles can be lifted out. Although not a ready-to-use coupler in the sense that a Kadee or a tension-lock is, the S&W is relatively easy to assemble and install and addresses many of the problems inherent in the typical British model railway. It may thus be described as an example of that truly British speciality, a Jolly Good Compromise. Nowadays, it is made and sold by Model Signal Engineering (MSE).

N scale couplings

The very first commercial models in this size – Lone Star's Treblo-Lectric 000 gauge trains of 1960 – used a miniature version of the tension-lock design, which was quite neat and reasonably effective. However, Arnold in Germany had other ideas and when N scale displaced 000 the Arnold Rapido design of coupler – a sort of chunky square knuckle designed to move vertically to engage and disengage – took over and has remained the standard N scale fitment to this day. This is a shame, as it's a hideous eyesore of a thing, far bigger in relation to the rolling stock than even the most obtrusive of 4mm scale couplers and giving a coupling distance between vehicles that is more than generous. That said, it works well enough in the coupling mode and – praise be – can be separated by simply lifting stock vertically, making it a fiddleyard-friendly design.

Above: Peco's take on the Arnold 'square knuckle' – not exactly discreet, although better than a lot of installations of this same design on European equipment. You can adapt these for magnetic uncoupling.

Below: The Peco N coupler is nice and short and gives a commendably close coupling distance. Steve Earle has tweaked these Taylor Plastic Models kit-built wagons a bit to close the gap even further, but those are standard Peco knuckles.

The Arnold coupler is a straightforward mechanical affair when it comes to remote uncoupling, using a simple ramp to lift one coupling in a pair. Peco market their own version of the design – the ELC or 'Elsie' coupler – which can be fitted with a small bent-steel lift arm for magnetic actuation using the Peco PL25 track electro-magnet. This last is unobtrusive and effective, but does not provide for any delay facility, which means you need an electro-magnet at every uncoupling location. To some extent, these limitations reflect the nature and scope typical of N scale layouts in Europe, which often tend to gravitate more to the 'trains passing by in a landscape' style of operation rather than concerning themselves over-much with the intricacies of shunting. In the USA, however, they're very struck with switching and the Arnold coupling design was soon found wanting; as well as its lack of operational facility, it was only suitable for truck-mounting – where its bulk, in conjunction with the lower riding-height of American rolling stock, often resulted in N gauge vehicles that sat far too high off their trucks.

Enter Kadee once more, with an N scale Magne-Matic coupler that had many of the virtues of its H0 counterpart, although it worked in a slightly different fashion and was made in nylon rather than being cast in tough zinc alloy. It still featured magnetic actuation and delayed action, as well as being supplied either ready mounted to scale-height trucks or self contained for body mounting. Kadee's N and Z scale products were eventually grouped into a new range, Micro-Trains Line, an independent company rather than just part of the general Kadee organisation and now a completely separate concern. This is where you'll find these products today; any search for 'Kadee N scale couplings' will draw a resounding blank!

The body-mounting Micro-Trains knuckle coupler would seem a good solution for the British N modeller wanting something both less obtrusive and more sophisticated than the Arnold device, but unwilling to take on the complexities of DIY couplers like the DG. The Micro-Trains device normally comes pre-assembled in its mounting box (although you can buy bulk packs in kit form) and, given that the usual snag facing US modellers is setting it high enough above rail level, the greater ride height of British N 1:148 stock compared to US-prototype in 1:160 shouldn't be a problem. The drawbacks are a rather high cost with restricted availability here, together with the physical difficulty of fixing the mounting box in place. It is moulded in a somewhat glue-resistant plastic and is best mounted with a small screw or a push-fit pin. Given that the Arnold coupler relies on a dedicated mounting moulded-in to the underframe or bogie-frames of vehicles, quite a bit of modification and preparation is usually needed to fit the Micro-Trains alternative. Also, there's no bogie-fitting variant – the US ready-truck-mounted couplers are rarely on bogie types suited to British rolling stock.

Finescale 2mm modellers have long looked elsewhere than Arnold for their couplers. Scale hooks and links not being a viable option, the usual solution has been a DIY variant of the basic hook-and-loop design, the DG, which is just as applicable to N equipment; it also finds favour in 3mm scale and with some 4mm modellers. The DG is similar to the Marklin coupler long used on much European H0 RTR equipment, having a fixed hook and a lifting loop. On the DG the loop is magnetically actuated and the coupler incorporates an ingenious mechanical 'delay' latch, making it a fully featured design. It is supplied in kit form as etched components with a jig to bend the loops around and is, it must be said, a little fiddly to assemble. But it's reliable, effective and relatively unobtrusive while, as it incorporates a buffing plate as part of the hook, it does not require the actual buffers on rolling stock to be anything other than decorative. Just as well, given the miniscule size of the average 2mm scale buffer! Like the Sprat & Winkle, the DG is produced and sold by MSE and is endorsed by the 2mm Scale Society.

Semi-permanent couplings

All this discussion of automatic couplings stems from the assumption that it will be necessary to provide for the coupling up or separation

Below: This is a lesser-known fully featured auto-coupler based on the hook-and-loop principle, the DG, popular for fine-scale use in 2mm and 3mm scales; it can also be used for 4mm scale, as here. Made from a combination of jig-bent wire and etched parts, it works well and is only moderately fiddly to make. The DG and the somewhat-similar B&B are neat and workmanlike and as unobtrusive as any coupling can be in such a small size.

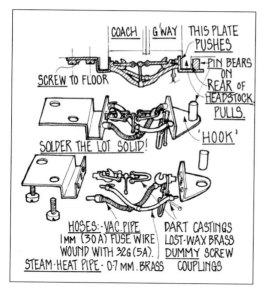

Above: Here's a sketch of a Pendon-style rigid drawbar coupler for coaches, incorporating full detail. You can get a cast version of this in brass from Bill Bedford Models.

Above: A simplified version of the 'Pendon' rigid draw-hook coupling for coaching stock which can be made from brass wire.

of every individual item of rolling stock on the layout. In many instances, however, this is not the case. Obviously, fixed-formation train sets like HSTs or DMUs are rarely broken up – usually only for maintenance – while many regular locomotive-hauled passenger workings were covered by dedicated rakes of coaches of which at least the core vehicles normally stayed together. Wagons, too, aren't always consigned individually and are often formed into block trains shuttling between two points; the Mendip stone trains already mentioned are an example of this, as are such workings as merry-go-round coal and bulk oil trains. Even wagons in general traffic weren't always shunted individually, often being consigned in cuts of from a pair of wagons up to a dozen or so. So, on the majority of layouts, it is by no means essential to fit every item of stock with auto-couplers; where stock normally stays together a much more basic manual design of coupling will suffice.

This is where the semi-permanent coupling comes into its own, used between vehicles in a cut or rake fitted with auto-couplings only at the

ends. These non-auto couplings generally take one of two forms: a rigid bar of some sort, or the use of scale screw or link couplings. The bar type is usually arranged in the form of an upward-facing hook that locates behind the bufferbeam of an adjacent vehicle; it is more usual with coaching stock and is often embellished with dummy vacuum brake and steam-heat connections to give the impression of prototype coupling arrangements – very effective when glimpsed beneath corridor connections. This arrangement, illustrated hereabouts, is often called a 'Pendon' coupling – the museum being an early user of the device.

I have used a similar type of rigid device between wagons of a vacuum-fitted express perishables trains, but with the usual loose-coupled freight train then the ploy of making up short cuts of wagons with scale three-links not only looks right but gives the characteristic uneven movement on starting and shunting. This is what I do on my own layout, using vehicles fitted with my 'Imprecise' auto-coupler at one end and a three-link at the other to top-and-tail each cut of wagons – typically

between two and five normal common-user types per cut. Auto-couplers are, however, still fitted at both ends of individual vehicles, such as brake vans, special traffic wagons or items of non-passenger coaching stock, and in other cases where the operational needs of the layout call for a particular wagon to be shunted solo.

Summary

The choice of a coupling system (or systems; you can use several in tandem for different purposes) is a very fundamental one. It is not just a matter of casual preference, either; the best coupling solution is very much bound up with the way you intend to operate your layout, as well as the nature of the actual layout itself and factors such as track curvature, type of fiddleyard and access (or lack of it) for manual manipulation. It's certainly an aspect of the hobby meriting careful consideration, plenty of practical experiment and a jolly good look at what everybody else is doing. Studying a layout akin to your own in the press or at a show

Above left and right: Semi-permanent rigid couplings have long been a popular way of coupling vehicles in rakes, where there is no operational requirement to divide trains. Usually associated with passenger stock, the same idea is equally relevant to goods workings. The twenty fitted vans making up the 'Perpot' (telegraphic code for the Weymouth–London express goods trains carrying Channel Islands produce – perishables and potatoes) on Andrew Duncan's layout are joined by the arrangement shown here. This incorporates the connected-up vacuum pipes and a representation of the screw links with a simple rigid hook that engages behind the bufferbeam of the adjacent wagon. The first and last wagons in the rake carry normal auto-couplers on their outer ends.

is a good way of both anticipating problems and learning about possible solutions. After more than forty years of fiddling, I'm still experimenting with couplers – and have yet to light on some 'Eureka!' solution that answers all my needs!

GLOSSARY OF TERMS AND ABBREVIATIONS

Availability

The percentage of the time for which a locomotive is available for traffic, determined by the servicing needs. Most steam locomotives had a relatively poor availability of around 50–60%; diesel engines are typically much better in this regard, with availabilities of 90% or more.

Block system

The fundamental safety feature under which all British railways operate, where the track is divided into individual block sections protected by signals, any one of which can only be occupied by one train at a time. More fully explained in Chapter 6.

BRMSB

The British Railway Modelling Standards Bureau, set up in 1940 to determine standards for the post-war development of the British hobby. Comprising the editors of the principal model railway magazines and other technical experts, the board laid out a range of standards covering 7mm, 4mm, 3.5mm (H0) 3mm (TT) and ³⁄₁₆in (S) scales. Unfortunately, no tolerances were quoted for adherence to the standard and there was no way of policing it, so many products were sold as to 'BRMSB Standards' when they were anything but, which regrettably undermined the whole exercise.

Cab control

The system of dc wiring most commonly used for British scale model railways, where the track is divided electrically into discreet sections, each of which can be independently switched to either turn them off (for isolation purposes), or to link them to any one of two or more controllers (or 'cabs', a term originating in the USA) in use on the layout.

Catch point

A point or set of point blades – often only a single blade – inserted in a running line to derail vehicles running away in the wrong direction or down a gradient. Where it is in a unidirectional line – as in normal double track – a catch point is normally sprung; where it is in a bidirectional or single track line, the catch point is worked from the signalbox controlling that section of track and would be linked to the signals such that they could not be cleared unless the catch point was closed to trains approaching in a facing direction.

CCE

The chief civil engineer – the man responsible for the railway's infrastructure – earthworks, bridges and structures, PW, signalling, buildings and all fixed plant and equipment except within locomotive depots, where the motive power department had a say. The CCE was generally regarded as the most senior engineering appointment within railway management, although locomotive engineers are generally better known.

Cess

The drainage ditch, usually filled with ash and

cinders, running along each side of the track formation.

CME

The chief mechanical engineer, responsible for all the movable plant of the railway – locomotives, carriages and wagons. In Britain, this usually included the design and construction of new locos or rolling stock. On major railways with large equipment fleets, the CME might be assisted by a motive power superintendent, who looked after maintenance and day-to-day running, and by a carriage and wagon superintendent to look after the rolling stock.

Common crossing

The assembly of components – a 'vee' combined with knuckle and wing rails – that allows a flanged wheel to cross over an opposing rail in a turnout. It is categorised by the angle of divergence of the rails expressed as a gradient, i.e.: a 1-in-8 crossing. That is, the crossing is of an angle such that 8 feet from the point of the crossing vee the diverging rails are one foot apart.

CTC

Continuous track circuiting. A length of line protected by continuous electrical train position detection by track circuit. The modern railway system is almost entirely under CTC for running lines.

CTC can also mean centralised traffic control. A term of American origin used to describe the system whereby a major district of lines or even a whole railway is controlled from a single central point. CTC operation aided by computers and automatic four-aspect signalling (and fed information as to train position by continuous track circuiting, just to confuse things) is the prevalent railway operating system in Britain – and the rest of the world – today.

C&W

Carriage and Wagon – the department responsible for the design, construction, purchase and maintenance of a railway's passenger and goods rolling stock. The C&W department might have a separate superintendent, but the position was often combined with control of the locomotive department, resulting in some CMEs rejoicing in the title of 'Locomotive, Carriage and Wagon Superintendent'.

Distant signal

A 'permissive' signal which can be passed at 'danger', as it serves merely as advance warning of the status of the next home signal, which is 'absolute' and can only be passed at clear. Distant signals have a V-notch in the end of the arm and are painted yellow on the face and white on the rear, with a black chevron marking on each face. The spectacle glasses are arranged to show amber when 'on' and green when 'off'.

Doll

A subsidiary post on a bracket signal. A 'dolly arm' is thus a signal arm mounted on a 'doll' rather than on the main post.

EM gauge

An intermediate track standard for 4mm scale modelling, using a track gauge of 18.2mm (which scales out at a full-size gauge of fractionally over 4ft 6in). Dating from 1954, EM (Eighteen Millimetre) was the first step towards modelling on a more accurate track gauge than 00, which actually represents a prototype track gauge of 4ft 1½in. EM standards were originally based on the BRMSB 'fine-scale 00' standard, but were refined and a new, finer wheel profile adopted in 1979.

Facing

A junction or individual turnout where the divergence faces the direction of traffic.

Facing turnouts

These are avoided in running lines where ever possible, the most usual exceptions being on single track or other bidirectional lines, at junctions and at the entry to lie-bye or platform loops. Facing turnouts in such situations are always protected by facing point locks (FPL) – mechanical devices on the point throw-bar linked to a track treadle operated by an approaching train or interlocked with the signalling and point-operating linkages. They lock the point blades in place to ensure that a facing point cannot move (or be moved) while a train is running over it. It is necessary to release the FPL before a facing point can be changed, and this is not possible unless the track is empty and all signals are at 'danger'.

A facing crossover is a pair of turnouts linking the up and down lines of a double-track formation such that trains approaching in the normal directions on the running lines can be diverted to the opposing line. This is very rare in British PW design on running lines, except at some junctions and within station approaches. Protected by FPLs and almost always subject to severe speed restrictions.

Finescale
Strictly, an approach to modelling that seeks to make everything as close to the true scale dimensions as is humanly possible. In a broader sense, it has also come to mean the pursuit of authenticity of appearance and fidelity to prototype – the 'finescale ethos'.

Fixed signal
A signal giving a permanent indication: speed restrictions, limit-of-shunt boards, 'do not pass' and 'all trains to stop and pin down brakes' are examples of notice-type fixed signals. The other common type of fixed signal is a normal semaphore arm which is literally 'fixed', being rigidly mounted to the post rather than pivoted, and having a lamp permanently showing one aspect colour. The distant on the approach to a minor terminus was usually fixed. 'Stop boards' or fixed home signals were sometimes used on the exit of mineral or industrial lines in which case trains would be brought to a stand, and then signalled forward by flag.

Formation
A term with several meanings, depending on context. As used by the running/traffic or C&W departments, 'formation' refers to the makeup of a particular train in terms of the number and type of vehicles included; strictly, the 'train formation'.

In a permanent way (PW) context, the term is used to describe a complete assembly. Thus the term 'track formation' refers to the complete ensemble of roadbed, drainage ditches, ballast, sleepers, chairs, keys, rails and fishplates that make up the whole permanent way. A 'point formation' is either an individual turnout or several turnouts together forming a junction, crossover or other complex piece of track; again, the term refers to the whole assembly of components making up the trackwork.

'Track formation' is also often used to describe the total layout of tracks at a particular location; again, the context is the complete thing from roadbed to railhead. Thus, one might state that 'the track formation at X consists of a double-track main line linked by a trailing crossover and having up and down lie-bye sidings.'

Freelance
In model railway terms, a layout based on a totally fictional subject. Nowadays, true freelance layouts are very rare; any 'fiction' usually only relates to the setting of the model (geographical location/landscape, place names, etc.). The railway itself will follow full-size practice closely, and the elements making up the setting are also normally modelled from life such that the whole thing will still be realistic and believable. This is probably the most prevalent style of layout today.

Older, truly freelance layouts, however, were often completely imaginary, the modeller designing his own locos and stock or mixing subjects regardless of origin or gauge. Imagination also provided the signalling, buildings, landscape and civil engineering features. The results often had great charm (the 'Madder Valley', 'Craig', 'Aire Valley', the 'West of England Railway') but were rarely convincing.

Frog
A commonly used term derived from American practice to describe the assembly – a 'vee' with

two knuckle rails and wing rails – that allows flanged wheels to pass over opposing rails in a turnout. The correct British PW term for this assembly is a 'common crossing'. A 'frog number' is the American description for the angle of the vee – a No. 8 Frog would have a 1-in-8 divergence. See 'common crossing' above.

Grouping/the Grouped companies

On 1 January 1923, following the end of the First World War, the independent, privately owned railway companies of Britain (which by that time numbered more than 160) were 'grouped' by Act of Parliament into four large companies centred on London, but broadly split geographically over the areas of England, Scotland and Wales that they served.

The 'Big Four' 'Grouped' companies were: the London, Midland & Scottish Railway (LMS) serving the English Midlands, North-West England, parts of Wales, Central and Western Scotland to the Far North (plus some railways in Northern Ireland). The London & North Eastern Railway (LNER) covering the eastern Midlands, East Anglia, Yorkshire (with a tentacle across Lancashire to Liverpool), the North-East, plus eastern and central Scotland together with a route to the West Highland port of Mallaig. The Great Western Railway (GWR), serving Wessex, the South and West Midlands as far north as Birkenhead on Merseyside, most of Wales, and the Welsh Borders and the whole of the West Country. The Southern Railway (SR), which had exclusive rights over the South-East and the South Coast as far west as Weymouth, large parts of Wessex and lines in the West Country as far as Padstow in North Cornwall.

Heel

The 'blunt' end of a turnout where the two roads diverge through the crossing, or 'frog'.

Home signal

The basic 'absolute' signal, which must not be passed when showing the 'on' or 'danger' indication, except by special authority of the signalman or by a subsidiary arm which can be cleared to permit certain specific movements, such as shunting moves. A home signal had

a square-ended arm painted red on the face and white on the reverse, with a white vertical stripe on the face and a black vertical stripe on the rear. The spectacle glasses were arranged to show red when 'on' and green when 'off'.

Interlocking

The linking together of various devices in a signalling system to prevent errors, inappropriate or dangerous actions on the part of the signalman. Typical interlockings would prevent conflicting signal indications – such as both routes through a junction being shown as 'clear' – or a lack of correspondence between the route set by turnouts and that indicated by the associated signals. Interlocking can be arranged by mechanical or electrical means.

Lie-bye

A siding or loop off of a running line designed to allow a slower or less important train to 'lie bye' while it is overtaken by faster or higher-priority traffic. An operating necessity where slow mineral and goods trains shared the same tracks as fast passenger workings.

Lost-wax casting

A sophisticated (but ancient) casting technique in which an original, which can be made of almost any material, is used to produce a 'cold' mould into which wax is injected to produce replicas of the required part. These waxes are then built up into a sprue or 'tree', which is mounted in a canister which is then filled with a very fine plaster to form a mould.

MOROP

A sinister-sounding organisation that seems to have slipped from the pages of spy fiction but is, in fact, a federation of model railway clubs that operates somewhat along the lines of the NMRA in America in covering most of Europe.

MOROP is based, appropriately, in Switzerland and promulgates standards through the NEM (see below) as well as organising events and promoting the hobby. The official title of the organisation is rendered in German as the *Verband der Modelleisenbahner und Eisenbahnfreunde Europas* and in French as the *Union Européenne des Modélistes Ferroviaires et des Amis des Chemins de Fer* (European Union of Railway Modellers and Railway Enthusiasts). Quite how you get from either of those official titles to MOROP is beyond me! (The term MOROP has been created from the German word MOdellbahn (for 'model train') and the French word 'EuROPe'. Ed.)

MPD

An abbreviation with two possible meanings. In common use, it stood for motive power depot – the correct term for a facility where locomotives could be serviced. Usually, but not always, this was an engine shed, but some MPDs did without the luxury of a building to house the locomotives.

The more formal meaning of MPD was the Motive Power Department, that section of the engineering hierarchy of the railway that had responsibility for the design, construction, maintenance and running of a railway's locomotive fleet. The MPD – often abbreviated as MP Dept. to avoid confusion, was headed by the motive power superintendent, or chief mechanical engineer (CME).

NEM standards

The *Normen Europäischer Modelleisenbahnen* or European Standards for Modelling is a set of standards for wheels, track and couplings developed from the early 1950s by the members of MOROP. The NEM wheel standard was very toy-like, with wide, flat treads and very deep flanges of a knife edge profile. This standard is now, thankfully, falling into disuse, being replaced by the much more refined and well-proven NMRA RP25 wheel. MOROP and the NMRA nowadays have close links which are providing positive benefits for the hobby worldwide.

One such benefit is the NEM universal coupler mount system, based on a highly ingenious device that is designed to open up coupler spacing on curves while maintaining scale spacing on straight track; it incorporates

a sleeve into which almost all current coupler designs, including American magnetic knuckle couplers like Kadee, can be simply push-fitted. This type of coupler mount will be found on recent RTR models from across Europe, including Bachmann and Hornby.

Passing loop

A double-track section on a single-track running line – often at a station – signalled and equipped to allow trains going in opposite directions to pass one another and to exchange the token, staff or other authority to occupy a single-track section.

Passing loops could also usually be used as lie-byes to allow a slow train on a single track to be overtaken by a faster one.

P&C

Point and crossing; those aspects of trackwork design, construction and maintenance concerned with individual items of pointwork and junctions of all kinds.

Pre-Grouping

The period of railway history up to the 'Grouping', or 'Amalgamation' of 1 January 1923. A pre-Grouping company was a railway in existence prior to the time of the formation of the 'Big Four': GWR, SR, LMSR and LNER.

Power classification

The two largest 'Grouped' companies, the LMS and the LNER, adopted a system of classifying all their locomotives by power capability and suitability for certain types of traffic. Power was rated on a scale of 0–9, with 0 the least powerful, while traffic potential was denoted by the suffixes 'P' (passenger), 'F' (freight) and 'MT' (mixed traffic). Thus, a 1F was a small goods or shunting engine, while a 7P was a large express passenger type. A 5MT was a medium-powered mixed-traffic loco while a 5P/4F was a loco which could work either type of traffic but was not rated equally for both.

British Railways adopted the system after Nationalisation on 1 January 1948 and applied it to all locomotives including the new BR Standard designs, the most powerful of which was the famous 9F class 2-10-0. The concept was carried forward to the early diesel era, with the use of 'Type' numbers to indicate prime mover horsepower. A Type 1 was a main line loco up to 1,000bhp, a Type 2 1,000–1,500bhp, a Type 3 1,500–2,000bhp, a Type 4 2,000–3,000 and the solitary Type 5 (the 'Deltic') 3,000+bhp.

PW

Permanent way. Strictly, the complete assembly of components and earthworks making up the track; roadbed, drainage cesses, ballast and track – although often used just to describe the latter two elements. The PW department of a railway was responsible for all matters relating to the track and its foundations (but not bridges or earthworks) and came under the direction of the chief civil engineer (CCE).

Refuge

A place where a man could stand safely clear of the tracks in restricted situations, as on a viaduct, in a tunnel or steep-sided cutting.

Refuge loop or siding

A siding or loop off a running line, controlled by signals and protected by a trap, where vehicles or complete trains could stand clear of the running lines within a block section.

Roster

This was a list of duties and the men and engines assigned to them, often written up on a large blackboard in the driver's mess or outside the depot manager's office at the motive power depot.

To 'roster' was thus to assign a locomotive and crew to a particular operational task. Driver Jones and Fireman Bloggs with engine No. 1234 would be rostered to work a specific duty, or turn, which might consist of a single run with one train or a whole series of linked jobs – working a goods train, then shunting for a couple of hours, taking another goods, parcels or even passenger train out, or returning light engine, as dictated by the WTT or the traffic foreman/traffic control department.

Route availability

This was the extent to which a locomotive type could be used over the various routes making up the railway network. Route availability depended on a number of factors, including overall weight, axle weight, hammer-blow (on steam engines), the tightest curve the engine could negotiate and the amount of fuel and water it could carry.

Route availability was often expressed in a code or classification system displayed on the loco. The GWR used coloured dots above the number plate, ranging from 'double red', the most restricted, to 'uncoloured' (no dot at all) – types which could go anywhere. The corresponding system on the LNER used a numeric code, with RA1 being the most restricted and RA5 the least. The LMS and SR did not use codes, but noted suitable locomotive types or restrictions against the various entries in the Working Time Table (WTT).

RTR

The abbreviation for Ready-to-Run, e.g., a model needing no assembly before use.

S&T

The signal and telegraph department was a division of the chief civil engineer's realm that dealt with the provision and maintenance of all signalling installations and their associated electrical apparatus, telegraph and phone lines and operating systems, including signalboxes.

Scratchbuilt

A model mostly constructed from raw materials, e.g., sheet or solid metal, card, wood or plastic sheet, strip and sections.

Toe

The 'sharp' end of a turnout where the two routes are set by the blades; the end away from the divergence of the tracks.

Throwbar

An American term to describe the bar linking the two point blades in a switch, by means of which they are both held in alignment and moved (or 'thrown') to set the route. The British PW term for this component is a stretcher bar or point stretcher. Modellers often refer to it as a 'tiebar' or 'point tiebar' – which is, strictly speaking, incorrect. A tiebar is actually used to hold rails in gauge, typically where longitudinal sleepers are employed (as on steel-deck bridges) or on sharp curves where the track tends to 'spread'.

Trailing

In a PW context, trailing refers to a junction or individual turnout where the diverging road joins from the same direction that the train is travelling. That is, the opposite of 'Facing'.

As a rule, almost all turnouts connecting to a double-track running line will be trailing, except for junctions, terminal station approaches and the entry to loops.

Trailing is also used to describe something that is behind in a train formation or within a loco or vehicle. Thus, a double-headed train will have leading and trailing engines, while a locomotive with several driving axles will have leading and trailing coupled wheelsets. Six-wheeled locos would have a centre set as well, while eight-coupled engines have leading, second, third and trailing wheelsets. A rear bogie, as on a 2-6-4T for example, would likewise be described as a trailing bogie.

Trap or trap point

A catch point or normal turnout inserted in the exit of a siding or loop where it joins a running line. It is linked to the turnout controlling the entry/exit to the siding or loop in such a way that when the turnout is set for the running line the 'trap' would derail any vehicle on the siding moving towards the running line.

Whitemetal castings

Components – often a complete locomotive superstructure, rolling stock or road vehicle kit or locomotive, rolling stock or scenic detailing parts, cast in low-melting point alloy. This is usually a mixture of tin, lead, bismuth and cadmium and is sometimes described as 'Pewter'. Whitemetal melts at around 130° C; parts made from it are either glued together with an epoxy resin or cyano-acrylate adhesive, or soldered with a special low-melt alloy with a 70ºC melting point.

WTT

A Working Time Table is the document, produced by the railway's traffic department, which sets out not only the times of all trains (passenger and freight) on a given line, but also any special instructions relating to those workings, such as requirements to shunt, wait for connecting services, or to exclude the use of unsuitable locomotives or rolling stock.

INDEX

Booklist and Websites

Many 'paper' sources were consulted in compiling this book; my own notebooks, long runs of back numbers of model railway magazines, old exhibition guides, manufacturers literature and catalogues and an extensive library of books – of which the following are just a selection. A few of these are older books of historical interest rather than sources of practical help; those marked with an * are out of print and will have to be sought secondhand through one of the specialist railway book dealers.

Today, there are hundreds of railway modelling titles in print from a wide range of sources. To get an idea of what's out there, the easiest approach is to browse the websites of a good specialist bookseller; try: British Railway Books (britishrailwaybooks.co.uk), Ian Allan/Midland Counties Publications (www.ianallanpublishing.com) or Kevin Robertson Books (www.kevinrobertsonbooks.co.uk)

7mm Modelling Parts 1 & 2, by Gordon Gravett. Wild Swan Publications.
Architectural Modelling. Dave Rowe. Wild Swan Publications.
Beginner's Guide to 2mm Modelling. 2mm Scale Association.
Carriage Modelling made Easy. David Jenkinson. Wild Swan Publications.
Cottage Modelling for Pendon, by Chris Pilton. Wild Swan Publications.
Finescale Track. Iain Rice. Wild Swan Publications.
Flexi-Chas: A way to build fully-compensated Locomotive chassis. Mike Sharman. Pub by author.
Indoor Model Railways*. E W Twining. Newnes, 1937
In Search of a Dream – the life and work of Roye England. Stephen Williams. Wild Swan Publications
Landscape Modelling, Barry Norman. Wild Swan Publications.
Locomotive Kit Chassis Construction. Iain Rice. Wild Swan Publications
Martin Brent – Master Model Maker. A collection of Martin's writings, published by the Missenden Abbey
    Modeller's Weekend.
Miniature Building Construction* and *Miniature Landscape Modelling**
both by John H Ahern. M.A.P./Argus Books – various editions.
Miniature Scenic Modelling*. Jack Kine. MAP , 1979
Modelling Buildings – Methods and Materials. Malcolm Smith. Pendon Musem (Booklet).
Modelling Diesels. Tim Shackleton. Hawkshill Publications/Mainly Trains
Model Loco Construction in 4mm Scale*, by Guy R Williams. Ian Allan, 1979
The 4mm Engine, by Guy R Williams. Wild Swan Publications
The 4mm Wagon (Series). Geoff Kent. Wild Swan Publications
Narrow Gauge Adventure. P D Hancock, Peco Publications
Narrow Gauge Railway Modelling, Peter Kazer. Wild Swan Publications.
New Developments in Railway Modelling*. Rev Edward Beal. A & C Black 1947
Plastic Bodied Locos. Tim Shackleton Wild Swan Publications
Plastic Structure Kits. Iain Rice. Wild Swan Publications
Railway Operation for the Modeller. Bob Essery. Midland Publishing.
Semaphore Signals. Mick Nicholson. Challenger Books
Whitemetal Locos – a kitbuilder's guide. Iain Rice. Wild Swan Publications

Model railways on the Internet.

The hobby of railway modelling has a very large presence on the internet, with literally thousands of websites covering every aspect of modelling and the prototype. It would obviously be impracticable to list all these sites or even a representative selection. Use of a search engine will winkle out sites relating to most specifics, while for general interest and browsing, starting from a site carrying a large number of links is the best approach.

Here are a handful of 'portal' sites or sites with extensive links; there are many, many others…

I-Rail: Index of railway and model railway websites UK/Ireland	www.irail.co.uk
Model Railways Online (resources page)	www.mrol.gppsoftware.com
UK Model Railways Web Community – WebRing	r.webring.com/hub?ring=modelrail
The UK Model Shop Directory	www.ukmodelshops.co.uk
RM Web: online railway modelling forum	www.rmweb.co.uk
3433 Railway links Portal (Prototype railways)	www.3443.co.uk
Rail Serve – US-based international model/prototype links site	www.railserve.com
Railway Register – UK prototype links	www.railwayregister.co.uk
Scalefour Society (links page)	www.scalefour.org.uk